Precolonial India in Practice

Precolonial India in Practice

Society, Region, and Identity in Medieval Andhra

CYNTHIA TALBOT

OXFORD
UNIVERSITY PRESS
2001

OXFORD
UNIVERSITY PRESS

Oxford New York
Athens Auckland Bangkok Bogotá Buenos Aires Cape Town
Chennai Dar es Salaam Delhi Florence Hong Kong Istanbul Karachi
Kolkata Kuala Lumpur Madrid Melbourne Mexico City Mumbai Nairobi
Paris São Paulo Shanghai Singapore Taipei Tokyo Toronto Warsaw

and associated companies in
Berlin Ibadan

Published by Oxford University Press, Inc.
198 Madison Avenue, New York, New York 10016

Library of Congress Cataloging-in-Publication Data
Talbot, Cynthia
Precolonial India in practice: society, region, and identity in medieval Andhra /
Cynthia Talbot.
p. cm.
Includes bibliographical references and index.
ISBN 0-19-513661-6
1. Andhra Pradesh (India)—History. 2. Social Change—India—Andhra Pradesh—
History—to 16th century. 3. Regionalism—India—Andhra Pradesh—History—
to 16th century. I. Title.
DS485.A55 T35 2000
954'.84—dc21 99-049890

1 3 5 7 9 8 6 4 2

Printed in the United States of America
on acid-free paper

Acknowledgments

This book is the culmination of many years of study and I have incurred numerous debts of gratitude in the process. My interest in medieval Andhra was first stimulated by V. Narayana Rao, at the University of Wisconsin-Madison, and led to a doctoral dissertation on the topic of religious gifts in Kakatiya Andhra, much of which is incorporated in chapter 3 of this work. A Fulbright-Hays doctoral dissertation grant funded the initial period of research in India. I am grateful to Sri Venkateswara University in Tirupati for providing an institutional affiliation, and to the directors and staff of the Chief Epigraphist's Office at Mysore and the Andhra Pradesh Department of Archaeology and Museums in Hyderabad for allowing access to many unpublished inscriptions. I especially wish to thank Prof. S. S. Ramachandra Murthy of Sri Venkateswara University for the many painstaking hours he spent reading through Telugu inscriptions with me.

My doctoral research was summarized in the article "Temples, Donors, and Gifts: Patterns of Patronage in Thirteenth Century South India," published in the *Journal of Asian Studies* (vol. 50, no. 2 [1991], pp. 308–40). Portions of it are reprinted here with permission of the Association for Asian Studies. I subsequently began to examine aspects of Kakatiya Andhra beyond religious patronage, resulting in chapters 2 and 4 of this work. Two interim analyses of Kakatiya society and polity appeared in the articles "Political Intermediaries in Kakatiya Andhra, 1175–1325" and "A Revised View of 'Traditional' India: Caste, Status, and Social Mobility in Medieval Andhra," in *Indian Economic and Social History Review* (vol. 31, no. 3 [1994]: 261–89) and *South Asia* (vol. 15, no. 1 [1992]: 17–52), respectively. I thank Sage Publication India Pvt. Ltd., New Delhi, India and the editor of *South Asia* for permission to publish revised versions of these articles here.

I am also indebted to Prof. Noboru Karashima, formerly of the University of Tokyo, for including me in a team project on Vijayanagara inscriptions that was funded by the Mitsubishi Foundation. While working on his project, I was able to return to India in 1991 and examine many of the inscriptions utilized in chapters 1 and 5. Additional materials analyzed in chapter 5 were collected in 1992 at the India Office Library with the partial assistance of a Bernadette E. Schmitt Grant for Research in European, African, or Asian History from the American Historical Association. I am especially grateful to the National Endowment for the Humanities for awarding me a fellowship in 1992–93, which led to the inception of this work in its present form.

Many other colleagues have assisted me over the years and it gives me great pleasure to thank some of them individually. For their comments on earlier drafts of the book, in whole or in part, I am very grateful to Peter Claus, Richard Eaton, Anne Feldhaus, Patrick Olivelle and his graduate seminar on classical Indian culture and society, Leslie Orr, John F. Richards, George Spencer, and Phillip Wagoner. I have also much appreciated the support extended by Susan M. Deeds, James Heitzman, Eugene Irschick, David Shulman, and Thomas R. Trautmann. I am also obliged to Phillip Wagoner and John Henry Rice for providing the photograph on the cover.

My greatest thanks go to my husband, Eric Schenk, whose love and encouragement helped sustain me during the seemingly interminable gestation of this book. Without Eric's nurturing, in addition to my labor, it might never have seen the light of day.

Contents

List of Maps and Tables

Note on Transliteration and Translation

Words from Indian languages are treated in two different ways in this work. While technical terms discussed in the text are transliterated with diacritical marks and always italicized, the names of places and people are given in standardized or simplified forms. Hence the common, Anglicized, spellings of place-names—Srisailam, Cuddapah, Visakhapatnam, and the like—are used throughout. Personal names, as well as some proper nouns, are transliterated in a simplified version that does not differentiate vowel length or consonant class (such as retroflex or dental) and according to which the vowel *ṛ* is represented by *ri*, *c* by *ch*, and both *ś* and *ṣ* by *sh*.

When words appear in italics, a more scholarly system of transliteration is employed with full use of diacritical marks. I therefore indicate long *e* and *o* vowels, not only in Telugu but even in Sanskrit words (although they are always long in the latter). Instead of using *ṃ* to indicate the Telugu *sunna* symbol, a circle that stands for all nasal sounds, I employ the appropriate nasal sign from Sanskrit orthography in order to better represent the actual pronunciation. Some readers may be unfamiliar with the transliterated form *ṟ*, used for a letter in medieval Telugu script that is now obsolete and replaced by the standard *r*. I also adopt the equal sign between compounded words in Sanskrit phrases to indicate that the following vowel has been subjected to euphonic change under the grammatical rule of *sandhi*. Nouns are generally cited in their root forms, without inflection—for example, *nāyaka* rather than the Telugu masculine singular form *nāyuḍu* or masculine plural *nāyakulu*. In the case of Telugu words of neuter gender, however, I generally append the medieval *mu* ending, as with *nāyaṅkaramu*; in modern Telugu, the final *u* of neuter words is usually dropped.

All translations from Sanskrit and Telugu are my own, unless otherwise indicated.

Abbreviations

APAS Andhra Pradesh Archaeological Series

- No. 3 = *Kannada Inscriptions of Andhra Pradesh*
- No. 9 = *Select Stone Inscriptions from the A.P. Government Museum*
- No. 31 = *Select Epigraphs of Andhra Pradesh*
- No. 38 = *Perur Inscriptions*

APRE *Andhra Pradesh Reports on Epigraphy*

ARE *Annual Reports on (Indian) Epigraphy*

CPIHM *Copper-Plate Inscriptions in the Hyderabad Museum*

CTI *Corpus of Telingana Inscriptions, Pt. 4*

EA *Epigraphia Andhrica*

EI *Epigraphia Indica*

HAS Hyderabad Archaeological Series

- No. 3 = *Inscriptions at Palampet and Uparpalli*
- No. 4 = *Pakhal Inscriptions of the Reign of Kakatiya Ganapatideva*
- No. 6 = *Kotagiri Plates of the Reign of Kakatiya Queen Rudramba*
- No. 13 = *Corpus of Telingana Inscriptions, Pt. 2*
- No. 19 = *Corpus of Telingana Inscriptions, Pt. 3*

IAP *Inscriptions of Andhra Pradesh* (series)

- C = Cuddapah District
- K = Karimnagar District
- N = Nalgonda District
- W = Warangal District

NDI Nellore District Inscriptions (*A Collection of the Inscriptions on Copper Plates and Stones in the Nellore District*)

SII *South Indian Inscriptions*

SS *Sasana Samputi*

TIAP *Temple Inscriptions of Andhra Pradesh*, vol. 1: Srikakulam District

TL *Topographical List of Arabic, Persian, and Urdu Inscriptions of South India*

TS *Telangana Sasanamulu*

TTD *Tirumala Tirupati Devasthanam Inscriptions*

Precolonial India in Practice

Introduction

Medieval India

A History in Transition

> From the scattered hints contained in the writings of the Greeks, the conclusion has been drawn, that the Hindus, at the time of Alexander's invasion, were in a state of manners, society, and knowledge, exactly the same with that in which they were discovered by the nations of modern Europe; nor is there any reason for differing widely from this opinion. It is certain that the few features of which we have any description from the Greeks, bear no inaccurate resemblance to those which are found to distinguish this people at the present day. From this resemblance, from the state of improvement in which the Indians remain, and from the stationary condition in which their institutions first, and then their manners and character, have a tendency to fix them, it is no unreasonable supposition, that they have presented a very uniform appearance during the long interval from the visit of the Greeks to that of the English. Their annals, however, from that era till the period of the Mahomedan conquests, are a blank.
>
> James Mill, *The History of British India* (1826, 2:146–47)

James Mill is virtually a caricature of the colonial project to construct a history of India, so extreme are his views.[1] Yet the opinion he expressed in the preceding passage represents a prominent strand of nineteenth-century thinking about India which portrayed it as fundamentally unchanging. According to Mill, India was "exactly the same" when Europeans began to arrive in the sixteenth century as it had been at the time of an earlier European intrusion, that of Alexander the Great, in the fourth century B.C.E. Nothing of consequence had occurred during the two millennia that had elapsed because India was "stationary." Karl Marx, like Mill a commentator on India who had neither visited it nor studied its languages, echoed the widespread Orientalist conviction that the Eastern Other was slumbering in a time warp when he characterized India as a civilization composed of self-sufficient villages in which the lifestyle of time immemorial was reproduced indefinitely (1972: 38–41). Despite the inherent absurdity of such a proposition and despite the concerted attack on Orientalism waged over the last two decades, the assertion that India was largely unchanging has not vanished from the secondary literature.[2]

Although Mill's book has been called the "oldest hegemonic account of India within the Anglo-French imperial formation" (Inden 1990: 45), not all colonial-era scholars shared his negative views on the entirety of Indian history. An alternate interpretation first emerged in the late eighteenth century which stressed the greatness of India in ancient times, as a major world power. This was the age of India's great empires under the dynasties of the Mauryas and Guptas, comparable both in time and in scope to classical antiquity in the Greco-Roman world. But the glories of ancient India could not be sustained, and, similar to events in the West, the Indian Middle Ages declined for a thousand years or more from the previously high civilizational standard. The indigenous belief that society had gradually deteriorated as the cycle of four ages (*yuga*) progressed contributed to the colonial perception that India had reached its apex long ago (Rocher 1993: 226; Trautmann 1997: 67). The notion of a medieval decline was incorporated into Vincent Smith's *Early History of India*, which superseded Mill's text in the early twentieth century, and it prevails even today among proponents of the Indian feudalism school, a branch of Marxist historiography.[3]

The middle period of Indian history fared poorly in both of these influential conceptions of the Indian past. From its initial depiction as a stagnant era in the unchanging India of James Mill and Karl Marx, medieval India became a dark age, a period when things actively regressed, in the subsequent model of a degenerate India. The exact periodization varied since the decline commenced in the seventh or eighth centuries according to some interpretations, or with the establishment of Muslim rule in North India from 1200 onward according to others. But the same symptoms of decay were widely cited: artistic standards declined as classical forms were overelaborated in a mindless replication, religious beliefs were corrupted by the accretion of folk superstitions, society was increasingly choked by the weight of a rigid caste hierarchy, and political instability resulted from the increasing fragmentation of kingdoms. Wildly differing reasons were advanced for this sorry state of affairs, ranging from the deleterious impact of Muslim rule to the stultifying effects of Oriental despotism and the Asiatic mode of production. A favorite culprit has been the caste system, regarded as a cancerous growth that undermined all attempts at political unity and thus led to the engulfing of the state by society.[4] Regardless of the cause, it was agreed that the medieval past had produced an ossified India resistant to reform and enfeebled by foreign conquest.

Medieval India is now being rehabilitated, historiographically speaking, and one of my primary aims is to contribute to this ongoing process. Far from constituting a moribund or regressive phase, the medieval era in my opinion was a period of progressive change, characterized by the extension of agrarian settlement, a rise in the number of religious institutions, an expansion of commercial activity, and an evolution of political systems and networks. As the agrarian frontier advanced farther and farther, it was accompanied by a culture that valued the making and recording of religious gifts. Although this process occurred throughout the subcontinent, simultaneously but at differing tempos, a multitude of permutations occurred on the main theme. The particulars of religious belief and practice varied from place to place, as did the specific configurations of the human communities who participated together in religious worship, as well as in the larger social, economic, and political spheres that intersected at the shrine or temple. Out of these many variables emerged the distinctive regional societies that comprise India today and it is the medieval history of one of them, Andhra Pradesh, that constitutes the subject of this book. As we increasingly recognize the nature and extent of the transformations that characterized the medieval past, our evaluation of the period has correspondingly altered—it is in this sense that we can speak of the history of medieval India as both a history *in* transition and a history *of* transition.

Some of the impetus for a reappraisal of medieval India arises from recent revisionist research on the eighteenth and early nineteenth centuries, the time span when British rule was first extended over parts of India. A number of scholars now argue that the "traditional" India recorded by later colonial observers represented neither the early colonial era nor its precolonial predecessor. This "traditional" India was allegedly an atomized civilization composed of self-sufficient villages, upon whom the ephemeral state systems of the subcontinent had little impact. Religion and kinship, rather than economics or politics, were the dominant principles ordering society and so the parameters of existence for the masses was dictated by the inflexible hereditary caste structure headed by brahman religious specialists. But the British commentators who identified these features of "traditional" India failed to realize how much change had already been wrought by colonial rule, according to the revisionist view.

Indeed, much of what was described as "traditional" was a product of the colonial presence. Revisionist scholars believe the indigenous social system was depoliticized in the early colonial period through elimination of the pivotal role of the king. British intervention, by removing the king from his focal position at the center of society, truncated the top levels of what had been an extensive redistributive system integrating the various sectors and thereby forcibly separated the hitherto joint economic, political, and social hierarchies. In the economic sphere, British rule thus resulted in the emergence of the self-sufficient village. Similarly, in the newly autonomous social sphere, the dislocations caused by colonialism led to the replacement of the king by brahmans as the arbiters of social order. If these assertions are correct, it follows that our conceptions of "traditional" India apply primarily to nineteenth-century India, a society transformed by colonial rule, and not to earlier periods of Indian history.[5]

Further grounds for reconsidering older interpretations of the medieval era come from new research that places India in a broader world-historical setting. Our enhanced understanding of India's importance within the larger Indian Ocean trade networks modifies traditional thinking about both the activities of Indian mercantile communities and the volume of domestic trade. Studies have shown that precolonial Indian merchants acted in an entrepreneurial manner in supplying commodities for export to distant domestic markets as well as international ones. In doing so, they stimulated the production of commercial goods and the expansion of overland and coastal trade routes that linked many portions of the subcontinent. These commercial networks existed even before the Europeans came to the Indian Ocean around 1500, extending both westward to the Middle East and eastward to Southeast Asia. The implications of such findings are obvious—medieval India can no longer be regarded as a world of isolated villages struggling on a subsistence economy.[6]

A final factor in the changing assessment of medieval India is the small but growing body of analytically oriented historical scholarship on South India, which implicitly contradicts earlier notions of a medieval decline in the realms of economics and politics while it simultaneously enlarges the scope of our historiographic gaze by shining light on the activities of peasants and merchants along with those of the more visible priests and kings.[7] Whether we are speaking of research on early colonial India, early modern India, or medieval South India, therefore, we find an emerging consensus that previous conceptualizations of precolonial or "traditional" Indian society and history are seriously flawed. This work seeks to add momentum to the current historiographic shift that is recasting the medieval past more and more in a dynamic and progressive form. In the process, it will fill in some of the blank spaces in the historiography of non-Muslim India, which James Mill believed had produced no historical records.

Regions and Regionalism in Medieval India

My reconstruction of the medieval past limits itself to the region of Andhra, one of the least studied parts of the subcontinent. Yet today Andhra Pradesh is the largest state in South India, with more than 100,000 square miles in land and a population of more than 66 million in 1991 (map 1). In European terms, it is roughly comparable to Italy in both size and extent of population.[8] Andhra Pradesh did not attain its current form until 1956, as a result of administrative reorganization of state boundaries along linguistic lines.[9] But defined not as the modern state called Andhra Pradesh ("Andhra province") but rather as the territory inhabited by the Telugu-speaking people, Andhra has a history stretching back more than a millennium. The broadest sweep of time surveyed in this book, the centuries from 1000 to 1650, corresponds to the era during which the geographic contours of the modern linguistic region were established. Several chapters focus more narrowly on the years between 1175 and 1325, the period when much of modern Andhra Pradesh was politically unified for the first time under the rule of an indigenous dynasty, the Kakatiyas. For centuries afterward, the Kakatiyas figured prominently in conceptions of the regional community they had helped create by consolidating the dry upland territories of Andhra with the older coastal zone of settlement.

Although a geographic focus on one region consigns developments occurring across a larger arena to the periphery of our historiographic gaze, there are good reasons for choosing a regional point of view. Regions did not exist in airtight compartments, of course, and the circulation of goods, people, and ideas throughout the subcontinent and beyond was an important source of medieval India's dynamism. In fact, the balance of power among the various kingdoms of early medieval India was significantly affected by shifts in the geographic foci of Indian Ocean trade networks, as André Wink has demonstrated (1990). But the growth of regional societies, as the most outstanding feature of the medieval period as a whole, demands our attention. Between 500 and 1500, there was a vast expansion in the territorial spread of "historic" society in India, the civilization that left behind monumental buildings and written documents. This civilization simultaneously took on more differentiated forms, as local elites appropriated features of pan-Indic culture in varying ways and local societies coalesced in diverse configurations. The internal dynamics thus differed from place to place, even if propelled by the same underlying

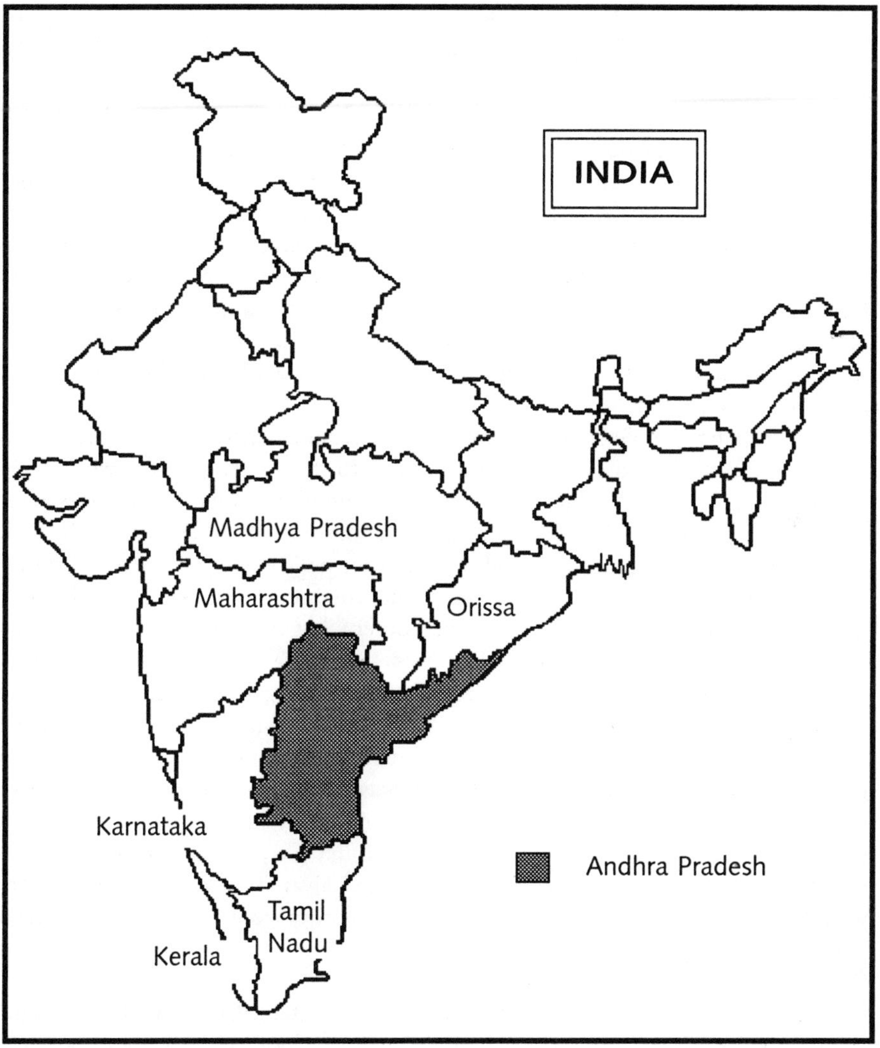

Map 1. Location of Andhra Pradesh

forces of agrarian expansion and demographic increase. Anything larger than a regional perspective would obscure the critical variables leading to the emergence of distinctive local societies, while anything less would fail to account for the regionally differentiated India of today. In the past decade, scholars of contemporary India have increasingly come to regard regional patterns of cultural practice as the significant units of study (e.g., Erndl 1993; Feldhaus 1995) and called for greater attention to the historical processes that led to their emergence (Leavitt 1992).

The interpretation of medieval India I advance here agrees in its basic thrust with that of B. D. Chattopadhyaya, whose research, centered on North India in the centuries from 700 to 1200, has consistently presented an alternative to the standard depiction of the medieval period as "a breakdown of the civilizational matrix of early historical India" (1994: 2).[10] Instead, Chattopadhyaya identifies three major historical processes that gained momentum from 700 onward: the expansion of state society both horizontally and vertically, the assimilation and acculturation of previously tribal peoples, and the integration of local religious cults and practices. Hermann Kulke's work on Orissa has led him to similar conclusions about medieval India (1978a, b, and c; 1982). Because of its large tribal population and many scattered centers of settlement, medieval Orissa provides an exceptionally vivid illustration of how the growth of regional polities proceeded hand in hand with the incorporation of indigenous deities and the "peasantization" of tribal societies. On that basis, Kulke has formulated a schema of the progressive stages of medieval state formation: from chiefdom to early kingdom to imperial kingdom (1995a).

The most noticeable sign of regional development during the medieval era is indeed the proliferation of polities. In contrast to the ancient period, when large portions of India were dominated by a single empire for several centuries, the states of medieval India were smaller and more numerous (Schwartzberg 1977: 218–21). They were also increasingly situated in areas that had not earlier produced states. The first indigenous polity in peninsular India, the Satavahana kingdom, did date back to the first two centuries of the common era, but its influence extended only over parts of the Deccan and not the far South. From the sixth and seventh centuries onward, the pace of state formation in the peninsula began to accelerate with the rise of the Pallavas in northern Tamil Nadu, the Pandyas in the southern tip of the peninsula, and the Chalukyas of Badami in central Karnataka, who each absorbed or enveloped other budding states along the way. The three-way struggle for power persisted until the middle of the ninth century, followed by a period of several centuries when two polities dominated South India (i.e., the Cholas of the Tamil country versus first the Rashtrakutas and later the Kalyani Chalukyas, both of whom were based in the Western Deccan). The diffusion of political centers was even more apparent by the thirteenth century, when no fewer than four major kingdoms flourished within the confines of the peninsula.

R. S. Sharma and other adherents of the Indian feudalism school of thought interpret the proliferation of states in early medieval India as evidence of political disintegration. The main culprit, in their opinion, was the growing popularity of royal land grants, the assignment of rights to income from land, which were first given as charitable endowments to brahmans and then later given in lieu of salary to secular officials. By alienating large tracts of land from royal control and thus fragmenting political authority, this practice allegedly led to the demise of strong central power. Officials increasingly turned into semi-autonomous feudal lords who encroached further and further on the rights of the peasantry, thereby producing a more stratified and less free society. Meanwhile, the medieval economy was becoming both demonetized and deurbanized as levels of trade dropped precipitously. Hence the proliferation of states, according to this thesis, was both a symptom and a cause of medieval India's regression into feudalism.[11]

But the phenomena that feudalism proponents interpret as medieval decline can be more readily explained in opposite terms, as indicative of the vitality of the

Middle Ages. The feudalism model assumes that political power was centralized in prefeudal times, for only then could new political bases represent a siphoning off of established political authority. Except in the core areas around their capitals, however, there is little evidence that the ancient empires exercised direct control over their subjects or territories. The supposedly extensive territorial dimensions of the ancient empires have also been questioned. Outside of the Gangetic heartland, there were huge tracts of forested land interspersed between the small pockets of settled agriculture. It is these scattered outposts of "civilization" that were incorporated into the ancient empires, and even then, in an indirect manner—that is, via the intercession of more localized authority.[12] With the premise that the ancient empires were centralized bureaucratic states controlling the bulk of Indian territory now thoroughly discredited, the entire Indian feudalism thesis falls apart.[13] The polities that appear throughout the subcontinent during the Middle Ages were not the dispersed fragments of a previous central government, but new formations arising out of the extension of agrarian settlement and the resulting growth of population. And the increasing number of political powers who figure in the historical record do not evidence the usurpation of royal power by a formerly dependent class, but instead the emergence of new political elites among the evolving societies along the agrarian frontier.

While agrarian development provided a material stimulus, state formation was also facilitated by the transmission of a pan-Indic royal ideology and idiom throughout the subcontinent and eventually beyond it into Southeast Asia. From the fourth century onward, this Indic discourse of kingship was typically expressed in the Sanskrit language and so Sheldon Pollock has labeled the elite world that shared it the Sanskrit cosmopolis. Through the medium of Sanskrit, an entire set of assumptions "about the nature and aesthetics of polity—about kingly virtue and learning; the dharma of rule; the universality of dominion" was circulated widely, creating a transregional "symbolic network" of vast proportions (1996: 230). At least in the public expressions of power, a homogeneity in practice and thought united the various political elites of the first millennium. A series of interrelated cultural appropriations—the assimilation of pan-Indic or Sanskritic ways of speaking and doing (including, most prominently, patronage of the brahman bearer of the Sanskrit language and tradition)—were integral to the emergence of numerous foci of political power in peninsular India during the second half of the first millennium.

As regional societies matured and became more self-confident in the early centuries of the second millennium, regional languages gradually took over many of the roles previously performed by Sanskrit. This displacement occurred not only through the composition of literary texts but also in the expanded use of the regional language for inscriptional purposes, as Pollock notes perceptively. The regional languages of the Deccan first appear in inscriptions centuries before any surviving literary texts. Telugu, for instance, dates back as far as the sixth century in inscriptional texts, whereas the earliest literary text belongs to the mid eleventh century. But regional languages were typically used only to document the details of religious endowments, while the poetic, or nonbusiness, portions of early medieval inscriptions (genealogies, eulogies of kings, invocations to the gods, etc.) were composed entirely in Sanskrit. The Sanskrit cosmopolis began to collapse when regional languages started to encroach on the discursive realm of Sanskrit, that is, when regional languages had achieved sufficient prestige and authority to assume symbolic and aesthetic functions in inscriptions.[14] At roughly the same time, the first important literary texts were produced in the languages of the Deccan.

The shift toward a regional idiom in inscriptions and literary texts indicates that medieval elites were becoming more localized in character. Both the composers and patrons of written works in a regional language were acting within a geographically circumscribed field of communication and meaning, in comparison to the pan-Indic scope of Sanskrit discourse. To be sure, the new literatures borrowed heavily from Sanskritic models and transregional literature continued to be written in Sanskrit and later in Persian. Nor were the worlds of the different regional languages mutually exclusive—the educated and experienced might well be versed in two or more languages, while the power of patronage could easily summon someone who was. But writing was increasingly directed to the regional audience in the late medieval age, surely a significant change in cultural practice. One reason for this is the expanded social range of people involved in the production of inscriptions and literary texts—people to whom, we might speculate, Sanskrit was impressive but only the regional language was accessible. Even kings and learned brahmans, who might have opted otherwise, participated in the burgeoning regional literary cultures, however. The regional world was the one that mattered most to the elite societies of the late medieval peninsula.[15]

Through the expanded use of regional languages in writing, regionally based communities of elites became more firmly demarcated and differentiated from each other. It is one of these elite communities, the society represented in Telugu inscriptions, whose activities are of chief interest to me. Language, in other words, sets the parameters for what is examined in this book, although inclusion in the Kakatiya political network (in other words, a common political culture) is an additional factor. By using language to define the unit under analysis, it might be argued, I am attributing an unwarranted coherency to the linguistic area of medieval Telugu. For example, Sudipta Kaviraj points out that linguistic regions have often replaced nations in discourse on precolonial India, even though they are just "as much a historical construction as the nation is" (1992: 22–23). Another possible objection is that I am implicitly privileging language as the central component of group identity, when it was but one of many elements. Let me anticipate these criticisms by saying more about the community constituted by a common literary language in medieval Andhra.

Our dependence on written source materials in reconstructing past societies means that we can observe only traces of the elite groups. The community responsible for the production of Telugu inscriptions and literary texts, whether as sponsors, composers, or engravers, was a select category. When I refer to the Telugu linguistic region in medieval Andhra, therefore, I do not mean the entire body of people who spoke languages or dialects that we might classify as Telugu today. Instead, I am alluding to the small portion of the population that was involved in some fashion with the composing and recording of written Telugu. Presumably these people were also Telugu speakers, but there was a considerable difference between written and spoken forms of the language in this period (and indeed until recently in the South Indian languages), a difference that was probably one of the main attractions of the literary language for the elite. The boundaries separating participants in literate Telugu discourse from those who operated in other discursive realms were no doubt "soft" (to use Prasenajit Duara's term, 1995: 65–66) or "fuzzy" (Kaviraj 1992: 25–26). Moreover, it was only within particular contexts that an allegiance or affiliation with written Telugu was meaningful, whereas in different contexts other bases of social identity would come to the forefront. The medieval linguistic region of my analysis thus bears little resemblance to the bounded enumerable community of modern Telugu speakers; nor did linguistic ties of the past have the focus and intensity of modern linguistic nationalisms.

There is no question that linguistic identities were operative in medieval peninsular India, however, no matter how restricted in their social circulation. At least at the level of elite cultural practice, there was a clear consciousness of affiliation with one regional language rather than another and even a certain degree of pride. "Of all the regional languages, Telugu is the most excellent," so the Vijayanagara king Krishnadeva Raya of the early sixteenth century was supposedly told by a god who calls himself the Telugu king and refers to Krishnadeva Raya as the Kannada king.[16] Nor is the notion of a linguistic region a *modern* construct, for medieval South Indian sources draw an explicit connection between language and region, as in the designation *dēśa-bhāṣā*, literally, "language of the land," signifying the regional languages or vernaculars. Even before the peninsular regional languages had fully emerged on the literary level, moreover, the ninth-century scholar Rajashekhara described the linguistic geography of India, associating particular places with particular styles of Sanskrit literature and speech practices (Deshpande 1993b: 91–92). Finally, the idea that linguistic groups constituted cultural communities was by no means introduced to India by the British (contra Washbrook 1991: 190), for language (more specifically, the Sanskrit language) was the main feature thought to differentiate the civilized from the barbaric in ancient India (Parasher 1991: 42–43). Language was thus important in Indian conceptions of culture, region, and community well before the modern age.[17]

To anyone familiar with precolonial India, it may seem that I am belaboring the issue of medieval literary communities and their significance. Nor would those individuals have to be reminded that large-scale identities prevailed primarily among the elites in premodern societies, creating what Anthony D. Smith has called "lateral-aristocratic *ethnie*," or forms of incipient ethnicity that united the upper classes over a widespread geographical area as opposed to the "vertical-demotic" forms more characteristic of the modern era (1986: 79–84). Yet my insistence that a consciousness of literary communities existed in precolonial India seems necessary given the tenor of recent post-Orientalist scholarship.[18] Much of this scholarship has been dedicated to challenging colonial constructs of caste and religious community, on the grounds that colonial policies and perceptions actually created these broadly based identities (e.g., Cohn 1984; Dirks 1989; Pandey 1990). In this process, post-Orientalists have questioned whether any supralocal allegiances existed at all in India prior to the late nineteenth century. Colonialism thus occupies the same role in post-Orientalist theory that modernity occupies in the theories of Benedict Anderson and other like-minded scholars, as the fomenter of widespread and self-conscious communities where none had existed before.

Both post-Orientalism and modernist theories of nationalism posit too radical a rupture between the "traditional" and the "modern," in my opinion.[19] The scale and exclusivity of modern communities may be a new development, but the processes leading to identity formation are much the same as in the past. Whether in medieval or modern India, various attributes or cultural practices like language, political allegiance, and a shared history were selectively deployed in order to mobilize the sense of community. Conceptions of a regional identity that merged linguistic and political affiliation were articulated during the era of the Kakatiyas (1175–1325 C.E.), when the territorial boundaries of the state were largely congruent with the Telugu-speaking area, and they continued to persist even after the demise of the Kakatiyas. The past and the present are hence united through the continued appropriation and redeployment of past constructions of community into the present, another reason why we should not emphasize too much the difference between them. And, just as in the present, historical actors in medieval Andhra belonged simultaneously to a number of communities and possessed a multiplicity of identities. Individuals represented themselves in inscriptions as members of specific social classes and as participants in particular polities, while their acts of endowment gave them entry into certain circles of religious worship. These other levels of community were generally encompassed within the linguistic region, however, for most temple networks were locally based and the typology of social classes was specific to the Telugu area. In the sense that many other allegiances were circumscribed by the linguistic region, therefore, we can point to language as the most important cultural affiliation in the medieval South.

My choice of Andhra runs counter to the predominant scholarly concentration on those regions that produced the earliest and largest political cultures. From the viewpoint of historiography, Andhra is not one of the more glamorous regions of India. It may have a larger areal extent and population today than either of its neighbors, Tamil Nadu and Karnataka, but its literary history commenced considerably later, and it never produced an empire that triumphantly subjugated other territories. The study of Tamil Nadu, in particular, has so overshadowed that of Andhra that the Tamil country is synonymous with South India in academic parlance. But Andhra is by no means anomalous in its relative paucity of historical documentation nor in its failure to generate a transregional polity. One could easily argue, in fact, that its historical experience is more representative of the subcontinent as a whole, since only a handful of core areas consistently dominated the historical stage in terms of their political, economic, and cultural impact. A similar case could be made for the time period 1175 to 1325 C.E., to which much of this book is devoted. As an era when no empires flourished in peninsular India, it is more typical of the medieval period overall than the ninth, eleventh, or sixteenth centuries when the polities of the Rashtrakutas, Cholas, and Vijayanagara reached their respective zeniths.

Unlike the densely populated and fertile nuclear zones of Indian civilization to which historians have devoted the greatest attention, much of Andhra and the rest of the subcontinent was less favored ecologically and slower to produce written sources. But precisely because it was still very much in the process of being settled, medieval Andhra exhibits many dynamic qualities, including a level of physical and social mobility not found in the older localities as well as a large degree of fluidity in the configurations of political power. In this era when regional societies were emerging throughout India, many other areas must have resembled Andhra in undergoing rapid change. If this assumption is correct, Andhra society serves far better as a gauge of the validity of standard characterizations of traditional India than the more commonly examined societies of areas like the Kaveri River delta or the mid-Gangetic plain. In adding to our knowledge of a poorly understood region and era, a case study of medieval Andhra also redresses the balance, in small measure, in a historiography of India skewed toward the imperial heartlands.

Inscriptions as Historical Sources

One of the hallmarks of this work is its heavy reliance on a particular kind of historical source material, medieval stone inscriptions. The use of contemporary data must be central to any effort to recover an alternative vision of medieval India, one that is not distorted by the prism of the colonial past. If nothing else, the critique of Orientalism has taught us to be cautious about adopting historical interpretations formulated in the colonial period. Nor can we trust much in ethnographic observations from the past century, for we can no longer assume that they pertain to the same India that existed in precolonial times. Projections backward from the early colonial era, though helpful, can obscure the changes of the intervening centuries. Our only recourse is to tease out what we can from the admittedly slim corpus of material that survives from the medieval period. And inscriptions are by far the most abundant of our original sources for a reconstruction of Kakatiya Andhra, the focus of much of this book.[20]

Because stone inscriptions from medieval South India typically record religious donations, a history constructed from their perspective assigns greatest weight to the documented activities of real individuals rather than to the normative ideals prevalent in much of the contemporary literature. Epigraphic texts describe the kinds of property given away and also provide other useful details: the date of the gift, the donor's name, his/her family background and personal accomplishments, and praise of the monarch. In other words, they tell us when, where, and what specific persons donated to Hindu temples. Inscriptions enable us to track individual actors in motion and are thus our primary source of information on what people actually did as opposed to what they were supposed to do. And the range of social groups represented in inscriptions is considerably more diverse than in the case of elite literary compositions—merchants, landed peasants, herders, and warrior chiefs, along with their wives, daughters, mothers, and sisters—figure among the donors whose beneficence inscriptions record, rather than just kings and brahmans.

Before proceeding any further, a concrete example illustrating both the kinds of information and donors appearing in medieval Andhra inscriptions might be helpful. In this portion of a longer inscription from coastal Andhra (SII 5.130), recording the gift of a veterinarian specializing in the treatment of horses, the essential details are narrated quite rapidly:

> May all fare well and prosper![21] In the 1,222th year of the Shaka era [1300 C.E.], on the 1st (day of the) bright (fortnight of the lunar month) Jyeshtha, a Friday;
>
> The doctor of horses Vasudeva Pandita, son of Ananta Pandita, of the Atreya *gōtra*, in order to endow the illustrious great lord Kshirarameshvara with a perpetual lamp for the religious benefit of his mother and father and the long life of his son Ananta Peddi; gave 50 milch cows and 2 *kha(ṇḍugas)* of our land south of Jiyani tank in Penamanchchili (village) as lamp-land.[22] Also, 5 *tūmus* to the north of the field-boundaries of Malluru (village) and 5 *tūmus* north of that in centrally located fields for a total of 3 *kha(ṇḍugas* of land).
>
> Having accepted these cows and this land, Donabola Kata Boya's son Nare Boya, Ramana Boya, and Pakka Kommana Boya's son Nare Boya, agree to supply one *māna* of ghee according to the *nandi-mānika* measure daily for as long as the moon and sun endure.[23] He who steals (endowed) land, whether given by himself or by another, will be reborn as a maggot in excrement for (the next) 60,000 years.

The medieval India witnessed from the vantage point of inscriptions—which includes donors like the horse doctor Vasudeva Pandita in its purview, along with herders and others to whom endowments were entrusted—is consequently considerably less uniform than the society depicted in much of the brahmanical and courtly literature from the first half of the second millennium, especially in texts composed in the Sanskrit language. To be sure, the *dharmaśāstra* lawbooks do not advocate the same behavior for the entire population, since different classes of people were held to different standards. Nor does the legal literature ignore local variations in custom, which were accepted as legitimate within a circumscribed sphere. But local norms were accommodated only within the larger context of the brahman project to extend their authority over an increasing number of local communities (Lariviere 1997). Despite the presence of divergent voices within the texts themselves (Olivelle 1999), the *dharmaśāstra* tradition consistently propagated the preeminence of brahmans and tended to suppress any contrary evidence. Historical uniqueness and particularity is even more successfully shrouded in royal Sanskrit biographies, which highlight the patron's resemblance to exemplary kings of the past. While greater variation can be glimpsed in the vernacular compositions of medieval court poets, even here we find the same cast of characters as in the older Sanskrit dramas and poems. Inscriptions, on the other hand, offer a more diverse group of actors who are engaged in a greater array of activities and exhibit a broader spectrum of beliefs.[24]

Perhaps even more important, inscriptions provide specific contexts of time and place that are lacking in many literary texts from the medieval period. Because the dominant Indian intellectual tradition adopted the model of the eternal character of religious truth for all forms of knowledge, it was largely unconcerned with the historical present or even with the notion of historical change (Pollock 1985, 1989). Instead it generally looked to the past, when truth and virtue had been more fully manifested in the world. This is why medieval court poets cast their royal patrons in the mold of bygone heroes and reiterated the ancient stories of the gods. It also explains why medieval *dharmaśāstra* commentators seldom acknowledged that authoritative texts might differ in opinion because they were composed at different times. Not only did medieval literary narratives frequently adopt a timeless scenario, but also the geographic location and date of these texts can seldom be pinpointed. In contrast, inscriptions capture and preserve discrete moments in time by their very nature as records of specific events. They are almost invariably dated and are generally situated where they were originally placed, usually on the walls or structural columns of a temple building or on a stone slab or pillar within the temple grounds. With inscriptions as our guide, therefore, a range of human agents and their diverse actions inevitably occupy the foreground of our historiographic gaze, within a definite geographic and temporal setting.

Because inscriptions are materially embodied records of practice, we can analyze them much in the manner of archaeological artifacts.[25] Inscriptions can be plotted on a space and time grid, not only individually but also en masse. A corpus of inscriptions can thus be compared to an archaeological assemblage, the total array of material artifacts found at one site or from one era. Like archaeological assemblages, sets of inscriptions have properties that pertain only to their entirety—properties like their chronological distributions or locational patterns. Inscriptions also resemble archaeological artifacts in that the sum of the whole is greater than the individual parts, because connections *between* components are revealed when, and only when, the entire complex is analyzed (Neustupny 1993: 26). When the multiplicity of inscriptions is collectively examined, we can therefore discern relationships that would not be visible otherwise. I exploit this advantage provided by inscriptions, using their patterns of distributions as a gauge of various cultural practices and as a basis for extrapolating related trends. In other words, historical processes can be tracked through the medium of inscriptions in a way that is not possible with medieval literary sources. Only because inscriptions are material objects whose texts comprise a large enough body of information and have a sufficient degree of variability can this kind of historical analysis, in aggregate, be conducted.

Unfortunately, our methods of studying Indian inscriptions for historical research are still unsystematic and undeveloped when compared to archaeological methodologies for dealing with artifacts. We have yet to establish even the rudimentary dimensions of the epigraphic phenomenon in most regions and dynastic eras of medieval India—that is, roughly how many inscriptions exist and when and where they were produced.[26] Until the 1960s, inscriptions were mainly read in order to build a chronological framework for non-Muslim dynasties, and so only the regnal dates and political events mentioned in them interested scholars. More recently, information relating to the functioning of temple institutions, the role of religious patronage, and the nature of political structures has also been extracted from the epigraphic record and occasionally subjected to statistical analysis. Some of these recent efforts, however, tend to sift through a mass of inscriptions in the quest for a single set of variables (certain terminology, for instance) or a narrow range of issues. If done too mechanically, this approach could isolate and objectify phenomena, a common criticism of quantitative methods in the social sciences.[27]

In advocating the aggregate analysis of inscriptions, therefore, I do not simply mean that we should examine large numbers of inscriptions. That is valuable, of course, in order to eliminate the obvious errors of ascribing uniqueness to what is common or, conversely, interpreting an unusual situation as representative. But it is also of critical importance that an entire body of material be studied for patterns of interrelated phenomena. A case in point is my classification of medieval Andhra temples into two basic types, the major and the minor. Although the primary criterion is the number of endowments received by a temple, a cluster of accompanying variables—the identity of the donor, location of the temple, and nature of the gift object—divide along similar lines. When we find such clusters of traits or interconnected patterns, we have identified an important nexus in the dynamic configuration of people and events that comprised a society. In other words, the subjectivity of a researcher's judgment can be tempered by searching for intertwined features and parallel or intersecting trends.

Furthermore, in organizing information drawn from inscriptions, it is important to apply categories that were meaningful to the people under study. Insofar as possible, I have therefore classified people in medieval Andhra society and polity by the titles and terms they themselves employed, instead of applying a preconceived model of sociopolitical structure. In this way we can minimize another widespread objection to quantitative approaches, that their classificatory schemes merely reflect the researchers' suppositions and have no empirical or conceptual validity. A good example of the distortions that can result from the imposition of a predetermined set of categories is the information compiled on caste by the British censuses in India (Cohn 1984; Pant 1987; Pederson 1986). They are virtually useless for anything other than an analysis of British conceptions of Indian society, since the Indian subjects could only identify themselves in ways that made sense to their British questioners.

Yet it is inevitable that some of our own categories will be imposed on the material and that some phenomena revealed in inscriptions will be misinterpreted. It is impossible for any scholar to transcend entirely the parameters of our modern conceptual framework and understand the medieval world solely on its own terms. Moreover, a certain simplification and reduction is inherent in any attempt at formulating higher-order generalizations about the historical record. Unless we restrict ourselves solely to microhistorical analyses or "thick" descriptions, we are inevitably creating abstract models of reality that suppress its complexity and ambiguity. But the drawbacks of an aggregate approach to the analysis of medieval Indian inscriptions are far outweighed by the problems with its alternative—the cut-and-paste method wherein isolated pieces of inscriptions are cited to support whatever thesis the researcher desires. Given the paucity of other types of source material for the period and the corresponding need to extract the maximum out of the relatively copious inscriptional corpus, it is irresponsible to reject aggregate methodologies outright. Instead, I hope to demonstrate throughout this work that a context-sensitive and systematic aggregate analysis of inscriptions can yield questions and conclusions that are both relevant and reliable.

Since inscriptions are not only material artifacts, they should also be comprehended through a more culturally oriented approach, one that concerns itself with "the production of meaning rather than the dispersion of objects" (Chartier 1988: 59). The tangible physical presence of inscriptions can easily dupe the historian into treating them as if they were neutral transmitters of facts from the past to the present. Certainly, the existence of an inscription at a given place is an empirical fact. And in most cases we can assume that the transaction documented in a stone inscription—the gift of property to a particular temple or group of individuals—did actually occur, because inscriptions were a means of publicly certifying the transfer of property.[28] Yet we must not forget that inscriptions are also literary texts of a particular type. Although they record certain past activities of interest to us, they do so in ways that were meaningful and useful to their contemporary audience. Inscriptions, just like medieval court literature, are forms of discourse containing representations of the self and the world. As such, the social and political aspirations they embody must be recognized along with the ideology they convey.

We can review the inscription written on behalf of the horse-doctor Vasudeva, to expand on this point. Preceding the previously translated Telugu lines are two verses in Sanskrit, which run:

> Salutations to the gurus! Salutations to (the god) Rameshvara! In the Shaka year enumerated as the months of the sun, the arms, and the eyes [1222=1300 C.E.],[29] on the first lunar day of the bright (fortnight) in the month of Jyeshtha, a Friday, when auspiciousness prevailed; the best of men called Vasudeva—who is the son of Ananta Arya, knows the Ayur Veda of horses, and is the repository of all good qualities—gave a lamp, like the day in brilliance, to (the form of the god) Shiva (known as) Kshirarameshvara.
>
> Vasudeva Arya—who excels in serving the feet of his mother, is the son of Ananta Arya, is praised by the discerning, whose desires are fulfilled through worshiping (the god) Shankara, whose head is forever cleansed with water from the lotus feet of brahmans—gave a lamp, with joy, to the lord of Kshirarama town in order to illuminate the world. This inscription of two verses to the lord Kshirarameshvara was composed by his son-in-law, Bhairava Suri.

This introductory Sanskrit portion of the inscription adds no information regarding the endowment to what the Telugu lines tell us in greater detail. Many scholars would entirely overlook them, finding such nondocumentary sections of inscriptions tedious and inconsequential (Pollock 1996: 242–43). Yet these verses serve a purpose—to highlight the donor and his allegedly good qualities. In this instance the rhetoric is uninspired and repetitive, but it attempts (rather feebly) to portray Vasudeva as a medically knowledgeable brahman. When all the social clues are read together, however, the inscription suggests that the status of a veterinarian was actually ambivalent. Vasudeva may use the scholarly brahman title Pandita, claim to be a member of the brahman Atreya clan (*gōtra*), and even have a relative who can compose Sanskrit of a sort, but were he unequivocally accepted as a brahman, he would not need to express piety toward brahmans in general.

Even this modest example illustrates how inscriptions can be fruitfully read for their representations of the social world and a person's place within it, an approach that is common among literary scholars but largely ignored by historians of medieval India. Because inscriptions are cultural products, I place much emphasis on the ways in which social and political identities are constructed within them—the heroic epithets, titles of ranks, and names borne by individuals, as well as the language that expresses political affiliation. For the same reason, I pay far more attention to the eulogistic portions of inscriptions than do other historians of precolonial India. The individual attributes of donors or their overlords that are praised, the collective symbols that are manipulated in praising them, the kind of genealogical information about the donor or king's family that is narrated—all of these aspects of the inscriptional *praśasti* (eulogy) indicate what was valued in the literate culture of medieval Andhra. Wherever possible, I also try to consider the interests served by inscriptional representations, as strategies for promoting the self as much as reflections of how people thought. I have not taken more than a small step forward in the formulation of a methodology for the cultural analysis of inscriptions. The study of inscriptional rhetoric and style is virtually in its infancy, and much more consideration is needed regarding the conditions of inscriptional production and their intended audiences. My intent is to alert readers to the possibilities and suggest how we might more imaginatively consult inscriptions as historical sources.

In short, inscriptions are a rich mine of information for a period of Indian history that is often thought to lack historical source material. To be sure, the non-Muslim elites of medieval India did not produce much in the way of standard historical writing—no "annals," as James Mill noted. But we have ample documentation in inscriptional form which can greatly enhance our historical understanding. Inscriptions cannot, of course, tell us everything we would like to know about medieval India, for they provide us direct entry into only one sphere of human activity—religious patronage. Nor can all strata of medieval society be witnessed in inscriptions, since only the relatively privileged could make a religious endowment or discharge one. Because of their "fragmentary" nature, inscriptions should be supplemented by other contemporary sources whenever these are available (Narayana Rao, Shulman, and Subrahmanyam 1992: 31). Indeed, ideally one should use both inscriptions and literary texts to explore the Indian past since both were cultural products that could shed light on each other (Walters 1997: 161). Whatever their deficiencies, however, inscriptions are a resource of unparalleled value for the methodical study of past practices and past processes, due to their sheer abundance. Although the religious gift made by Vasudeva Pandita may not have endured as long as the sun and the moon, in the very act of recording it he and the others like him in medieval Andhra who commissioned inscriptions have left behind a rich legacy for posterity.

Plan of the Book

Because the history of medieval Andhra is a history of transition, different chronological parameters are adopted here in order to best capture the various dimensions of its vitality. The broadest perspective is taken in chapter 1, which examines the distributions of Andhra inscriptions during the long span of time from 1000 to 1650 C.E. within the context of its political history and physical environment. In tracking the changing localities of epigraphic production over time, other long-term processes are highlighted: the gradual demographic movement toward the interior territories, the consequent shift of political power away from the coast, and the increasing salience of a Telugu cultural identity that spanned the lowlands and uplands. This overview of inscriptions provides the most dramatic illustration of the degree of change that occurred in the medieval period. By treating the making of inscriptions as a demonstrable and measurable cultural practice, it also uncovers a clear correlation between high levels of epigraphic production and the existence of strong polities.

The temporal focus is narrowed in chapters 2, 3, and 4 to the years from 1175 through 1324, the time span when the Kakatiya polity flourished and the largest quantity of inscriptions were produced. Each of these chapters focuses on a different facet of the expansionistic and vigorous world of Kakatiya Andhra that is revealed in inscriptions: the society in chapter 2, temple worship and patronage in chapter 3, and polity in chapter 4. Chapter 2 presents a social typology of class derived from inscriptional titles, and ultimately based on occupation, which was by no means fixed or rigid. In a period and place where opportunities for economic or political advancement and occasions for physical mobility were widespread, I argue, social identities fluctuated according to individual action and effort. Patronage of temples was one means through which new social identities and communities were formulated and chapter 3 takes a closer look at this as well as other consequences of religious endowment in the Kakatiya era, including the expansion of agricultural productivity and the strengthening of political ties. The practice of religious gift-giving not only diverged significantly from the norms laid out in Sanskrit literature but also varied considerably between the upland and lowland subregions because of their different developmental trajectories. The great achievement of the Kakatiya dynasty was the uniting of these two subregions into one overarching polity, a process that is carefully plotted in chapter 4. In analyzing both the strategies of the rulers and the changing composition of their network of subordinates, I advance an interpretation of medieval polity and political culture that emphasizes its heroic values and militaristic foundations more than previous scholarship has.

Chapter 5 looks retrospectively at the Kakatiya era from the vantage point of later times. Rather than trying to reconstruct the past directly via the medium of inscriptions, here I ask how subsequent generations of Andhra people transmitted and appropriated memories of the Kakatiyas and their period. Since the ways in which the Kakatiya past were made meaningful to Telugu society over time is the topic, I consult literary texts and early colonial accounts along with inscriptions. The concerns and methods of this chapter hence represent a departure from those of the earlier portion of the book. Through this comprehensive analysis of the historical traditions pertaining to a single Indian dynasty, I compare indigenous perceptions of the Kakatiya period's significance with my own interpretation. Additionally, I am able by this means to illustrate the vigor of precolonial India's historical imagination, which creatively recast the past in light of the changing circumstances of the present. Thus, as the regional society of Andhra continued to develop, so too did its sense of its own past as a community continue to evolve.

1

Andhra's Age of Inscriptions, 1000–1650

Although stone inscriptions can be found in various areas of the subcontinent from the third century B.C.E. onward, they were most abundantly produced in South India between approximately 1000 and 1650 C.E. As a cultural practice, therefore, the production of inscriptions is most characteristic of the medieval South. The large number of stone inscriptions issued throughout South India in these centuries visibly differentiate it not only from North India but also from both the classical South Indian society that preceded it and the early modern South Indian society that followed. The era of epigraphic efflorescence is thus a distinct phase in South India's development, and I have chosen the period from 1000 to 1650 as the chronological focus for this chapter on that basis, in a deviation from the common practice of identifying eras of Indian history solely on the basis of political factors.

The most notable feature of the age of inscriptions is, of course, the impulse to document religious gifts in a permanent form, for the great majority of stone inscriptions are records of substantial religious endowments. But this practice is in turn an index for a complex configuration of socioeconomic processes and cultural meanings. The rising popularity of the religious patronage of gods and brahmans is testimony to the spread of a pan-Indic culture that valued the expression of piety in such forms. The flurry of epigraphic activity was also predicated on economic development, however, for without an expansion of the agrarian base it was not possible for numerous localities to support temples and brahman villages. And, as explained in the discussion that follows, surges in state formation stimulated the production of inscriptions. By tracking the proliferation of the material artifact that is the stone inscription, we can trace the trajectories of a number of interrelated historical processes. Hence the aim of this chapter is to establish when and where inscriptions were issued within Andhra during the 650-year period from 1000 to 1650, so that we may better understand the overall developments in this age of inscriptions.

Implicit in my methodology is the assumption of a meaningful correlation between the distribution of inscriptions and the occurrence of other societal trends. There are some problematic features of this assumption, I admit. Since only inscriptions that have survived the vagaries of weather and changes in political control over the past few centuries are included in the corpus, we cannot assume that the current distribution of inscriptions is an exact reflection of the conditions in earlier times. It is quite probable, for instance, that a higher percentage of inscriptions once existed in northern interior Andhra (Telangana), which has often been under Muslim hegemony since 1323. The capital of the Kakatiya kingdom, Warangal, was attacked repeatedly after the fall of the dynasty and many inscriptions have undoubtedly been lost at the site of the original Kakatiya fort. Furthermore, many of the Kakatiya-period temples in Telangana are no longer living temples in the sense that they no longer house images that are actively worshiped (Wagoner 1986: 145–46). We may speculate that other abandoned temples were dismantled and their components used for building new structures, in the course of which valuable inscriptions would have been lost.

Another potential distortion arises from the process of epigraphic collection. Agencies of the government of India, and more recently of the state government of Andhra Pradesh, send out teams to gather ink rubbings of inscriptions, but these teams go on tour for short periods only and concentrate on areas where inscriptions are known to exist. New findings are still being reported today and the end is not in sight. Due to the unsystematic nature of the collection process, there may be an uneven pattern of surveyed localities with inscriptions in the relatively sparsely settled interior being overlooked But in view of the length of time that has passed since collection of inscriptions was begun, it seems unlikely that the figures are significantly skewed on this account.[1]

The best way to compensate for variables that may have differentially affected the survival of inscriptions is to collect as many inscriptions as possible. The larger the overall pool of sources, the better the chance it will resemble original distributions. I have made every effort, therefore, to be exhaustive in my collection and analysis of epigraphic sources.[2] The results should not be construed as definitive, nor do I claim any such status for them. But even a rudimentary sketch of the broad contours of Andhra epigraphic distributions is a great advance, given our current state of ignorance. At the minimum, it allows us to make some basic comparisons between Andhra and other areas of South India as well as to differentiate subperiods within the 650 years under consideration. At best, the surveying of inscriptions enables us to trace the progression of a series of dynamic and intertwined processes: agrarian settlement, the assimilation of tribal and pastoral peoples, and the emergence of an Andhra variant of a pan-Indic civilization.

I begin the chapter with a brief sketch of Andhra's geography and history prior to 1000 C.E., to provide a backdrop for the subsequent examination of inscriptional distributions in the 650 years after 1000. Only once the temporal and spatial dimensions of inscriptional distributions have been fully explored do I proceed to the issue of what we can infer from the patterns of epigraphic occurrence—that is, the factors shaping Andhra's age of inscriptions.

Physical Environment and Early History

The two most important environmental variables differentiating localities within Andhra are the elevation of land and the amount of rainfall. Because the Deccan plateau on which Andhra is situated tilts gently down in an easterly direction, the elevation gradually lessens as one traverses Andhra from the interior toward the coast. The undulating peneplains of the uplands of western Andhra range between approximately 1,000 and 2,000 feet in height, gradually decreasing to between 500 and 1,000 feet midway across the state (map 2). Intersecting this west-to-east drop in elevation are the Eastern Ghats, which run northeast to southwest through the state. Many geographers prefer the term Eastern Hills to describe this broken series of hills and ridges that do not form a continuous chain. Considerably lower than the Western Ghats, the Eastern Hills range from about 4,000 feet in the north to between 1,500 and 3,000 feet in the south, where several sets of hills can be differentiated, including the Nallamalas, Palkondas, and Velikondas. The Eastern Hills are breached in the middle by a wide deltaic stretch formed by the Godavari and Krishna Rivers. This deltaic area extends as far as 50 miles inland and constitutes the core of the coastal lowland region, the last major type of terrain in Andhra. North and south of the Krishna-Godavari River delta, the coastal lowlands are considerably narrower.[3]

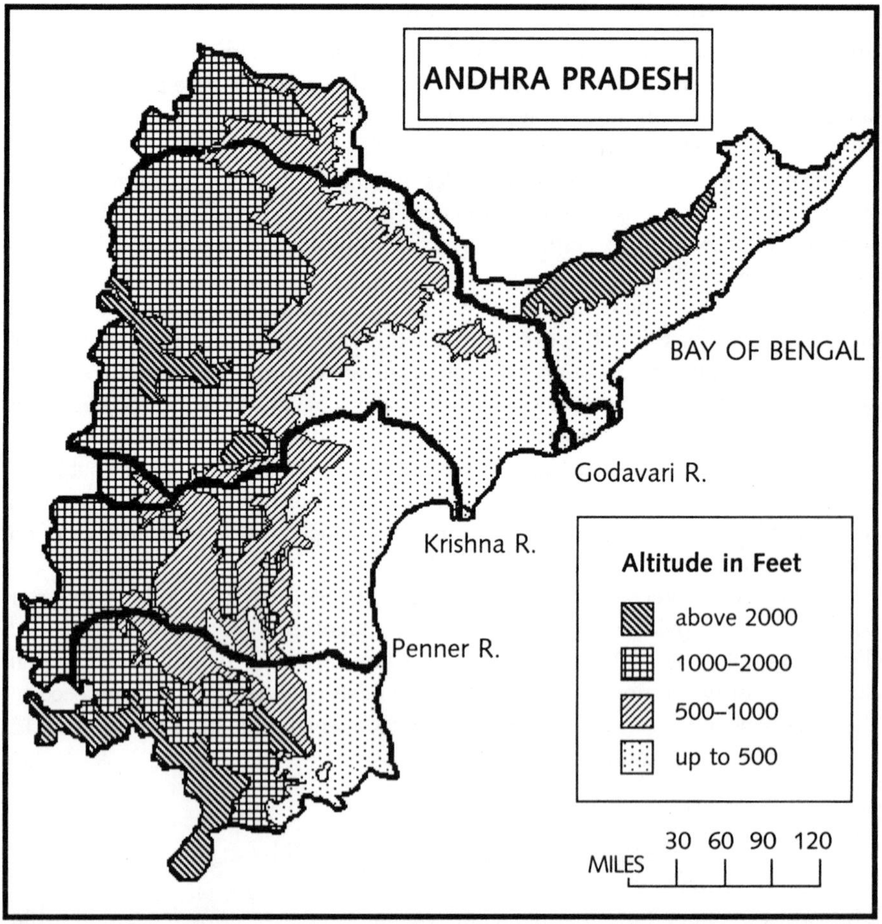

Map 2. Elevation and Major Rivers in Andhra

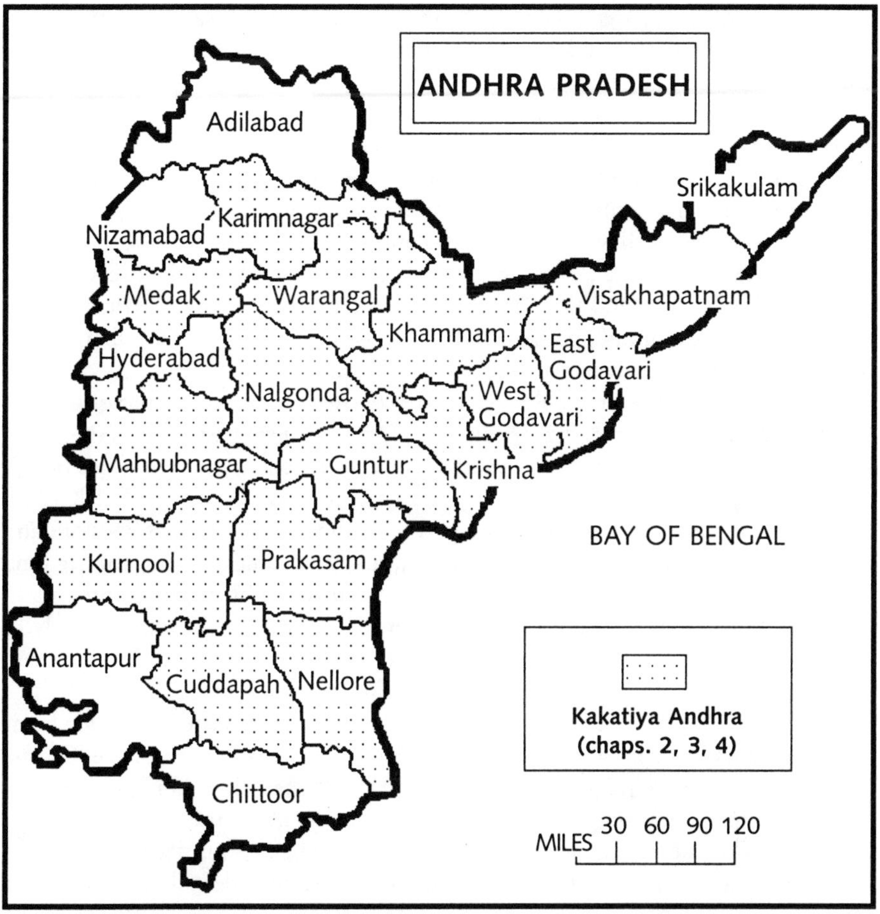

Map 3. Districts of Andhra Pradesh

Unlike the elevation of terrain that diminishes from west to east, rainfall contours in Andhra run in a north-south direction. Generally speaking, the highest amounts of rainfall are to be found in the northeastern districts, decreasing gradually to the southwest (Raychaudhuri et al. 1963: 1). Andhra north of the Krishna River receives the bulk of its precipitation during the southwest monsoon period between June and September, whereas southern Andhra gets most of its rain from the retreating or northeast monsoons from October to December (Vasantha Devi 1964: 18). Based on annual rainfall amounts, three basic zones can be distinguished within Andhra. The zone of heaviest rainfall, which receives between 40 and 45 inches annually, comprises the northern coastal districts, as well as a few of the northern interior districts (Adilabad, Nizamabad, and Khammam—see map 3 for location of districts). Less favored is the moderately dry zone of 30 and 40 inches of annual rainfall, encompassing some of the southeastern districts (Guntur, Nellore, and Chittoor) and several districts in the northwestern interior (Karimnagar, Medak, and Hyderabad). Less than 30 inches of rain fall in parts of central Andhra (Mahbubnagar, Nalgonda, Warangal, and Prakasam Districts) and in southwestern Andhra (Anantapur, Kurnool, and Cuddapah districts)—the latter being the driest zone in Andhra.[4] The southwestern districts are arid because they lie in a rainshadow region reached by neither the southwestern nor retreating monsoons (Vasantha Devi 1964: 18).

Proximity to sources of water is critical for agricultural production in Andhra, due to the general paucity of rainfall. Unfortunately, most streams dry up during the hot season, since they are rain-fed in contrast to the snow-fed rivers of North India. One example is the Penner or Pinakani River (map 2), which enters Andhra in Anantapur District and flows through Cuddapah and Nellore Districts, with a total length in Andhra of approximately 350 miles. The intermittent character of most rivers accentuates the importance of the Krishna and Godavari, the only two perennial rivers in the state. Rising in the Western Ghats of Maharashtra, the Godavari flows through Andhra for almost 500 miles. Once past the upland region where it often forms narrow channels, the Godavari broadens out to a width of $3^1/_2$ miles around the town of Rajahmundry and splits into five branches. The Krishna River also originates in Maharashtra but enters Andhra from Karnataka state and flows another 384 miles. At Vijayavada city, about 45 miles inland, the Krishna crosses a low ridge and then spreads out into a delta, splitting into three main branches. Since ancient times canal irrigation has drawn on the steady supply of water from these two major rivers but was practical only in the lowlands, where the rivers broadened and slowed before emptying into the Bay of Bengal.[5]

Besides benefiting from the accessibility of perennial water, the coastal lowlands were blessed with the most fertile soils in the state. The alluvial soils of the Krishna and Godavari River deltas, periodically renewed by silt, are richest in plant nutrients. Older alluvium containing less organic matter is found along the coast both north and south of the deltas. Somewhat less fertile are the black soils derived from lava flows and characteristic of the upper Deccan. In Andhra deep black soils exist primarily along the northern border of the state or where they have been introduced by rivers. Deposits of shallower black soil are also located in pockets in the southern portion of the state. Because of its high clay content, black soil is very moisture-retentive and can be used to grow crops like cotton without the need for irrigation. Most of Andhra, however, is covered with the less fertile red soils that developed in situ from the underlying peninsular bedrock. Almost 70 percent of the total area of the state has these red soils, which are highly permeable and of limited fertility without a regular and copious supply of water.[6]

Because of its agricultural productivity, the zone encompassing the Krishna and Godavari River deltas has been identified as the most crucial locale in Andhra, its "core" area. Core areas, alternatively called "nuclear regions," are defined by geographers as "bases of power which are perennially significant in Indian historical geography" (Spate 1954: 148). Proximity to water, enabling intensive agriculture and thus denser populations, was a fundamental feature of nuclear regions. But other factors such as ease of travel also played a part in determining where the earliest historic settlements would emerge. In Andhra, urban centers first developed in the lower Krishna River valley, rather than around the Godavari. Since a large part of the Godavari's course (from Khammam District westward) is through a densely forested and faulted trough, it was avoided by travelers who instead sought the wide opening of the Krishna River's passage through the hills (Geddes 1982: 86). By the early centuries C.E., plow cultivation and irrigation were widespread in the lower Krishna valley and two major urban centers emerged at Amaravati/ Dharanikota and Nagarjunakonda.

Other locales within the larger Krishna-Godavari delta soon joined the lower Krishna valley in developing denser settlements and producing historic source materials. Geographer David Sopher has remarked that where a culture core is spread over a broad territory with little change in physical environment, there is a tendency for centers of power to shift around (1962: 122). We witness this trend in Andhra from the fourth through sixth centuries, as several minor ruling families established their capitals outside the lower Krishna valley, although still within the Krishna-Godavari deltaic region. Among them were the Salankayanas of Vengipura, generally identified as the modern Peddavegi village near Eluru in West Godavari District, roughly midway between the Krishna and Godavari Rivers (Gopalachari 1941: 167). The city of Vengi retained its importance in succeeding years as the capital for three centuries of the long-lasting Eastern Chalukya rulers. The term Vengi gradually developed several other referents: Vengi-vishaya or Vengi-mandala designated the region surrounding the capital, while Vengi-desha and Vengi-nadu denoted the Eastern Chalukya kingdom (Mangalam 1979–80: 101). The entire deltaic region extending between the Krishna and Godavari Rivers was also often referred to as Vengi. By the last few centuries of the first millennium, the broad expanse of the Krishna-Godavari deltas had thus been established as the nuclear zone or core area of Andhra. Even today, the subregion of Andhra Pradesh known as Coastal Andhra (map 4), which includes the Krishna and Godavari deltas, is the most populated and wealthiest portion of the state.

Historic settlement proceeded at a much slower pace outside of coastal Andhra. Less suited for the intensive agriculture of wet rice cultivation, the interior portions of Andhra—Telangana in the north and Rayalasima in the south (map 4)—have hosted pastoral lifestyles since prehistoric times. Neolithic peoples left behind clear evidence of their cattle-raising in the form of huge ash-mounds, marking the sites of ancient stockades where cattle dung accumulated and was burnt off. Almost all of the ash-mounds have been found within a specific ecological zone in northern Karnataka and western Andhra, a semiarid region receiving less than 25 inches of annual rainfall (Allchin 1963; Murthy and Sontheimer 1980). The societies of the Iron Age were also based in the dryer upland expanses of the region, covered with poor savanna scrub. The Iron Age Pandukal culture, named after its distinctive "megalithic" burials, lasted from about the third century B.C.E. to the second century C.E. Its sites in Andhra are concentrated in the interior districts, as well as in the upland taluks (subdistricts) of Guntur (Leshnik 1974 and 1975). During the second half of the first millennium C.E., historic sources begin to appear in the interior. Minor local dynasties like the Renati Cholas of Cuddapah District and the Vaidumbas of the Cuddapah-Chittoor border figure in inscriptions from Rayalasima, whereas in Telangana most inscriptions were issued by people affiliated with the imperial dynasties of Karnataka. But far less is known about the early history of Rayalasima and Telangana than of coastal Andhra.

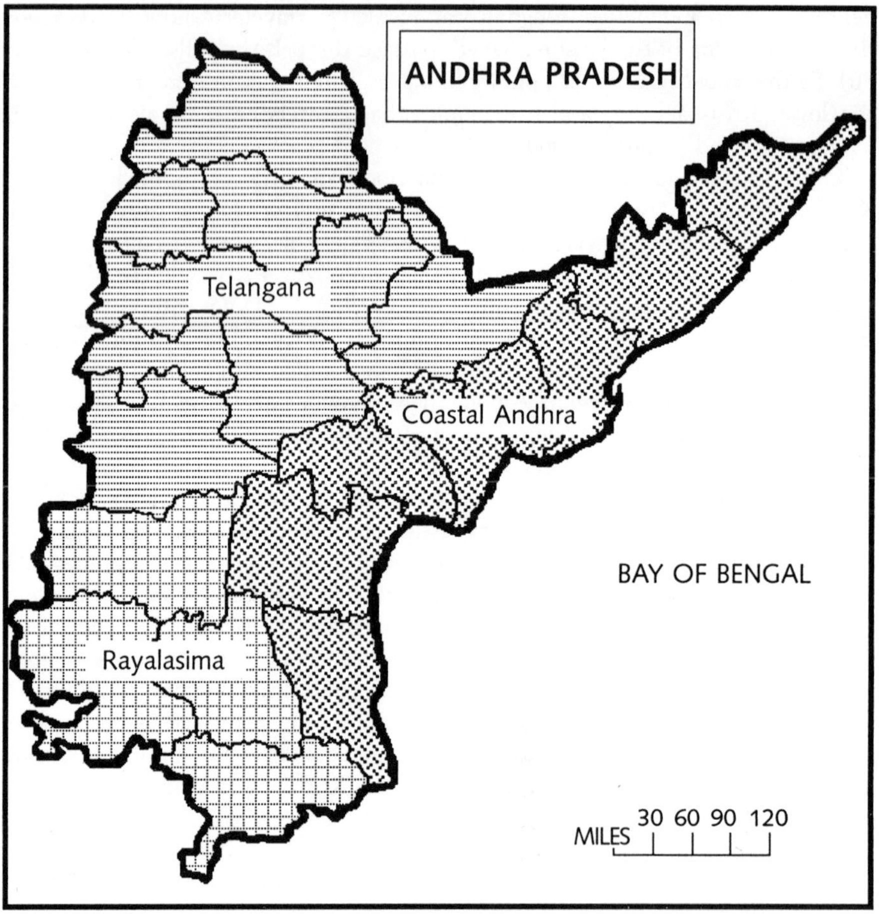

Map 4. Andhra Subregions

The only significant indigenous polity in Andhra prior to 1000 C.E. was that established by the Eastern Chalukyas beginning in 642. For the remainder of the first millennium C.E., the Eastern Chalukyas continued to control portions of coastal Andhra from their base in the fertile area of Vengi. But the extent of their territories and the degree of their independence fluctuated greatly, depending on the strength of polities based elsewhere in the peninsula. The Eastern Chalukyas initially faced little threat from the outside, because they were a junior branch of the powerful Badami Chalukyas of Karnataka. After the Badami Chalukyas were overthrown by the Rashtrakutas in the mid eighth century, however, Andhra was no longer insulated from interregional struggles for power. It soon became a contested zone between polities based in the Western Deccan and those in the far south. For much of the era of Rashtrakuta dominance in Karnataka (753–973 C.E.), the Eastern Chalukyas were either their acknowledged subordinates or were struggling to keep them at bay. Andhra also suffered from numerous campaigns on its territory fought by the Rashtrakutas and the Tamil power to the south (first the Pallavas of

Kanchipuram and later the Cholas of the Kaveri River delta). In 973 C.E. the Rashtrakutas were replaced as the dominant Karnataka dynasty by the Chalukyas of Kalyani, but the basic pattern of northwest-southeast conflict in the peninsula persisted and armies from other regions continued to fight over Andhra.

Distribution of Andhra Inscriptions

Andhra's age of inscriptions began slightly later than in the neighboring regions of Tamil Nadu and Karnataka, for the rise in the number of Andhra inscriptions does not begin until midway through the eleventh century. High rates of inscriptional production were reached by the early twelfth century in Andhra and were maintained, with some fluctuations, until the seventeenth century.[7] The two centuries yielding the largest quantities of inscriptions are the thirteenth and the sixteenth, coincidentally also the eras when strong polities existed in Andhra—the Kakatiya, in the case of the former, and Vijayanagara during the latter. Breaking down the 650-year span of time under consideration into century-long units would make our analysis of inscriptional distributions unwieldy, however. Instead, I have chosen to subdivide the age of inscriptions into four smaller units or subperiods corresponding roughly with changes in Andhra's political situation. This is not only less complicated than using century-long units of time but also enables us to gain a better perspective on the Kakatiya period from 1175 through 1324, the topic of the following three chapters. Moreover, as discussed in the pages that follow, dividing the entire time period into four smaller units reveals a correlation between epigraphic production and political stability: the Kakatiya and Vijayanagara states reached their zeniths during the same periods when the greatest number of inscriptions were issued.

The first of our (smaller) periods of analysis comprises the years from 1000 through 1174—in other words, from the commencement of the age of inscriptions until the era of Kakatiya hegemony. The time span when the Kakatiya dynasty rose to paramount status within Andhra constitutes the second period, from 1175 through 1324. The third period spans the years 1325 to 1499, and the fourth period encompasses the remainder of the age of inscriptions, from 1500 through 1649, when the Vijayanagara state was most closely involved with Andhra affairs. Table 1 displays the number of dated inscriptions issued during each of these periods

Table 1. Distribution of Andhra Inscriptions by Period

Period	Dates	Telugu[a]	Other[b]	Total
I	1000–1174	887	173	1,060
II	1175–1324	1,385	133	1,518
III	1325–1499	908	73	981
IV	1500–1649	1,159	308	1,467
All	1000–1649	4,339	687	5,026

a. Includes Sanskrit inscriptions in Telugu script.

b. Includes Sanskrit inscriptions in Kannada, Grantha, and Nagari scripts.

within the territory that now constitutes the modern state of Andhra Pradesh.[8] The inscriptions are divided into two categories: "Telugu," which covers all inscriptions composed solely in Telugu, in a combination of Telugu and Sanskrit, or solely in Sanskrit language but written in Telugu script;[9] and, second, "Other," which includes inscriptions composed in Persian, Arabic, and regional Indic languages other than Telugu, as well as Sanskrit-language inscriptions written in non-Telugu scripts.[10] Whether we look only at the "Telugu" category or at the total number of all dated inscriptions from Andhra, the second and fourth periods in table 1 stand out as the times of maximum epigraphic production.[11]

The significance of periods II and IV can only be appreciated within the larger context of Andhra's geopolitical history, for unlike Tamil Nadu and Karnataka, Andhra has seldom been politically unified nor powerful within the peninsula as a whole.[12] We have seen that Andhra was caught between two expansionist empires in 1000 C.E., when Period I commences. Both the Kalyani Chalukyas and the Cholas sought to dominate coastal Andhra by backing competing contenders to the Eastern Chalukya throne. A brief interlude of peace was ushered in when Kulottunga I, a Chola on the maternal side and an Eastern Chalukya on the paternal side, ascended the Chola throne. During the reign of this famous ruler (1070–1122), there was a strong Tamil presence along the Andhra coast, where several of Kulottunga's sons acted as viceroys. Shortly before Kulottunga's death, rivalry between the Kalyani Chalukyas and the Cholas resumed. The Cholas were assisted by small Andhra princely families situated along the coast, most importantly the Velanati Chodas. Andhra chiefs of the interior, on the other hand, fought in coalition with the Kalyani Chalukyas. As incessant warfare weakened the once mighty imperial Chola and Chalukya dynasties, these minor Andhra princes and chiefs began to act in an increasingly independent fashion. By approximately 1160, the Velanati Chodas assumed their own imperial titles. One of the main chiefly lineages of interior Andhra was the Kakatiyas, who declared their independent status in 1163.

Period II (1175–1324) marks the rise of the Kakatiyas to a hegemonic position within the region. Beginning from their base in northern inland Andhra, the Kakatiyas gradually built up a political network that at its height encompassed roughly two-thirds of the territory within the modern state. While the Kakatiyas were forced at times to repel invading armies, they were never subjugated by any other South Indian polity, unlike the Eastern Chalukyas. The good fortune of the Kakatiyas resulted from the division of peninsular India in this period into four regional kingdoms that were equally balanced in power—the polities commanded by the Yadavas or Seunas of southern Maharashtra and northern Karnataka, the Hoysalas of Mysore, and the Pandyas of the Tamil country, in addition to the Kakatiyas of Andhra. Armed incursions of the Delhi sultanate disrupted the peninsular balance of power beginning in the late thirteenth century and eventually brought about the collapse of all four regional kingdoms. The Kakatiyas survived several earlier sultanate campaigns before succumbing in 1323, when their capital Warangal was captured and their political network destroyed.

Period III (1325–1499) began in a time of great turmoil, when existing political networks were entirely overthrown. Several new Telugu warrior lineages managed to carve out small areas for themselves during the second half of the fourteenth century, although they always had to contend with threats from polities based outside Andhra. By the early fifteenth century, however, these Telugu chiefdoms had largely disappeared and their place was taken by more powerful, and nonindigenous, states. One of the outside polities was the Bahmani sultanate of Gulbarga and Bidar, founded in 1347, who now dominated large portions of western interior Andhra. The Vijayanagara kingdom of southern Karnataka, whose establishment is traditionally dated to 1336, controlled much of southern interior Andhra. Another strong power—the Gajapatis of Orissa—entered the fray around 1450 and seized the coastal strip of Andhra. In the last 50 years of the period, Andhra witnessed constant vacillations in the balance of power (and territory controlled) between these three kingdoms.

In the first half of Period IV (1500–1649), all of southern Andhra was incorporated into the Vijayanagara kingdom. The greatest of all Vijayanagara kings, Krishnadeva Raya (r. 1509–1529), launched a sustained campaign against the Gajapatis who were thereby pushed back into northern Andhra. The Vijayanagara kingdom now comprised a contiguous stretch of territory extending from the Western Ghats in Karnataka to the Andhra coast south of the Krishna River in the east. Meanwhile, the Qutb Shah dynasty broke off from the Bahmani sultanate and displaced the Gajapatis as the dominant power in northern Andhra by the 1530s. The most momentous event of Period IV occurred in 1565, when the Vijayanagara capital was sacked by a coalition of Deccani sultanates. The Aravidu dynasty of Vijayanagara retrenched within its native southern Andhra territory, and a brief resurgence of glory occurred during the reign of Venkata II (r. 1586–1614). Thereafter, however, Aravidu power waned rapidly and by 1650 most of Andhra was under the hegemony either of the Adil Shah kingdom of Bijapur (in Karnataka) or the Qutb Shah kingdom of Golkonda and Hyderabad.

How do the tides of political fortune I have just narrated correspond to the production of inscriptions? Period I (1000–1174) can be summed up as a politically unstable era lacking a dominant political configuration, a time when Andhra was recurrently enmeshed in the larger power struggles of the peninsula. Fewer Telugu inscriptions were issued during Period I than in any other, but even the inclusion of non-Telugu inscriptions gives Period I only a ranking of second from the lowest in number. In marked contrast, Period II (1175–1324) was characterized by the sway of one polity, the Kakatiyas, for much of the time. Period II is unusual both in its political unity and in the fact that the paramount power was an indigenous dynasty. It yields both the largest numbers of Telugu inscriptions and of all inscriptions added together.

During Period III (1325–1499) Andhra once more experienced much political disturbance. The overall number of inscriptions issued during Period III is even lower than in Period I. This must be attributed at least partially to the destabilization of the region caused by the incursions of the Muslim armies from the North. It is difficult to explain the sharp drop in epigraphic levels after the fall of the Kakatiyas otherwise, particularly when we see that epigraphic levels rebound in Period IV. That is, once the age of inscriptions was inaugurated, we might expect to see a slow increase in inscriptions as long-term trends such as agricultural expansion gradually unfolded, if no other factors were involved. But rampant political instability and specifically the absence of a powerful polity encompassing large portions of Andhra seem to have adversely affected epigraphic production.

The Vijayanagara empire never controlled as much territory within Andhra as did the Kakatiyas, nor was Vijayanagara strength in Andhra as long-lasting. But Period IV (1500–1649) was an era of political unity for southern Andhra, especially prior to 1565. Although the Vijayanagara polity was originally based outside of Andhra, during the sixteenth century it became increasingly Telugu, in terms of both its military personnel and political culture. After the destruction of the Karnataka capital in 1565 and the subsequent withdrawal of the Vijayanagara kings to bases within Andhra, Vijayanagara became a solely Telugu enterprise. In this way, Vijayanagara after 1500 can be viewed not as a foreign kingdom but as an indigenous Andhra polity. These similarities between the Kakatiya and Vijayanagara eras may explain why Period IV yields almost as many records as Period II, in a remarkable resurgence from the low levels of epigraphic production found during Period III.

Although inscriptions continue to be issued at a modest rate in subsequent centuries, Andhra's age of inscriptions was well nigh over by the seventeenth century. Scholars of Tamil Nadu have similarly observed a substantial drop in inscriptions once Vijayanagara's power had been sharply curtailed (Narayana Rao, Shulman, and Subrahmanyam 1992: 89; Ludden 1985: 70–71). The continuing scarcity of inscriptions throughout South India after 1600 seems to reflect a fundamental transformation that transcends the correlation between political scale and epigraphic production. It may be that the rates of demographic and agrarian growth had leveled off throughout the peninsula, after four centuries of escalation.

Aside from such economic causes about which we can only speculate, we also have firm evidence of a change in patronage patterns. In the late sixteenth and seventeenth centuries, the preferred object of religious gift was no longer land, nor a herd of milk-bearing animals, nor even lump sums of cash to be invested. Instead, the kings and chiefs of post-Vijayanagara South India favored the ostentatious feeding of gods and brahmans (*annadāna*), an ephemeral form of religious charity that was not permanently documented on stone. The growing liquidity of the early modern economy, which was highly monetized and commercialized, has been correlated with this shift in religious practice (Narayana Rao, Shulman, and Subrahmanyam 1992: 67–72).[13] The ending of the era of copious epigraphic documentation thus corresponds to a momentous change in the political economy of South India and represents the transition from a medieval to an early modern world.

We have established a clear correspondence in medieval Andhra between the presence of strong polities and high levels of epigraphic activity, yet the reasons for this phenomenon have not yet been explored. Extensive royal patronage of temples is not the answer, despite the emphasis in the secondary literature on the connection between Hindu kings and temples. In fact, the religious beneficence of Kakatiya and Vijayanagara kings was quite limited.[14] Rather than overlords, their political subordinates were responsible for many of the gifts recorded in Andhra inscriptions. The same pattern has been noted for the Tamil country under the Chola dynasty

(Heitzman 1997: 115; Stein 1980: 230). Although local leaders and minor chiefs existed in all periods of medieval Andhra history, it was during the eras when such individuals were incorporated into larger polities that they left behind the greatest quantity of inscriptions. This strongly suggests that political intermediaries utilized inscriptions, if not religious gift-giving itself, to attain political objectives within the supralocal world of the large kingdom.

I further examine motivations for religious gift-giving in chapter 3, but let me briefly mention several points that are relevant to our present discussion. Upwardly mobile political intermediaries in late medieval South India often sought to endow temples in order to enhance their own prestige and legitimacy. This was especially common when they moved into newly acquired territories, since gift-giving was a primary method for achieving integration into a locality (Appadurai 1977). Competition between various local notables participating in the same political network could result in flurries of temple-building and other forms of religious patronage (Ludden 1985: 31). Subordinates frequently expressed solidarity and allegiance to an overlord in their inscriptions (Stein 1960: 171) and may have been more inclined to record their religious benefactions because they could offer homage to their lord in doing so. Another possible incentive may have been the desire of political intermediaries to protect their resources from state taxation. Endowments made to temples, which were taxed at lesser rates, were sometimes left in the management of their original proprietors, who thus retained a measure of control (as well as profit) over them. The greater complexity of large polities may also have encouraged more people to document their endowments in the form of imperishable stone inscriptions, so that they could have public proof of the transfer of rights over valuable property. The abundance of inscriptions from the early part of the sixteenth century that confirm prior endowments is striking in this respect. After decades of turmoil in the late fifteenth century, representatives of the Vijayanagara state in Andhra sought to reassure temples and others of their secure property rights and tax exemptions by this means.

The chronological correlation between high levels of inscriptions and the presence of large stable polities indicates that epigraphic production was a social act directly linked to the growth and vitality of political networks. But, we have not yet investigated another aspect of inscriptional distributions—their geographic location. The addition of this second dimension to the pattern of epigraphic occurrence immediately makes it apparent that neither inscriptions nor polities were uniformly dispersed within the region of Andhra. Indeed, shifts in the geographic sites of inscriptional production over the four subperiods of the age of inscriptions are as dramatic as the fluctuations in numbers of records over time.

Prior to 1000 C.E., as previously explained, the core area of Andhra was situated along the coast, specifically the strip of coastal lowland stretching from the Godavari to Krishna River deltas. In contrast, much less is known about the early history of interior Andhra. The historical record remains spotty for much of interior Andhra even into the beginning of the second millennium. This can readily be seen in map 5, which displays the expanse of territory within which inscriptions dating from Period I (1000–1174) have been retrieved. Because it is not possible to identity the exact location of every site, maps 5 through 8 depict each taluk or subdistrict

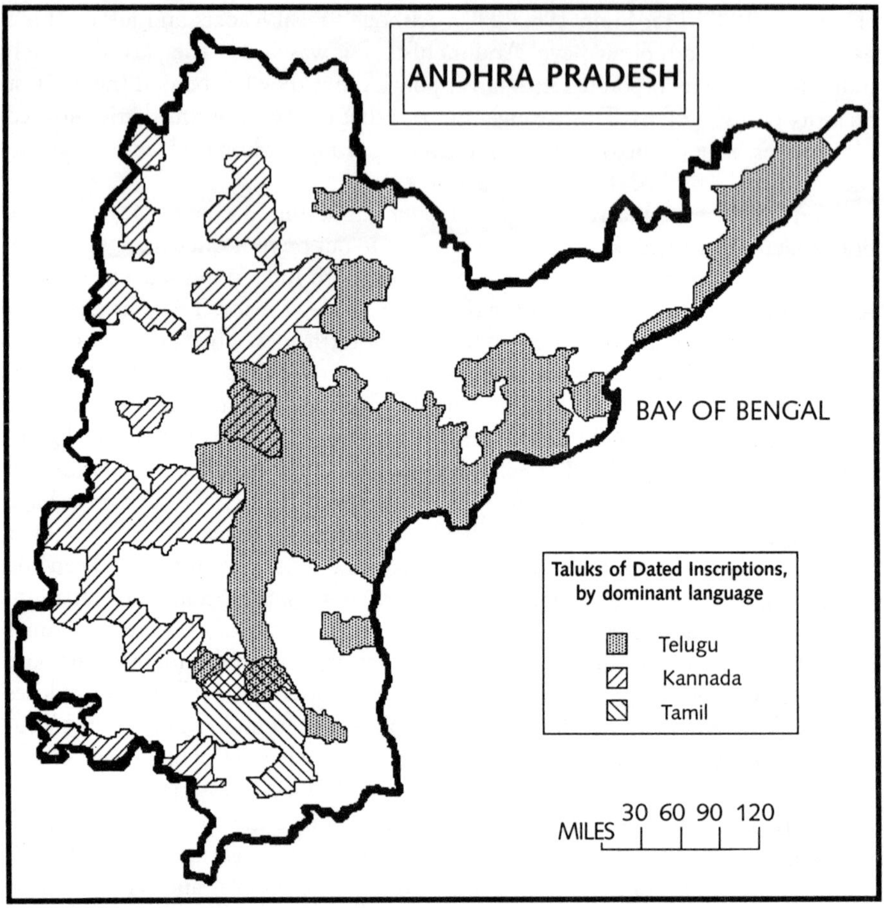

Map 5. Geographic Distribution of Inscriptions, 1000–1174

where an inscription has been found.[15] The most noticeable feature of map 5 is the empty space—the blank area lacking inscriptions along the northern, western, and southern borders of the state. Epigraphic find-spots are concentrated along the northeastern coast and in the central part of the state, in contiguous blocks. In western and southern Andhra, in contrast, several areas yielding inscriptions were geographically isolated.

There was a noticeable extension of epigraphic production during Period II (1175–1324), as shown in map 6. Considerably more of the modern state's territory was encompassed in the inscription-creating culture. The majority of taluks (subdistricts) yield inscriptions from this period, with the exceptions being situated primarily along the northern and western borders. Furthermore, the taluks yielding inscriptions are now contiguous to one another rather than being isolated, as they sometimes were earlier.

We witness a southerly shift in the territory where inscriptions were issued during Periods III (1325–1499) and IV (1500–1649), displayed in maps 7 and 8,

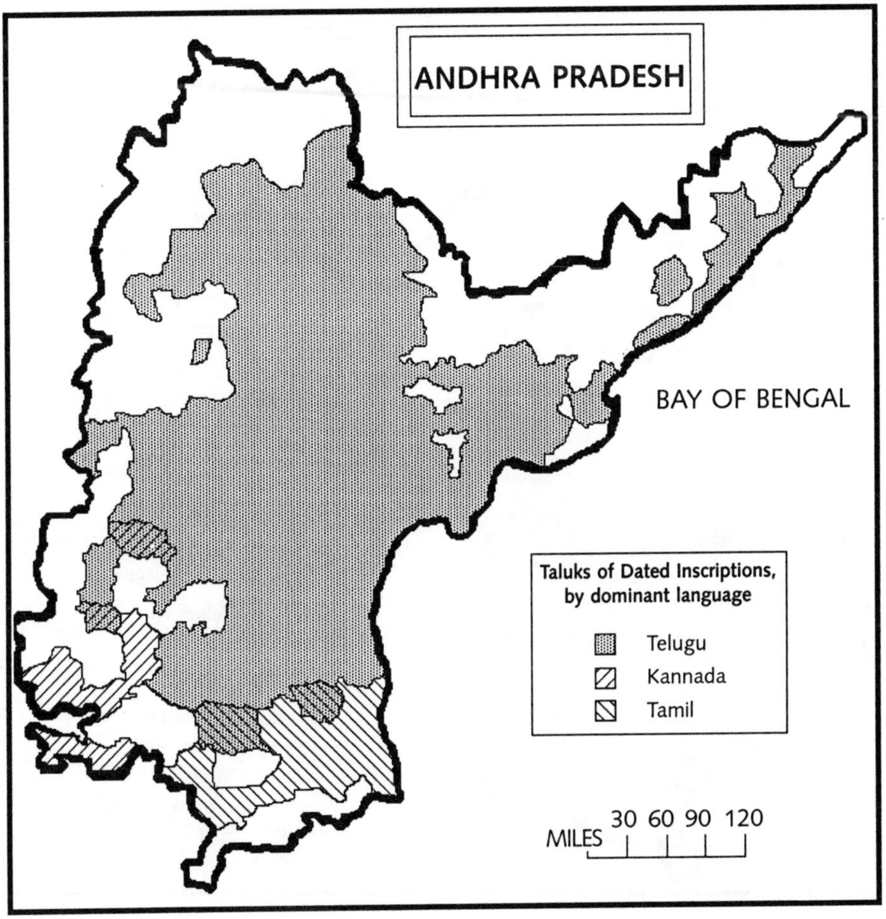

Map 6. Geographic Distribution of Inscriptions, 1175–1324

respectively. A somewhat larger number of localities in Rayalasima produced inscriptions during Period III, and by Period IV virtually all of Rayalasima is encompassed within the inscription-making culture. This gain in southern Andhra is more than offset, however, by a marked contraction in the area yielding inscriptions in northern Andhra. Particularly striking is the shrinkage in the spatial spread of Telangana inscriptions during Period III. Telangana rebounds to a certain degree by Period IV, but to nothing like its former levels during Periods I or II. Once Qutb Shah control of Telangana had stabilized, in other words, epigraphic levels rose slightly. But clearly, the religious patronage of Hindu temples did not appeal as much to the political subordinates of the Qutb Shah state as it did to those affiliated with Vijayanagara. Meanwhile, northern coastal Andhra remains fairly consistent in its areal extent of epigraphic production throughout all four periods, with some slight loss during Period IV.

Looking at all four maps, we can see the gradual movement of inscriptional activity from the core region of coastal Andhra in Period I, to the northern

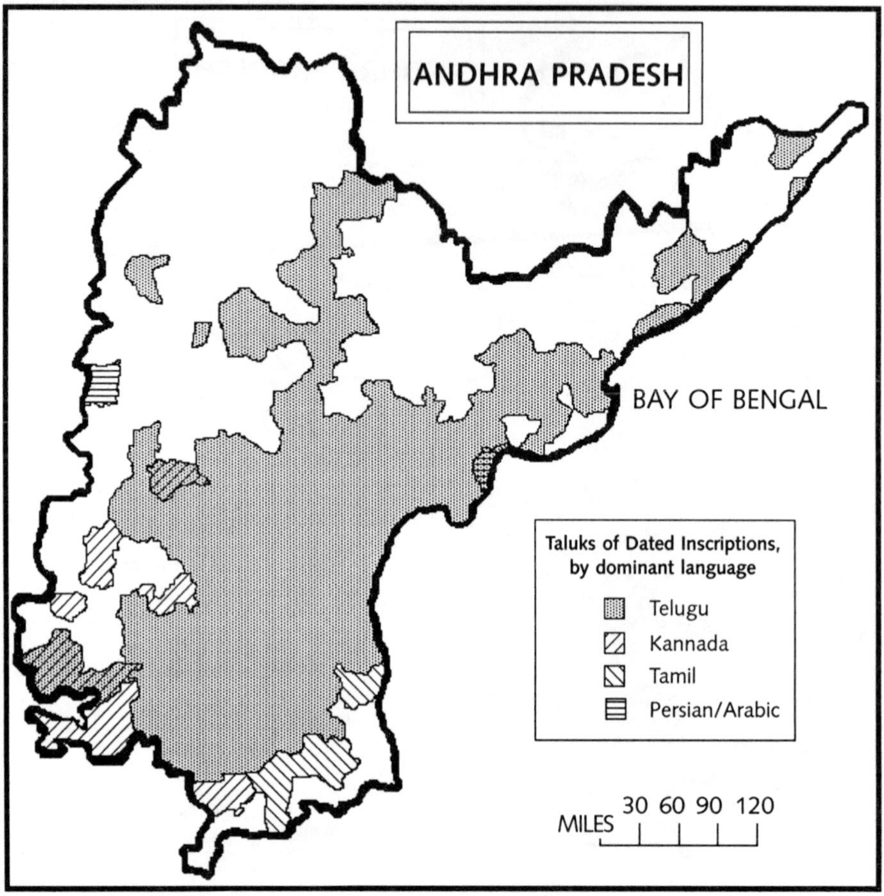

Map 7. Geographic Distribution of Inscriptions, 1325–1499

interior in Period II, and subsequently to the southern interior in Periods III and IV. During the age of inscriptions, different subregions of Andhra took turns as the locus of inscriptional production. For Telangana, Period II (1175–1324) was the era of the maximum geographic extent of inscriptions, but it was only in Period IV (1500–1649) that Rayalasima's production of inscriptions achieved its largest territorial expanse. Once again, changes in political control offer the most obvious explanation for this differential distribution. Period II is the era of the Kakatiya polity, based in Telangana, whereas the major polity of Period IV was that of Vijayanagara, based in southern Andhra. Thus, our analysis reveals that the geographic spread of inscriptions was influenced by shifts in the location of the centers of political power, which reinforces the connection between political activity and epigraphic production that we noted in relation to the chronological distribution of inscriptions.

Overall, during Period II (1175–1324), or the Kakatiya period, the largest amount of territory in Andhra was producing inscriptions and also yielding the largest

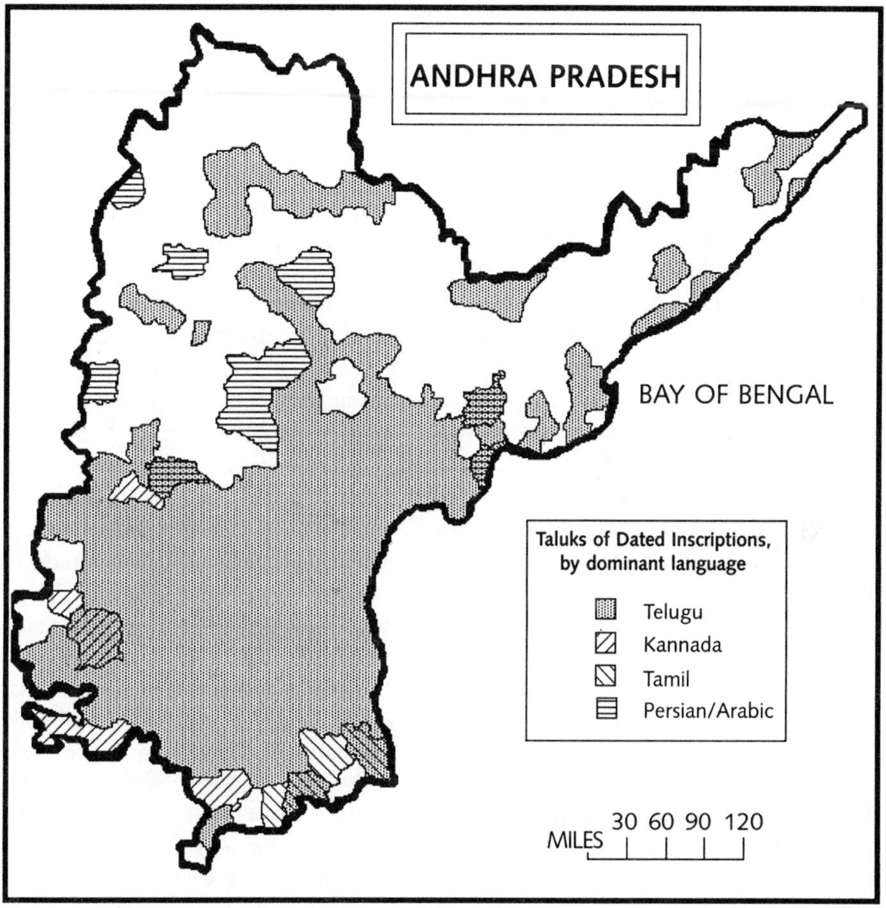

Map 8. Geographic Distribution of Inscriptions, 1500–1649

quantity of inscriptions. There is some connection between these two patterns of epigraphic distribution, of course. It is not surprising that high numbers of inscriptions result when many localities are involved in their production. On the other hand, high levels of inscriptions do not necessarily have to originate from a wide region. Only 50 fewer inscriptions come from Period IV than from Period II, although the area involved during Period II is substantially bigger. The method of mapping inscriptional locations used here is not very precise, of course. If the actual village sites were shown rather than the taluks where inscriptions are situated, we might see a greater discrepancy in the maps illustrating the geographical spread of inscriptions during the various periods. But the fact that the maximum territorial dispersion of inscriptions—their largest perimeter—was attained during Period II (1175–1325) would not change. The large size of the Kakatiya political network, which eventually controlled much of Andhra, was a clear factor in the unusually extensive expanse of inscriptional production during Period II.[16]

The Telugu Linguistic Region

Because the modern state of Andhra Pradesh was created on the basis of its linguistic unity, it is easy to forget that languages other than Telugu were formerly spoken within the state's boundaries. In fact, the current distribution of Telugu is a fairly recent phenomenon. If we limit our perspective to records inscribed in Telugu and/or Sanskrit in Telugu script, the geographic expansion of epigraphic production during the Kakatiya period is even more striking. Prior to 1000 C.E., Telugu inscriptions had been issued in some parts of inland Andhra, notably in Cuddapah and Chittoor Districts.[17] But the bulk of Telugu epigraphic activity was centered in coastal Andhra, whereas large portions of upland Andhra were part of the Kannada or Tamil epigraphic spheres. The patterns of the first millennium persisted until the late twelfth century, as we can see in map 5. Between 1000 and 1174, Telugu and Sanskrit inscriptions in Telugu script were quite restricted in scope, appearing primarily in the central core of Andhra—Vengi and its immediate hinterland as well as the northeastern districts bordering Orissa. Less than half of modern Andhra Pradesh's territory yielded Telugu inscriptions in this earliest period.

The Telugu area virtually doubled in Period II (1175–1324), when much of southern Andhra and considerably more of Telangana were absorbed in the Telugu inscriptional sphere. By the end of the Kakatiya era, approximately three-quarters of the modern state were participating in a culture of religious endowment and epigraphic documentation in the Telugu language (map 6). The southerly trend of inscriptional production continues in Period III (1325–1499). The territory encompassed by Telugu inscriptions begins to approach modern state boundaries in the south and southwest but recedes in Telangana (map 7). Telangana is somewhat more active in Period IV (1500–1649), when the greatest southern and western extent of Telugu records can be observed (map 8). In this last era Telugu inscriptions are also found beyond the modern state boundaries in the western and southern directions.[18]

The greater range of the Telugu language area partly results from the displacement of other epigraphic languages. Prior to 1175 Kannada was prevalent over much of western Andhra. In southern Andhra, Kannada was interspersed with Tamil, the other major epigraphic language found within Andhra at this time.[19] Not until the Kakatiya period (1175–1324) does Telugu become the ascendant epigraphic language in Andhra, primarily at the expense of Kannada. Telangana largely shifted from using Kannada in its inscriptions to using Telugu during the Kakatiya era. Kannada was now the dominant epigraphic language in only a few areas of Rayalasima, within Kurnool and Anantapur Districts. It took a little longer for Telugu to have much impact on Tamil usage, which began to diminish in Period III. The impact of the establishment of Muslim polities in the Deccan can be seen in the appearance of Persian and Arabic inscriptions in portions of Telangana after 1500 C.E. (Period IV).

What does the growth of Telugu as an epigraphic language signify? One of the primary factors behind the sharp increase in Telugu use in Telangana was a change in the political situation. This is suggested by the rapidity with which Kannada was abandoned in the mid twelfth century when almost all of Telangana adopted Telugu for the purpose of inscribing records. Previously Telangana had been part of a larger Kannada inscriptional culture, extending into Maharashtra from its core area in Karnataka. But as the influence of the Kalyani Chalukya empire based in Karnataka waned, so too did the number of Kannada inscriptions issued within Andhra. Of the 130 dated Kannada records from Telangana issued between 1000 and 1649, only 9 were composed after 1150. All over Telangana, minor kings and chiefs switched to Telugu inscriptions in the last decades of Period I.

The Kakatiya dynasty's epigraphic practices exemplify this rapid transition caused by a shift in the balance of power. The Kakatiyas first issued inscriptions in Kannada that were very closely modeled on those of their imperial overlords, the Chalukyas of Kalyani. The same general inscriptional format was used by Chalukya subordinates elsewhere in the Deccan interior as well as in Telangana.[20] But once the Kakatiya dynasty terminated its allegiance to the Kalyani Chalukyas, beginning with Kakatiya Rudradeva's reign (r. 1158–1195), the language of their inscriptions changed. Before the time of Rudradeva, all records belonging to the Kakatiyas or their followers cited a Chalukya king as the overlord. Only two of these twelve inscriptions are in Telugu, with the remainder being composed in Kannada or Sanskrit and Kannada.[21] From the time of Rudradeva onward, however, the Chalukya dynasty was no longer referred to and all records are in Telugu and/or Sanskrit.[22]

The Kakatiya example illustrates how the political elites of interior Andhra switched their epigraphic usage from the Kannada of their previous overlords to Telugu as they gained stature and autonomy. The speed and thoroughness with which Telugu was adopted suggests that it was already the spoken language of eastern and central Telangana, the Kakatiya base. When the languages used by political elites for cultural production were not those widely spoken, their impact was far more limited.[23] Hence, in shifting their allegiance from Kannada to Telugu, the Kakatiya rulers were both expressing their political independence and their own distinct identity as members of the Telugu literary community.

The early dominance of Kannada inscriptions in western Andhra is only one sign of the pervasive contact between the Kannada and Telugu cultural spheres in this era. Until the twelfth century, Telugu and Kannada shared the same script (Rama Rao 1974: 2, 77). Even today there are strong resemblances between the Telugu and Kannada scripts, although the languages themselves are quite distinct.[24] Many other Karnataka cultural traits were widespread in upland Andhra. Western Telangana's temples were almost identical in form to those of northern Karnataka, while eastern Telangana architectural styles were closely related.[25] As various chiefs in Andhra began to issue their own coins in the late twelfth century, they borrowed both names and forms from the Karnataka currency tradition (Chattopadhyaya 1977: 133–34). Religious trends also mirrored those of Karnataka. Jainism, the favored religion of the Hoysala rulers of southern Karnataka through the early twelfth century, was patronized until that time in Telangana as well.[26] Subsequently the Kalamukha sect of Shaivism received considerable support both in Andhra and Karnataka.[27]

In many ways, therefore, western Andhra was part of the larger Kannada cultural universe during Period I, at least at the level of political elites. Telangana inscriptions of the early second millennium were not only composed in the Kannada language but followed the conventional format and rhetorical style of Kannada inscriptions.

Some elements of the Kannada epigraphic style lingered on into the Kakatiya period. The impact of Kannada and Karnataka on Andhra has not been much remarked upon, perhaps because few scholars have studied interior Andhra. In contrast, the Tamil influence on Andhra has received far more attention because most historians of South India specialize in the Tamil region.[28] Yet for Andhra as a whole, Karnataka was an equally important stimulus in the early medieval period. The abandonment of Kannada in favor of Telugu, for composing inscriptions, signifies the breaking away of Telangana from the Kannada cultural sphere and its growing incorporation into the Andhra or Telugu cultural sphere centered in Vengi on the coast. With the expansion of Telugu epigraphic usage during the Kakatiya period, the contours of the modern linguistic state were beginning to take shape.

Even in the beginning of Andhra's age of inscriptions, we find that the region of Andhra is clearly associated with the area within which the Telugu language was spoken. Because of this mutual connection, the term *āndhra bhāṣa* (the language of Andhra) is used as a synonym for Telugu in the Nandampudi inscription of 1053.[29] The composer of the inscription, Nannaya Bhatta, states that the brahman recipient of the grant was a poet in the Sanskrit, Karnata, Prakrit, Paishachi, and Andhra languages (Iswara Dutt 1967: iii). The phrase "Andhra language" reappears in later inscriptions like the Amaravati inscription of 1226 (SII 6.221) and the Malkapuram inscription of 1261 (SII 10.395). In these bilingual Sanskrit and Telugu records, the explanation "and now it will be stated in the language of Andhra for clarity's sake" (*adhunā spaṣṭ=ārtham-āndhra-bhāṣay=ōcyatē*) appears after the long introductory portion in Sanskrit. In such expressions, Andhra is characterized as having its own mother tongue and so its territory is implicitly equated with the extent of the Telugu language.[30] The equivalence between the Telugu linguistic sphere and the geographical space of Andhra is also brought out in an eleventh-century description of Andhra's boundaries. Andhra, according to this text, was bounded in the north by the Mahendra mountain in the modern Ganjam District of Orissa and to the south by the Kalahasti temple in Chittoor District. But Andhra extended westward only as far as Srisailam in the eastern portion of Kurnool District, about halfway across the modern state (Sundaram 1968: 1). This description of Andhra's boundaries corresponds roughly to the maximum spread of Telugu inscriptions between 1000 and 1174 C.E., shown in map 5.

The noted Andhra historian M. Somasekhara Sarma believes that a consciousness of unity based on the use of Telugu began to grow stronger in the late twelfth century. Before the Kakatiya era, most geographic references in Telugu literature were to distinct subregions within the state. But from the late twelfth century onward, the label Andhra to designate the entire territory inhabited by Telugu speakers appears more frequently in literary sources. Examples can be found in the writings of the thirteenth-century Telugu author Tikkana, who refers to the Andhra populace, and the fourteenth-century Vidyanatha, who called the last Kakatiya king Prataparudra "the lord of the Andhra realm" (Somasekhara Sarma 1945: 2). The correspondence of the Telugu language and the Andhra region is also now expressed in a more explicit manner. The two words were virtually congruent and so could be used interchangeably, as in a mid-fourteenth-century inscription that equates the Andhra country (*dēśa*) with the Telugu country (IAP-W.103)—the language, the physical territory, and the culture are all conflated into one. As the Telugu linguistic realm expanded during the second period in the age of inscriptions, so too did the conception of Andhra's territorial extent. Telangana was now encompassed within the Andhra region, as is clear in Kakatiya-period inscriptions from Warangal that praise it as the best city within all of Andhra up to the shores of the ocean (EI 36.27, vv. 1 and 21). By the time Kakatiya Prataparudra is called the lord of Andhra in the early fourteenth century, the Andhra region was thought to include large expanses lying to the west of Srisailam and was therefore a much larger area than it had been in Period I.

The continuing expansion of the Andhra region as a conceptual space is evident from an inscription dated in 1403, less than a century after the fall of the Kakatiyas. It describes Andhra as the land in which the Godavari, Krishna, Malapaha, Bhimarathi or Bhima, and Tungabhadra Rivers flowed (Sarma and Krishnamurty 1965–66: 168).[31] The Bhima River is a tributary of the Krishna that joins it at the border between modern Mahbubnagar District of Andhra Pradesh and the neighboring state of Karnataka. The confluence of the Tungabhadra and the Krishna occurs a little further to the southeast, between the Andhra districts of Mahbubnagar and Kurnool. The conceptual dimensions of the Andhra country in the early fifteenth century had by this time expanded westward to its modern boundaries, in contrast to the situation in the eleventh century when the western border of Andhra had been conceived as extending only about halfway as far from the coast. As time passed and the Telugu language area gradually grew larger, we therefore find a corresponding enlargement of the region considered to be Andhra—a striking correlation between linguistic practice and cultural theory.

For Andhra, the most important era in establishing the linguistic and, ultimately cultural, unity of the region was Period II, or the Kakatiya era (1175–1324). The transformation of Telangana from an area of mostly Kannada inscriptions to one that was predominantly Telugu in character during the Kakatiya period meant that inland Andhra was increasingly united with the earlier heartland of Telugu culture along the coastal territory. Andhra as we know it today thus began to take shape in Period II. The same thing can be said of the Marathi-speaking region, which began to take form in the late twelfth century when the first Marathi inscriptions appeared as a result of the rise of the Yadava dynasty (Eaton 1978: 5–6). With the emergence of Marathi, the basic contours of the modern-day linguistic distributions of peninsular India were largely set. Not only had four of the five languages existing today in the peninsula developed their own epigraphic spheres and literatures by the Kakatiya era,[32] but they had also found political expression in the form of a regional kingdom—the Marathi-speaking area in the case of the Yadavas, the Telugu-speaking area of the Kakatiyas, the Kannada area of the Hoysalas, and the Tamil area for the Pandyas. Once the identification of languages with regions had been firmly articulated in the era of regional kingdoms, it continued to persist in subsequent centuries even after the loss of political unity. And so we find that Andhra inscriptions from Periods III and IV routinely label the various rulers flourishing within Andhra as Telugu kings and differentiate them from the rulers of other linguistic regions, such as the Odda kings (i.e., the kings of the Oriya-speaking region) or those of the land of the Kannada language, Karnata (e.g., SII 4.659 and 6.905).

Settlement of Interior Andhra

While political factors have much to do with the growth of Andhra as a cultural region during the Kakatiya era, the most important long-term trend behind the increasing unity of coastal and interior Andhra was the continuing settlement of Andhra's inland territories from 1000 C.E. onward. We have seen that only a fraction of the territory now included in Andhra Pradesh state was part of the culture that built temples and recorded endowments to them on stone at the commencement of the second millennium. Over the next 650 years, inscriptions were issued in more and more Andhra localities, in a gradual movement outward from the earlier core area along the coast. The political center of Andhra similarly shifted gradually from the coastal subregion into the interior during the same time period. These two phenomena can be interpreted as signs of growing population and agricultural settlement in inland Andhra during the second millennium, since temple institutions and brahman villages flourished only within an agrarian economy. This is not to suggest an inevitable correlation between agrarian development and the founding of temples, since various religious and social incentives played a big role in individual decisions regarding the making of charitable donations. In addition, religious endowments often themselves contributed to the expansion of a locality's agrarian base, as I discuss in chapter 3. But without an agrarian sector it was not possible for a locality to support temples or brahman villages and so a certain level of agricultural development was a necessary, if not sufficient, condition for the spread of the inscription-making culture.[33]

In one of the few systematic analyses of South Indian inscriptional distributions that has been conducted to date, it was discovered that the density of medieval Tamil inscriptions corresponded quite closely to the densities of population recorded in the 1911 Census as well as to high percentages of irrigated land and other measures of economic productivity (Trautmann et al. 1985: 21). The authors of this study conclude that the main settlement patterns of the Tamil country were already in place by the eleventh and twelfth centuries (i.e., during the height of the Chola period), when half or more of these Tamil inscriptions were composed. The correlation between modern demographic and medieval epigraphic distributions cannot be sustained for Andhra, where much of the agrarian settlement occurred later in time. But the evidence of this study of Tamil inscriptions supports a general interpretation of epigraphic occurrence as an indicator of both population density and the employment of intensive agricultural techniques (and especially wet rice cultivation). Although epigraphic patterns can be inflected by the contours of political power, as we observed in the preceding two sections, they also broadly reflect the levels of economic development within a region. On the whole, endowments to temples and brahmans occurred more frequently in localities that were more agriculturally advanced and had larger populations. The diversity of ecological conditions thus affected the progress of epigraphic production in the different subregions of Andhra.

Although the most fertile localities of South India had already been densely settled by 1000 C.E., large-scale settlement of the drier upland territories did not begin until the second millennium. Throughout the peninsula, we witness the spread of settled agriculture into the hinterland in the centuries from 1000 onward. This process has been tracked for Salem District, an arid region in northwestern Tamil Nadu, by the geographer Brian Murton. He notes that two successive phases of colonization took place in Salem, where there were few agrarian settlements prior to 900. The first phase occurred between 900 to 1350 when numerous villages were established in the river valleys of Salem. A second phase of colonization occurred after 1550, during which time villages were founded in the driest portions of Salem. The two stages observed in Salem reflect growing demographic pressures that compelled people to settle in increasingly less favorable areas. First to be developed were the localities where some irrigated cultivation was possible, followed much later by the more arid sites (Murton 1973: 59–62).

The South Indian ecological typology developed by David Ludden helps clarify the progression of settlement in Salem from the more to the less desirable areas. Ludden distinguishes three main kinds of ecological zones: the wet, the mixed, and the dry. Agricultural settlement proceeded from the wet zone, through the mixed zone, and then to the dry zone. In the wet zone, regular water supplies are available for irrigation. Wet zones are typically either deltaic or adjacent to major perennial rivers. The presence of water enables intensive forms of irrigated agriculture and dense population concentrations. In the case of Tirunelveli District in Tamil Nadu, the focus of Ludden's analysis, the main patterns of wet zone settlement had already been set before 1000 and few changes in the ethnic or social composition of the wet zone population transpired in subsequent times. This situation resembles what we have found for Vengi in Andhra, where there was little expansion in the territory producing inscriptions after 1000.

The opposite of the wet zone is the dry zone, where agricultural activities depend almost exclusively on rainfall, with the occasional supplement of well water. Due to insufficient water, rice cannot be grown on a large scale and instead millets are the major grain. The Tirunelveli dry zone studied by Ludden typically has either black soils or sandy soils and was colonized only after the fourteenth century by migrants from other regions, including interior Andhra. The mixed zone stands somewhere between the wet and dry zones, both in the extent of irrigated land and in the period of settlement. Tirunelveli's mixed zone is characterized by red soils, considerable elevation, and moderate rainfall. Reservoir-type tanks were constructed by using the slope of the landscape, enabling some microzones to support wet rice cultivation. Other localities within the mixed zone are restricted to dry agricultural techniques, and so the mixed zone supports the widest range of crops and agricultural landscapes (Ludden 1978: 3–8).

Because there is substantial variation from locality to locality, it is risky to generalize about Andhra's ecological zones. The absence of detailed geographic and agricultural studies of the various Andhra subregions, when compared to states like Tamil Nadu, compounds the problem. On a general level, however, we can describe coastal Andhra as a zone of wet agriculture, Telangana as a zone of mixed agriculture, and Rayalasima as most typically a dry farming zone. To be sure, numerous exceptions exist within each of these three subregions. In reference to coastal Andhra, the eastern lowlands that border the sea have to be differentiated from the generally more elevated western portions. Despite these local variations, however, the coastal districts can still be broadly characterized as constituting an ecologically wet zone. This is most true of Vengi, the stretch from East Godavari through Guntur Districts, where the current proportion of irrigated land is well over half of all land sown (62 percent for East Godavari District, 83 percent for West Godavari, 73 percent for Krishna, and 59 percent for Guntur).[34] The typical form of irrigation in these districts utilizes canals to draw on the Krishna and Godavari Rivers and their tributaries.

While it is fairly easy to discern wet zones and dry zones, a mixed zone is less easy to pinpoint. Neither Telangana nor Rayalasima contain large wet zones, that much is obvious. And agricultural conditions appear to favor Telangana over Rayalasima. Currently, a greater amount of cultivated land is under irrigation in Telangana than in Rayalasima, despite the several irrigational projects constructed over the past century in the latter subregion. The most highly irrigated district in Telangana is Karimnagar, where the proportion of net area irrigated to net area sown is 56 percent, followed by Warangal (50 percent) and Nizamabad (54 percent). Moderate ratios of irrigated land are found in Khammam (38 percent) and Nalgonda (33 percent) Districts. These proportions are lower than what we find in coastal Andhra, but still higher than proportions in Rayalasima. The highest proportion of irrigated land in Rayalasima is found in Chittoor District with 33 percent, followed by Cuddapah with 32 percent. Less than 20 percent of the fields of Anantapur (19 percent) and Kurnool (17 percent) are irrigated. The current situation thus warrants the classification of Telangana as a mixed ecological zone and Rayalasima as a dry one.

The greater levels of rainfall in Telangana are one reason that more irrigation occurs there than in Rayalasima. Telangana's terrain is also a contributing element. The undulating character of its landscape facilitates the construction of tanks (Telugu, *ceruvu*; Sanskrit, *samudra*), which are basically reservoirs created by erecting stone and/or mud embankments across the valleys of small seasonal streams. Water that drains from catchment areas during the rains collects in these ponds and is stored for use in the dry season. Although tank irrigation is found throughout the state, it is most widespread in northern Andhra, where the underlying bed of metamorphic rock assists water retention. Irrigation is particularly beneficial for the predominantly red soils of Telangana, which are not very productive under a dry farming regime. With a regular supply of water, these red soils can be transformed into fertile lands where rice and "garden" crops thrive on a large scale.[35]

Today Telangana is renowned as the "tank-district" of Andhra, most especially the rice-producing Warangal, Karimnagar, and Nalgonda Districts (Venkataramanayya and Somasekhara Sarma 1960: 679). Nizamabad is the fourth of the comparatively well irrigated and fertile Telangana districts today, but as much of the total irrigated area there depends on modern canals drawing upon the Godavari River as on tanks (Alam 1968: 300–301). Almost every village in the Telangana districts of Warangal, Karimnagar, Nalgonda, Nizamabad, and Khammam is reputed to have at least one tank (Parabrahma Sastry 1978: 206). In these areas, the average tank irrigates between 1,000 and 2,000 acres. Elsewhere, in Mahbubnagar and Hyderabad Districts, tanks are typically somewhat smaller, irrigating between 400 to 500 acres (Chaturvedi 1968: 65).

Tank irrigation was not widespread in Telangana before the second half of the twelfth century, and the storage tanks were small. During the next 150 years (1175–1325), numerous tanks were constructed in central and eastern Telangana, of which many still exist. Some huge ones are called lakes more accurately than tanks. Pakala Lake in Warangal District, for example, which collects water from a drainage area of 80 square miles and can irrigate about 17,000 acres, was built in the first half of the thirteenth century by the son of a Kakatiya minister (Parabrahma Sastry 1978: 205). Believing that this was a highly meritorious religious act, many kings and chieftains in Telangana sponsored the construction of such tanks during the twelfth and thirteenth centuries and, in the process, significantly augmented the prosperity of their inland region.[36] Epigraphic activity during the Kakatiya period followed the movement of political power and was more prevalent in central Telangana than in those districts adjacent to Karnataka where it had abounded earlier. Period II inscriptions from Telangana appear in a broad belt running from Warangal in a crescent toward the southwest through Nalgonda and Mahbubnagar Districts, corresponding roughly to the main areas of new tank construction.

Rayalasima's agricultural conditions, less favorable than those in Telangana, explain its failure to produce as many inscriptions in the early centuries of the second millennium. Even in the Kakatiya era, Rayalasima inscriptions are quite restricted geographically, since about 60 percent of them come from the single district of Cuddapah.[37] Although Cuddapah is the most hilly district in Andhra, except for the agency tracts of the northeastern hills, it also contains an extensive stretch of flatlands, the Cuddapah basins, which actually begin at the confluence of the Krishna and Tungabhadra Rivers in central Kurnool District to the northwest of Cuddapah. Cuddapah also possesses more irrigable streams than other districts in Rayalasima, for almost all of the district is drained by the Penner and its numerous tributaries. A third reason why Cuddapah District has the largest number of inscriptions from Rayalasima during Period II, aside from its flatlands and irrigable streams, may be the suitability of its terrain for tank construction. Eastern Cuddapah has a series of valleys running north-south between the main Velikonda and Nallamala ranges, where water running down from the hills can easily be dammed by building a bund or embankment (Sivasankaranarayana 1967: 5–21; Spate 1954: 676–82). Within the larger arid territory of Rayalasima to which it belongs, Cuddapah's mixed zone of agriculture is clearly an exception.

The case of Cuddapah illustrates the problems in applying the categories of wet, mixed, and dry to territories as large as the three subregions of Andhra, since there is considerable ecological variation at the local level. For a rigorous testing of the thesis that agrarian settlement in Andhra gradually progressed in stages from the wet zone through the mixed zone to the dry zone, as it did in the Salem and Tirunelveli areas of Tamil Nadu studied by Murton and Ludden, we would need to carry out microstudies of Andhra ecology on a much smaller scale. But we can obtain a general confirmation of this thesis through considering the differing densities of inscriptions in coastal Andhra, Telangana, and Rayalasima in the early centuries of the second millennium. Whereas maps 5 through 8 portrayed the differing spatial distributions of inscriptions from period to period, table 2 shows the number of inscriptions produced in each subregion during each of the four periods. Localities with higher numbers or densities of medieval inscriptions were

Table 2. Epigraphic Production by Subregion and Period

	No. of Inscriptions by Period				
Subregion	I	II	III	IV	Total
Coastal Andhra	849	1,215	755	470	3289
Rayalasima	48	134	197	844	1,223
Telangana	163	169	29	153	514
Total	1,060	1,518	981	1,467	5,026

associated with a larger population and a high incidence of wet rice cultivation in the modern period in the study of Tamil Nadu conducted by Trautmann and his team of scholars. By that measure, we find a clear hierarchy during Period I with coastal Andhra yielding an overwhelmingly large proportion of all inscriptions (80 percent), while Telangana falls into the intermediate range (15 percent), and Rayalasima ranks at the bottom (4.5 percent). The contrast between subregions is less dramatic if we instead examine the number of village sites where inscriptions were issued between 1000 and 1174, shown in table 3, although the same overall ranking obtains. As one would expect, the more densely settled subregion of coastal Andhra domintes the epigraphic activity at the beginning of the age of inscriptions, followed in descending order by Telangana and then Rayalasima.

But tables 2 and 3 also testify to the continuing expansion of inscriptional production in coastal Andhra into Period II, the Kakatiya era. Both the numbers of inscriptions and of village sites in coastal Andhra rise substantially in the second period, which seems to contradict our assumption that the settlement patterns of the wet zone had already largely been established by this time. When examined more closely, the apparent anomaly disappears, for much of the increased activity in coastal Andhra during Period II is occurring not in its most fertile taluks but in the drier localities. Palnad is perhaps the best example of this trend. This most westerly taluk (subdistrict) within Guntur District is a semiarid and hilly area resembling Telangana far more than eastern Guntur. Palnad experienced a tripling of the number of inscriptions produced between Period I (18 records) and Period II (60 records). Similarly, we witness a considerable rise in epigraphic production during Period II in the two southern coastal districts of Prakasam and Nellore, where the area of alluvial soil is far more restricted than in the Krishna-Godavari deltas farther to the north.[38] Furthermore, the main increase in activity within Rayalasima during Period II occurs in Cuddapah District, a zone of mixed agriculture. The examination of the densities of inscriptions, when differentiated on a smaller scale, thus suggests that there was a major expansion of agrarian settlement during the Kakatiya era into the mixed zone localities found in every subregion of Andhra.

Perhaps the most striking trend revealed by tables 2 and 3, however, is the slow but steady growth of Rayalasima as a producer of inscriptions. In this most arid subregion of Andhra, both the numbers of inscriptions and of village sites gradually rose from period to period until a dramatic peak of epigraphic activity was reached in Period IV. By the sixteenth century, Rayalasima's epigraphic production exceeded that of coastal Andhra by a considerable margin, a phenomenon that must be

Table 3. Village Sites of Inscriptions by Subregion and Period

	No. of Village Sites by Period			
Subregion	I	II	III	IV
Coastal Andhra	182	327	169	298
Rayalasima	39	82	125	428
Telangana	67	104	23	39
Total	288	513	317	765

partially attributed to the Vijayanagara state's presence there. But we must also recognize that the increase in Rayalasima's epigraphic activity over time reflects the ongoing process of agrarian settlement and development into the least favorable ecological environments. Anantapur and Kurnool, the two driest districts of Rayalasima, were the last to yield inscriptions in substantial numbers. Not until Period IV (1500–1649) are inscriptions found in most of their taluks.

The Frontier in Andhra History

As the tempo of agricultural settlement in upland Andhra quickened, the balance of power within Andhra tilted in favor of the interior. Andhra's political center moved from the wet zone of the Vengi coast to the inland mixed zone of Telangana during the Kakatiya period and ultimately to the drier subregion of Rayalasima, where Vijayanagara power was centered. From the late twelfth century onward, Andhra's frontier zone had more political influence than did the long-settled coastal strip, with its greater agricultural fertility and denser population. This represents one of the most momentous transformations in the geopolitical history of Andhra, eclipsed only by the original emergence of historic settlement there.

All over peninsular India, the same trend was gaining force. Old political centers waned, and new or reinvigorated kingdoms were constituted in their stead. By around 1200 the long-standing geopolitical pattern in South India had been altered forever. Instead of two rival imperial powers in the northwest and southeast with Vengi caught in between, the peninsula witnessed the rise of four regional polities during the thirteenth century. Like the Kakatiyas who were based in the mixed zone Telangana, the other regional polities of the time were based outside the most cultivable lands. The ability of the Pandyas to control thirteenth-century Tamil Nadu was a reversal of the centuries-old dominance by the Kaveri River delta—the Chola heartland and the Tamil country's prime wet zone. The Hoysalas were much like the Kakatiyas, in being a lineage of recent origin and centered in a zone that had previously been of marginal political importance. Dorasamudra, the Hoysala capital, was located in the western portion of Mysore just north of Coorg, far further south than any previous Karnataka dynasty of note. From their starting point in that forested and hilly subregion, the Hoysalas spread throughout the Mysore Plateau. The thirteenth century was in many ways a watershed in the history of the peninsula because at that time "a shift of dominance in peninsular politics from the old riverine core kingdoms of the earlier medieval age to the large zone of upland, dry" territory occurred (Stein 1989: 21).

Why was it possible for the mixed zones, with their fewer economic resources, to dominate the older wet zone regions? One must first realize that although agricultural settlement spread outward from an original nucleus in the wet zone, the end result was not uniform sociologically. That is, the society of upland Andhra was not simply a replica of the earlier wet zone civilization. The differing ecological conditions, preexisting peoples, and histories of colonization combined to produce distinctly different societies. Indeed, both Burton Stein and David Ludden postulate a connection between a certain type of ecological setting and a corresponding sociopolitical structure. Ludden's schema more directly addresses the problem of explaining mixed-zone political dominance.

According to Ludden, the society of a wet zone was highly stratified with caste status determining an individual's access to economic resources. Wet zones typically had high proportions of brahmans as well as a dominant peasant class, both of whom controlled land but did not work it themselves. Actual cultivation was done by low-status, landless laborers. Dry zones, where many inhabitants were recent immigrants, had far less of a social hierarchy. Power was wielded by families who built up large factions of clients and monopolized positions as village headmen and accountants. In the dry zone, kinship and patronage were at least as important as caste status, if not more so. In the mixed zone of agriculture, people with authority over the areas of irrigation had a less secure status and resource base than similar individuals in the wet zone. As a consequence, land controllers in the mixed zone often attempted to extend their political power over cultivators of dry land in order to enlarge their economic base (Ludden 1985: 81–96). The leaders of a mixed zone were the most likely to be expansionistic, in Ludden's view, because of inherent economic insecurity.

Burton Stein's classificatory system uses somewhat different terminology, for it arises out of an analysis of Tamil subregions of the Chola period (tenth to twelfth centuries). During the time of the imperial Cholas, a number of territorial units known as *nāḍus* were recognized within the Tamil country. In the *nāḍus* that were central to the Chola power and economy (equivalent in their ecological characteristics to Ludden's wet zone), an "elaborately hierarchical" society was found, with large brahman villages, urban mercantile settlements, and a dominant peasant group who controlled agricultural resources. The political elite of the central *nāḍus* was closely integrated into Chola kingship symbolically. In intermediate *nāḍus*, the association with Chola kingship was weaker. These *nāḍus* were in areas of the interior upland where the water supply was insufficient for extensive irrigation, similar to Ludden's mixed zones. Political control in intermediate *nāḍus* was concentrated in the hands of hereditary local chiefs, who represented peasant communities organized on more egalitarian kinship lines. The peripheral *nāḍus*, where conditions resembled Ludden's dry zone type, were also characterized by the rule of strong local chieftains. Most inhabitants of peripheral *nāḍus* shared a common identity, resembling tribes more than the caste society depicted in modern ethnographies of India (Stein 1980: 134–40). Perhaps because his main interest was in this older era of wet zone dominance, Stein did not pay much attention to explaining how wet zones were later superseded.

Brian Murton has cautioned against too simplistic an application of this type of model, because it can easily be reduced to a crude form of geographic determinism. First of all, he argues that there is far greater environmental variation in actuality then is implied by the tripartite scheme of wet, mixed, and dry zones. In Murton's area of study, Salem District, at least ten different ecological types can be identified. Furthermore, environmental conditions have shifted considerably over the last two thousand years. Nor is there an absolute correlation between an ecological zone and the degree of political power wielded. Parts of Salem, generally regarded as a peripheral region, were incorporated into the core area of the Karnataka dynasty of the Western Gangas and thus achieved substantial political clout. Murton also rejects the notion of an invariable relation between ecological type and political structure, pointing out that intermediary chiefs exist in all areas (Murton 1989).

Certainly, one must take Murton's caution to heart. My differentiation of zones in Andhra is very roughly sketched, as I have already indicated, and there may be far more diversity than implied by a tripartite scheme. Although any combined typology of ecological zones and sociopolitical formations is merely an abstraction, there are some benefits to the approach. The primary advantage is that it forces attention to regions outside the earliest centers of settlement and thereby highlights the diversity of social types within the peninsula. Up to now, historical interest has been overly focused on the core areas of South Indian civilization, almost invariably wet zones. These are the regions where the fullest elaboration of caste society and of agricultural mentalities have existed. Outside the wet zones, other kinds of social organizations and cultural values have emerged, based on differing productive regimes. Large portions of the peninsula were inhabited until the Middle Ages, if not longer, by social groups whose main livelihood came from animal herding. Nor should one forget the role of shifting cultivation, practiced widely in areas where permanent settled agriculture was not viable. Murton notes the long history of shifting cultivation in Salem, present almost as long as pastoralism. Even after pockets of irrigated lands were developed, pastoralism and shifting cultivation remained economically significant there until the late eighteenth century (Murton 1989).

The expansion of epigraphic production in Andhra must therefore be viewed within the context of the extension of "historic" civilization throughout an ever larger portion of Andhra society and territory. Andhra's regional variant of Indic civilization—a cluster of practices and ideologies that found concrete expression in the building of temples and inscribing of documents—was based on intensive agricultural techniques. As it grew larger, it encroached upon and absorbed nonsedentary and nonagricultural peoples. This long-term process, sometimes called "peasantization," is still not complete today, as evidenced by the survival of tribal peoples who by definition stand outside Hindu caste society. According to the 1971 census figures, almost 4 percent of Andhra Pradesh's population were tribal, considerably higher than the situation in Tamil Nadu (0.8 percent), Karnataka (0.8 percent), or Kerala (1.3 percent). In terms of sheer numbers, Andhra Pradesh had the ninth largest population of scheduled tribe members in India (Hasnain 1983: 234). By the 1981 census, the tribal proportion of Andhra's population had risen to 6 percent (Babu 1990: 122).

The main concentrations of tribal peoples today are found in northern Andhra

Pradesh, both along the coast near the border with Orissa (Visakhapatnam and Srikakulam Districts) and further inland along the Godavari (Khammam, Warangal, and Adilabad Districts). This is one of the most impenetrable areas of the peninsula, because of dense forest and the geologically complex nature of the landscape with its many faults (Geddes 1982: 89). The vast majority of tribal peoples have been forced to adjust to a settled agrarian lifestyle within the last two centuries, but as late as the 1940s the Kolams of Adilabad continued to practice slash-and-burn cultivation combined with food gathering (Furer-Haimendorf 1985: 40). While tribal populations have persisted in this northern region, largely inaccessible and undesirable to the dominant caste society and its agriculturalists, only remnants exist in other hilly locales within the state where tribal peoples must once have been populous. One well-known example, the Chenchus of the Nallamala Hills of southern interior Andhra, maintained a hunting and gathering economy until the mid twentieth century (Furer-Haimendorf 1985: 8–9). In light of the resilience of tribal economies and lifestyles, one can assume that tribal peoples were far more widespread in earlier times and helped shape the Andhra we know today.

Pastoralists are a second large group that should not be overlooked. Unfortunately, historians seldom give them credit. According to Gunter-Dietz Sontheimer, who has conducted extensive research on Deccan pastoralism, "The substantial part which groups of nomadic shepherds, and cattle-herders, and village-based cattle herders (perhaps transhumant) have played in India, especially regarding their long existence parallel to settled agricultural communities, their spatial separatedness, their economy, and their contributions to the formation of Indian culture, have been generally ignored" (Sontheimer 1975: 143). We know that upland Andhra has hosted pastoral communities since the prehistoric era of the second millennium B.C.E. and material artifacts from the protohistoric Pandukal culture of cattle-herders have been recovered. Herders often appear in medieval donative inscriptions, either as patrons of temples or more commonly as the trustees of milk-bearing animals endowed to these institutions. In such records, the growing accommodation between settled agriculturalists and pastoralists can be traced. Outside the zones of settled agriculture, there must have been numerous communities of pastoralists who had little or no contact with cultivators and their literate society, and who are thus invisible to us.

Even in the twentieth century, a substantial part of inland Andhra's population has consisted of practicing pastoralists and communities traditionally associated with pastoralism (Sontheimer 1989: 8). Inland Andhra's sizable rates of sheep per person are also suggestive, for the raising of sheep tends to be a specialized economic activity restricted to pastoralists, unlike cattle-keeping which is widespread in modern rural India. High sheep ratios currently exist only in western India, according to David Sopher, and in "a compact southeastern zone comprising the Rayalaseema and Telengana regions of Andhra Pradesh; eastern Mysore; and Tamil Nadu except for the Kaveri delta and the Nilgiris" (1975: 189). Several groups in modern Andhra Pradesh who are now shepherds are thought to have been cattle raisers in earlier times.

The Dhangar communities of Maharashtra were similarly once herders of both cattle and sheep, before turning exclusively to the rearing of sheep (Sontheimer 1975: 156–57). Ajay Dandekar believes that the Dhangars used to live exclusively in the semiarid plateau to the east of the Western Ghats where they followed a fully nomadic lifestyle. He notes that this is the same region of Maharashtra where hero-stones that commemorate deaths in defense of cattle from the tenth through twelfth centuries are concentrated. The pastoral character of the region at the time is further evidenced by the absence of any land grants issued by the Yadava kingdom in this part of Maharashtra (Dandekar 1991: 316, 320–21). If hero-stones recording the deaths of men in the course of cattle raids can indeed be taken as an indicator of pastoralist lifestyles, as would seem logical, we then have confirmation of widespread herding activities in early Andhra, at least for the subregion of Rayalasima where the great majority of such memorials are found (Chandrasekhara Reddy 1994: 70–72). Most of these were issued in the centuries before 1000 C.E., and are inscribed in both Telugu (e.g., IAP-C 1.77 Devapatla 4 and 8) and Kannada (e.g., ARE 726, 734, 746–48, and 759 of 1917). Aside from revealing the importance of cattle in the local economies, inscriptions of this type also shed light on the prevalence of armed conflict in upland society and the corresponding premium placed on fighting skills.

As it grew, therefore, the new and vibrant society of upland Andhra assimilated former hunter-gatherers, animal herders, and those engaged in shifting cultivation, along with ambitious migrants from coastal Andhra. The resulting mixture of peoples possessed a distinct character—more mobile and martial in quality than the culture and society of Vengi. The greater sociopolitical dynamism of the mixed zone contrasts with the status quo of the wet zone, the difference due possibly to the more conservative attitudes typical of rice-growing areas (Williamson 1931: 624). Chapter 2 treats the society of Kakatiya Andhra more fully. But we can surmise that frontier peoples were less averse to risk-taking, more likely to move in search of personal advantage, and more accustomed to fighting in order to acquire what they wanted. For whatever reason, the Telugu warriors of upland Andhra became major political actors in the late Kakatiya period. In subsequent centuries, they not only continued to dominate local affairs within Andhra but migrated to other regions within South India as well. The critical era of transformation in these ongoing historical processes was Period II, the years of Kakatiya hegemony from 1175 to 1324.

The spread of epigraphic production into an ever larger expanse of Andhra is synonymous with a dynamic historical process of migration and agricultural settlement. Although we are accustomed to think that technological innovations affect the whole of a society within a restricted time period, in actuality these economic developments and their accompanying social transformations have not yet permeated all of the Indian population. Well into the medieval era, sizable expanses of Andhra territory were not yet settled by agriculturalists practicing intensive techniques.[39] The agricultural frontier was hence in constant motion. This was not only a movement outward from the coasts into the semiarid upland zones but also involved increasing intrusion into the less favorable niches within the settled territories. With a high degree of physical movement as a major feature of medieval South Indian history, social and political dynamism were the resulting corollaries. The dynamism of medieval Andhra is one of the central themes of this work, to which I return repeatedly in subsequent chapters.

2

The Society of Kakatiya Andhra

Stone inscriptions have rarely been utilized in attempts to understand the social structure of precolonial India, although they record the names and activities of many thousands of people who made religious endowments. Instead, much of our reconstruction of Indian society before the advent of colonial rule has been based on two types of sources: the brahmanical literature (especially the *dharmaśāstra* [law books]) and modern ethnographic studies. The fact that brahmanical literature presents only the normative views of one segment of society has long been recognized; yet, because of the presumed centrality of the brahman in "traditional" Hindu India, scholars have continued to rely heavily on such works. Similarly, the projection of present-day ethnographic realities back into the precolonial period has been justified on the grounds of the alleged continuity of Indian society. Both types of sources are attractive in the relative richness of their information, since the lawbooks offer a detailed indigenous conceptualization of social organization while ethnography provides insights into actual social interaction not readily available elsewhere. The fragmentary glimpses into the social system obtained via inscriptions are, by contrast, far less immediately rewarding as sources of knowledge.

Recent research on the early colonial period has, however, increasingly called into question the accuracy of images of "traditional" South Asia derived from ethnographies and brahmanical literature. In the revisionist view, brahman dominance was greatly heightened by colonial policies of the nineteenth century. The cultural hegemony of the brahman was strengthened by the colonial creation of a legal system applied to all Hindu communities which was based on the brahmanical norms expressed in the *dharmaśāstra*. The legal validation of brahman authority, accentuated by British employment of large numbers of brahmans as clerks and assistants in their administration, extended the influence of the caste system into areas where it had not previously intruded. The British suppression of the alternative lifestyles and values of pastoralist and martial communities further contributed to the elevation of the brahman during the nineteenth century.[1] If these assertions are correct, it follows that the modern caste-dominated social system does not reflect the precolonial situation but instead is a colonial product. A further implication is that neither brahmanical literature nor modern ethnography can be accepted as reliable guides in reconstructing India's precolonial past.

Inscriptions offer an alternative means for recovering the social world of precolonial India, one that is not distorted by the transformations caused by colonial rule nor restricted to the viewpoint of the elite brahman. What little evidence is available on the production of inscriptional texts does suggest that their composers were often brahmans, although at other times temple scribes may have been responsible for their composition. The strong linkage between brahman status and literacy in precolonial India thus accounts for a certain commonality in rhetorical expression throughout the subcontinent, most notably in Sanskrit inscriptions. Yet the fact that medieval inscriptions may have been composed by brahmans, who therefore framed regional discourse at least partially through the lens of the Sanskrit cosmopolis, does not mean that inscriptions reflected solely, or even primarily, the brahman perspective. The desires of the people who commissioned these documents displayed in highly visible public arenas of social interaction had to be accommodated by epigraphic composers, who were after all only hired hands. Whereas the documentary portion of donative inscriptions—specifying the exact nature of the object gifted, as well as its purpose and its recipient—was largely technical and thus not amenable to much variation, the representation of a donor's identity in an inscription was undoubtedly dictated by the donor's wishes.

My reconstruction of medieval Andhra society hence begins with an examination of how individuals and groups commissioning inscriptions chose to have themselves described in these public records. It is largely immaterial for our purposes whether the status claims of inscriptional patrons were widely accepted by other parties, since in either case we learn what social identities were considered pertinent in Kakatiya Andhra. The social typology implicit in the names and titles borne by donors of religious endowments should inform our own models of medieval social organization, rather than preconceptions derived from brahmanical texts or from more recent data. Thus, a second theme of this chapter concerns the way in which the picture of Andhra society derived from inscriptions differs from standard constructions of traditional India in its greater social fluidity and emphasis on earned status instead of ascribed rank. Third, to anticipate my conclusions, I argue that the degree of dynamism in medieval India has been underestimated largely because the actual extent of social and physical mobility has not been sufficiently appreciated.

But first a word on the scope of the chapter, which like chapters 3 and 4 is restricted to the spatial and temporal dimensions of Kakatiya Andhra. This limits the time span under consideration to the years between 1175 and 1324, corresponding to the heyday of Kakatiya power. Our analysis in chapter 1 emphasized the significance of the Kakatiya age, the second of the four periods in the time span from 1000 to 1650 C.E. Not all of modern Andhra Pradesh was encompassed by the Kakatiya political network, however. Among the areas excluded is the northeastern territory bordering on Orissa, today two districts known as Srikakulam and Visakhapatnam. Throughout the Kakatiya period, this subregion of the modern state, along with neighboring areas in Orissa, constituted a separate political and cultural sphere, Kalinga. Other districts on the peripheries of Andhra Pradesh—

namely, Adilabad, Nizamabad, Hyderabad, Anantapur, and Chittoor—produced no more than a handful of Telugu inscriptions in this era. The geographic parameters of Kakatiya Andhra comprise the vast bulk of the modern state's territory but only 14 out of its 21 districts (see the dotted area in map 3).[2] The approximately 1,000 inscriptions from this place and time constitute our primary evidence in this and the two following chapters, which are devoted to a study of the nature of the society, religious patronage, and polity of Kakatiya Andhra.[3]

Varṇa, Jāti, and Clan in Andhra Inscriptions

Any discussion of the people of precolonial India must address the issue of caste, for caste has been most persistently and consistently presented as the essence of Indian society in the secondary literature. The typical portrayal of Hindu society recognizes two major levels in the caste system: the four *varṇas* and the myriad subcastes, or *jātis*. The *varṇa* system described in classical Sanskrit literature—with its orderly division of society into the four ranks of the brahman (priest and scholar), *kṣatriya* (king and warrior), *vaiśya* (herder, trader, or cultivator), and *śūdra* (menial servant)—bears little resemblance to the complex realities of modern society. Whether the theory of the four *varṇas* was ever an accurate description of social divisions is a moot point; at any rate, it is evident that the identification of specific groups as *kṣatriya*, *vaiśya*, or even *śūdra* has been ambiguous for over a millennium (Thapar 1974: 103, 117, and 120). Hence, many modern commentators regard the *varṇa* scheme as an idealized paradigm of societal functions. In contrast, the subcaste (*jāti*) is largely ignored in ancient social theory and appears to be a comparatively late phenomenon (Basham 1959: 148).[4] This social grouping—whose boundaries are demarcated on the basis of endogamy, commensality, and hereditary occupation—is seen as the true operative unit of the Hindu social system in more recent times.

If *varṇa* and *jāti* were indeed the two most significant aspects of social organization in traditional India, we would expect to find numerous references to them in medieval Andhra inscriptions. Yet few of the donors of the endowments recorded in these documents choose to describe themselves in these terms. Instead, persons figuring in inscriptions commonly only provide their names and those of their parents, and occasionally the names of their overlords and patrons. In the relatively rare instances when *varṇa* status is indicated in inscriptions, the individual involved is usually a brahman. Brahman *varṇa* claims are often indirectly expressed by phrases such as "born of the mouth of (the Creator) Brahma" (SII 10.318) or through reference to membership in a brahmanical *gōtra*, sometimes along with further mention of the Vedic school (*śākhā*) and scripture (*sūtra*) in which the person was trained. Far fewer people made claims in these records to royal *kṣatriya* or mercantile *vaiśya* rank. In only a couple of cases did people say they were *vaiśyas* (SII 10.357 and 446). Genealogical links with the ancient lunar and solar dynasties of kings described in the Puranas and other Sanskrit literature were the means by which *kṣatriya* rank was most often asserted. The alleged *kṣatriyas* were usually members of minor princely lineages in Andhra, with names derived from the great imperial families of South India such as the Chalukyas, the Pallavas, and the Cholas.[5]

One peculiarity of Andhra society is that many of the leading warrior families made no pretensions to *kṣatriya* status but instead proudly proclaimed their descent from the creator Brahma's feet. This is an allusion to the famous origin myth first found in the Rig Veda wherein the four *varṇas* are said to have originated from different portions of the body of Purusha, the primordial man (e.g., SII 6.95, SII 10.281). It was from the creator's feet that the fourth, or *śūdra*, class sprang, and another way of expressing *śūdra* status was to say that one belonged to the fourth order of society (e.g., HAS 19 Mn.46, SII 4.1053). The pride in *śūdra* origin is especially prominent in two records from the second half of the fourteenth century, in which *śūdras* are said to be the best of the four *varṇas* because they are the bravest (CPIHM 1.17 v.8) or the purest (EI 13.24 v.7).[6] Families in what was theoretically the lowest social category, and not the *kṣatriya* lineages of the coastal subregion, possessed the greatest degree of actual political power in medieval Andhra, despite their relatively humble ancestry.

The prevalence of *śūdra* ranking among politically prominent lineages in medieval Andhra is exemplified in the case of the Kakatiya dynasty. The majority of inscriptions in which the Kakatiya genealogy is presented make no specification of their *varṇa* affiliation. But when a *varṇa* ranking is assigned to them, in most cases the Kakatiyas are said to have been born in the fourth class, that which emanated from Brahma's feet. The following excerpt is representative of the general tenor of Kakatiya Sanskrit inscriptions:

> The four-faced Brahma, having sprung from the center of Vishnu's navel-lotus, created the celestial beings. Then from his own mouth, arms, thighs and lotus-feet, he produced the brahman, the king, the *vaiśya*, and the *śūdra*, respectively. The Kakatiya dynasty, praised by the entire world and belonging to the fourth *varṇa*, then came into existence. In it was born the king named Prola, who was renowned for being exceedingly judicious. (HAS 13.34)

Only a handful of records, almost all inscribed on copper plates, attempt to provide this ruling family with a more illustrious ancestry.[7] In these inscriptions the Kakatiyas are linked with the solar dynasty of the ancient *kṣatriyas*, stemming from Ikshvaku through Dasharatha and Rama, in what seems to be an imitation of the genealogy of the imperial Chola rulers (see Spencer 1982).

The lack of consistency regarding the *varṇa* rank of the Kakatiya dynasty is noteworthy, as is the fact that their *kṣatriya* claims were put forth primarily in documents associated with gifts to brahmans. Other records of the thirteenth century produced by families possessing political power similarly reveal little interest in asserting high *varṇa* rank. Had this rank been crucial to social recognition and prestige during that time, we would observe a greater number of royal and chiefly lineages advancing claims to *kṣatriya* status. That they did not indicates the relative insignificance of *varṇa* for nonbrahmans in the thirteenth century. In other words,the classical *varṇa* scheme was meaningful primarily to those who considered themselves brahmans. Current research suggests that consciousness of *varṇa* became stronger during the colonial period, partially as a result of the listing of castes according to *varṇa* affiliation in the Census of India (Cohn 1984; Pederson 1986).

Jāti is, if anything, even less visible in thirteenth-century records than *varṇa*. In modern South Asia, the term *jāti* is employed in a wide range of applications.

Besides designating an endogamous group, *jāti* also refers to categories of persons differentiated by language, regional origin, and religion. In effect, *jāti* simply signifies a kind, category, or sort of person. We also find this broad usage of the word in thirteenth-century Andhra. On the rare occasions when the term *jāti* figures in the epigraphic sources, it has a very general meaning. The phrase *padunenmidi jātula praja*, literally meaning "the people of the eighteen *jātis*," is equated with the more frequently occurring *aṣṭādaśa praja*, or "the 18 (kinds of) people" (e.g., HAS 19 Km.6 and 7).[8] A few lists in contemporary literary sources name the units comprising the collective of 18, but the lists do not agree with each other (Somasekhara Sarma 1948: 276). Thus the number 18 appears to be formulaic, indicating either a variety of (unspecified) communities or the totality of social groups in a locality or village.[9]

In the general scholarship on South Asia, *jāti* is depicted as a social group with a definite character, clear-cut boundaries, and an immutable quality. However, the accuracy of the common Western perception of *jāti* and the caste system (in the sense of a ranked social order composed of a number of *jātis*) is questioned, even for the modern period, by specialized works on caste. While a closed marriage-circle may indeed exist as the outcome of a succession of discrete marriage choices, the *jāti* as such may have little concrete reality in the eyes of its participants, according to some observers (Kolenda 1978: 18 and 20; Gough 1981: 21). Other scholars dispute the very notion that an actual marriage-circle can be specified, despite the perception of participants that such groups of people exist (Quigley 1993: 165). Lower-ranking communities today, particularly those in service occupations, are often said to lack a clear *jāti* organization of their own and have less defined forms of endogamy (Beck 1972: 72, 87, and 90; Dirks 1987: 267–69).

Not only is the word *jāti* rarely found in thirteenth-century inscriptions from Andhra, but there are also no references to specific subcastes by name. Particularly notable is the failure to mention the territorial divisions of the dominant landed castes of modern Andhra, although Burton Stein has alleged that all major landed communities in South India were territorially subdivided into local segments (1989: 106). Given a situation today where the subcaste unit may be amorphous, it is most likely that well-articulated social organization at this level had not yet developed in thirteenth-century Andhra, even among higher-ranking groups. To be sure, the absence of references to specific *jātis* in thirteenth-century inscriptions does not prove that distinct subcaste units were also nonexistent in this period but, rather, it shows us that subcaste membership was not an outstanding or memorable feature of an individual's identity in his/her transactions with the larger society. This "argument from silence" can thus attest to the irrelevance of subcaste affiliation for the purpose of enhancing prestige in publicly displayed records.

There are other social units besides the *varṇa* and the *jāti*—clans and lineages, for example—whose study has languished because of the academic preoccupation with *jāti*. Some of these other social categories may prove to be of greater significance in certain localities than the *jāti*. For example, Dennis McGilvray's research among the so-called Ceylon Tamils of eastern Sri Lanka reveals the centrality of the matriclan in their social system. The exogamous matriclan was formerly clearly delineated through its corporate possession of political office, management of temples, and sponsorship of festivals. Although the various matriclans have distinct identities in the minds of the people, their subcaste affiliation is not always consistent. That is, the same matriclan might be assigned to different subcastes in different localities. Instances of high-status individuals marrying across putative subcaste boundaries are also encountered (McGilvray 1982: 47–48, 61, 70–72). In other words, *jāti* identity is not the determinant factor in Ceylon Tamil social relations.

The clan is also an important level of the social structure elsewhere in South Asia. Variously known as *gōtra*, *kula*, or *vaṃśa*, the clan generally includes a number of patrilineages that are believed to share descent from a common ancestor. Either the lineage or the clan in its entirety serve as the basic exogamous unit, depending on the community. For most castes in Tamil Nadu, the patrilineage is exogamous while the clan group (*kula)* as a whole is endogamous (Bayly 1989: 27). The lineages that comprise a clan may be dispersed over a wide area, but in parts of North India the clan is an organized body of people living in the same territory (Kolenda 1978: 14, 15, 18). Such is the case with the *birādarī* of Uttar Pradesh, who are said to form a discrete and well-defined social unit, a concrete group with a known membership (Cohn 1971: 116). In other parts of India, it is not unusual to find hierarchically ranked lineages, which occasion considerable divergence in status within the larger clan (Inden 1976: 41; Dirks 1987: 72).

Numerous references to clans occur in Andhra inscriptions of the thirteenth century. *Kula* is the term most widely used, with at least seven different *kulas* named in the records.[10] These *kulas* appear to be broad groupings of lineages with alleged kinship ties that stem from a shared eponymous progenitor. Thus, Durjaya is cited as an ancestor by many chiefly lineages from Telangana—including the Kakatiyas (IAP-W.29), Malyalas (HAS 13.8), Viryalas (IAP-W.27)—as well as by lineages from coastal Andhra such as the Konakandravadis (SII 4.780), the Ivani Kandravadis (SII 10.253), the Kondapadmatis (ARE 346 of 1937–38), the Parichchhedis (SII 10.430), and the Chagis (SII 4.748). *Kula* may also denote a social unit far larger than a clan, as when it is used in connection with the solar and lunar divisions of the ancient North Indian *kṣatriya varṇa* (SII 5.61, IAP-C 1.137). So claims to membership in a particular *kula* may simply reflect status aspirations, rather than any actual belief in ancestry.

Some individuals in Kakatiya Andhra cited their *vaṃśa* name, in addition to that of their *kula*, implying that these two words denoted distinct levels of kinship or group affiliation (SII 6.588; SII 10.265, 278, and 442). *Vaṃśa* is sometimes glossed as "race" in English and is the word most closely associated with the solar/lunar distinction among *kṣatriyas*. But occasionally *kula* and *vaṃśa* are used interchangeably to refer to the same named group (SII 10.398). No systematic differentiation between *kula* and *vaṃśa* can therefore be made since these two terms do not consistently apply to different units of social organization. Some overlap of meaning is also witnessed with a third term for clan, *gōtra* (e.g., SII 5.55, SII 10.197 and 312). On the whole, however, *gōtra* affiliation is more straightforward, with a few princely families of *kṣatriya* rank using the names of brahmanical *gōtras* like Bharadvaja, Kashyapa, and Manavyasa. Nonbrahmanical *gōtras* are cited by a number of individuals who were merchants, some with the title Lord of Penugonda.[11] This community of merchants, who resided in the coastal territory, considered themselves *vaiśyas* and are regarded as the precursors of the modern Komati community (Sundaram 1968: 57–64).

The way people appearing in the epigraphic records identified themselves tells us much about the social categories that were considered important at the time, and in thirteenth-century Andhra the clan and/or lineage was the most frequently mentioned kinship unit. Donors who cited clan names in inscriptions, with the exception of the few merchants noted above, were almost always members of lineages that possessed political and military power. Their political prominence places them in a position homologous to the dominant castes of modern ethnography, among whom strong clan and lineage organization is characteristic (Kolenda 1978: 18; Fox 1971: 17). As in more recent times, the people in medieval Andhra who were most likely to possess a strong identity as members of a clan or lineage had the greatest control over land and landed income. This comes as no surprise since, in Laurence W. Preston's words, "while anyone can construct his biological genealogy (given, of course, adequate historical records or traditions), only with a shared descent of property does this have a social relevance" (1989: 69).

The absence of well-articulated social groups above the lineage or clan level in thirteenth-century Andhra inscriptions may result from the instability of the period. Much of inland Andhra was newly settled, and local societies were still in the process of emerging. The physical movements of people migrating to frontier areas would naturally have led to a great degree of social fluidity in the hinterland. But even the local societies of the delta region were affected by the changing balance of power and the intrusion of warrior lineages from the inland territories. Research on lineages elsewhere in India suggests that kinship networks were more restricted in the earlier phases of their history. So, for instance, kinship ties were less significant among Rajput lineages in the initial stages of power building, for often the founder of a lineage would have migrated to a new territory with a small number of kinsmen. Only in the later stages of the developmental cycle of a Rajput lineage, when it had succeeded in dominating a sizable area of land, did a large body of kinsmen organized into stratified and distinct tiers appear (Fox 1971: 70, 75). The same phenomenon was observed in the Pudukkottai region of the Tamil country. Separate kin groups who migrated into Pudukkottai gradually began to form larger affinal networks because of their territorial proximity. Through these marriage ties, originally separate groups of families gradually developed into a subcaste unit (Dirks 1987: 222, 244). Hence, it is possible that clearly defined subcastes had not yet emerged from among the evolving lineages of Kakatiya Andhra.

On the other hand, doubt has also been expressed about the presence of the caste system in Tamil Nadu during the Chola era, from the ninth through thirteenth centuries.[12] Since the wet zone of the Tamil country was more densely populated and had a longer history of agrarian settlement than did most of Andhra, it should exhibit signs of organized subcaste activity if stable political conditions typically led to the formation of subcastes. In this connection, Ronald Inden's statement that castes "in something resembling their modern form [do not] appear until the thirteenth or fourteenth century, at the earliest" is worthy of further consideration (1990: 82). Whether or not we believe the caste system, as such, existed in late medieval India, it is obvious that we need to pay greater attention to the lineage level of social grouping.

A Typology of Statuses

We have seen that neither *varṇa* nor *jāti* was a prominent element in the public identity of individuals who figured in religious endowments from medieval Andhra. The only markers that are consistently found, the only items that would situate a person in a social context, are sometimes a lineage but most often just the individual's name and those of his/her parents. Hence names are the most direct form of social identification available, as labels or signifiers invariably possessed by every person. Admittedly, though names cannot tell us a great deal, particularly about social relations among groups and individuals, they do constitute a significant method by which people represented themselves to the society at large. Given the emphasis placed on naming in the ancient Indian tradition and the widespread belief in an ontological correspondence between a person's name and the person himself, we must assume that names were considered highly meaningful by medieval Andhra elites (Kane 1938; Schopen 1996: 66–72). Because men's names generally contained components beyond the merely personal (i.e., what we would consider a first name), analysis of them gives us some insight into the social classifications that were prevalent in medieval Andhra.

Names possessed by men varied considerably in length and in structure. The following inscription provides three examples, each somewhat different:

> In the 1,218th year of the Shaka era [1296 C.E.], on the 5th (day of the) dark (fortnight of the lunar month) Chaitra, a Sunday, at the time of *uttarāyaṇa-saṅkrānti*;[13]
>
> Tammili Bhimaya Raddingaru's son Chodaya Raddingaru gave land to the illustrious great lord Kshirarameshvara for a midday service, for his own religious merit. Fields in the lands of the village Pallavadapalli were purchased from Hanungi Kuchenangaru (to wit): a plot of 1 *kha(ṇḍuga)* in the fallow land to the south of the village and 2 *kha(ṇḍugas)* to the east of Udukula canal. Another *kha(ṇḍuga)* in the lands of Peddavipara near the village Modalikudulu was purchased from Hanungi Kuchenangaru. Out of this total of 4 *kha(ṇḍugas)* of land, I (Chodaya Raddingaru) will supply 1 *tūmu* of paddy grain for the food offering and 3 *gūnas*[?] 1 *sōla* of butter daily to the temple of the lord, for as long as the moon and sun endure.
>
> Also given by Chodaya Raddingaru for this midday service: a metal plate (weighing) 3 *visya* 14 *pa(lamu)*, a large censer weighing 2 *visya* 2 *pa(lamu)*, a plate for burning camphor (weighing) 10 *pa(lamu)*, a bell (weighing) 1 *visya* 4 *pa(lamu)*, and a conch shell (weighing) 1 *visya* 10 *pa(lamu)*. (SII 5.131)

According to this inscription, a man called Chodaya Raddi (*gāru* is a Telugu honorific) purchased land from Hanungi Kuchena, ostensibly to give to the Kshirarameshvara temple at Palakol in West Godavari District. In reality, however, the terms of the endowment reveal that Chodaya Raddi would retain the land and instead supply a stipulated amount of foodstuffs to the temple. He also gave a number of ritual implements for use in the worship of the deity. Chodaya Raddi's father is said to be Tammili Bhimaya Raddi.

The father and son pair, Tammili Bhimaya Raddi and Chodaya Raddi, share a common last component to their names—Raddi, a variant of the better-known Reddi. This component is known as the *gaurava-vācakamu* (literally, "honorific word") in modern Andhra, a term I translate as "status title."[14] Immediately preceding the status title are the men's personal names, Bhimaya and Chodaya. In the case of the father Bhimaya we also find an extra prefix, Tammili. This was an *iṇṭi-pēru*, "house-name," derived from the place-name of the family's ancestral village or from an illustrious predecessor (Somasekhara Sarma 1948: 260). The third man also had an *iṇṭi-pēru* (Hanungi) and a personal name (Kuchena) but possessed no status title as a suffix. The individuals figuring in this record thus had up to three components to their names: *iṇṭi-pēru*, personal name, and status title.[15]

Eminent persons often had an administrative title that preceded all other parts of the name. The administrative title indicated possession of an "official" position such as that of general or minister, as we see in the case of Mahapradhani Mallala Vemadri Raddi (SII 4.1333). This man had the official or administrative title *mahāpradhāni*, which showed that he was a minister; the *iṇṭi-pēru*, or house-name, Mallala; and the personal name Vemadri followed by the status title Raddi. It was not uncommon for men to bear administrative titles in lieu of *iṇṭi-pēru* (e.g., Mahapradhani Muppadi Nayaka, NDI Kandukur 25), as well as in addition to them. The length of the name was not always a marker of prominence, for some important subordinate chiefs under the Kakatiya rulers of Telangana lacked administrative titles.[16] Some men also placed their father's name prior to their own personal name, so that we find instances like Marayasahini Rudradevaningaru—the man Rudradeva who was the son of Maraya Sahini (ARE 307 of 1934–35).

Of the various components of masculine names in medieval Andhra, the last element, the status title, is the most useful in establishing a social typology. Personal names are numerous and, with a few exceptions, seem to bear no status connotations.[17] The house-name may have been used to regulate marriages, for nowadays lower-ranking Andhra subcastes (who lack clan organization) prohibit marriage between families with the same *iṇṭi-pēru* (Tapper 1987: 30; Thurston 1975, 3: 314). Except in the case of a few powerful lineages, however, for whom it functioned as a dynastic label, the house-name was of limited significance in medieval Andhra. Administrative titles are fairly rare in Kakatiya Andhra inscriptions and their exact meanings are unclear. Status titles, on the other hand, are both widespread and limited in number, which makes it possible to conduct statistical analyses and attempt categorization of them. Of the 723 individual male donors represented in the body of data from the Kakatiya period, 514 men (71 percent) have this component in their names. (Status titles are very rarely possessed by women.) Table 4 provides information on the variety and distribution of status titles found among men who made religious endowments, as well as on male donors without titles and on female donors.[18]

Particular sets of status titles were adopted by men in roughly the same type of occupation. This becomes especially evident when we examine the titles used by medieval Andhra brahmans, who differentiated themselves according to the means of their livelihood. One set of titles, the Sanskrit terms *bhaṭṭa* and *paṇḍita*, were reserved for individuals knowledgeable in religious matters. Charakurikardi Narayana Bhatta is one of these brahman religious specialists who is said to have performed the Vajapeya sacrifice (SII 6.205). Another example is Mahadeva Bhattopadhyalu, whose brahman rank is alluded to by his claim as belonging to the Bharadvaja *gōtra* (SII 10.452). A second set of status titles seems to have been used for brahmans of a more secular bent. *Pregaḍa*, *amātya*, and *mantri* all had administrative or clerical

Table 4. Classification of Individual Donors

Title	Donors No.	Donors %	Endowments No.	Endowments %
Nāyaka	114	14	129	13
Rāju	86	11	131	13
Reḍḍi	77	10	92	9
Mahārāja	53	7	95	9
Seṭṭi	50	6	56	5
Bōya	46	6	51	5
Pregaḍa	20	2	23	2
Śivācārya[a]	14	2	26	3
Leṅka	10	1	12	1
Cakravarti	8	<1	16	2
Bhaṭṭa	5	<1	5	1
Misc. titled men[b]	31	4	45	4
Untitled men	209	26	229	22
Women	87	11	109	11
Total	810		1,019	

a. Includes Shaiva sectarian leaders with other titles such as *rāśi*, *śambhu*, and the like.
b. Includes the titles *amātya*, *bhakta*, *camūpati*, *dāsa*, *dēsaṭi*, *mantri*, *ōju*, *paṇḍita*, *rautu*, *sāhiṇi*, *sēnāpati*, and *vaidya*.

connotations and thus imply literary skills. Considerable indirect evidence indicates that these three titles were restricted in their social range, since men with these titles often claim brahman *varṇa* rank or cite their membership in brahman *gōtras*.[19] It seems likely, for this reason, that the status titles *amātya*, *mantri*, and *pregaḍa* could only be borne by brahmans with nonreligious means of livelihood.

We also find a number of individuals claiming to be brahmans who bear the status title *rāju*,[20] the Telugu equivalent of the Sanskrit *rāja* and most often used by members of noble or princely lineages. *Rāju* could also designate an individual employed by a lord or prince, however. Of the 86 men called *rāju* in the body of data, 50 can be identified as having royal or noble descent (whom I label royal *rājus*), while the remaining 36 are ministerial or clerical (and almost certainly brahman) *rājus*. The distinction made in modern Andhra between brahmans engaged in secular occupations, known as *niyōgi*, and those who are religious specialists, called *vaidiki* (Vedic brahmans), is reflected in the two sets of status titles possessed by medieval Andhra brahmans. The religious specialists were known as *bhaṭṭa* or *paṇḍita*, while the secular brahmans were variously called *amātya*, *mantri*, *pregaḍa*, or *rāju*. The interchangeable character of titles within a given set is shown in the case of the man Induluri Annaya, who bears the status title *pregaḍa* in one inscription (SII 5.110) and *mantri* in another (EA 4.12).

Similarly, there are a number of titles associated with royalty. The most well-known, *mahārāja*, was used by the Kakatiya dynasty and by several other noble lineages located south of the Krishna River or in the interior portion of Andhra.[21]

The Telugu variant *rāju* was the preferred appellation among royal families of the northern coastal territory.[22] The more elegant Sanskrit word *cakravarti* (universal emperor) was adopted by minor lineages descended from the imperial Eastern Chalukya kings who still flourished in East Godavari and West Godavari Districts during the twelfth and thirteenth centuries.[23]

A last set of titles has military connotations. *Camūpati*, *sāhiṇi*, *sēnāpati*, and *rautu* all point to command of armed forces of some type. *Leṅka* also refers to a warrior, although it seems to mean a member of a lord's own private troops rather than a commander. The *leṅka* lived, fought, and died with the lord to whom he had sworn his services (Venkataramanayya and Somasekhara Sarma 1960: 670). The most prevalent status title of all—*nāyaka*, literally meaning "leader"—is part of this military set. One individual in our sample was known both as Jaya Senapati (SII 6.214) and as Jaya Nayaka (EI 5.17). *Nāyaka* is an ambiguous term, however, that also encompassed local notables, as well as military leaders (Stein 1980: 407). The majority of the *nāyaka* men in the corpus of inscriptions mentioned the name of their royal overlords, and roughly one-third of them possessed administrative titles such as *mahāpradhāni* (minister), *sāmanta* (allied subordinate or feudatory), and *sēnāpati* (general). *Nāyakas* hence ranked below kings and princes, to whom they generally owed allegiance. Because the title *nāyaka* was adopted by a wide range of important persons, variant versions of it—*nāyuḍu*, *nāiḍu*, *nāik*—are employed today in the names of diverse castes in South India and Orissa (Thurston 1975, 5: 38–40).[24]

Up to this point I have been describing sets of status titles that circulated within certain specific social classes—Vedic brahmans, secular brahmans, royalty, and the military elite. The status titles themselves are obviously not the names of distinct castes since they have overlapping referents. For instance, the titles *pregaḍa* and *mantri* were borne by the same person, as were *nāyaka* and *sēnāpati* by another man. Even if the status titles are not the actual labels of specific castes, however, they could be taken as indicators of caste allegiance. That is, one could argue that the various social types signified by status titles represented different castes or caste-clusters. This argument is strengthened by the nature of the three remaining widespread titles found in medieval Andhra inscriptions, *reḍḍi*, *seṭṭi*, and *bōya*.[25] None of these three are interchangeable with other titles, and both *reḍḍi* and *seṭṭi* are widely regarded as caste names today. In modern Andhra Pradesh, *reḍḍi* is a name associated with a powerful landowning cluster of subcastes, while *seṭṭi* forms part of the caste-name of many South Indian merchant communities. Additionally, although the term *bōya* is no longer in use, one of the synonyms for *bōya* in the inscriptions is *golla*, the name of a widespread caste-cluster of modern Andhra pastoralists.[26]

Whether the interpretation of status titles as signifying caste affiliation is accepted or not depends a great deal on how one defines caste. Clearly the status titles do not correspond to the four *varṇas* of the classical Sanskrit tradition. Nor do modern scholars generally mean *jāti* when they speak of caste. Caste is often used to refer rather to a level of social organization at least one step above that of the *jāti* or subcaste. Some castes are said to be aggregations of just a few subcastes who know about each other and sometimes act in concert (Mandelbaum 1970: 20). Members of this type of caste have substantial social interaction, in forms like the sharing of food or possibly even the exchanging of daughters in marriage, because they reside in a fairly compact territory. In this restricted definition of caste, there would commonly be a sense of shared origin—that is, a belief that the constituent subcastes were somehow related. It is evident that the status titles do not refer to communities of such limited character because of the diversity of people using any given title.

The breadth of social groups encompassed by a status title is particularly well illustrated in the case of the term *seṭṭi*. In medieval times this title was used by the Teliki community of oilmongers in Andhra and by various artisan groups throughout South India, as well as by purely mercantile communities (Sundaram 1968: 39). Even today we find that *seṭṭi* and its Tamil equivalent *ceṭṭi* are utilized by a whole series of merchant, moneylending, and trading groups (Rudner 1987: 372n.11). For instance, Kathleen Gough reports the presence of the Telugu Komati Chettiars in Tanjavur, along with the Nattukottai Chettiar caste of Madurai (Gough 1981: 30). Because this title is used by communities of different geographical origin and linguistic background, *seṭṭi* cannot be interpreted as specifying a caste. It should be understood instead as the label of an entire social class, designating any person involved in the production and sale of commercial goods. Similarly, *reḍḍi* was a title originally held by village headmen regardless of their hereditary background (Thurston 1975, 6: 230; Somasekhara Sarma 1948: 75). Hence, although it had associations with agriculture, *reḍḍi* did not signify a specific hereditary group of peasants in medieval times. And the fact that the words *gōpa* (the Sanskrit word for "cattle herder") and *golla* (the Telugu equivalent of *gōpa*) are used as synonyms of *bōya* underlines the term's significance.[27] The title *bōya* referred to the occupation of herding, rather than to a particular community.[28]

Status titles thus indicated membership in an overall occupational class rather than a localized community. Some scholars might still assert that the status classes represented castes, if they define caste broadly as a sociocultural category rather than more narrowly as an organized and interrelated group. The various endogamous subcastes that form a caste, in this broader definition, typically share no more than a name and occupation and perhaps some customs (Kolenda 1978: 20; Cohn 1971: 116). (The term "caste-cluster" is sometimes used to designate this level of social grouping.) The reality of a caste exists more in the mind of the outside observer than in actuality, even though members of similar subcastes usually accept the assertion of common caste affiliation (Dumont 1970: 63; Cohn 1971: 126). Since there are generally no attributions of kinship ties nor even any social interaction between the several subcastes in the larger caste unit, the main factor by which others identify them as a single social group is their shared occupation. In the words of Louis Dumont, "One may conclude that profession is one of the differences, perhaps the most indicative difference, whereby a group seen from the outside, a caste, is designated" (Dumont 1970: 95).

If a similar occupation is the primary criterion for the inclusion of *jātis* in a caste, the second, broader, definition of caste (or caste-cluster) would seem to greatly resemble that of *varṇa*. Since the various subcastes that are combined under a common caste name might have no hereditary or kin link, surely a genealogical connection cannot be considered the defining feature of a caste. The entire system may be predicated on the principle of membership by birth in the constituent subcaste units, but caste identity derives from perceived similarities among subcastes based primarily on a shared societal function or occupational identity (such as potter, weaver, merchant, etc.). The four *varṇas* of Sanskrit literature are also social classes defined by occupational function. If caste merely denotes a grouping of social units that share a similar profession and status, then a caste (cluster) resembles a *varṇa* as a functional rather than genealogical classification.

Of course, much of the difficulty in defining caste occurs because there is no exact equivalent in indigenous languages. This is not to deny the existence of marriage-circles or hierarchical relations in Indian society. But well into the colonial period, if not even now, people in India had complex social identities in which, depending on the situation, one or another element would take the foreground. When colonial censuses attempted to ascertain caste affiliations, therefore, the responses ranged from names designating endogamous groups or occupations to titles and surnames. No single category to which people claimed affiliation corresponded to the Western construct "caste." But the colonial classificatory systems assumed that castes were coherent and homogeneous entities whose populations could be enumerated and whose characteristics could be specified. As Rashmi Pant astutely observes, the large mass of details accumulated about caste through the censuses and similar surveys were considered as confirmation of its existence, and so "the theoretical question 'what is caste' was increasingly hidden by the substantiality of caste beings" (1987: 161).

The modern sociological discourse on caste derives from colonial practices and conceptualizations. Caste, in the sense of a large bounded community composed of interrelated subcaste units, is increasingly viewed as a theoretical construct (particularly for the precolonial period) rather than an observable reality.[29] This explains why anthropologists have disagreed on how to define a caste *grouping*, as distinct from the caste *system*. As we have seen, many scholars have now fallen back on occupation as the main criterion in establishing caste affiliation. In fact, European visitors of the seventeenth and early eighteenth centuries also classified Indian social groups primarily on the basis of occupation, as well as region of origin (Dharampal-Frick 1995: 89–94). And, indeed, occupation appears to be the key factor in attributions of group identity among Indians themselves. The peoples known as Gollas in Andhra today, for instance, comprise a heterogeneous conglomeration of endogamous groups linked only by the similarity of their traditional livelihood (Sontheimer 1975: 142). S. Westphal-Hellbusch (1975) describes several instances of name shifts among pastoral groups occurring through assimilation. When segments of the cattle-breeding Rabaris of Saurashtra and northern Gujarat moved to eastern Gujarat and switched to sheepherding, they were no longer known as Rabari but instead were named for the local shepherd community, Bharvad. Conversely, another camel-breeding group that moved into Rabari territory has now been absorbed by the Rabaris and lost their distinctive name. In both cases, the critical criterion for classification was the type of animal husbandry practiced. Along similar lines, G. D. Sontheimer has shown how both the occupation and name of the Gavli pastoralists of Maharashtra were assumed by another group that adopted the Gavli lifestyle (1989: 105).

In other words, indigenous thought does differentiate broad categories of people even though concrete social entities corresponding to what we now call castes may not have existed. Often these social types are signified by the use of the same title. Dirks points out that titles associated with specific subcaste groups in Tamil Nadu were often adopted by other subcastes with similar occupations because of their prestige (1987: 174n.17, 248). The Vellalar title "Pillai" was usurped by other communities in Tanjavur including the Kallars, Maravars, and Agambadiyars (Gough 1981: 300). Likewise, in North India many unrelated groups have adopted the names or titles of locally prominent ones. Hence, no common ethnic identity, kin relation, or social interaction necessarily motivated the use of the same title, which essentially identified a social category formed through the coming together of diverse groups that perceived commonalities between themselves or aspired to the prestige of an already-established group (Fox 1971: 16–22, 44–46).

I would argue that the status titles of medieval Andhra similarly reveal the existence of broad social categories based primarily on occupation. Although each particular title did not necessarily designate a distinct class, much less a bounded community or a hereditary grouping, various sets of these titles differentiated social types marked by a common status and shared occupation. The inscriptional status titles can be grouped into the following seven categories:

bhaṭṭa/paṇḍita	=	Vedic brahman
amātya/mantri/pregaḍa/rāju	=	secular brahman
cakravarti/mahārāja/rāju	=	royalty or nobility
seṭṭi	=	merchant, trader, artisan
bōya	=	herder, pastoralist
reḍḍi	=	village headman, warrior-peasant
nāyaka/camūpati/sāhiṇi/ sēnāpati/rautu/leṅka	=	military leader, local chief

Taken as a whole, the status titles should be understood as a medieval Andhra form of social typology. They do not, of course, reflect all the multiple social identities that a single individual might embody, whether sectarian, linguistic, and kin-related or territorial and political. Nonetheless, since the titles appear in the same context, that of a publicly displayed inscription, there must be some consistency in what they signify. The social typology inherent in the status titles does not encompass all existing social groups. Those of inferior status and occupation do not appear in this scheme, for the simple reason that almost all medieval inscriptions document transfers of property to Hindu temples and hence only record the names of persons who owned something of value. Obviously, other classes besides those enumerated above existed. The issue is not to describe every existing social group but rather to note the salient fact of the medieval Telugu social universe's conceptual division into discrete functional orders or estates.[30] The significant point for our discussion here is the centrality of occupation in determining how people were classified.

Social Mobility and Individual Achievement

If a social typology based on function and occupation underlies the use of status titles as surnames in medieval Andhra, this implies that what people actually did played a significant role in determining their social identity. That is, the names of the people mentioned in inscriptions suggest that their public personas were derived from the activities in which they were engaged. Persons with a common source of livelihood were grouped together in the social class associated with that occupational function. References to *varṇa* and *jāti* in thirteenth-century inscriptions, as noted in the preceding discussion, may therefore be scarce because hereditarily ascribed rank was less important than earned status. Certainly, there were spheres of life in which one's membership in a particular family or marriage-circle would have been of foremost importance. But the stone temple inscription was a public domain, an arena for the enhancement of personal reputations. In this specific setting, social identities appear to have drawn more heavily on individual achievements. We can test this thesis by examining the extent to which titles were passed on from father to son, for if high achievement was crucial to social prestige, we would expect to find fluctuations between generations.

Although we can seldom trace families over several generations, many donors do cite their father's name. Our sample provides us with 342 sets of names for fathers and sons. A statistical analysis of the similarities and differences between the two generations is provided in table 5.[31] In over two-thirds of our cases, fathers and sons are alike in either possessing the same status title or not possessing a status title at all (column "Same"). However, this means that there is some difference between father and son in nearly one-third of the instances. We must be cautious in interpreting these data, for epigraphic names were not officially binding. A name was a customary practice rather than a legal description. When a person issued more than one inscription, therefore, changes in their status titles could occur. For example, Madhava, a Yadava chief from Addanki, used both the status titles *mahārāja* (NDI Ongole 76) and *nāyaka* (NDI Ongole 88). The Chalukya prince Indushekhara sometimes issued inscriptions without any status title (EI 38.16) but at other times

Table 5. Father-Son Status Titles

Son's Title	No.	Same[a]	F Titled[b]	S Titled[c]	Changed[d]
Nāyaka	44	38	0	2	4
Reḍḍi	46	41	0	1	4
Rāju	35	28	0	5	2
Seṭṭi	31	29	0	2	0
Bōya	23	20	0	1	2
Mahārāja	20	9	0	3	8
Pregaḍa	13	9	0	1	3
Misc. titles	32	21	0	4	7
Untitled	98	44	54	0	0
Total	342	239 (70%)	54 (16%)	19 (6%)	30 (9%)

a. Both father and son have the same title or neither has a title.
b. Father has a status title but son does not.
c. Son has a status title but father does not.
d. Both father and son possess a status title but not the same one.

called himself a *cakravarti* (SII 5.147). But no more than a handful of such deviations occur in the data; typically, people used the same status title in all of their records. While changes in personal preference or scribal error may account for some of the discrepancies in status-title possession noted in table 5, they cannot all be explained by such factors. Since variation between father and son occurred in 30 percent of our examples, it is evident that status titles were not automatically transmitted from generation to generation.

The most common difference between fathers and sons had to do with possession of any status title at all. Sixteen percent of the time, a son did not have a status title although his father did (column "F Titled" in table 5). The reverse situation also occurred occasionally (6 percent), when a son had a title but his father did not (column "S Titled"). This kind of fluctuation in the use of status titles occurs across the board, regardless of status type. The title was obviously not inherited from one's father, although many father-and-son pairs did share one. Further proof that the status title was not a hereditary marker comes from the instances when fathers and sons were both titled but in different ways (column "Change"). Bhima Reddi, for example, was the son of Malli Nayaka, and Kalari Pinnamari Nayaka was the son of Prole Boya (SII 4.1178 and SII 10.319). Altogether, this sort of switch in titles between father and son occurred in 9 percent of the pairs.[32]

Because titles were not always inherited, they must have been related to an individual's own activities. They were probably a type of honorific, reflecting a certain measure of accomplishment or prominence.[33] While it may have been easier for sons whose fathers were eminent to attain a similar stature, not all of them managed to do so. Some sons were more successful than their fathers and acquired titles even though their fathers lacked them. Other men presumably changed their occupations and so used titles unlike those of their fathers.

Although family members of different generations could vary in their earned stature and might even switch occupations, there were limits to the degree of change that could take place. Looking more closely at the cases where status titles differed between father and son, we find the following range of fluctuations:

SON	FATHER
mahārāja	*rāju*
rāju	*mahārāja, nāyaka*
nāyaka	*bōya, camūpati, reḍḍi*
reḍḍi	*nāyaka, leṅka*
bōya	*nāyaka, seṭṭi*
leṅka	*reḍḍi, bōya*
pregaḍa	*mantri, rāju, bōya*
amātya	*rāju*
bhaṭṭa	*paṇḍita*
bhakta	*seṭṭi*
dāsa	*reḍḍi, rāju*

The left-hand column lists the titles of sons, whereas the right-hand column portrays the various statuses associated with their fathers. For example, the top line shows that some *mahārājas* had fathers with the title *rāju*. Sons of *bōyas* did not become *mahārājas*, however, nor did sons of *mantris* become *reḍḍis*.

An analysis of the variations listed confirms the existence of distinct social classes within which specific sets of titles circulated. One set are the secular brahmans who used the titles *pregaḍa*, *mantri*, and *rāju* interchangeably. Only once did a person whose father had another status title (*bōya*) enter into this largely exclusive category. A circumscribed royal or noble class in which the titles *mahārāja* and *rāju* rotated can also be distinguished. Two sons of *nāyakas* were able to enter this group, however (SII 10.331 and 444). *Seṭṭis* (merchant-artisans) formed another fairly restricted set, with just one case of a crossover (a *seṭṭi* father with a *bōya* son). The most fluid of all were the *reḍḍi*, *bōya*, and *nāyaka* categories. *Nāyaka* and *leṅka* fathers could have *reḍḍi* offspring, while *nāyaka* and *seṭṭi* men produced *bōya* sons. *Nāyakas* could come from *reḍḍi*, *bōya*, or *camūpati* (lit., "head of an army") families.

The traversing of boundaries between these status groups also characterizes female donors in inscriptions. We have one example of a woman whose father was a *nāyaka* but who was married to a *reḍḍi* (SII 5.153). Another had a *nāyaka* husband but was the daughter of a *bōya* (SII 10.311). A third woman was the sister of a *nāyaka* and the wife of a *reḍḍi* (HAS 13.42). Marriage patterns thus indicate much interchange among members of the *nāyaka*, *reḍḍi*, and *bōya* statuses. Additionally, several *nāyaka* daughters became the wives of *rājus*, *mahārājas*, and *rautus* (IAP-K.37; SII 10.260 and 290).

In short, there were restrictions to the movement possible among certain classes of people demarcated by status titles. The two kinds of brahmans, the merchant-artisans, and royalty were largely discrete social groups in which membership was acquired primarily by hereditary means, although there are most definitely exceptions to the rule. In contrast, there were few limits to the movement between the remaining classes. *Nāyakas*, *reḍḍis*, and *bōyas* comprised 46 percent of the (113) men in the father-son sample with titles. While many members of these three statuses retained the title borne by their fathers, it was not at all unusual for them to acquire one of the other two titles instead or, alternatively, a military title such as *leṅka*, *camūpati*, or *rautu*. Some of them, especially *nāyakas*, also moved upward into the ranks of the nobility. That there was considerable social fluidity among roughly half of the titled male population, all nonbrahmans, raises further doubts about the validity of applying the standard hierarchical caste model to Kakatiya Andhra society.

The possibilities for social advancement based on what a person actually did explain why many medieval Andhra inscriptions emphasize an individual's achievements above his family background. This is true even when the person's ancestry was quite distinguished, as was the case with Ambadeva, a member of the powerful Kayastha lineage. An inscription issued by him in 1290 devotes far more space to his exploits than to praise of his predecessors. It begins with the standard praises to the gods. The next few verses deal with Ambadeva's genealogy:

> From the body [*kāya*] of the lotus-born god Brahma was born the clan of certain kings called Kayastha. From that clan arose the great lord Gangaya, the subduer of horses, like the celestial tree Parijata from the ocean.
>
> After him, the two-armed Janardana, the child of that king's sister, came into existence like an embodiment of great glory appearing, with the royal fly-whisk clearly displayed, resembling an ornament (on the trunks) of the elephants who were guardians of all the cardinal directions.

> His brother was Tripurarideva, who with the heat of the vigor of his arms, which surpass Mt. Meru in strength, turned back the course of the sun from traversing the entire earth whose girdle is the ocean.
>
> Like Upendra, the younger brother of the lord of the gods Indra, his younger brother [Ambadeva] obeyed the injunction to be charitable, even going to the extent of fetching the wish-fulfilling tree.[34] Ambadeva, whose arms were skilled at wielding a sword, protected the earth which had been brought under the control of his commands in all directions, with righteousness. (vv. 4–7 of SII 10.465)

Ambadeva's successes in battle are narrated in the following nine verses. Although mythological allusions are abundant, each verse relates victories over specific historical figures, as shown in the following selections:

> Ambadeva, who having defeated King Shripati Ganapati in battle by displaying his ferocious abilities, has taken away from him the honor symbolized by possession of the epithet "Champion over a Thousand Kings" [*rāya-sahasra-malla*].
>
> Because of Ambadeva's arms, King Eruva Mallideva fell from a moving horse in battle along with his pride and the host of his allied troops. Having cut off Mallideva's head, Ambadeva then cast down his own weapon and through repeatedly knocking the head around the ground with his feet, as if kicking a playing ball, he who was never tired finally grew weary.
>
> Ambadeva, having made King Keshava flee accompanied by Somideva and Allu Ganga, has seized all their horses as the reward for his valor. (vv. 8, 10, 13 of SII 10.465)

A final two verses asking for the god Shiva's benediction end the Sanskrit verse portion of the inscription. The praise of Ambadeva's deeds is not over, however, for the record continues with a list of approximately 50 titles (*biruda*) that he possessed, many of them earned in battle. Some epithets, such as "the hero who has taken the head of Eruva Mallideva" (*Ēṟuva-mallidēvani tala-goṇḍu-gaṇḍa*), refer to events narrated in the earlier Sanskrit verses of the inscription. Others refer to different accomplishments, like the tribute from distant kings ("he who is adorned with shining ornaments of gold and gems sent as gifts by the king of Devagiri," *Dēvagiri-rāya-prasthāpita-prabhṛta-maṇi-kanaka-bhūṣaṇa*).

Although Ambadeva's inscription is unusually long, the highlighting of a warrior's own feats rather than his inherited prestige is typical of the period. This kind of publicly acknowledged individuality is what Mattison Mines calls "the individuality of eminence" in a recent study of modern South Indian society. A leader's reputation, he suggests, rests on his ability to distinguish himself through his own deeds (Mines 1994: 40–43). Because leadership in medieval Andhra was so closely bound to victory in battle, ambitious warriors had to repeatedly prove themselves in action. The uncertainties of warfare were important in the social dynamism of medieval Andhra, since they could lead to dramatic shifts in a military career. And the premium placed on military success resulted in the foregrounding of individual achievements over family background in many of the inscriptions of Kakatiya Andhra.

In the preceding few pages, I have pointed out the inscriptional emphasis on an individual's agency and the evidence of changes in titles between fathers and sons. Combined, these features of the inscriptional corpus refute the widespread depiction of precolonial India as a static and closed society in which people underwent little change in rank, status, or occupation. To be sure, rampant social movement was not typical of medieval Andhra and one cannot deny the strength of hereditary privilege and kinship bonds. Alterations of occupation and status tended to take place within certain limits, and the majority of men followed in the footsteps of their fathers. But, in this sense, precolonial India was not unlike other preindustrial societies, which were characterized by limited social change and the use of heredity to determine status (Crone 1989: 108). The ways in which people described themselves in medieval inscriptions, however, reveal that individual accomplishments were honored and could alter one's social position.

While the secondary literature on precolonial India has always acknowledged that individual social mobility could occur, the phenomenon has been regarded as rare. Other than in a few exceptional circumstances, such as the seizure of royal power through military conquest, individuals were allegedly unable to effect significant improvements in their own status (e.g., Stevenson 1954). According to M. N. Srinivas's influential model of Sanskritization, upward movement in the social scale was possible only when an entire corporate group (generally, the subcaste) adopted a more Sanskritized or brahmanical lifestyle (Srinivas 1971). The insistence that social mobility was a group phenomenon is a logical corollary of the paradigm of Indian society as a fixed hierarchy ordered on the principle of purity and impurity. Because rank would be ascribed primarily by birth in such a system, individual attainments could have only an ephemeral impact on social status. Unless the marriage-circle to which the person belonged revised its customs and claimed a purer status, any upgrading in position would not be lasting.

Yet ample evidence of fluidity in the social system can be found; how to reconcile this with the notion of a set hereditary hierarchy has been a recurrent problem in South Asian scholarship. Louis Dumont, the best-known proponent of the concept of a hierarchy based on purity and impurity, himself acknowledges the major weakness in his formulation: "Anticipating the study of actual observable status rankings, we admit in advance that they give power a place which is not allowed for by the theoretical hierarchy of the pure and the impure" (1970: 77). More recent research on South Asian society has drawn attention to values other than purity and impurity, such as auspiciousness (Marglin 1985: 300–303), or to the ritual centrality of the dominant caste rather than the brahman (Raheja 1989: 82). Nicholas B. Dirks argues that "caste was embedded in a political context of kingship" and hence concern with royal authority, honor, and power was far more prevalent than notions of purity-impurity (1987: 7). Furthermore, Patrick Olivelle points out that the "ideology of purity/impurity that emerges from the [brahmanical] Dharma literature is concerned with the individual and not with groups, with purification and not with purity, and lends little support to a theory which makes relative purity the foundation of social stratification" (1998: 214).

Proverbs found throughout India show that the popular culture has always been aware of the possibilities for individual social mobility. It was said in nineteenth-century North India that "last year I was a Jolaha; now I am a Sheikh; next year if prices rise, I shall become a Saiyad" (Kolff 1990: 18). A somewhat similar Bengali proverb runs, "The first year I was a Shaikh, the second year a Khan, this year if the price of grain is low I'll become a Saiyid" (Eaton 1993: 315). Folk sayings of this sort are found all over India—one example from the South pertains to the Kallars, often defamed as bandits, who turned into Vellalar land-owning peasants. In fact, everyone can eventually rise to the position of Vellalar, according to the Tamil adage, "Slowly, slowly, they all become Vellalar" (Hellman-Rajanayagam 1995: 127n.65). In Maharashtra it is said that "when a Kunbi prospers he becomes a Maratha" (O'Hanlon 1985: 10). Older scholarly constructs of Indian society acknowledge that individual acts may affect ranking but only detrimentally, by causing an individual to lose purity or caste status. Popular perception in India, in contrast, affirms the positive potential of individual agency.

The Militarism of Kakatiya Society

The instances of *nāyaka* sons becoming *rājus*, as noted in the earlier discussion, illustrate how military activity could serve as an avenue for social mobility in medieval Andhra. Through success in battle, a warrior could move up in the world and even aspire to kingly status. The most notable example of a meteoric rise in fortunes during the Kakatiya period is the Kayastha family, who figure in approximately 50 inscriptions. P. V. Parabrahma Sastry believes that the Kayasthas were recruited from Western India by the Kakatiya king Ganapati, due to their expertise in cavalry warfare (1978: 157). That all the female members of this family had names ending in "bai," a typically Western Indian suffix, serves as evidence for their alleged Western Indian origin, along with the generous grant made by the first member of the family known to be in Andhra, Gangaya Sahini, to a brahman resident of Dvaraka for the worship of Krishna there.[35] In his earliest record from Palnad Taluk, issued ca. 1239 C.E., Gangaya Sahini bears no administrative titles or marks of high rank (ARE 69 of 1929–30). By 1251 he is said to be ruling the area from Panugal in Nalgonda District down to Marjavadi in Cuddapah District and possesses numerous lofty titles, including *mahāmaṇḍalēśvara*, and two Kakatiya insignia bestowed on him as a sign of their special favor (SII 10.334). His growing prominence seems to have resulted from his involvement in the Kakatiya campaigns in southern Andhra to restore the Telugu Choda king and Kakatiya ally, Manuma Siddhi, to his throne at Nellore.[36] Between 1251 and 1258 Gangaya Sahini figures in no fewer than 11 inscriptions.[37]

Three of Gangaya Sahini's nephews followed him, in succession, as leaders of the family.[38] Whereas Gangaya never used a status title more grand than *sāhiṇi* or *sēnāpati*, his successors called themselves *mahārājas* from the outset. Ambadeva, whose achievements were narrated at such great length in his inscription of 1290, was the third of Gangaya Sahini's successors and the first to break away totally from the Kakatiyas. By 1290 he was firmly entrenched in southern Andhra as an independent king who resisted Kakatiya attempts to subjugate him. In a period of approximately 50 years, the Kayasthas evolved from elite cavalry warriors to the intermediary rank of subordinate chiefs and, in the end, achieved independent royal status for a short time. The memory of their humble origins is erased in Kayastha inscriptions shortly after the death of Gangaya Sahini. While three earlier

Kayastha inscriptions name Gangaya Sahini's father and grandfather, neither of whom distinguished himself in any notable way,[39] in his 1290 record (partially translated in the previous section of this chapter) Ambadeva goes only as far back as Gangaya Sahini, just one generation removed, in narrating his ancestry. There must have been countless other warriors like Gangaya Sahini, only less successful, whose martial abilities won them recognition and whose descendants accordingly enjoyed an elevated status.

Probably the main reason that the actual degree of social mobility in precolonial India has not been well-perceived to date is because we have considerably underestimated the extent of military skills among the population. In a provocative analysis of North India from 1450 to 1850, Dirk Kolff has recently argued that military skills and weapons were widespread among the peasantry, many of whom took up occasional military service. For these peasants, service in one of the plentiful armies of the period was not only a significant source of income but could be "a major generator of socio-religious identities" (1990: 58). In Kolff's view, many labels that are today considered caste or ethnic designations were originally military identities acquired through membership in a war-band. One could become a Rajput or Afghan through military service, since these identities were open status categories rather than closed hereditary communities. According to Kolff, the demand for military labor in early modern Hindustan therefore generated considerable social dynamism.

The Kakatiya inscriptional corpus does not allow us a glimpse into the social stratum of the run-of-the-mill peasant, of course. But the mention of so many warriors certainly evidences the importance of military activities and skills. Warriors of various sorts form the single largest block of donors in Kakatiya Andhra. Many of them were known as *nāyakas*, a term that literally means "leader." More than any other title in medieval Andhra, *nāyaka* encompassed persons of varied backgrounds. A study of northeastern Andhra in the medieval period notes how individuals as diverse as brahmans and artisans adopted this title (Ramachandra Rao 1976: 217). Very few *nāyakas* in Kakatiya Andhra claimed to belong to the *kṣatriya varṇa*, nor do they provide many details on their ancestry, in sharp contrast with men holding the titles of *mahārāja* or *rāju*. Like the Rajput of Kolff's analysis, *nāyaka* was a status that could be acquired, regardless of origin, and move a man up the social ladder. *Nāyaka* was essentially an honorific title borne by prominent individuals who participated in military activities.

Several other status titles denote martial skills and experience. *Leṅka* is the most commonly found military title after *nāyaka* (see table 4). Explained as "soldier, servant" by Iswara Dutt (1967: 259), the *leṅka* was a special kind of soldier: one who fought in the king's personal forces and took an oath to serve his lord unto death (Venkataramanayya and Somasekhara Sarma 1960: 670). Some *leṅkas* in Karnataka are known to have taken this vow so seriously that they committed suicide upon their lord's death (Settar 1982: 197). *Sāhiṇi* has been equated with the Sanskrit term *sādhanika* (the master of the royal stables; Sircar 1966: 285). It is sometimes found in conjunction with the word for "elephant," *gaja*, to indicate a commander of the elephant corps. A *rautu* was also a cavalry leader, while *camūpati* simply means "general" or "army leader" (Iswara Dutt 1967: 257; Sircar 1966: 67).

The warriors described so far all enjoyed an elevated status as either military leaders or royal bodyguards. Common soldiers called *baṇṭu* also figure occasionally as donors, either individually or in groups. *Baṇṭus* are differentiated from the horse-riding *rautus* in several inscriptions and are twice assessed lower rates for their religious gifts (*Bhārati* 54: 56, HAS 19 Mn. 19). They may have been foot soldiers.

Status titles are not the sole markers of a man's engagement in martial activities. Even more revealing are the lists of epithets (*biruda*) recorded in inscriptions, which are often of a heroic or martial character.[40] Consider, for example, the epithets borne by the donor in the following inscription:

> May all fare well! In the 1,157th year of the Shaka era [1235 C.E.], (corresponding to the cyclic) year Manmatha, on the 2nd (day of the) dark (fortnight in the lunar month) Margashira, a Wednesday;
>
> May all fare well! The dependent on the lotus feet of Anungu Maharaja who has obtained all five of the Mahamandaleshvara honors, the king's cavalier Vishaveli Masake Sahini, son of Devai Sahini and grandson of the illustrious Master of the Robes Vishaveli Kunte Sahini, who is a Narayana among the king's cavaliers, who possesses all the praiseworthy (titles such as): a perfect Revanta amongst those mounted on the most unruly horses,[41] beloved of the goddess of heroes, purifier of the clan, the crest-jewel of his relatives, like a son to the women of others, the hero of heroes, true to his word, fierce in combat, a lion among men, like a tidal wave in force;
>
> Gave 25 cows for a perpetual lamp to the glorious lord Tripurantaka, having been victorious in the battle of Chintalapundi mounted on (the horse) Punyamurti. By accepting these (cows), Pasem Brammana and his sons and grandsons agree to supply butter at the rate of 1 *mā[na]* daily (for) as long as the sun and moon (endure). He who steals (endowed) land, whether given by himself or by another, will be reborn as a maggot in excrement for (the next) sixty thousand years. (SII 10.283)

Often, men with status titles that are not specifically warriorlike also proclaim martial epithets in their inscriptions. This is quite common among *reḍḍis*, to mention only one example. Or we have individuals like Malyala Kata and Malyala Chaunda who bear no status titles yet possess military epithets. Several of the Malyala family's titles derive from specific campaigns in which members engaged and were probably awarded for their military service by Kakatiya rulers. One of Malyala Kata's epithets is *Kōṭa-gelpāta*, "the conqueror of Kota," referring to the town Dharaṇikota (Guntur District), which was attacked in the reign of Kakatiya Rudradeva. During the king Ganapati's reign, Kakatiya forces subjugated the chief of the coastal territory, Velanati Prithvishvara. Malyala Kata's participation in the campaign garnered him the title *Pṛthvīśvara-śiraḥ-kanduka-krīḍā-vinōda*, "he who played with the ball that is Prithvishvara's head." The conquest of the island Divi in the mouth of the Krishna River led to his epithet *Divi-cūṟakāra*, "the plunderer of Divi" (Parabrahma Sastry 1978: 149–50). The specificity of the Malyala epithets, pertaining to a particular battle or conquest, contrasts with the general nature of the heroic epithets born by Vishaveli Masake Sahini in the inscription just translated. But in both cases, the epithets identify them as warriors.

Not all of the men I am calling warriors would have been occupied full-time with military activities, obviously. Still, it is striking how widespread martial skills were during this era or, at least, how widespread were claims to possess these abilities. Even at the level of status titles, we find a considerable proportion of men who were tagged as warriors. Individual *nāyaka* donors comprise 22 percent of all men with status titles (114 out of 514). When *leṅkas*, *sāhiṇis*, and the like are added in, men with military status titles constitute 25 percent of all individual male donors with titles. But, as I have just explained, this omits the many other men—either with different titles or no titles at all—who can be classified as warriors on the basis of their epithets. In addition, of course, there are the numerous *mahārājas* and royal *rājus* who conducted military campaigns in their capacity as kings. Half or more of the privileged men of Kakatiya Andhra may have engaged in fighting at some point in their lives, at a conservative estimate.

It is no coincidence that Andhra's two great martial epics, *Palnāṭi Vīrula Katha* (Story of the Heroes of Palnad) and *Kāṭama Rāju Katha* (Story of Katama Raju), are both set in the Kakatiya period, given the widespread militarism of the era. While the historicity of the *Kāṭama Rāju Katha* (discussed further following) cannot be established with any certainty, the *Palnāṭi Vīrula Katha* (epic of Palnad) is based, however loosely, on an actual conflict that occurred in the late twelfth century.[42] The Kakatiyas themselves were in no way involved, for the central struggle was occasioned by a succession dispute over the Haihaya throne of Palnad, a small kingdom located in the semiarid interior of Guntur District. The chief characters in the epic are not the Haihaya nobles nor any of the other high-ranking figures, but rather the warrior Brahma Nayudu, his son Baludu, and their various associates—collectively known as the 65 or 66 "heroes."

Although the epic in its present form is quite recent, since it was transmitted orally for centuries before it was ever written down, the heroes of Palnad were already worshiped by the early fourteenth century. In 1315 the prominent Kakatiya general Devari Nayaka made a gift of land on their behalf at Macherla, one of the main sites in Palnad associated with the events of the heroes' lives (SII 26.617). Temples to the heroes were established elsewhere as well, as an early-fifteenth-century record from Donakonda village in Darsi Taluk, Prakasam District, demonstrates (NDI Darsi 19). The continuing popularity of the epic is attested in the *Krīḍābhirāmamu*, usually attributed to the author Vinukonda Vallabharaya of the early fifteenth century.[43] In this Telugu satire, which purports to describe the Kakatiya capital Warangal during the reign of its last king Prataparudra, the epic of Palnad is said to be both recited regularly and depicted in pictorial form. Both the epic and the cult of the Palnad heroes still flourish today, particularly in the Palnad area. As is the case in several other hero cults, such as the *teyyam* cult of Kerala, the Palnad heroes are worshiped today in the form of weapons enshrined in small structures (Roghair 1982: 27).

The Palnad epic reveals a level of ruthlessness and bloodthirstiness that is not apparent in the rhetoric of medieval inscriptions, but which nonetheless must have comprised an aspect of precolonial Andhra's martial ethos. Insults easily lead to blood feuds, supposed allies are treacherously sent forth to death to avenge old hostilities, and each possibility for peace is destined to fail. A truce almost averts the final tragedy until Baludu is presented with the bloody sacred thread of his brahman brother-in-arms, who committed suicide when he was deviously prevented from joining the battle. In the end virtually every character in the epic meets a gory death. Among the most gruesome is the fate of an enemy beheaded by Baludu, who cooks the head with rice and water and has this rice-flesh flung up into the air as he triumphantly marches to the battlefield (Roghair 1982: 342). Echoes of this vengeful world of the Palnad epic are heard in the family history of the Velugoti clan, where victors offer rice cooked with the blood and bones of their enemies to the spirits and where effigies of the defeated are affixed to spittoons or anklets (Somasekhara Sarma 1948: 248–50). In comparison, the dark underside of war is only rarely exposed in inscriptions, as when the Reddi king Vema is said to have a formidable sword surrounded by the ghosts of the men he had killed on the battlefield (CPIHM 1.16).

The cult of the Palnad heroes is but the most developed manifestation of the widespread custom of commemorating heroic death. As far back as the third century, Andhra warriors who died in battle were honored through the erection of an inscribed memorial pillar (section 6.B of EI 35.1). These gradually evolved during the following centuries into a fairly standardized form—the hero-stone bearing a pictorial representation of the man who died in some heroic manner, either while defending a village's cattle from attack or fighting on behalf of a lord. Elsewhere in the peninsula, hero-stones were regularly offered food and flowers, and the family of the dead was often given land (Kasturi 1940: 206–7). Although similar practices must have been observed in much of Andhra, they are attested only in Kannada inscriptions from the region, some of which record land grants for the specific purpose of conducting worship of a hero-stone (e.g., ARE 1918: 176). In the absence of a systematic study of Andhra hero-stones, one can only roughly estimate their quantity and spatial distribution based on the published reports of the few that also bear inscriptions. Inscribed hero-stones are considerably more numerous in Andhra in the era before 1000 C.E., although they were still being created during the Kakatiya period (e.g., IAP-C 2.3; SII 10.391; ARE 771 and 772 of 1917). This is not attributable to a decline in martial activities, however, nor to reduced respect for dead warriors after the turn of the second millennium. But as the temple cult grew in popularity, the custom of erecting hero-stones seems to have been increasingly displaced by those of consecrating images or establishing perpetual lamps in temples on behalf of those who died in battle (e.g., APAS 31.30 and IAP-C 1.128).

Andhra society's reverence for martial heroism manifested itself in one new development of the Kakatiya period—self-beheading as a form of expressing devotion to a god or goddess. This most extreme manner of displaying one's piety was regarded as a great act of courage and accordingly memorialized in numerous hero-stones, found primarily in centers of Shaiva worship (Murthy 1982: 212–17). But a more militant attitude toward religious devotion in general is also witnessed in the Virashaiva sect, which was founded around the beginning of the Kakatiya period and spread from Karnataka to inland Andhra in the next century. Its virulently anti-brahman adherents were not averse to using violence against those who opposed their beliefs, at least as portrayed in the *Basava Purāṇamu*, a thirteenth-century Telugu text that narrates the events of the saint Basava's life (Narayana Rao 1990: 12). The Vaishnava creed of the main characters in the epic of Palnad has been dubbed "Viravaishnavism" by some modern commentators, who view it as a militant counterpart to Virashaivism (Prasad and Sambaiah 1983: 239). And, interestingly, the chief antagonists in the Palnad conflict are cast as sectarian rivals, Shaivas opposing Vaishnavas in armed combat (Roghair 1982: 123).

The existence of martial epics, hero-stones, and militant sectarian groups—although discussed all too briefly here—suggests how deeply Andhra culture was imbued with a respect for warriors and martial heroism in this era. Coupled with inscriptional testimony of the many male donors who possessed social identities derived from military activity, we cannot doubt the pervasiveness of armed skills at this time nor the attractiveness of a warrior lifestyle. While social mobility surely would have been limited due to the costs of equipping oneself as an elite warrior, military service must have offered many aspiring young men in Kakatiya Andhra an appealing opportunity for raising their social status.

Physical Movement in a Changing Landscape

A second reason that the extent of social dynamism and fluidity in medieval India has been seriously underrated is the misconception that precolonial Indians were immobilized in geographic space. Just as its social structure was previously depicted as inflexible due to the dictates of a caste system based on the principle of purity and impurity, so too were its people thought of as permanently stuck within a myriad of self-contained villages. Because each one possessed its own division of labor, Indian villages were regarded as self-replicating and almost entirely autonomous—with every place a microcosm of the whole, there was little need for contact with each other.[44] The social rigidity of the precolonial populace was thus matched by its stationary physical position, and both of these factors accounted for India's lack of historical change, in older interpretations of India's past.

Since the late 1960s, however, the characterization of precolonial India as a solely sedentary and agrarian civilization has been severely undermined, with important implications for the corresponding assumptions regarding social stagnancy and historical inertia. Once scholars began to look beyond the confines of the Indian village in recent years, they quickly realized that vigorous regional networks linked the various agricultural localities. Pilgrimage, marriage alliances, and commerce all mobilized people and goods throughout the physical landscape. Nor was precolonial India an entirely agrarian world, as a spate of works on merchants, artisans, and trade have amply demonstrated.[45] Beyond the merchants, craftsmen, and peasants documented in the historical sources, the tribal and pastoral peoples are only now starting to be appreciated for their role in Indian history.[46] Before colonial policies forced mobile communities to settle and before population pressures largely eliminated open spaces, the proportion of nonsedentary peoples must have been far greater. And if, as we now believe, precolonial people were often in movement and in contact with diverse others, then their social identities and affiliations were more likely to be altered or transformed.

Perhaps the most obvious error in older models of a sedentary Indian civilization is that they overlook indigenous mercantile communities. The well-studied expansion of trade in South India after 1500 was preceded by an earlier period of mercantile growth in the thirteenth century. An increase in the number of inscriptions issued by merchants, more frequent references to commercial taxes and tolls, and a higher level of monetization all point to a boom in the commercial economy of the peninsula (Abraham 1988: 10; Sundaram 1968: 49–50; Chattopadhyaya 1977: 124–25, 134). Sanjay Subrahmanyam has suggested that agrarian expansion, and the demographic increase that resulted from it, were major causes for the growth of trade in the two centuries after 1500 (1990: 357–63). The extension of agrarian settlement, a process already well under way during the Kakatiya period, may similarly have figured into the increase in trade activities during the thirteenth century. External stimulus may have been another influence, for there was a remarkable efflorescence of international trade throughout Eurasia between the mid thirteenth and mid fourteenth centuries (Abu-Lughod 1989).

The importance of long-distance trade was clearly recognized by the rulers of Kakatiya Andhra. One indication that they wanted to encourage maritime trade comes from the famous Motupalli inscription issued by King Ganapati in the mid thirteenth century. The text of the record, the beginning portion of which is translated below, was intended to reassure traders from elsewhere that they were welcome in the Kakatiya realm:

> This inscribed guarantee has been granted by His Majesty the King Ganapatideva to seatraders going back and forth en route to all continents, countries, and towns. In the past, kings forcibly seized all the cargo such as gold, elephants, horses, jewels, etc. when sea-going vessels journeying from one region to another were caught in storms, wrecked, and cast on shore. But We, for the sake of our reputation and religious merit and out of pity for those who have incurred the grave risk of a sea-voyage thinking that wealth is more valuable even than life, give up all but the customary tariff.[47]

Motupalli must have been the chief port in Kakatiya Andhra, to judge by this inscription and by the fact that it is the one place in Andhra which the Venetian traveler Marco Polo claims to have visited, just decades after King Ganapati's edict was inscribed (Nilakanta Sastri 1972: 174–75).[48]

The Motupalli inscription proceeds to specify the rates assessed on a variety of items, including scents such as sandal and civet, camphor, rose water, ivory, pearls, coral, a range of metals (copper, zinc, and lead), silk, pepper, and areca-nuts. This list gives us a good idea of the types of luxury goods that were being exported and imported through Motupalli port to other Indian regions along the coast, as well as to foreign territories. Many of the same commodities are enumerated in a record issued by merchant groups who traded in the main market of the Kakatiya capital Warangal (HAS 13.14). The range of merchandise is even greater in the Warangal inscription, because the inland trade included foodstuffs and other bulky items in addition to the precious goods transported by sea. The number of agricultural products offered for sale in Warangal is particularly notable—from rice, wheat, and other grains to assorted vegetables, coconuts, mangos, tamarind and other fruits, sesame seeds, green lentils, mustard, honey, ghee, oil, turmeric, and ginger. This and similar inscriptions attest to the presence of a commercial component in the thirteenth-century agricultural economy.

All of these trade articles had to be hauled from the places where they were produced to the point of sale, whether that was a periodic market, permanent market, or seaport. Boats were used to move commodities when this was feasible, especially along the lower Krishna River (e.g., EI 3.15). Carts pulled by bullocks were another form of transport. But inscriptions more frequently mention loads carried by pack-bullocks or by people themselves. The quantities of bullocks could be quite large, as was the case in Tripurantakam where the temple had 300 pack-bullocks in the mid thirteenth century (SII 10.304). Goods transported into the temple town on these bullocks were exempted from tolls (*suṅkamu*). Who was handling the transport is unclear, although this record mentions *kāmpulu* (a general term for agriculturalists) who carried things on carts.

Most probably, trading and herding activities were combined by some of the transporters. Pack-caravan traders figure in the subcontinent's past as far back as the early historic period, and by Mughal times references to such communities are found frequently (Allchin 1963: 112; Habib 1990). Conveying goods by pack-bullocks is less efficient than using bullock carts, but much cheaper if the bullocks are moved in herds and allowed to graze as they go along. Problems with difficult terrain can also be reduced by resorting to pack-bullocks rather than carts. Throughout much of early modern India, the term for people who were both pastoralists and transporters of goods was Banjara, applied to a variety of different ethnic and linguistic groups. One Banjara community that has been active in the Deccan over the past few centuries is the Lambadis, or Lamans. Aside from their regular carrying trade, Lambadis were often engaged in transporting supplies for the numerous armies of the peninsula.[49] By virtue of their very mobility, such people are less likely to be recorded in the epigraphic sources. But it is noteworthy that modern pastoralist communities in both Andhra Pradesh and Karnataka (the Gollas and Kurubas) share traditions relating to the folk-deity Mallana or Mailara which place him in the company of itinerant traders and their bullock caravans (Sontheimer 1989: 322–23).

Long-distance trade was loosely coordinated by associations of merchants like the Pekkandru (literally, "The Many") who figure in the following inscription:

> May all fare well and prosper! In the auspicious 1,191th year of the Shaka era [1269 C.E.], (corresponding to the cyclic) year Shukla, on the 5th (day of the) bright (fortnight of the lunar month) Kartika, a Thursday;
>
> May all fare well! The celebrated Pekkandru of the Enamadala locality—who are preservers of the Vira Balanjya way, famed among the people of the entire world, possessors of 500 hero-inscriptions, adorned with an army of (good) attributes, sincere and unsullied in conduct and character, well-versed in the ways of courtesy; and who are the licensed traders[50] of the Pakanadu-21,000, the Vengi-16,000, and the Hanumakonda metropolitan area—have levied a tithe [*magama*][51] for the ritual worship of the illustrious lord, the great Shiva-linga Gaunishvara-deva, the specifics of which are as follows:
>
> — 1 *kēsari-pātika*[52] per bullock-load[53] of areca-nuts
> — 2 *vīsa* per bundle of areca-nuts
> — 1 *kēsari-pātika* per cart-load of sesame seeds
> — 2 *vīsa* per cart-load of grain
> — 1 *kēsari-pātika* per bale of cotton
> — 1 *vīsa* per bullock-load of grain
> — 50 betel leaves per bundle of betel leaves
> — 2 *vīsa* per bullock-load of oil
> — 1 *vīsa* per head-load
> — 2 *vīsa* per miscellaneous load
> — a ladleful whenever oil is measured out (for retail sale)

> An extra *kēsari-aḍḍugu* is to be added to this tithe on the occasion of special worship-services. The Ubhaya Nanadeshi will make donations according to the terms set forth (here), for perpetuity.[54] Should anyone be obstructive, he will be (considered) a traitor to the convention [*samaya*].[55] (SII 4.935)

The inscription enumerates the exact rates of a tithe, or voluntary contribution, to a temple in Enamadala, to be calculated according to the quantity of merchandise brought into town for sale. This is a rather unusual case, in that the religious donations of merchant groups were usually calculated as a fraction of total sales or of a sales tax.[56]

The inscription translated above shows us that even a group of merchants based in one locality might have trading rights over a fairly large territory. Enamadala, where this particular collective was situated, is a town in Guntur Taluk, approximately 25 miles south of the Krishna River and 8 miles north of the Bay of Bengal. Its Pekkandru is said to have operated in several other localities in Andhra—in Pakanadu and Vengi, which are coastal areas adjacent to Guntur District, and in the more distant Hanumakonda, the first Kakatiya capital in far-off Telangana. Even more intriguing than this glimpse of the wide-ranging geographic activities of a single set of merchants is the inscriptional reference to the Vira Balanjya way (*dharma*) and the use of standard epithets associated with the Vira Balanjya. The Vira Balanjya are often traced back to a corporate body known as the Ayyavole 500 from the name of their place of origin in Karnataka. Beginning in the eleventh century, the Ayyavole 500 start to figure in records scattered throughout the Kannada and Tamil areas, with a consistent set of titles. Only in the thirteenth century, however, do mercantile inscriptions bearing these same epithets but using the name Vira Balanjya instead appear in Andhra (Abraham 1988: 41; Sundaram 1968: 69–71). Vira Balanjya affiliation is sometimes claimed by individuals and at other times by groups; there are scattered references to *balañjya-seṭṭis* or *balijas* as well.[57] Vira Balanjya traders employed fighters to protect their warehouses and goods in transit, also acted as toll farmers for local lords, and in later times used the status title *nāiḍu* as well as *ceṭṭi* (Sundaram 1968: 76–82; Thurston 1975, 1: 136). The Ayyavole 500, Vira Balanjya, and similar merchant organizations are often dubbed guilds in English, but it would be more accurate to think of them as a network of traders and merchants who shared a set of standard business practices and could thus cooperate over long distances. The Vira Balanjya network eventually extended throughout much of South India, evidence for not only the large-scale circulation of trade goods and traders in the thirteenth century but the emergence of a common mercantile culture.

The pastoralists of Kakatiya Andhra are more of an enigma than the merchants. They are visible in the inscriptional corpus both as donors of religious gifts and as caretakers of livestock endowed to temples. Curiously, however, their presence is epigraphically attested primarily in the coastal territory rather than in the semiarid inland zone that is most ecologically suited for pastoralism. Nor can we confirm the level and range of their migratory activities. Today the so-called pastoral communities of the Karnataka-Andhra region are actually settled in villages. At most their movements consist of a young male's herding of a flock a short distance away from his home base. The anthropologist Peter Claus, who is studying the Kurubas and Gollas of the Karnataka-Andhra border, believes that these communities are not remnants of some age-old pastoral ethnic or tribal group, but instead became classified as pastoralists by acquiring rights to grazing land and by actively taking care of cattle for others.[58] If Claus is correct, herding is no more than a village occupational specialty, as pottery or weaving once were.

The archaeological record confirms the ties between farming and cattle-herding in Neolithic South India. The earliest practitioners of (shifting) agriculture, who were concentrated in the dry uplands, simultaneously engaged in animal husbandry. Cattle were the predominant livestock, although sheep and goats were also raised (Rodgers 1991; Murthy 1993). Today several communities in the Deccan interior are considered to be shepherds rather than cattle-breeders, including the Dhangars of Maharashtra and the Kurubas of Karnataka. During the Kakatiya period, ewes were more commonly the objects of religious gifts than cows, and Marco Polo observed that Andhra sheep were the largest in the world (Ratnagar 1991: 181). But Andhra's modern herding community, the Gollas, have traditionally been linked with cattle in popular perception. Because cattle require better pasturage than sheep and are less able to withstand unfavorable conditions, in all likelihood it became increasingly difficult to maintain large herds of cattle as the amount of uncultivated land decreased. In any case, livestock were obviously valuable resources in the slash-and-burn and dry farming regimes of the interior Deccan, where crop productivity was much lower than in the zones of irrigated cultivation.

The regions in the Deccan where herding was combined with some form of cultivation correspond broadly to the territories within which hero-stones are most abundantly found. Systematic searches for hero-stones have yielded large numbers in most Karnataka districts, and in the Tamil districts of North Arcot, Dharmapuri, and Salem. Hero-stones are also widespread in the Maharashtra districts of Poona, Kolhapur, and Satara (Settar 1982). Unfortunately, there has been no such attempt to survey Andhra Pradesh on the ground, with the result that we know only about inscribed hero-stones, most certainly far fewer than those that simply bear a pictorial image of a warrior. The inscribed hero-stones I have noticed come primarily from Cuddapah and Anantapur Districts, while Chandrasekhara Reddy claims to have identified the greatest number in Chittoor District (1994: 77).[59] Even with the limited knowledge that we currently possess—which points to Rayalasima as the subregion of greatest activity—the overlap between local cultures that produced hero-stones and the more arid zones of the interior where pastoralism was so important is clearly demonstrated. The martial character of inland South Indian society, perhaps forged through the need to protect livestock, has been noted by numerous scholars.

The potential for conflict between herders in search of pastures for their animals and peasants engaged in intensive agriculture is a central motif in the *Kāṭama Rāju Katha* epic. One of the main episodes in the story concerns the war between Katama Raju, leader of the Yadavas (i.e., herders), and the Telugu Choda king Manuma Siddhi of Nellore, a historic figure of thirteenth-century Andhra. The oral narrative tells us that Katama Raju brought his large herds of cattle to Nellore where he requested grazing rights from the king. The king agreed, saying "all the grass that is born out of the water is yours, and all the male calves born from the cows are ours" (Narayana Rao 1989: 111). But Katama Raju cunningly understands the king's words as license to graze his cattle in the fields where rice grew, on the grounds that it too was a form of grass born out of water. This was the ultimate outrage in an agrarian society that prized rice above all, and so the outcome could be none other than war. A short and somewhat garbled version of the Katama Raju story is contained in an inscription whose date we cannot ascertain (NDI Kandukur 26). In this rendition the war is said to have been occasioned by Katama Raju's refusal to pay the standard grazing fee (*pullari*) to the king. The events are placed in the reign of Kakatiya Prataparudra, who ruled from 1289 to 1323.[60]

In both the oral and inscriptional narratives, Katama Raju and his people are said to own large herds and to have migrated to Manuma Siddhi's Nellore kingdom in search of pastures. The migration was caused by drought, according to the inscriptional account. While quite possibly not a memory of a historic event, the story of the war between the pastoral Katama Raju and the king of the fertile agrarian zone may accurately record the tensions between the conflicting requirements of wet rice agriculture and animal husbandry. We might also interpret it as evidence for the prior existence of herding on a much larger scale than occurs today. Deccan pastoralists may not have moved continuously in the manner of Central Asian nomads, but it is likely that they frequently traveled farther distances in the medieval period than did full-time peasants. When faced with conditions of drought, moreover, they could be forced to entirely new territories.

The origins of many villages in Rayalasima—the most sparsely settled region of Andhra, or, more precisely, the last of the three regions to be incorporated into the temple-building and inscription-recording culture—date back to immigrant herders. Ravulakollu is said to have been founded by the shepherd Manikela Basi Nayudu, who migrated from the north to this village in Siddhavatam Taluk of Cuddapah District. Similarly, the village Aluvakonda in the present Koilkuntla Taluk of Kurnool was established by some Yadavas (pastoralists), according to village tradition. It was a cattle-herder called Machana who supposedly first settled Machanavolu in Cuddapah Taluk and gave the village its name.[61] These men may have been fleeing from drought, or they may have been pushed out of their earlier localities by the extension and intensification of agrarian settlement. We should not discount the lure of unclaimed land as a possible motive either, for many peasants likewise carved out new villages in Kakatiya Andhra. But whatever the reason, the widespread presence of livestock and herding in inland Andhra added another dimension to the complex world that was being forged during the medieval period through the incorporation of diverse peoples into one social web.

This brings us back to the village, where we began. We have seen that certain segments of the population—traders, pastoralists, and warriors—routinely made forays out of their homes into the larger world. But it would be a mistake to draw too great a contrast between them and others whose livelihood derived primarily from agriculture. For in an age when large tracts of land were still unsettled, there was plenty of scope for the agricultural entrepreneur. The colonization of interior Andhra was a long-term process that served as a backdrop for the events of the medieval period. The founders of villages were men with considerable labor resources in that they generally migrated with a band of family and followers. In return for their initiative, they were commonly granted a privilege like the position of village headman or *reḍḍi* (e.g., ARE copper plate 4 of 1960–61). This was typical of sixteenth- and seventeenth-century Maharashtra as well, where men who founded villages became the village headmen (Gordon 1993: 22–23).

Villages, once established, did not necessarily become permanent fixtures in the agrarian landscape. They could be abandoned for causes as varied as famine, drought, or disease, and they were sometimes subsequently resettled. This cycle of depopulation and repopulation does not often show up in inscriptions, which are typically records of religious endowments.[62] Occasionally, however, disputes over land rights or village boundaries were resolved by a king and recorded permanently on stone. In one such instance from Cuddapah District in 1257, the local conflict arose out of the temporary abandonment of a village by part of the population (ARE 580 of 1907). Nonbrahman peasants had gradually settled on lands belonging to the brahman village Perungadura, some migrating from elsewhere due to political unrest and others to avoid an outbreak of disease. The understanding was that the nonbrahman cultivators would pay annual revenues to the brahman proprietors. When famine struck the village some years later, the brahmans temporarily moved elsewhere. Upon their return, they found the nonbrahmans unwilling to resume payments. The king ordered an investigation and ultimately regranted the village to the brahmans (ARE 1908: 70–71; Venkataramanayya 1929: 17).

Heavy taxation was another major motivation for leaving one's home, at least during the Vijayanagara age. Several records from that period were issued in order to announce the remission of taxes and encourage the deserters to return. Certain taxes levied on village accountants (*karaṇālu*), brahmans, and temple servants were canceled in a sixteenth-century inscription from Guntur (SII 16.160), which states explicitly that those taxes were unjust and had resulted in migration out of the locality. Artisans and merchants also might opt to move away rather than pay excessively high taxes. An inscription issued in 1533 in Anantapur District (SII 16.104) contained assurances that certain taxes, which had caused the artisans of thirty-two villages to move elsewhere, would henceforth no longer be levied.[63] Warfare was another incentive to move. Soon after the town was annexed by Qutb Shah forces, a Telugu edict was issued at Mangalagiri (Guntur District) that enumerated the tax rates on merchants, weavers, and others (SII 4.711; 1593 C.E.). The accompanying Persian inscription asks that the former residents of the town return.

With all this evidence of movement in and out of the village, which could exist at some points of time and be nonexistent at others, it may not even be safe to speak of a fixed village population. Eugene F. Irschick's (1994) fascinating study of early colonial South India suggests that villages were indeed ephemeral. Prior to colonial rule, land-controlling peasants in the region around what was to become Madras repeatedly relocated themselves in response to external circumstances. Should they return to their former villages, they could expect to face considerable opposition to any effort to regain their former privileges. The colonial project to develop a stable tax base was premised on the continual occupation of land, however, and played a major role in curtailing peasant mobility over the nineteenth century. Irschick believes that East India Company officials and local land-controllers jointly produced the construct of a past Tamil society composed of immutable villages inhabited by the original settlers. Their motives may have been different, but both the British and the local landed elite had a vested interest in "restoring" the chaotic contemporary world to its presumably pristine state, where everyone knew their proper place (sociologically and geographically) and stayed there. In the process, they created a new world and a false knowledge of the past.

Contrary to earlier views, the people in precolonial India often moved from place to place, sometimes to escape from adverse circumstances—drought, disease, oppressive taxation, or political unrest. Other times they moved to improve their lot in life, and yet other times they traveled as a routine part of their livelihood. The precolonial Indians were thus by no means rooted to their villages of birth. Two features of medieval Andhra—the expanding agrarian frontier and the demand for military labor—accentuated the trend toward physical mobility. Regardless of their reasons for migrating or traveling, the mobile individuals of Kakatiya Andhra would have inevitably come into contact with new peoples and new ideas. With the greater opportunities opened up by the possibility of moving, a person could experience considerable change in fortune over a lifetime. By denying that physical mobility was an inherent part of precolonial India, we have discounted one of the major forces for social creativity. The fluidity of social identities that I believe constituted a critical feature of Kakatiya Andhra can only be fully explained in the context of abundant physical movement and change.

Fresh Perspectives: Collectives and Women

An advantage of using inscriptions as a basis for historical reconstruction, as opposed to literature, is their relatively broad scope. With hundreds of records available from Kakatiya Andhra, we are able to view a range of lifestyles and social groupings. Some are familiar to us, because of the wealth of information concerning them or because they are documented in other types of sources. But inscriptions also offer us traces of less familiar peoples, institutions, and values. While limitations of space prevent an examination of every anomalous sociological feature, two further aspects of medieval Andhra inscriptions illustrate the utility of inscriptions for rethinking our models of precolonial society. The first is the presence of collectives that are not kin-or caste-based. The existence of many such groupings of people belies both the Orientalist construct that caste was of paramount importance in traditional social organization and the current modernist stance that precolonial Indians had no meaningful loyalties beyond the narrow confines of family and village. Second, the status and activities of women figuring in inscriptions refute the insignificant position to which precolonial women are generally relegated in the secondary literature. How people actually behaved was often not how the *dharmaśāstra* said they should behave. And such discrepancies make the study of inscriptions particularly rewarding.

The alleged group-orientation of traditional Indian society is not reflected in the patterns of religious endowment in Kakatiya Andhra. The great majority (86 percent) of gifts were given not by families or other social units but by individuals, the prime initiators and actors in religious patronage, a phenomenon that supports my earlier discussion on the premium placed on individual deeds and achievements. Nonetheless, a sizable number of religious endowments originated from groups of people. In some cases several individuals whose names are enumerated came together to make a single endowment. These I call joint donors, since the collaborative nature of the act is evident but the donors do not constitute a corporate organization of any sort. Larger, more anonymous groupings of people also engaged in religious gifting—these I call collective donors since their individual names are not listed in the inscriptions. It is instructive to examine the kinds of people who collaborate in religious endowments for evidence of the nature of group affiliations in medieval Andhra.

Kinship connections did unite many of the joint donors in the 101 instances contained in the Kakatiya Andhra corpus. About half of these were made by brothers, a father and son(s), a brother and sister, or a mother and her son(s). In another quarter of the joint gifts, the donors possess the same status title. Some of them may have been relatives, others are clearly not. Status titles could vary among members of the same family, as discussed previously in the analysis of the names of fathers and sons. This is confirmed by several joint donors who were brothers with different status titles—one pair of brothers were a *nāyaka* and *bōya* (SII 10.765), another had the titles *rāju* and *nāyaka* (SII 10.444), a third were a *mahārāja* and a *rāju* (IAP-C 1.134), and a last set of brothers held the titles *rāju* and *pregaḍa* (NDI Ongole 70). Joint ties of military service also brought together some donors in the sample. Vilemu Rudradeva and Anumakonda Amnu Lenka, who call themselves subordinates of the Kakatiya king Prataparudra (*tat-pāda-padm=ōpajīvulaina*), united to give several plots of land to the deity of Manuru in Medak District (HAS 13.53). Pallinanti Vikkari Nayaka made a gift with one of his warriors (*baṇṭu*), and both are said to have been members of the retinue (*parivāra*) or war-band of Gundaya Nayaka (HAS 19 Mn.20).

Bonds of shared military service also occasioned a number of the 69 endowments made by collective groups in the Kakatiya Andhra inscriptional corpus.[64] Gundaya Nayaka's war-band figures in two other instances, and another troop of warriors (*baṇṭu*) who served the lord Kolani Mandalika Keshavadeva Raju was also active. Several inscriptions were issued by sets of warriors known as *ekkaṭīlu*. M. Somasekhara Sarma believes that the *ekkaṭī*, "single-handed," in their name comes from the fact that they engaged in one-on-one combat (1945: 240–41). In the Kakatiya-period records, *ekkaṭīlu* are either associated with a particular village or carry a numerical designation, a common practice with corporate bodies. This raises the possibility that they were military garrisons in command of certain villages, like the *paḍaipaṟṟu* towns of Tamil Nadu where the troops controlled all agricultural lands (Tirumalai 1981: 37). Because military skills were so prevalent and battle so common, collectives of warriors must have brought together men of varied origins (Venkataramanayya and Somasekhara Sarma 1960: 669).

Some indication of the heterogeneous nature of war-bands can be found in the famous Andhra epic, the *Palnāṭi Vīrula Katha* (Story of the Heroes of Palnad). A leading character in the narrative, Baludu, has a small war-band of devoted companions from diverse backgrounds. One is a brahman, while others—a blacksmith, a goldsmith, a washerman, a potter, and a barber—are drawn from the service and artisan communities. Baludu and his cohorts are so committed to each other that they are called brothers, and their kinlike relations are justified by the story that their births resulted from their mothers' sharing of a divine fruit granted as a boon (Roghair 1982: 103, 244). The greatest testimony to the strength of the bonds created by fighting together appears in the well-known episode of their intercaste dining. Just before they set out for battle, Baludu's mother prepares a meal for all the "brothers" with her own hands. But she serves each one his food on a different kind of plate (earthen, bronze, leaf, etc.) and is rebuked for making such distinctions by her son, who says that caste must be set aside when one goes to war. And so the "brothers" all eat from each other's plates, in defiance of convention but in recognition of their joint fate (Roghair 1982: 309).

Sectarian allegiances inspired other bodies of donors. Shaiva devotees were called *māhēśvaras* or *bhaktas* (SII 7.735; ARE 273 of 1952–53; SII 10.459). Groups of Shrivaishnava adherents also existed (SII 5.70). One designation for Vaishnava followers was the status title *dāsa* in the names of joint and individual donors. Four *dāsas* came together on one occasion to establish the deity Varada-Gopinatha in the village Alugadapa (Nalgonda District; HAS 19 Ng.2). Three of them say they are members of different brahman *gōtras*, while the fourth calls himself a Komati, the name of a Telugu mercantile community. Elsewhere, two *dāsa* brothers say they belong to the (Vira) Balanjyas of Enamadala town, another mercantile group (SII 10.435). The evidence suggests that membership in a sectarian organization could supersede or overlay other social identities and unite diverse peoples.

Merchant and artisan associations are numerically the largest category of collective donors. Common interests in metalworking, trade in perfumes, the production and sale of oil, or weaving brought certain groups together (HAS 13.11; IAP-W.61; SII 10.209, SII 10.533). The remaining commercial organizations fall into two divisions—*nagaram* and *pekkaṇḍru*.[65] K. Sundaram believes that the *nagaram* was the caste assembly of the Komatis, Telugu merchants who describe themselves as *vaiśyas*. Whereas the Komatis operated primarily within Andhra, he thinks the *pekkaṇḍru* represented long-distance traders drawn from several communities (1968: 69–70). In his analysis of trade in Chola-period Tamil Nadu, Kenneth R. Hall makes a similar distinction between local networks of merchants, who comprised the *nagaram*, and the itinerant traders who had inter-regional networks (1980: 141–51). The fact that one Andhra inscription differentiates the Balanji (Balanjya) *seṭṭis* from the *nagaram* supports the view that these were distinct groups (HAS 19 Km.6). But the difference may not have been based solely on the size of their trading networks, since the *pekkaṇḍru* could either be associated with a single locality or, conversely, with several localities (ARE 277 of 1934–35).

The greatest difficulty in understanding the character of collectives like the *pekkaṇḍru* and *nagaram* lies in the anonymity of their members, whose individual names are typically not specified. We are therefore fortunate in having one record from a Vira Balanjya *pekkaṇḍru* that includes a long list of its members (SII 10.473). It was inscribed in the temple-town Tripurantakam in 1292 when the *pekkaṇḍru* met to settle corporate affairs (*samaya-kāryamu*). Many men with the status titles *reḍḍi* and *seṭṭi* are named as having assembled on this occasion, as well as one *bōya* and a few *nāyakas*. Together they decreed that a levy be assessed on all grain sold in two villages and on several items bought and sold in Tripurantakam, as a gift to the god of Tripurantakam to be administered by the chief temple-priest Nandashiva. Parabrahma Sastry has interpreted the inscription to mean that these men obtained a trade monopoly in Tripurantakam from the priest Nandashiva and made their gift in gratitude (1978: 245–46). Whatever the case may be, this record makes the heterogeneous character of the *pekkaṇḍru* amply evident. Rather than thinking of the *pekkaṇḍru* as a permanent and fixed corporate body, it may be better to regard it as a loosely bound commercial network linking local merchants with traders in other areas. Any given *pekkaṇḍru* may have been a limited business partnership that was convened only for a specific purpose and that existed as a collective unit only within that context.

The last type of collective documented in the Kakatiya Andhra inscriptional corpus pertains to the village or locality. Several related terms are used: *aṣṭādaśa-praja* or *padunenmidi jātula praja*, both meaning "the 18 kinds of people," or simply *samasta-praja*, "all the people."[66] Each of the variants implies the totality of residents in a designated place—the number 18 is no more than a convention. At times, some of the groups who are included among the *praja* are specifically named. In one case, these are the brahmans (*mahājanālu*), land-controlling peasants (*kāmpulu*), *nagaramu*, and *balañji-seṭṭi-kāṇḍru* (HAS 19 Km.6). Herders (*golla-vāru*), goldsmiths, Komati merchants, and toddy drawers figure in another inscription (HAS 13.30). The intent of enumerating specific groups was to ensure that all inhabitants would make some contribution, usually to the local temple. Peasants with proprietary rights in land would hence donate a certain proportion of their harvest, while nonlanded people like merchants, weavers, and herders would instead vow to make yearly contributions of money, with the rates being set by occupation (HAS 13.26). The *praja* typically represented the people of a single village but could also cover the larger territory of a *sthala*.[67] Common residence was hence one bond that served as a basis for cooperative action by different types of people.

I have gone into perhaps greater detail than necessary in order to make my point—that a multiplicity of social foci existed in Kakatiya Andhra. Both kinship ties and territorial proximity were important in creating linkages among people. But collectivities of interest could also arise from the bonds generated by shared military service, a common sectarian membership, or similarities in occupation. In chapter 3 I also demonstrate that members of political factions often acted together in their religious gifting. The profit motive may even have united people in temporary business arrangements. None of this is particularly shocking or unknown to scholars of the medieval period. Yet the perception that the social horizons of "traditional" India were limited to kin and village is still widely propagated by others. To be sure, the wide-ranging social networks of modern India—the caste associations, trade unions, and religious organizations—were largely absent. But the reason is not that precolonial people were incapable of conceptualizing or actualizing social affiliations that transcended their immediate setting. The differences are a matter of scale, occasioned by the more restricted nature of precolonial transportation and communication linkages. In Kakatiya Andhra people could and did unite in joint action out of shared interests beyond the commonalities of family or village.

Another striking feature of the inscriptional corpus is the relatively large number of women represented within it. Women comprise 11 percent (87 in number) of all individual donors (see table 4). This is certainly less than a proportional representation, but it is much higher than one might expect given the limits placed on women's personal property (*strīdhana*) in the legal literature. In ancient India, *strīdhana* was restricted to jewelry and other such movable goods. Land, in particular, was regarded in the lawbooks as an inappropriate possession for women, although by medieval times the scope of women's property had broadened. In the event that land had been given to a woman, by her parents at the time of marriage, for example, it was not supposed to be alienable. She enjoyed usufructory rights, but proprietary rights passed on to either her husband or her brothers (depending on which family the rights had come from) upon her death. In theory, then, women were unable to transfer land rights to others.[68] In practice, numerous women in Kakatiya Andhra made land grants to temples. That at least some of this property was given to them in dowry is suggested by two inscriptions from the period. The first records that Kundamba, one of the Kakatiya King Ganapati's sisters, granted a village given to her at the time of marriage by her father (IAP-W.58). In the second, another princess, this time from a minor coastal dynasty, received an orchard of five hundred areca-nut trees from her father as her marriage portion (*araṇam*; SII 10.349). In addition to land grants, female donors made gifts of virtually the entire range of objects commonly endowed in Kakatiya Andhra, such as livestock, temple buildings, metal items used in ritual worship, irrigational facilities, and cash.

Many of the women appearing in the Kakatiya Andhra inscriptional corpus were members of the ruling elite, and such aristocratic women—the queens, princesses, and others whose male kin typically bore the titles *mahārāja* or *rāju*—appended the term *dēvi* to their names. The most prolific donor among them was Kaketa Mailamadevi, the sister of a Kakatiya king and the wife of an allied Telangana chief, who had sufficient resources to establish several new temples in different villages.[69] But we also find many other female donors whose names end in the suffix *-sāni*. Like Valyasani, the daughter of a *seṭṭi* (ARE 397 of 1932–33), women of this class had menfolk with the titles *bōya*, *nāyaka*, or *reḍḍi*.[70] Few women called *sāni* left behind more than one inscription, nor were their gifts grand. But they were able to make religious endowments as individuals in their own right. The ability to alienate property through religious patronage is thus characteristic of women in all the social categories that figure in inscriptions.

Inscriptions also reveal that the impact of marriage on a woman's social identity was less dramatic in fact than in the doctrine of the lawbooks. According to orthodox ideology, a marriage of the ideal *kanyādāna* (gift of a daughter) type severed a woman's ties to her natal family and led to her incorporation into her husband's family. Many women in the Kakatiya Andhra inscriptional corpus did, of course, describe themselves as the wife of so-and-so. But in almost one-third of the sample, women only cited the names of their fathers and/or mothers (Talbot 1994).[71] It seems hardly credible that all of them were unmarried. We can only infer that a woman's social identity in medieval Andhra encompassed not only her status as someone's wife but also her status as someone's daughter—a clear indication that natal ties remained strong and socially relevant even after marriage (Talbot 1995b: 412–20). A woman could choose to highlight either of her two families, depending on the situation. One female donor made her gift for the merit of her mother, who is therefore explicitly named, but there was no need to list any other relative in this situation (SII 5.1280). The greater fame of a woman's natal family in the locality of a temple might also have led her to foreground her connection with them.

The roles that women could assume in medieval society were not solely domestic, as one might believe from reading the *dharmaśāstra* texts. The temple institution was the primary public arena for women in Kakatiya Andhra.[72] There they could hold honored positions as officials in charge of the treasury (EI 6.15; SII 6.89 and 228), as well as serving as temple dancers (SII 4.700, SII 5.140). In several temples of coastal Andhra, endowments were administered by the collective body of temple women known as the Sani 300 (e.g., SII 5.161). Most of these temple women, or *guḍisāni*, were daughters of respectable men like *nāyakas* and *seṭṭis*. In at least one instance, a temple woman had been married as well (SII 5.1102). These tantalizing hints demonstrate the vast differences between the temple women of medieval Andhra and the *dēvadāsi* of the nineteenth century, who are commonly depicted as temple prostitutes. Political authority could also be publicly wielded by aristocratic women. Such cases are admittedly rare, yet less so than in later centuries. At least 4 women in the Kakatiya Andhra corpus (out of a total of 87) acted as the heads of their families, adopting, in their inscriptions, the heroic epithets to which the lineage was entitled. With the glaring exception of Kakatiya Rudramadevi, who succeeded to her father's position as ruler, the other women who assumed political authority were the wives of dead kings or chiefs (Talbot 1995b: 404–9). The very fact that this was an option, however, proves that patrilineal principles could be overruled by pragmatic political considerations—most notably the desire to retain power within the immediate kindred.

The glimpses into women's lives that inscriptions yield are frustratingly limited. There is enough, however, to prove that they acted in ways that did not conform to orthodox strictures. Most women in most times and places may have assumed the role of dutiful wives as the norms dictated. But not all of them did so. We cannot know what it meant to be a woman in precolonial India if we have no idea of the full range of possibilities. Deviations in normative patterns reveal alternatives and thus disclose the dimensions of action open to women. While the lack of information on women in the Indian past is often deplored, a concerted effort to collect the data available in inscriptions can go a long way toward dispelling the simplistic construct of the traditional Indian woman that one derives from both the legal and epic literatures.

Summary: The Fluidity of Social Identities

In the many debates over the true nature of precolonial Indian society, information drawn from inscriptional sources has been conspicuously lacking. The long dominance of structuralist approaches is certainly partially to blame. The messy details of actual behavior seemed irrelevant to those searching for the underlying structures that were thought to generate practice, just as grammar generated speech activity. Behavior that deviated from the ideal paradigm was no more than a lapse, an absence of culture. Inscriptional evidence of variation in cultural practice was thus no more significant than the linguistic divergences of epigraphic Sanskrit, which was similarly regarded as substandard. No allowance was made for regional variation, since it was assumed that the subcontinent constituted a single unified cultural zone. Nor have current, post-Orientalist approaches much improved our understanding of the precolonial past. Reconstructions of India before the British arrived are still often derived from colonial data, albeit from the early colonial period, and the many centuries of prior history collapsed into a monolithic and changeless traditional India.

I reiterate the point I have made before—inscriptions are not the optimal source material. They tell us what kinds of resources the privileged people of the period possessed, but not how they got them nor from whom. As a form of discourse, inscriptions are similarly limited in the range of their producers and consumers, for few people were literate or had recourse to the literate. The social identities inscribed in this form did not constitute the totality of existing identities, nor did they necessarily correspond to concrete social entities. The representations of the self offered in inscriptions might very well have differed from representations in other contexts. With all these limitations, inscriptions can never assume the role of sole informants on past life. To the extent that it is available, other information should certainly be used in conjunction with inscriptions. At the same time, we cannot deny that inscriptions give us access to a small slice of the past. If we are sincere in wanting to reconstruct precolonial society without the distorting effects of colonial constructs or of hegemonic brahman discourse, how else can we possibly proceed?

What we learn from Kakatiya Andhra inscriptions is that social identities, at least within this context, were not expressed in terms of *varṇa* or *jāti*. Instead, we find a social typology embedded in the use of titles appended to male names. Specific sets of titles were associated with particular occupations. Not all men possessed these titles nor did they necessarily assume the same titles as their fathers. On this basis I believe that the titles represent earned statuses rather than ascribed rank. The emphasis in inscriptions on individual achievements reinforces my contention that social standing was not based solely on hereditary attributes but could be considerably altered by an individual's accomplishments. Success in a military career may have been the easiest way for a man to move upward in the world, and the number of men with military skills and experience in Kakatiya Andhra was substantial. The opportunities for social mobility were reinforced by the considerable physical mobility of the medieval Andhra population. Furthermore, although individuals—including many women who had independent rights over property—generally acted on their own in patronizing temples, they could also come together out of collective interests beyond that of kinship or locality. The Andhra that one sees in inscriptions thus bears little resemblance to the rigid, tradition-bound society implied by the common model of a social system composed of hierarchically ranked and hereditary *jātis*. Indeed, the reputed centrality of caste in precolonial India is undermined by the inscriptional evidence.

An alternative model of the indigenous social system has been advanced by Nicholas B. Dirks and other scholars in the past decade. They believe that the precolonial society was actually centered around the king, rather than being a hierarchical system based on levels of ritual purity. Depoliticization occurred after the British eliminated the pivotal role of the king—who had integrated an extensive redistributive system that united the various sectors of society. His disappearance caused the economic, political, and social hierarchies to differentiate, which in turn gave rise to villages that were far more self-contained, each with their own *jajmāni* division of labor—a remnant of the original redistributive network, but not an inherent feature of "traditional" India itself (Fuller 1977: 105–8; Dirks 1989: 65–72). Similarly, the displacement of the king caused the social sphere to become autonomous and led to brahman ascendance in the social order (Dirks 1987: 10).

Dirks's work has had the salutary effect of displacing the brahman as the "central ordering factor in the social organisation of caste" in favor of the king (1989: 59). Yet the small early colonial kingdom of Pudukkottai in southern Tamil Nadu that was the basis of his study may not be representative of many precolonial conditions. Certainly, thirteenth-century Andhra society was not as systematically organized or densely settled as Dirks's Pudukkottai, with its strong kin- and territory-based social structure. Nor was Kakatiya Andhra so thoroughly permeated by royal power as was Pudukkottai, where many of the ruling elite belonged to the same subcaste as the Tondaiman king. Pudukkottai, if it is typical at all, stands at the end of many centuries of precolonial development. There is little evidence for such well-developed subcaste groupings or clearly articulated territorial hierarchies in medieval Andhra. Kakatiya Andhra's minor kings and chiefs may have sought to establish themselves as the focal points of local society, but it is doubtful whether either they or the Kakatiya kings stood at the undisputed apex of a fixed social hierarchy.

Kakatiya Andhra far more resembles the medieval Bengal that Richard M. Eaton has recently described (1993) than the Pudukkottai of the eighteenth century. Large portions of eastern Bengal (the modern Bangladesh) were yet to be brought under the plow prior to the sixteenth century. Along with an advancing agrarian frontier, Bengal was simultaneously experiencing moving frontiers of political control and religious affiliation. In this situation of extreme flux, socioreligious identities were still very much in the process of coalescing.[73] Not until the late precolonial period did the eastern Bengali physical and social universes begin to approach their current configurations. Like Bengal, medieval Andhra was characterized by agrarian expansion, the migration of agrarian peoples to new lands, and the growing assimilation of nonagrarian peoples. Public identities stressed occupation and individual achievements far more than caste or territorial affiliations, suggesting that the dominant, territorially based subcastes described by Dirks and others had yet to emerge in full-blown form in Kakatiya Andhra. Nor do they appear to have developed in Pudukkottai before the mid seventeenth century, according to Dirks's own discussion of the region's history prior to Tondaiman rule. The transformation of occupational identities such as *kā(m)pu* and *reḍḍi* into hereditary "caste" labels did not occur in Andhra until at least the late Vijayanagara period (ca. seventeenth century), if even then. Throughout much of the medieval period, the abundance of land and the ever-changing patterns of agrarian settlement fostered flexibility in social relations and mutability in definitions of community.

3

Temples and Temple Patronage in Kakatiya Andhra

Stone inscriptions tell us more about temples than about any other aspect of Kakatiya Andhra. Since stone inscriptions generally record gifts of lasting value made to temple deities, we can learn much about forms of temple worship, the economic resources possessed by temples, and the identities of temple donors. The sheer abundance of data from temples emphasizes their importance; this impression is reinforced by the paucity of other types of information that were not thought worthy of such permanent documentation. From the perspective of inscriptions, all paths appear to lead to the temple. It is thus easy to exaggerate the centrality of the temple, which is often represented in the secondary literature as the single most crucial institution of medieval South India (e.g., Breckenridge 1985a: 53). We should retain a healthy dose of skepticism toward such claims, recognizing that our reconstruction of the past is skewed by the nature of the extant primary sources. The rhetorical submission of a king to a deity, made within the context of a temple inscription, may not signify his submission outside the setting of the temple, to cite just one example.[1]

While we may doubt that the temple was the epicenter of medieval society, there is no question that the patronage of temples was a highly significant practice with repercussions for many facets of social, economic, and political life. The desire to support the worship of temple gods resulted in the erection of numerous costly stone structures throughout Andhra and the alienation of substantial economic assets on their behalf. In the process, both the geographic and social landscapes of Andhra were considerably transformed. While the building of new temples reflected the agrarian expansion that was occurring in inland localities, it simultaneously stimulated more economic growth. Moreover, temples offered arenas for the formation of new sociopolitical identities, and the patronage of specific temples was often motivated by such factors. The patronage of temples can hence be viewed as both a symptom and a cause of the dynamism of medieval Andhra society: it both reflected ongoing processes and helped shape their further evolution.

How and why all these consequences could result from the act of endowing a temple is the main subject of this chapter. I begin with an overview on the ideology of the religious gift and the ways in which religious gift-giving differed in praxis, for there are substantial differences between literary norms and the patterns revealed in stone inscriptions. The manner in which agrarian expansion was encouraged by the construction of temples and their accompanying tanks is a second topic, followed by a discussion of the types of objects given to temples and how they enabled the temple to act as a redistributive center. Significant variations in the temple institutions and endowment practices of coastal and inland Andhra are examined next, pointing to the differing developmental trajectories of these two subregions. In the fifth section, I return to the question of the multiplicity of motives fueling temple patronage and the various purposes hence served by the temple as an institution situated within the larger world of Kakatiya Andhra.

The Religious Gift in Theory and in Action

Both the beliefs inspiring temple patronage and the actual forms of religious endowment recorded in Kakatiya Andhra inscriptions bear scant resemblance to the classical Sanskrit norms of religious gift-giving. In the Sanskrit literature on *dāna* (the religious gift), the brahman is designated as the proper recipient, a role that seems to have evolved out of the fee (*dakṣiṇā*) paid to brahmans for the ritual performance of Vedic sacrifices. Gifts or hospitality to brahmans gradually became incorporated into a range of other religious practices, such as the *śrāddha* funerary ceremonies. As the centuries progressed, the variety and cost of items that were recommended as gifts to brahmans increased, and so we find mention of clothing, gold, and cows in the *dharmaśāstra* legal literature and the *Mahābhārata* epic. The culmination of this trend was reached in the second half of the first millennium C.E., with the formulation of a series of complex gift rituals known as the *mahādānas*. They were modeled on the Vedic sacrifice, with its construction of a sacrosanct area, attendance of several priests, use of *mantras*, and giving of *dakṣiṇā* (ritual fee). But the core of the *mahādāna* ceremonies was the giving of lavish quantities of gold and precious stones to brahmans (Hazra 1940). The best-known *mahādāna* is the *tulāpuruṣa*, in which the donor gives away his weight in gold, recorded in South Indian inscriptions from the sixth century onward (Mangalam 1976–77: 91).

The *mahādāna* rituals were intended to be sponsored by kings, for who else could have afforded such expensive gestures of faith? The importance of gift-giving for kings, as opposed to sponsorship of Vedic sacrifices, increased in the second half of the first millennium (Dirks 1976). In both literary and epigraphic sources, the king emerges as the primary patron of brahmans and the religious donor par excellence.[2] Hundreds of royal grants inscribed on copper plates were issued during this era, to record the granting of land rights to brahmans. The oldest existing copper-plate charter in South India (which is also the first recorded land grant to a brahman) comes from late-third-century Andhra.[3] From this time onward until ca. 1000, the great majority of Andhra inscriptions record land grants to brahmans on copper plates. The purpose of the copper-plate grants was to support brahmans well-versed in Vedic knowledge so that they could both perform the rituals and transmit their teachings to the younger generation, which in turn was meant to increase the spiritual prosperity of the realm. At times the revenues from entire villages were alienated so as to establish settlements of learned brahmans, in Andhra commonly known as *agrahāras*.

The literary emphasis on the *mahādānas* and on brahman recipients of the gift continued into the second millennium C.E. By this time a distinct genre of Sanskrit literature was dedicated to the norms of religious gift-giving (*dāna-dharma*) and huge compendiums drawing on earlier works were compiled, often in a court setting and for a court audience. For instance, Hemadri, minister of the Seuna kings Mahadeva and Ramachandra of Devagiri during the late thirteenth century, devoted a lengthy section of his *Caturvarga-cintāmaṇi* to the subject of the religious gift. Known as the *Dānakhaṇḍa*, Hemadri's text on gift-giving came to be considered authoritative throughout South India within decades of its composition (Kane 1975: 755). Several Andhra kings of the fourteenth and fifteenth centuries claimed to have followed Hemadri's injunctions in extending generous patronage to brahmans.[4]

Despite the continuing literary emphasis on giving to brahmans, however, inscriptions issued after 1000 show that this practice was rapidly waning in popularity. Rather than copper-plate grants to brahmans, we find an ever-increasing proportion of stone inscriptions recording gifts to temples. By the Kakatiya period, copper-plate grants had become a rarity.[5] Brahmans still received some gifts, but no longer in order to perform Vedic rituals for the good of the universe. They might instead, in the thirteenth century, have received land as a reward for priestly services. The performance of funerary rites for Queen Kota Ganapamadevi's dead husband at Gaya in North India earned the brahman Rudrapeddi the gift of a village as his fee, we are explicitly told (EA 4.11). Other inscriptions similarly record gifts to brahmans in return for traveling to holy sites like Gaya and Rameshvaram to conduct rituals (CPIHM 1.10; HAS 13.51) or for carrying out vows as the donor's substitute.

But most brahmans in Kakatiya Andhra received endowments because they were associated with a temple in some manner.[6] When a temple was established, an attached brahman village was frequently also set up or separate plots of land were given to brahmans. In these cases, it is clear that the brahmans were subsidiary to the temple, for they are mentioned only at the end of the inscription and are sometimes not even named. Because the *gōtra* clan membership or Vedic affiliations of the brahman grantees are rarely specified, they were most probably priests rather than scholars or Vedic sacrificialists. Another type of brahman recipient during the Kakatiya period was the Shaiva sectarian leader. Most of this category were affiliated with the same school or monastic order, the Golaki Matha of the Shuddha Shaiva or Shaiva Siddhanta sect of Shaivism. Two Golaki Matha leaders served as spiritual preceptors to the Kakatiya kings in thirteenth-century Andhra, and several Golaki Matha monasteries were established at major pilgrimage sites (Talbot 1987).

The eclipse of the brahman in our records is attributable partly to the vast expansion in the number of documented religious patrons after 1000. While the brahman land grant inscribed on copper plates had been out of the economic and political grasp of all but the most powerful in the realm and was made primarily by kings and their officers (Sircar 1965: 74), more modest gifts could be given to the god at his temple abode. To be sure, kings were still important sources of religious patronage, but they were now overshadowed by the hundreds of nonroyal donors. Members of land-controlling groups joined merchants, artisans, and herders in making endowments, and the recipients of their gifts were temple deities. These people may still have made occasional gifts to brahmans, as well as other religious specialists, of objects like cows, cash, food, and clothing, but this type of impermanent object was not documented in imperishable form. Clearly, the growth of *bhakti* devotionalism within a temple context relegated brahmans to second place as religious-gift recipients just as it diminished the royal role in religious patronage.

The majority of the endowed deities in thirteenth-century Andhra were Shaiva. On a statewide level, the 247 Shaiva temples constituted 67 percent of all institutions documented in the corpus. Vaishnava temples, comprising 19 percent of the sites statewide, are most numerous south of the Krishna River. The farther south the coastal district, the larger the proportion of Vaishnava temples—23 percent of Guntur District's Kakatiya-period sites, 34 percent of Prakasam District's, and half of Nellore District's temples. Sheer proximity to the Tamil region, where Vaishnavism was rapidly gaining ground subsequent to the reforms of Ramanuja (1016–1137 C.E.), was probably a factor in the greater proportion of Vishnu temples in southern coastal Andhra (Hanumantha Rao 1973: 254–57).[7] The remaining 14 percent of temples either enshrined images of both Vishnu and Shiva, or independent goddesses, or minor gods like Karttikeya, the son of Shiva.

In temple worship the god or goddess is essentially treated as an honored guest. Thus, the traditional customs observed in welcoming a respected brahman are transferred to the temple setting (Goudrian 1969–70: 209). After a number of preliminary rites of purification, the service culminates in a series of offerings made to the deity. Commonly known as the 16 attendances (*ṣōḍaśōpacāra*), these offerings vary in content and sequence from place to place (Diehl 1956: 95–148; Goudrian 1969–70: 161–215). At the Jagannatha temple in neighboring Orissa state, the first step is the offering of a seat to the deity, who is then welcomed with an invocation. The next few offerings all involve water—for cleansing the feet, for sprinkling on the image, and for rinsing the mouth. A sweet refreshment is then presented, followed by more water for mouth rinsing. The image is bathed, dressed in clean garments, and adorned with ornaments. Sandalwood paste or other perfumes are then provided, as well as flowers and incense. A lamp is waved in front of the deity, who is then given a substantial food offering (*naivēdya*)—the main course, so to speak. The ceremony ends with an obeisance to the image (Tripathi 1978: 297–300).

Most endowments in Kakatiya Andhra were given for general worship of a deity—*aṅga-raṅga-bhōga*—and do not specify the exact rituals to be performed. In its narrowest meaning, *aṅga-bhōga* refers to the decoration of the image which takes place during daily worship (Sircar 1966: 20). By extension, it acquired the broader sense of all the various daily services performed for the main image (*mūla-bēra* or *mūla-sthāna*). Daily ritual worship was conducted at specific junctures of the day known as *sandhya*, in the Kakatiya period typically at daybreak and twilight.[8] *Raṅga-bhōga*, in contrast, denoted the worship services undertaken on special festive occasions, for *raṅga* refers to the special hall (*raṅga-maṇḍapa*) where the processional image of a god (*utsava-bēra*, *utsava-mūrti*) was worshiped (Sreenivasachar 1940:

201). When the purpose of a gift was to support the performance of a specific ritual, it is the food offering that is most often mentioned.[9] A good number of inscriptions expressly state that land was granted in order to raise crops for the food offering (ARE 338 of 1934–35; HAS 19 Km.15 and Mn.27–B).

The fact that thirteenth-century inscriptions do not mention a range of different worship services suggests that the elaborate rituals of later centuries had not yet developed. Most noticeably, there are few references to festival rituals, which involve carrying an image outside the temple precincts in procession. Because of the accessibility of the deity on these occasions and the public nature of the activity, ceremonies such as the annual enactment of the deity's marriage were to become highly popular. At both Tirupati and Simhachalam (a Shrivaishnava temple in Visakhapatnam District), festivals figure more frequently in inscriptions beginning in the fourteenth century (Sundaram 1969: 131–32; Viraraghava Charya 1982: 43–57). A corollary to the modest scale of worship at Kakatiya-period temples is the relatively small size of the temple staff who serviced their needs. Although few endowments were intended to support members of the temple establishment, in most cases arrangements for their payment were made internally. Only in the larger temples of coastal Andhra do we find mention of different classes of temple employees, such as the *sthānapati* administrators, the *māni* officials like treasurers and accountants, the *sāni* temple women,[10] and the more lowly *nibandhakāru* cooks, sweepers, conch-blowers, artisans, and watchmen (Parabrahma Sastry 1978: 284–87).

The temple cult of Kakatiya Andhra exhibits traces of past Buddhist practices. For one thing, several temple complexes were probably erected in places that had previously been Buddhist centers. This is certainly true of Amaravati in the lower Krishna valley, the most famous of Andhra Buddhist sites. As late as the twelfth century, the Buddha continued to attract endowments at Amaravati (EI 6.15), but the site now boasted a large Hindu temple that superseded the Buddhist establishment in popularity. It is quite likely that Hindu temple worship in Andhra also had Buddhist antecedents. Andhra was a major center of Buddhism in the early historic period and was studded with *stūpas* from Salihundam in the north to Ramatirtham in the south. The *stūpas* themselves appear to have been worshiped with garlands, flags, and the like, if sculptures from Amaravati are any indication (Ramaswami 1975: 9, 30). M. Rama Rao also believes that fruit, flowers, and lamps were offered on the balconies of Andhra *stūpas* (1967: 56). Some such similarities may derive from a common "folk" source and therefore not be attributable to any specific religion. But the very fact that both early Buddhist and medieval Hindu religious patronage took place in an institutional setting distinguishes them from the classic Sanskrit patronage of an individual learned brahman. Moreover, the classical Sanskrit land grant to brahmans was a royal act, whereas nonroyal donors were prominent in both Buddhist *stūpa* and Hindu temple worship. In terms of practice, therefore, significant resemblances between religious gift-giving to Buddhist and Hindu institutions have been overlooked due to the scholarly differentiation of the two religions on the basis of doctrine.

We note further deviations between classical Sanskrit theory and Kakatiya Andhra practice when we turn to the motivations for religious gift-giving. According to the ideology of the gift expounded in Sanskrit legal literature from the first millennium onward, the pure gift known as *dāna* was utterly different in character from the *dakṣiṇā* fee paid to the brahman for his performance of a ritual. True *dāna* could never be construed as payment for services, since the merit from the gift arose precisely because the giver held no expectation of reward. Complicated Mimamsa techniques were applied in this argument that only the disinterested gift could yield the maximum spiritual fruit (Trautmann 1981: 278–88; Kane 1941: 837–88). In most Kakatiya-period inscriptions, the purpose of the gift is similarly said to be a generalized spiritual merit (*dharma* or *puṇya*). The merit resulting from the gift could be transferred to others—another practice that originated in the Buddhist period—and was customarily dedicated to parents or other relatives in the thirteenth century.[11]

But because temple patronage was oriented toward a specific deity, temple endowment was often undertaken either in return for some perceived mercy already extended by a deity or in hopes of a future boon. One man who was grateful for the boon of a son from the god Bhavanarayana endowed a perpetual lamp at Sarpavaram in East Godavari District (SII 5.8). A warrior thankful for his success in battle made another gift of a lamp, in an inscription translated in chapter 2 (Vishaveli Masake Sahini, SII 10.283). The religious motives for temple endowment thus resemble other Puranic Hindu practices such as vows and pilgrimages more than those of the classic *dāna* gift, which required that the giver expect no reward or benefit in return. Many temple patrons wanted specific assistance from a god or goddess rather than the indeterminate religious merit accruing from *dāna*, especially in its form as a brahman land grant. Using inscriptions, a historian of religion could reconstruct the growing popularity of Hindu devotional practices and the ways in which orthodox brahmans adapted to this trend, both by carrying out vows and pilgrimages for patrons and by affiliating themselves with temples.

Puranic beliefs are also revealed in the many references to heaven in Kakatiya Andhra inscriptions. A significant number of gifts aimed to secure residence in heaven, commonly for a father. Because thirteenth-century Andhra temple worship was largely Shaiva, the word used for "heaven" is typically *śiva-lōka* (realm of Shiva).[12] The general idea is that the religious gift would enable a person to reach heaven:

> When the excellent king Beta, after ruling with her the great kingdom and acquiring everlasting merit, departed to the court of the king of gods (Indra), she had golden pinnacles placed on top of the brilliant lord Amareshvara's holy shrine at Shri Dhanyakapura. Her husband obtained the joy of an everlasting and pleasurable residence in the world of Shiva, after she had a temple of the lord (Shiva) named after the king Beta built in this city.[13]

In the inscription just translated, the recipient of the gift's merit—Beta, husband of Queen Kota Ganapamadevi—was evidently deceased. A temple endowment could thus complement or replace other types of religious observances for the dead such as the *śrāddha* funerary ceremony. This aspect of medieval religious practice and ideology has received very little scholarly attention. What little we do know suggests that love and reverence for a deceased relative was a compelling motivation for religious gifting. Some of the later Puranas describe a yearlong process during which the soul of a deceased person evolves through three types of bodies before finally going to either heaven or hell (Kane 1953: 265). This notion of permanent residence in heaven, particularly strong in the widespread hero-cults of South India and the Deccan, presents an alternative to the orthodox doctrine of reincarnation and dates back to the beginnings of Indian civilization (Thapar 1981: 306, 308; Filliozat 1982: 3). Gifts made at the time of dying were especially efficacious in leading a soul to heaven, although those made subsequently could still be of benefit (Kane 1953: 182–84; *Garuḍa Purāṇa* 1978–80: 821, 868). Medieval literature even enumerated different types of heavens that could be attained through making specific kinds of gifts (Rangaswami Aiyangar 1941: 114).

Since most Kakatiya-period inscriptions that document gifts given so that another could attain heaven were intended to benefit a father, the beneficiaries were most likely dying or deceased. We know that gifts might be given immediately before death, as when Enapotana Ketana dedicated the merit of a *sandhya* lamp to his younger brother who was on his deathbed (SII 5.186), or soon after death, as when Annaya Lenka endowed a tank just after his elder brother had passed away (HAS 19 Mn. 18). Temples themselves were increasingly constructed as a method of commemorating the dead.[14] An inscription commissioned by the prince Soma is explicit in stating that his chief queen had recently died ("Annama Mahadevi, having abandoned Lord Soma, has assumed leadership of the women of heaven," in SII 10.262). In order to make absolutely sure of her blissful afterlife in heaven, the prince had a temple built for the god Rameshvara of Duttika (West Godavari District). Those who died in battle were now sometimes recognized in this manner, rather than simply through the erection of hero-stones. So, for instance, Nalam Brolayandu consecrated a *liṅga* on behalf of his sons who had gone to the "world of the gods" in 1298 (APAS 31.30). Close by is a hero-stone bearing an image of two heroes holding bows, which possibly depict the sons referred to in the inscription. Records of religious endowments made to honor heroic deaths were occasionally left at the site of the death itself rather than at the endowed institution, perhaps as a carryover from the earlier practice of erecting stones where a hero had died (IAP-C 1.128).

Anxiety over the welfare of a loved one and fear of what lay beyond this worldly existence were hence among the greatest impetuses for temple patronage in Kakatiya Andhra, a fact we should keep in mind as we examine other aspects of temple patronage in the pages to come. It is all too easy to fall into the trap of analyzing ostensibly religious behavior as "a bowlful of strategies," as Richard M. Eaton warns us, and discount religious devotion and piety as causal factors (1992: 235). Many goals could be subsumed into the act of religious patronage, but the justification for these activities was always the desire for religious well-being, for oneself or for another.

Agrarian Expansion through Temple and Tank Construction

The rise in the temple cult's popularity is evidenced materially by the many new physical structures erected during the Kakatiya period.[15] Twelve percent (120) of the total 963 epigraphs in the Kakatiya temple corpus record the founding of new temples.[16] But the construction of new temples must also be understood as a reflection of the expansion of Kakatiya Andhra's agrarian resource base—it was motivated by devotion but made possible by economic growth. Establishing a new temple meant far more than merely providing the image of a god with a stone residence. The human caretakers of the god also had to be supported, and the rituals of worship required continual supplies of foodstuffs and other material offerings. Almost always, therefore, the construction of a new temple also entailed the endowment of rights to land. The ability of donors to alienate such important property rights in favor of a temple indicates that economic development in their localities had advanced to the point of a surplus in agrarian production. High levels of temple construction thus characterize regions experiencing high rates of economic change. In turn, as the following discussion makes clear, the founding of temples stimulated further agrarian expansion.

The construction rates of new temples show that inland Andhra was undergoing the most dramatic transformation. The highest number of new temples are found in Guntur District (25) and Prakasam District (18), as shown in table 6. But these are also the two districts with the largest numbers of inscriptions overall. More revealing is the proportion of new temples in any given district, calculated in column "% Founding" of table 6. The frequency of new temples is notably higher in the Telangana and Rayalasima subregions than in coastal Andhra. In these inland districts, the percentage of temple foundation records runs from a peak of 47 percent in Warangal to a low of 22 percent in Nalgonda and Cuddapah Districts. New temples were erected at considerably lower rates in the coastal subregion, with a

Table 6. Temple Founding by District

District	All Records	Founding[a] Records	% Founding	Temple Sites	% Sites New
Warangal	38	18	47	31	58
Karimnagar	14	6	43	8	75
Medak	7	2	29	6	33
Kurnool	7	2	29	5	40
Khammam	11	3	27	9	33
Mahbubnagar	34	8	24	15	53
Nalgonda	64	14	22	29	48
Cuddapah	18	4	22	14	29
Nellore	36	7	19	18	39
Prakasam	160	18	11	56	32
Guntur	230	25	11	114	22
Krishna	152	8	5	32	25
W. Godavari	116	3	3	23	13
E. Godavari	76	2	3	10	20
Total/Average	963	120	12%[b]	370	32%[c]

a. Refers to the establishment of a new temple.
b. 12% of all inscriptions are founding records.
c. 32% of all sites are new.

gradual decreasing trend the further north one goes. No more than 3 to 5 percent of all religious endowments involved the construction of a temple in the three most northerly coastal districts—East Godavari, West Godavari, and Krishna. Far from being evenly spread throughout the state, therefore, the founding of temples was occurring at a much higher rate in the interior, and specifically in Telangana, than in the northern coastal area.

In Telangana entire villages were sometimes created expressly to provide for the deity enshrined in a new temple. Mailamba, the sister of the Kakatiya ruler Ganapati, was responsible for the founding of at least three new villages in Yellandu Taluk of Khammam District (APRE 193, 197 and 198 of 1965). These new settlements were dedicated to deities Mailamba had just installed in temples. At each site she had a tank excavated which would then irrigate the land being transformed into a village for the deity. Through her donation land that was forested or unproductive prior to irrigation was brought under cultivation. Presumably Mailamba possessed some sort of proprietary right over this territory, probably acquired as part of her dowry or marriage portion. Because the villages were named after her mother, her *guru*, and her second son, their creation and endowment was a form of honoring these individuals. In this way a religious incentive could simultaneously extend the agricultural resource base.

At other times new temples were established in already-existing settlements. This is illustrated in an unusually short and simple foundation inscription from Inumella in Vinukonda Taluk, Guntur District:

> May all fare well! In year 1176 of the Shaka era [1254 C.E.], the illustrious Kalapa Nayaka, who possesses all the praiseworthy titles such as upholder of the kingdom of the Cholas, ornament of the Manma clan, he whose mighty right arm is formidably skilled with the bow, the husband of the goddess of victory in fierce battles, ruler of the Vengi territory, a potent procreator, like the sun in sincerity, worshiper of the divine and illustrious lotus feet of the god Malleshvara of Bejavada [Vijayavada], subduer of the armies of the foes, rescuer of Kulottunga Rajendra Chola of Velanadu, lord of the excellent city Manyapura in Kandavadi and of Bejavada, a Ravana in courage;
>
> Having consecrated the lord Chenna Keshava in Inumella and having had a temple built, gave land to the extent of 5 *kha(ṇḍugas* of unirrigated land) for the food offering and perfumed ointment of the Lord Keshava. For the worship outside the sanctum of the god, he gave land to the extent of 10 *kha(ṇḍugas* of unirrigated land) and 1 *maṟturu* (of irrigated land) behind Chintala tank to the east of that village and a flower garden; for the religious merit of Virayadeva, who rules over him, and of (Kakatiya) Ganapatideva Maharaja.
>
> The land given by Kessava Gopala-dasi is....[boundary details are illegible]. Whether given by oneself or by another....[17] (SII 6.602)

The person who had the temple built in this case also provided it with land to allow for the performance of certain daily and festive rituals. The endowed lands may have been situated on the outskirts of the existing settlement, as was usual in Chola-period Tamil Nadu (Heitzman 1997: 107). By bringing uncultivated land into production, the founding of a new temple in an established village could still be a means of extending agrarian activity.

The quantity and quality of arable land was often enhanced through the common practice of providing a new temple with a tank.[18] When this was done, at least a portion of the land irrigated by the tank would be set aside for the temple's needs. All the land irrigated by the two tanks built by Nami Reddi of the Recherla family was given to the deity he consecrated and named after himself at Pillalamarri, Nalgonda District (HAS 13.41). In contrast, Vrekkanti Malli Raddi donated only some of the land irrigated by the Mailasamudra tank he had constructed at Bekkallu, Warangal District (IAP-W.38). He seems to have retained proprietary rights over the remaining land. Tanks were also built for established temples. For example, the donor Guddali Vaitama Setti is said to have built a tank and demarcated the resulting wet lands around it, a portion of which were given to the deity (NDI Ongole 139).

One of the most explicit inscriptions recording the simultaneous founding of a temple and a tank comes from Karimnagar District (IAP-K. 38, from Chittapur, Metpalli Taluk, dated 1303). The donor in this instance was a man named Bairi Setti, a Vira Balanjya merchant-trader affiliated with the famous Ayyavole 500 organization that had originated in Karnataka. Only one-third of the land brought under irrigation through construction of his tank was to go to the new temple, while the remaining two-thirds was designated as *rācādinamu*, possibly meaning "crown land" (Parabrahma Sastry 1978: 198–99). The inscription expressly stipulates that this ratio 1:2 between the temple's land and the other land be maintained regardless of the total amount of land under cultivation—in other words, in the future, even if the tank was extended or further channels to convey water from it were dug, the irrigated land was to be divided in the same proportion.

Bairi Setti does not seem to have directly benefited, except in a religious sense, from the tank that he had constructed. He could not have been a local land-controller, since he had to purchase fields from brahmans in order to endow the temple. But his financing of a tank would have benefited the local ruler, whose lands were now far more productive. For this reason, the Andhra epigraphist P. V. Parabrahma Sastry believes that Bairi Setti must have received some concession from the local ruler either in the form of a trade license or a percentage of the sales tax from the local market (1978: 245). If Parabrahma Sastry's conjecture is correct, what we have in this inscription is an early example of agrarian entrepreneurship. In the most widespread mode of agrarian enterprise during the later Vijayanagara period, individuals who financed irrigational facilities received either a share of the produce grown on the newly irrigated land (Stein 1980: 425–26) or a plot of tax-free land comprising one-tenth of the area irrigated by the tank, hence the "ten" (*daśa*) in the name of the arrangement, *daśavandha* (Venkataramanayya and Somasekhara Sarma 1960: 680). Although the *daśavandha* contract is most widely noticed in later inscriptions from Rayalasima, the term twice appears in Kakatiya-period records from Telangana (CTI 41 and HAS 19 Mn.27).[19] Stein calls the initiative displayed by the individuals who undertook tank construction "rural development entrepreneurship," because it resulted in expanded productivity for the locality as well as personal gain for the entrepreneurs themselves (1980: 425–26).

Enhancement of the agricultural resource base through construction of irrigational facilities has been most closely studied in reference to the Tirumala-Tirupati temple complex in Chittoor District. Fifty-one grants of irrigational facilities (mainly tanks and channels) were received by this group of temples, primarily in the second half of the fifteenth century. The number of direct endowments of irrigational facilities decreased after that time, but the number of cash grants rose sharply (Jayasree 1991: 97–103). Much of that money was used to improve the temple's agricultural lands through the provision of water, and so cash grants in this case also extended the acreage of irrigated land (Stein 1960: 167). The growth of the Tirumala-Tirupati temple complex was relatively late, reflecting Rayalasima's general lag in agrarian development. Its endowments are concentrated in the short span of time from the second half of the fifteenth century through the third quarter of the sixteenth century (Subrahmanya Sastry 1930: 1–3). Earlier donors were almost solely local notables, but the patronage circle began to expand after Saluva Narasimha became the Vijayanagara governor of Chandragiri province in 1456. He subsequently usurped the Vijayanagara throne, and his successors continued to patronize the temple. Stein has remarked on the high proportion of what he calls "state" donors (that is, individuals associated with a particular polity) at Tirupati during the sixteenth century and suggests that state resources were being allocated to land development in this indirect manner (Stein 1960: 176).

Because Tirupati has been regarded as the paradigm for Andhra temples by many scholars, the scale of irrigational investment in Kakatiya-period Telangana has been generally overlooked. One example is the statement by Carol Breckenridge, "It is in the Vijayanagara era that South Indian temples and irrigation technology became, in some special, if not essential, way linked one to the other" (1985b: 41). This is true of Tirupati, the focus of Breckenridge's study, and for many other localities in Rayalasima. But if one's perspective is broadened to include Telangana, then the seminal period would have be identified as that of the Kakatiyas. Tank irrigation is only one of the many phenomena that are typically identified as characteristic of South India in the Vijayanagara period, but whose origins can be traced back earlier in Andhra. The main reason continuities with Kakatiya Andhra are not more widely recognized is the Tamil orientation of most historians of South India. Since practices associated with the drier upland areas of Andhra (and the peninsula at large) are not prominent in Tamil historical sources until the Vijayanagara period, they are usually regarded as originating in that era.

The momentum of agrarian expansion into dryer zones may indeed have accelerated during the Vijayanagara period for South India as a whole, but in the case of northern Andhra (and probably Karnataka as well) the trend was firmly established by the thirteenth century. Among the most important groups responsible for financing the development of inland Andhra were the many intermediary chiefs and officials who formed part of the Kakatiya political network. The same pattern is found throughout South India during the medieval period. Tanks in the dry Pandya country of southern Tamil Nadu were also financed mainly by local or subregional chiefs (Ludden 1979: 352). Even in tenth- and eleventh-century Tamil Nadu, when agrarian expansion occurred primarily in the wet zone, the instigators were mainly local notables (Heitzman 1997: 52–54). During the Vijayanagara period, local chiefs known as *pāḷegāḍu* (Telugu) or *pāḷaiyakārar* (Tamil) were responsible for much agrarian expansion through the provision of irrigational facilities (Subrahmanyam 1990: 330–32).

Two of the largest tanks in Telangana were built under the direction of Kakatiya subordinate chiefs. One is the Ramappa Lake, adjoining the well-known Ramappa temple at Palampet in Mulug Taluk, Warangal District. Formed by a ring of hills on three sides, it has a colossal bund only on one side that extends 2000 feet in length and rises up to 56 feet (Gopala Reddy 1973: 63; Parabrahma Sastry 1978: 205). The construction of this tank in 1213 was instigated by Recherla Rudra, a *sēnāpati* (general) of the Kakatiya King Ganapatideva (HAS 3.1). Pakala Lake in Narsampet Taluk of Warangal District is even larger, with a dam composed of laterite pebbles and earth that is one mile long from which 40 artificial channels have been extended (Parabrahma Sastry 1978: 205). It was also constructed during Kakatiya Ganapati's reign (1199–1262) by a subordinate, Jagadala Mummadi, who was the son of a minister (*mantri*; HAS 4).

Temples were not the recipients of all 38 tanks documented in inscriptions from Kakatiya Andhra.[20] Sometimes they were given to brahmans, as when Malyala Gunda had a tank constructed near Bothpur (Mahbubnagar Taluk) in 1272 and donated the land irrigated by the new tank to 13 different brahmans, as payment for rituals they had performed on his behalf (HAS 13.51). In several other instances, as with the Ramappa and Pakala tanks just described, no recipient is named. Similarly Loki Reddi documented the construction of a tank named after himself in 1215 but does not tell us whose property the tank was (APAS 31.26). Like the temple, which belonged to the god rather than to a person, tanks were not necessarily regarded as personal property. The gift of a tank was praised along with several other donations that benefited the public at large, in the following verses of a Telangana inscription:[21]

> That great soul of great prosperity beautified land by big tanks (which had) deep, extensive and good waters and (which) gave happiness to numerous living beings.
>
> He planted for the sake of Dharma groves of cool shades, very pleasant with shining sprouts filling the quarters with the fragrance of the flowers, beautiful with the humming of bees, bent (under the weight of) tasteful and excellent clusters of fruits, and (in fine), enjoyable and giving pleasure to all senses.
>
> In his wonderful alms-houses, people from various parts of the country, having eaten to their heart's content well-cooked food rich in good pulses, noteworthy ghee, along with vegetables of various tastes, buttermilk and curd, utter forth (i.e., praise loudly) amidst people, in their extreme joy, his good qualities in manifold ways.
>
> In his water-sheds containing cool water, constructed for the sake of numberless thirsty people, the fatigue of travelers quickly disappears even in the terrible summer and happiness arises. (HAS 13.41)

The donor's munificence and his concern for the people are highlighted in the preceding quote, and he is said to have been praised by the ones to whom he brought happiness in this manner.

While many other gift objects were cherished for their economic value, the gift of water had an even deeper value as an object necessary for survival, especially in the harsh heat of the hot season. The emphasis on tank building as a form of religious charity is apparent in a peculiarly Andhra conception, that of the *sapta-santāna* (seven offspring). Like the procreation of a son, the other six activities on the list also perpetuated one's name and fame for future generations. There is some discrepancy in the various accounts of the *sapta-santāna*, but all of them include building a tank, installing a god in a temple, commissioning a poem, and planting a grove or garden among the seven, in addition to having a son of one's own.[22] The other two commonly listed acts are arranging a marriage for a brahman or establishing a brahman village and hoarding treasure.

The provision of water sources was so desirable that it came to be considered a commendable religious act even when devoid of any explicit religious association. The true number of tanks built in Andhra between 1175 and 1324 must be many times more than what the 38 records of tank construction we have from that time span would suggest. The existing documents all appear to be inscribed on loose pieces of rock—a stone slab or pillar—and while many are located around the precincts of a temple, others were discovered in fields or set up next to a tank. The likelihood of destruction of a tank foundation inscription would have been heightened in the case of tanks that stand ruined today. And if small temples are sometimes bereft of any record of foundation, we can surmise that the creation of many small reservoirs, ponds, and the like were similarly undocumented. Indirect testimony of the high levels of irrigational investment comes from the many place-names ending in-*samudra*, -*sāgara*, or -*ceruvu* (all meaning "tank") in contemporary inscriptions, as well as traditional village accounts that describe the thirteenth century as an era of extensive tank construction (Parabrahma Sastry 1978: 203). The multitude of historical traces confirms that a boom in the building of tanks occurred in inland Andhra while the Kakatiyas were ruling.[23]

When the spurt in tank construction is viewed in conjunction with the high rates of new temple foundation, we can safely assert that Telangana was rapidly developing economically and also, most probably, profiting from its newly ascendant political position. The same can be said to a lesser degree of the Rayalasima districts Kurnool and Cuddapah and of Nellore in southern coastal Andhra. In contrast, the three northern coastal districts of East Godavari, West Godavari, and Krishna, which comprise the long-settled Vengi core area of Andhra, were in a static phase during this time. Presumably, the rates of population increase and agricultural expansion had slowed down in Vengi by the twelfth and thirteenth centuries. Telangana, not the well-established coastal strip, was undergoing the greatest degree of change. The twin processes of tank and temple foundation resulted from demographic increase in the interior and, at the same time, contributed to further growth by improving agricultural productivity. New settlements were being established, forest land was being reclaimed, and the quantity of arable land was being enlarged through irrigational investment in this frontier zone of Andhra.

The Temple as a Redistributive Center

Western scholarship since the 1960s has stressed the significance of religious gift-giving as the main integrative force in medieval South Indian society. Impelled by a variety of religious, social, and political incentives, a diverse range of patrons gave generously of their valuables to temple institutions. In societies without highly developed state structures or public spheres, this type of gift-giving along with the exchange of hospitality and women served as the fundamental binding mechanism, according to the theories of Marcel Mauss (1967) and other French sociologists. Hence, a number of historians have argued that the various strata of society in medieval South India were interconnected primarily through the large-scale giving of religious endowments and the subsequent redistribution of economic resources and honors back to the community.

The model of redistributive exchange is an anthropological one, clarified largely by Marshall Sahlins (1972), who contrasts it with reciprocal exchange. Reciprocity, characteristic of relatively simple and unstratified societies, consists of a direct one-on-one exchange. Redistribution, on the other hand, is found in more complex societies such as chiefdoms. With the emergence of strong leaders, the resources of a society accumulate at certain foci (i.e., in the hands of chiefs) and are then passed back out in the form of extravagant feasts and the like. Hindu temples, which acted as magnets in attracting valuable property, were the main centers of accumulation in medieval South India and the conduit through which exchange occurred: material goods were transformed into the symbols of prestige and influence known as temple honors (Appadurai and Breckenridge 1976). By providing employment to artisans, peasants, and herders, South Indian temples in turn redistributed resources garnered from the wealthy to other segments of society.

Beyond this function of economic redistribution, temples additionally served as social and political integrators. They incorporated members of different communities into one community of worship—the main nexus through which the disparate elements of medieval society were bound together to form one social fabric. And in the absence of an extensive administrative structure, the cohesion of the state system derived primarily from the religious networks created by donations. This is how, in Stein's (1977) view, the semi-autonomous localities were loosely woven into a larger segmentary state, presided over by ritual sovereigns. I discuss the issue of social integration further on in this chapter (and look at the model of the segmentary state in chapter 4). But here my primary concern is the economic dimension. To better understand how temples operated as redistributive centers, we must first examine what resources they controlled and to whom these resources were later allocated.

The prime gift object recorded in stone inscriptions was land—the most valuable and most enduring of all items. Without land, no temple could function, and an abundance of land ensured the proper honoring of the god with lavish ceremonies. In thirteenth-century Andhra, land was the donation preferred by an overwhelming margin. Plots of land alone comprised 39 percent of all gifts made in our corpus (table 7, column "Entire Corpus"). The more prized type of land was the low-lying land irrigated by a tank, canal, or well and called wet (*nīru-nēla*, also *nīrnēla*) because the soil is kept well soaked in water while crops are being cultivated. In contrast, dry land (*veli-volamu* or *veli-cēnu*) is found on a more elevated level and cultivation depends solely on rain for the water supply (Sreenivasachar 1940: 208). In addition to plots of wet or dry land, a third category of lands given to temples was known as *tōṇṭa-bhūmi* (or *tōṇṭa-polamu*). Generally translated as "garden" land, this was not only for growing vegetables, fruits, and flowers but for orchards of palmyra, coconut, and mango trees.

Unlike the more detailed land grants of the Tamil country, Andhra inscriptions

Table 7. Gift Items at Andhra Temples

	Entire Corpus		Major Temples		Minor Temples	
Gift Object	No.	%	No.	%	No.	%
Land plot	454	39	56	17	113	49
Livestock	308	27	193	57	18	8
Village	66	6	17	5	17	7
Implement[a]	49	4	28	8	6	3
Building/pillar	47	4	14	4	8	3
Miscellaneous[b]	47	4	7	2	11	5
Garden	35	3	2	1	14	6
Tax income	38	3	3	1	15	7
Group tithe	40	3	2	1	12	5
Cash	34	3	11	3	4	2
Irrigation	21	2	1	0	6	3
Tax remission	17	1	3	1	6	3
Total	1,156	99%	337	100%	230	101%

a. Refers to a metal object used in ritual worship.
b. Includes gifts of oil presses, salt pans, timber, and foodstuffs.

do not typically clarify the exact boundaries or locations of donated land. We see this rather cavalier attitude in the following gift of land:

> May all fare well and prosper! In the 1,243rd year of the Shaka era [1321 C.E.], (corresponding to the cyclic) year Durmati, on the 2nd (day of the) bright (fortnight of the) intercalary Ashadha (lunar month), a Thursday;
>
> May all fare well! For the religious merit of the illustrious Mahamandaleshvara Kakatiya Prataparudradeva Maharaja, Malayankaru, the minister of Mottupalli Bhaskaradeva, gave one *puṭṭi* of dry land (to provide) for the food offering of the lord Kedaradeva, the main deity of Kunkalakuntta, and .... [unclear] one oil press, to be maintained as long as the sun and moon (endure), to the lord Kedaradeva, the main deity of Kunkalakuntta. (SII 6.592)

A last type of land grant involves the gift of an entire village, rather than just a field or a garden—this generous donation constitutes 6 percent of all gifts recorded in the corpus. The term used in Andhra to designate lands endowed to a deity is *dēva(ra)-vritti*, the god's *vritti* (from the Sanskrit *vṛtti*, "means of subsistence or livelihood"). Brahmans could also possess *vrittis*, as did a few warriors.[24] Rather than having any religious meaning, therefore, *vritti* most probably indicates a special, reduced, tax status. Parabrahma Sastry believes that taxes were still levied on land and villages given as religious endowments to temples and brahmans, though at a concessional rate (1978: 212). This view is confirmed by several records in which a temple's land is exempted from the payment of specific taxes (SII 10.492, 499, 509, 521, and 540). Without such an exemption, one gathers, temples would have been assessed some taxes.

The exact terms of the tenure rights transferred to a temple in an endowment of land or a village is never specified in Kakatiya Andhra inscriptions. In the case of Tamil Nadu under the Chola dynasty, Noboru Karashima states that land grants to brahmans conveyed the right to actual possession whereas land grants to temples conveyed only the right to enjoyment of revenues (1984: xxxi). That Andhra brahmans who received land grants obtained full rights of proprietorship, as in Tamil Nadu, is evidenced by the numerous inscriptions that record the gift of land after it was purchased from an individual with a brahman personal name or other brahman marker (e.g., HAS 13.55; IAP-W.92; SII 10.422 and 478). The situation with temple land grants is less clear. It may be that most temples only obtained the rights to revenues from endowed land, but at least in some instances they had rights approximate to possession. For one thing, land given to temples as *vritti* was on occasion sold, as several records from Pushpagiri in Cuddapah District reveal (IAP-C 1.147, 1.148, 1.149, 1.151).

Although details are scanty, it appears that land belonging to temples was either cultivated under the direct management of temple staff or farmed out to local agriculturalists on lease. An inscription from Katukuru, Khammam Taluk, the most informative record, tells us that the village assembly levied a cess on all double-cropped wet land, which was intended to provide for ritual services in the local temple dedicated to Gopinatha, a form of Vishnu (HAS 19 Km.6). Certain exceptions were made to this cess, for it did not have to be paid on land belonging to the Shiva temple whether it was cultivated by Shaiva priests or by peasants (*kāmpulu*). On the land belonging to the Vishnu temple, the cess was waived if the land was cultivated by Vaishnava priests but had to be paid if cultivated by peasants. Since the priests certainly did not engage in actual cultivation themselves, the reference to the lands they cultivated must mean the lands others cultivated under their supervision. In contrast, the land cultivated by *kāmpus* must have been leased to them. Another inscription stipulates the exact amounts of rice and other crops that *kāmpus* should pay a temple yearly in exchange for their use of temple lands (NDI Atmakur 25). The individual to whom donated land was to be given on lease (*gutta*) is named in a different record (NDI Atmakur 7).

There was yet a third, occasional alternative to direct management of land or leasing. A donor could formally make a gift of land but actually retain the management of it in his own hands, giving only a portion of the produce to the temple. In other words, while "proprietorship" of the land would be officially transferred, immediate control of it was not. Such grants may have been motivated by not only piety but also the desire to evade taxes from which temple lands were exempt. An example of this type of situation was translated in chapter 2—the inscription of Tammili Chodaya Raddi, who said he was granting land but was actually just promising to supply foodstuffs produced on the land (SII 5.131). Chodaya Raddi had purchased this land from another man, which he might not have been able to do had its proceeds not been intended to benefit the temple. Although this sort of land grant wherein the donor undertook to supervise the land himself is quite rare, many herders adopted the similar practice of formally donating livestock to a temple while retaining actual possession of the animals in their own hands (e.g., SII 10.330 and 441).

Because so much land was donated to temples, these institutions were inextricably enmeshed in local agricultural networks. Whether their land was cultivated by hired laborers, tenants, or former proprietors, the end result was similar—a forging of links between temples and agriculturalists in the vicinity. Popular temples that attracted patronage from far and wide might have linkages with villages and lands in numerous scattered localities.[25] A whole series of individuals, who might have no occasion to interact otherwise, were thus connected through participation in a common economic web. Wealthy temples in some areas could also serve as a source of capital for neighboring villages. Cash donations received by the Rajarajeshvara temple at Tanjavur (Tamil Nadu) during the eleventh century were sometimes loaned out to village assemblies or merchant associations at a standard rate of interest (Spencer 1968: 287–88). At Tirupati during the late fifteenth and early sixteenth centuries, cash endowments were invested in irrigational improvements to the temple's own lands. Stein believes the increased productivity benefited not only the temple but the cultivators of its lands as well (1960: 167–69).

Pastoralists were similarly brought into close relations with temple institutions through the endowment of livestock. After land, the most popular category of gift in Kakatiya Andhra was that of milk-bearing animals—ewes, she-goats, and cows—comprising 27 percent of all donations. The gift of livestock was almost invariably intended to furnish fuel for lamps. Two types of lamps are referred to in Kakatiya-period records. The more popular was the *akhaṇḍa-dīpa* (lit., "lamp without a break") or perpetual lamp, meant to be continually replenished with ghee so that the flame would never go out. Stands for these perpetual lamps were commonly donated to the Draksharama temple along with livestock (SII 4.1092 from 1369). One of the most characteristically South Indian form of votive lamps was modeled on the human figure, with the cup that held the oil and wick being carried in the hands. These lamp-bearing statues were sometimes actual portrayals of the donor and even otherwise were meant to symbolize his or her personal devotion, expressed here as the rendering of a perpetual service to the Lord (Sivaramamurti 1962: 38). *Sandhya-dīpas* were also occasionally endowed. Because endowments for these lamps required far fewer animals than did an *akhaṇḍa-dīpa*, *sandhya-dīpas* must have been lit only at the two or three times a day (*sandhya*) when ritual services were conducted.[26]

Many inscriptions that recorded the gift of livestock for a perpetual lamp are very short, and each large temple had its own characteristic format for this type of donation. An example from the village Yenamalakuduru, documenting an endowment to the Malleshvara temple at Vijayavada, dates from 1241:

> May all fare well! In the year 1163 of the Shaka era [1241 C.E.], on the occasion of the winter solstice; Jakki Raddi gave 25 cows to the illustrious great lord Malleshvara of Bejavada [Vijayavada] for a perpetual lamp as a meritorious deed for (the religious benefit of) his mother and father. Having taken (charge of) these (cows), Male Boyundu's son Sure Boyundu and Nannaya Boya's son Kommana Boyundu, and their descendants after them, are to supply a *māna* of butter daily for as long as the moon and the sun (endure). (SII 6.92)

For each of these perpetual lamps a standard number of animals—normally 25 cows as in the record above, or 55 sheep (SII 4.685), or 50 goats (SII 10.327)—were handed over to *bōya* herders, who were then held responsible for providing a stipulated amount of butter for the maintenance of the lamp. Once the *bōya* had received charge of the herd, he had to ensure that its size did not fall below the minimum required. Any decrease in the number of animals would have to be made up by him, if his contract with the donor was to be honored. What would happen in the event that the herd grew larger is clarified in a record dated 1291 C.E. from Malyala village, Kurnool District (ARE 323 of 1937–38). The inscription stipulates that cows were never to be sold, and any transgression of this prohibition resulted in a cash penalty per animal. Regardless of the number of calves born that year, two male calves were to be raised as breeding bulls annually. The other male calves could, however, be castrated and sold as bullocks, to the profit of the herder. In essence, what this is means is that all female (i.e., milk-yielding) animals were to be reserved for the temple whereas all except for two males a year were regarded as the herder's property.

Inscriptions recording livestock donations to temples are essentially contracts between the donor, the temple, and one or more herders. They set up long-term arrangements for supplying one kind of service to a deity, the provision of lamps—note that in the inscription above, which is typical, the descendants of the herders are obligated to maintain the terms. The contractual nature of the agreement is also indicated by the specificity with which the herders are identified. That is, the herder's father's name is almost always stated along with the herder's own personal name, to clarify who was responsible. More than one *bōya* is usually involved, perhaps as another means of ensuring that the contract would be honored. In fact, each separate livestock endowment at any given temple appears to have been entrusted to a different herder or group of herders.[27] The requirements of ritual worship thus ensured that hundreds and perhaps even thousands of pastoralists and their families were drawn into temple economic networks during the Kakatiya period.

Numerous other categories of gift items existed during the Kakatiya period, in addition to those of land and livestock. On occasion, all the taxes on particular goods in a particular marketplace were endowed (see "tax income," table 7). For example, in one endowment made at Velpuru, taxes levied on the buyers of horses, oxen, carts, reins, sesame, and grain were donated along with other minor imposts (SII 10.314). The inscription is translated here:

> May all fare well and prosper! For the sake of the religious benefit of the illustrious Mahamandaleshvara Kakatiya Ganapatideva Maharaja who is endowed with all the praiseworthy titles such as the Mahamandaleshvara who has acquired the honors known as the five great sounds, the human lord of the city of Hanumakonda, exceedingly devoted to Shiva, he whose actions are for the good of his overlord, one for whom modesty is an ornament;
>
> To the glorious great lord Rameshvara of Velpuru, in the 1,169th year of the Shaka era [1248 C.E.], (corresponding to the cyclic) year Plavanga, on the 15th (day of the) dark (fortnight of the lunar month) Magha, a Sunday;
>
> The son of Dochena Pregada, Ganapaya—who is foremost in carrying out his appointed duties and is comparable to (the minister of Chandragupta Maurya) Chanakya in his understanding of policy—gave as a religious endowment the fees assessed on the following items purchased within the limits of the licensed marketplace of Velpuru where he has recently been appointed:
>
> When a horse is purchased, when an ox is purchased, when a cart is purchased, when a rope is purchased, when a *varu* [meaning unclear] is purchased, when sheep

are purchased or sold, when a marriage is performed, when sesame is purchased, when grain is purchased or fetched from afar and sold, as well as the registration fee and periodic tax on oil presses.

I have pledged (the Kakatiya king) Ganapatideva Maharaja that these terms will be met.

The donor in this example was presumably authorized by the Kakatiyas to collect taxes and tolls, and his endowment represented a loss of income either for the state or for the donor. Through the donation of tax revenues, resources extracted from many diverse individuals were rerouted to central collection points, the local temples.

Corporate bodies undertook a similar activity, for they often levied a tithe on themselves that consisted of a percentage of the taxes on goods sold and bought in a local market ("group tithe," table 7).[28] These groups, usually mercantile, would voluntarily contribute an extra amount over and beyond the existing taxes on items such as grain, oil, or areca-nut and betel leaves (e.g., ARE 313 of 1932–33; EA 4.14; SII 10.495). Instead of cash, sometimes a percentage of goods that were brought into the marketplace was given (e.g., ARE 277 of 1934–35; SII 10.473). The cess might be levied on bulkloads of transported goods, in the manner of tolls, rather than on goods bought and sold, as when a coastal merchant association voluntarily decided to donate a small amount of money for each boatload passing through the town (EI 3.15).

Sometimes a tax revenue due from a temple was simply remitted and the temple was declared exempt from payment of that tax ("tax remission," table 7). Generally, revenues from land belonging to the temple were remitted. In order to celebrate success in a recent military campaign, a warrior named Bolneningaru exempted all the land owned by a Vishnu temple from payment of the *panga* tax (SII 10.540). The money that would have gone toward the tax obligation was to be used for offerings of food and perfumed ointment to the deity instead. In another instance, five taxes on temple land were remitted by a man called Rudradeva:

In the 1,233rd year of the Shaka era [1311 C.E.], (corresponding to the cyclic) year Virodhikrit, on the 15th (day of the) dark (fortnight of the lunar month) Ashvayuja, a Thursday;

For the religious merit of his mother and father, Rudradevaningaru, the son of Mayideva Lenka, remits the *upakṣiti*, *paṅgamu*, *puṭṭi-māḍalu*, *kānika*, and *dariśanamu* (taxes), for as long as the sun and moon (endure), (that is), for all time, on those lands in the villages of the Konduri *nāyaṅkuṟamu* (territory) which are currently and which will henceforth be (endowed as) the subsistence lands [*vritti*] of the glorious Chenna Keshava Perumal of Penunguduru, no matter how much anyone should give (in the future). (SII 10.499)

Some individuals preferred to donate sums of money (see under "cash" category in table 7), often in order to provide for perpetual lamps. In most cases the money was invested and the interest from it used to purchase the necessary oil or butter, as is stipulated in NDI Kavali 25, where the Vaishnava priests were entrusted with a gold coin by the donor for this purpose. In addition to tanks, other kinds of waterworks ("irrigation" in table 7) were also donated to temples—wells (*bāvi*), canals (Telugu, *kāluva*; Sanskrit, *kulyā*), sluices (*tūmu*), and ponds (*kuṇṭa*). Under the rubric "building" I have counted various architectural additions, ranging from the erection of a major temple edifice such as a *maṇḍapa* pavilion, or the gift of a pillar, to repairs and rebuilding of a main shrine. Further minor categories of endowments include metal vessels or plates used for the sixteen offerings to the deity, gold and jeweled ornaments for the image, and metal lamp-stands on which perpetual lamps were kept burning ("implement," table 7). "Miscellaneous," a further category, groups together diverse kinds of gift objects: images of gods and goddesses, a metal torch for temple processions, and timber for a water pulley.

The wide range of goods donated to temples represented the variety of economic resources of the propertied classes of the Kakatiya period. Pools of wealth were thus formed at certain nodal sites, to be parceled out in turn to numerous other individuals, pastoralists as well as agriculturalists. In this manner, expanding circles of economic interdependence were created, which brought both diverse peoples and diverse localities together. The size and ecological setting of these redistributive centers varied considerably, however, and the assemblies of people being integrated differed from place to place. These subjects are further discussed in the next sections.

Diversity of Temple Types

Our model of the "traditional" South Indian temple has been derived from scrutiny of a few select sites—the Tirupati temple in southern Andhra, the Minakshi temple in the Tamil city of Madurai, the Tanjavur temple of the Chola period, and the Jagannatha temple in Puri, Orissa.[29] These famous temple complexes were situated in either royal centers or places that had been considered sacred for centuries. By their very nature, these sites are unusual and this special status is reflected in the large number of donations recorded at each one. In turn, the copious documentation at famous institutions has attracted scholarly interest and made them popular subjects of study.

Most of the thousands of temples found in South India are far more humble, in levels of both patronage and extant documentation. Yet it is generally assumed that they resemble the larger temples in their structure and functioning, being merely smaller replicas of them. Little attention has been paid to possible variations in temple types, because of the assumption that the same principles were operative on all levels, from the most unassuming local shrine to the most magnificently endowed pilgrimage center. This is part of a larger trend focusing on homologies of all kinds, inspired primarily by Stein's (1977) segmentary model that envisions the Chola state as composed of a pyramidal series of essentially uniform segments, the semi-autonomous localities. Whether the subject is temples, kings, or state systems, the various units have been regarded as being structurally similar regardless of scale (Dirks 1982, Breckenridge 1985a).

In the process, the great range in temple sizes has generally been overlooked, as well as the considerable diversity in types of terrain and in resulting socioeconomic formations. Given the marked variations in temples, can we really assume that they were all functionally identical? A related question has been raised by C. J. Fuller in reference to temple cults. He points out the noteworthy distinction between temple cults with Sanskritic deities and those with non-Sanskritic ones. Analysis of temple rituals shows that the power of the non-Sanskritic deity in a local caste temple is thought to extend only to a specific locale and social space, while the realm of a Sanskritic deity such as the goddess Minakshi of Madurai is conceived as limitless and universal. Such differences have led Fuller to call for greater investigation into the significance of variations in temple cults (1988: 65–66). In a similar vein, I suggest that we look more carefully at the diversity of temple types and their possible functions.

The uneven distribution of patronage is in fact the most striking feature of the temple corpus of inscriptions. An astonishingly high percentage of records—29 percent—come from just 10 sites within the area of the state under consideration (all districts excluding Srikakulam, Visakhapatnam, Hyderabad, Nizamabad, Adilabad, Anantapur and Chittoor; see map 3). Since 370 sites possess undamaged inscriptions from the years 1175–1324, this means that slightly less than 3 percent of the sites account for over one-quarter of all the records. Conversely, at 188 temples only one endowment was recorded during this period; in other words, 51 percent of the sites yield only 20 percent of the inscriptions. The remaining sites constitute 46 percent of all temples and account for 52 percent of all records in the corpus. In order to clarify the significant variations between temples, I concentrate on the two most disparate types of institutions in this section—the 10 heavily endowed sites and the 188 poorly endowed sites.[30]

Map 9 displays the location of the most popular sites of Kakatiya Andhra, what I call "major" temples for the sake of convenience. The two temples with the greatest number of extant inscriptions from the period are the Tripurantaka-Mahadeva temple at Tripurantakam (Markapur Taluk, Prakasam District) and the Bhimeshvara temple at Draksharama (Ramachandrapuram Taluk, East Godavari District). They both commanded pilgrimage networks encompassing all of Andhra and must have owned a staggering amount of property in view of the numerous donations documented at each temple—68 at Tripurantakam and 52 at Draksharama. In addition to these gifts, many pilgrims undoubtedly made donations of movable property that went unrecorded.

The Shiva temple at Tripurantakam derived much of its popularity and sacred character from its association with the renowned Shaiva center at Srisailam (Atmakur Taluk, Kurnool District), of which Tripurantakam is considered to be the eastern doorway or gateway. Srisailam and its four satellites constituted the most important sacred region (*tīrtha-kṣētra*) of inland Andhra in this era. Because earlier inscriptions at Srisailam were apparently destroyed in the early fourteenth century, Srisailam itself yields few Kakatiya-era records. Many pilgrims who visited Srisailam during the medieval period performed a circumambulation of it that included a visit to each of the four gateway temples. The central shrine at the current temple complex at Tripurantakam was built during the Kakatiya period, but the site is certainly much older (Parabrahma Sastry 1982: 17; Rama Rao 1966: 41).

The second most heavily documented site is Draksharama, where the main temple is said to have been erected by the Eastern Chalukya king Chalukya Bhima I (r. 890–922) and the deity named after him (Hultzsch 1896–97: 227). Sanskrit and Prakrit literary references to the site suggest that a temple may have existed there even earlier (Srinivasachari 1971: 217). The high regard accorded to

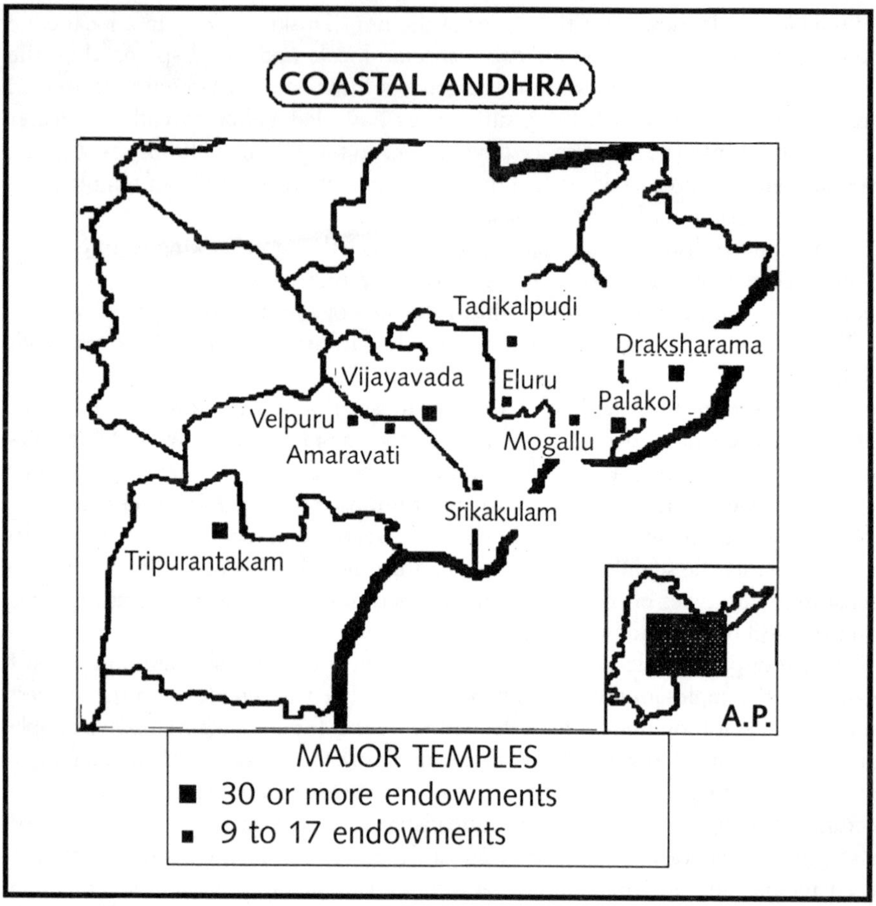

Map 9. Location of Major Temples

Draksharama is evident from its inclusion in two of the most famous classifications of Shaiva holy sites in Andhra—the *triliṅga* and *pañcārāma* schemes.[31] The scheme of the five *ārāmas* dates back to at least the eleventh century, when it is referred to in an epigraph (Sundaram 1968: 46). According to legend, each of the five *ārāmas* marks a place where a piece of the skull of the demon Taraka descended to earth when he was killed by Shiva's son Kumarasvami. Since Taraka was a great devotee of Shiva, these pieces were considered sacred and temples were founded at the places where they landed (Rao 1973: 221).[32] The popularity of the *ārāma* scheme during the Kakatiya period is obvious in the data at our disposal. In addition to Draksharama, two other *ārāma* temples are among the 10 major temples: the Kshirarameshvara temple at Kshirarama (modern town of Palakol) and the Amareshvara temple at Amaravati, ranking fourth (with 30 endowments) and fifth (with 17 endowments), respectively.[33]

At least four of the *liṅgas* at these five *ārāmas* are unusual in shape: tall (15 to 25 feet high), cylindrical, and made of marble or marblelike stone.[34] The resemblance of these *liṅgas* to the *āyaka* pillars that are a unique feature of Andhra Buddhist *stūpas* is one reason for believing that these places have a long and hallowed history as religious sites. Amaravati was an important Buddhist site in the second and third centuries and some scholars believe that Draksharama and Palakol were also originally Buddhist centers (Ramesan 1962: 88, 114–15). While not directly attributable to the king Chalukya Bhima I, who was responsible for the construction of temples at the other three *ārāmas*, the central shrines at Palakol and Amaravati also date back to the late Eastern Chalukya period of the tenth and eleventh centuries (Rao 1973: 221–22; Meister and Dhaky 1986: 165).

The temple with the third largest number of endowments (51) in the corpus is that of Malleshvara at Vijayavada. It was also a well-known pilgrimage center as far back as the Eastern Chalukya period, when the current shrine appears to have been built.[35] Vijayavada's Malleshvara is the special deity of the Teliki (oilmonger) community in Andhra, collectively known during the early medieval period as the Teliki-1,000 (Sundaram 1968: 30–39). Situated on the north bank of the Krishna River, Vijayavada has been acclaimed for its sanctity as a Varanasi of the south (Ramachandra Murthy 1983a: 307).

The other major temples, in sequential order from sixth to tenth in the number of their endowments, include the Rameshvara temple at Velpuru in Guntur District (15 endowments); the Vallabha temple at Srikakulam in Krishna District (12 endowments); the Someshvara temple at Eluru in West Godavari District (12 endowments); the Bhimeshvara temple at Mogallu in West Godavari District (10 endowments); and the Aruneshvara temple at Tadikalpudi in West Godavari District (9 endowments). These sites have received less scholarly scrutiny. Although there was certainly active worship at these sites prior to the thirteenth century, the dates of the temple structures themselves are not known. During the Kakatiya era, they received a fair amount of patronage from local princely families and were situated in localities of some political significance.[36]

The 10 major temples hence all predate the Kakatiya period. In most cases the main structures were probably built in the tenth or eleventh centuries, sometimes at sites sacred since Buddhist times. They share another similarity, for all but Tripurantakam are situated in the Krishna-Godavari deltas. Draksharama, the northernmost temple, is located very near the Gautami River, one of the seven branches the Godavari River splits into as it nears the coast (Ramana 1982: i). The village Palakol is similarly near another branch of the Godavari River. Mogallu, Tadikalpudi, and Eluru are all squarely in the middle of the broad Krishna-Godavari deltaic area. The four villages of Velpuru, Amaravati, Vijayavada, and Srikakulam are situated in the vicinity of the Krishna River. Only Tripurantakam lies at any considerable distance from the other major temples. It is situated in uneven terrain approaching the Nallamala Hills where Srisailam is located. Tripurantakam is the sole place among the 10 that is not close to a sizable center of population today, and the temple is currently in a semiruined condition. With the exception of Tripurantakam, the major temples are all located in Vengi, the longest-settled territory in Andhra Pradesh.

It appears that the great religious prestige of the major temples, acquired over the centuries and justified through association of their deities with pan-Indic

Table 8. Major and Minor Temple Inscriptions by District

District	All Records	Major Records	(%) Major	Minor Records	(%) Minor
E. Godavari	76	52	68	3	4
W. Godavari	116	61	53	2	2
Krishna	152	63	41	14	9
Mahbubnagar	34	0	0	5	15
Prakasam	160	68	43	26	16
Nellore	36	0	0	8	22
Nalgonda	64	0	0	14	22
Guntur	230	32	14	65	28
Kurnool	7	0	0	3	43
Karimnagar	14	0	0	6	43
Cuddapah	18	0	0	9	50
Warangal	38	0	0	21	55
Khammam	11	0	0	7	64
Medak	7	0	0	5	71
Total/Average	963	276	29%[a]	188	20%[b]

a. 29% of all records are major records.
b. 20% of all records are minor records.

mythology, granted them a special status and ability to attract religious gifts. Almost one-third of all donations recorded in the area of the state surveyed went to these 10 institutions. In their own local territories, the dominance of these coastal institutions was even more marked. Endowments to major temples comprise from 41 to 68 percent of all extant donative inscriptions in the coastal districts north of the Krishna River—East Godavari, West Godavari, and Krishna—as shown in table 8. In other words, the major temples acted as focal points in a very concentrated network of religious patronage. Few other sites possessing inscriptions from this period exist in the three districts north of the Krishna River, so strong was the appeal of the major temples. East Godavari District, for example, has only seven temples with documented donations from the years 1175 to 1324, besides the Bhimeshvara temple at Draksharama. These seven temples are located in just five different villages, all outside the subdistrict or taluk where Draksharama is situated. Because of the intensity of donative activity at their major temples, the northern coastal districts have very high ratios of endowments per site.

The focused pattern of endowment found in East Godavari, West Godavari, and Krishna Districts can also be seen in Visakhapatnam and Srikakulam Districts. These two districts at the extreme northeastern corner of modern Andhra Pradesh state also yield many Telugu inscriptions from the Kakatiya period but formed part of the Kalinga cultural and political sphere. Although they have not been included in the present study of Kakatiya Andhra for that reason, the donative patterns found in Visakhapatnam and Srikakulam resemble those of other districts in coastal

Andhra. Thus, the Kurmanatha temple at Srikurman in Srikakulam Taluk possesses 85 reasonably undamaged inscriptions that record gifts to the temple from the years 1175–1324. Only 3 other temples in Srikakulam District besides Srikurman bear inscriptions from the Kakatiya period. (One of these is at Mukhalingam, the dominant site of Srikakulam District in the two centuries before the Kakatiya period.) In the case of Visakhapatnam District, the premier institution of the thirteenth through fifteenth centuries was the Narasimha temple at Simhachalam.[37] It possesses 66 donative inscriptions in good condition from the Kakatiya period. Elsewhere in Visakhapatnam District, we find only eight temple sites. As was the case in Vengi, these areas of Kalinga had large, well-endowed temple complexes that inhibited patronage at other sites in their vicinities.

Because major temples were so prominent in the northern coastal districts, these areas have few temples with only one inscription from the period—what I call minor temples (column "% Minor" in table 8). Less than 10 percent of all endowments in East Godavari, West Godavari, and Krishna Districts were made at such institutions, although on a statewide basis minor temples received 20 percent of all gifts. At the other extreme are several districts situated in the northern and southern peripheries of Kakatiya Andhra. Gifts to minor temples accounted for roughly 40 to 70 percent of all donations in Kurnool, Cuddapah, Karimnagar, Warangal, Khammam, and Medak Districts. This is two to three times the statewide figure and is similar to the share of endowments garnered by the major temples in the northern coastal districts.[38] None of these interior districts contained any major temples.

The two types of temples I differentiate, major and minor, characterize different geographical areas of Andhra. The major temple, a large complex dating back at least to the Eastern Chalukya period and renowned as a pilgrimage site, flourished in the northern coastal districts. Conversely, the minor temple, a local institution attracting little patronage and of recent origin, was most commonly found in the interior portion of the state. Many of the minor temples were established during the time span 1175 to 1324—30 percent of the 188 minor temple records are foundation inscriptions, whereas the overall average of inscriptions documenting the establishment of temples is only 12 percent. In other words, a large number of minor temples were established during the Kakatiya era.

More than just varying patronage levels, age and location separated these two institutional types, however, for the social background of their donors and the kinds of gift objects they received also show a marked divergence. The kinds of people being incorporated into the temple's community of worship are dissimilar at the major and minor institution, in other words. With different sorts of resources at their disposal, the redistributive roles of major and minor temples were quite distinct. That entire clusters of opposing traits define the major versus the minor temple confirms the thesis that they represent two separate donative patterns or styles and justifies the distinctions drawn between the religious cultures of coastal and interior Andhra. It also suggests that the two kinds of temples served different functions in their respective areas.

To understand the integrative role of temples as institutions, it is crucial to know the identity of the chief patrons. Thus far, we have considered only who was

Table 9. Donor Types at Major and Minor Temples

Type	All Records	Major Records	(%) Major	Minor Records	(%) Minor
Bōya	39	21	54	1	3
Woman	92	46	50	11	12
Seṭṭi	54	22	41	6	11
Royal Rāju	70	26	37	11	16
Clerical Rāju	39	13	33	7	18
Reḍḍi	78	25	32	16	21
Mahārāja	53	13	25	15	28
Nāyaka	122	21	17	34	28
Other	282	75	29	56	20
Total /Average	829	262	32%[a]	157	19%[b]

a. 32% of all records are major.
b. 19% of all records are minor.

entrusted with the assets of temples, rather than who was providing them to begin with. The main categories of donors figuring in the temple inscriptions of the Kakatiya period, which accounted for two-thirds of all individual donations, are listed in table 9.[39] The classes of donors who gave the greatest proportion of all their gifts at major institutions are listed first in the table: *bōyas*, women, and *seṭṭis*. Between 41 and 54 percent of their donations went to deities at major temples, in contrast to the 32 percent norm for all individual donors. An intermediate set of donors—comprising royal *rājus*, clerical *rājus*, and *reḍḍis* (Vengi kings and princes, secular brahman officials, and peasant leaders, respectively)—made gifts to major temples at roughly average rates. The last two social categories, *mahārājas* and *nāyakas*, appear less frequently as donors at major temples. These non-Vengi lords and military leaders are underrepresented as patrons of major temples, having made only a small proportion of their gifts at those institutions.

The 10 temples with the greatest number of extant inscriptions from Kakatiya Andhra hence attracted an unusually high level of gifts from herders, women, and merchant-traders and a disproportionately low level of gifts from lords outside of Vengi and from military leaders. This varying distribution of patronage would not be so remarkable in itself were it not mirrored in reverse by the patronage patterns of minor temples. At minor temples—those institutions with only one recorded endowment from the period—we find the antithesis of major temple patronage (see column "% Minor" in table 9). The prominent donors at minor temples were *mahārājas* and *nāyakas*, the two groups who gave less to major temples than any other social group. Both of them made 28 percent of all their donations at minor temples, in comparison to the 19 percent norm among individual donors. Conversely, the least generous minor temple donors were *bōyas*, women, and *seṭṭis*, the primary donors at major temples. Only 3 to 12 percent of their gifts went to minor temples.

The inverse correlation in the social composition of donors helps explain another difference in the patronage patterns at major and minor temples—the predominant type of gift donated to them. The variety of goods and revenues given to Kakatiya-period temples was discussed in the previous section in general terms. Land and livestock were found to be the most popular gift items overall, but at minor temples the gift of land was far more popular than livestock (see column "Minor Temples," table 7). At major temples, on the other hand, the incidence of land grants was much lower than the norm whereas livestock grants were very abundant. The characteristic gift object received by the two types of temples was hence different—livestock in the case of major temples versus land in the case of minor temples. The scarcity of land donations at major temples may be partially due to the scarcity and expense of land in their vicinities. The major temples were in localities where intensive agriculture had been practiced for many centuries, and rights to the cultivable lands in their neighborhoods would have been well-established and difficult to acquire. But minor temples were typically located in the interior districts of Andhra, regions that were more recently settled. Much unclaimed land must therefore have been available near the minor temple sites.

Another reason that major temples received relatively few land endowments, however, has to do with the identity of their donors. The social groups most closely associated with major temples were also the categories of people least likely to make land grants. In table 10 the proportions of the various gift items donated by each of the primary donor types is displayed. Only 20 to 27 percent of all merchant-trader (*seṭṭi*), herder (*bōya*), and women's gifts in Kakatiya Andhra consisted of plots of land, considerably below the 40 percent average for all donations. Instead, merchants, herders, and women were much more likely than average to make gifts of livestock. The high levels of livestock donations at major temples can thus be largely attributed to the close association of major temples with patrons who favored livestock to land when making endowments. Conversely, the main patrons of minor

Table 10. Gift Items by Individual Donor Type

	Percentage of Endowments								
Item	Nāyaka	Reḍḍi	Royal Rāju	Rāja[a]	Clerical Rāju	Seṭṭi	Woman	Bōya	All
Land plot	50	44	37	36	44	27	27	20	40
Livestock	18	23	35	13	33	49	43	66	28
Village	2	5	10	29	7	2	4	0	6
Implement	5	5	5	5	0	6	5	0	4
Building	6	6	0	2	0	3	5	0	4
Misc.	7	2	1	0	5	3	4	5	4
Garden	3	1	5	5	2	0	4	0	3
Tax income	2	5	5	4	7	5	0	0	3
Irrigation	3	2	0	5	0	0	2	2	2
Cash	3	7	1	0	2	5	3	7	3
Tax remission	2	1	1	2	0	0	2	0	2

a. *Rāja* is an abbreviation for the title *mahārāja*.

temples were among the social groups who most frequently gave land in Kakatiya Andhra. As the figures in table 10 demonstrate, *nāyakas* endowed plots of land at a higher rate than any other group, followed by *reḍḍis* and royal *rājus*. If village grants are also considered, however, the most land-oriented donors turn out to be *mahārājas* and *nāyakas*, precisely the two categories most closely connected to minor temples.

In view of their primary occupations, herders and merchants would not be expected to have easy access to land, which they typically had to purchase first before donating to a temple.[40] Nor does brahmanical legal literature condone the ownership of land by women, although it is clear from our data that such prohibitions were routinely ignored. However, it seems likely that the bulk of women's personal property then, as now, consisted of movable goods such as jewelry. Compared to the formalities involved in purchasing land, granting livestock for the purpose of lamp maintenance must have been more straightforward. Since each temple had a set number of livestock (e.g., 55 ewes or 25 cows) laid down for each lamp, it is quite possible that the donor had only to furnish cash or goods deemed equivalent in value to the animals. Although not agriculturalists, *nāyakas* and *mahārājas* obviously had rights over land as did *reḍḍi* village leaders and *rāju* lords or ministers. Since kings, military chiefs, and influential villagers all ultimately subsisted on the proceeds of agriculture, they would logically be more likely than merchants and pastoralists to either possess land that could be alienated or have the authority to transfer revenues from land.

In summary, we can formulate two abstract models of the representative institutions of the coastal and interior regions of Andhra based on aggregate data. In doing so, I inevitably exaggerate the differences between the two types of temples. What is typical of one is not necessarily unknown at the other. This is especially true of the characteristic donors and gift items, since we are actually talking about predominant trends rather than absolute cleavages. Any analysis of the diversity of temples as institutions requires the use of such ideal types, however, in order to highlight the significant variations that are witnessed in the data. With this caveat in mind, let me reiterate the distinctive attributes of the major and minor temples. The major temple had a large number of endowments, was located in the Krishna-Godavari delta, and dated back to at least the tenth or eleventh centuries. The abundance of donations at the major temple meant that a variety of social groups were involved in their patronage, but they were uniquely favored by nonlanded donors. Partially as a consequence, the typical gift at the major temple was livestock. The minor temple received only one endowment, was located in upland regions of the state, and was of relatively recent origin. The range of patrons was obviously limited, given the very definition of a minor temple. On the whole, minor temples were favored by land-controlling donors and typically received gifts of land.

Motives for Temple Patronage

It is easy to see why older temples located in the fertile delta would be the institutions most successful at attracting patronage. But what was their special appeal for social groups that did not control land? Conversely, why were land-controlling chiefs and military leaders so partial to the minor temple? Before we can differentiate between the motives of these two broad classes of donor, we must examine the issue of the benefits accruing from temple patronage in general. Beyond the obvious religious incentives for gift-giving, how else did temple patrons benefit? In the standard model of the medieval South Indian temple, the economic integration created by resource distribution is seen as only one of its unifying aspects. The temple also fostered social solidarity through the incorporation of diverse groups into a single community of worship. Additionally, it brought about political cohesion through the legitimacy conferred on kings and local power elites.

Prestige is most often cited as the motivation behind large-scale gift-giving by the propertied classes of medieval South India. The desire to publicize generous benefactions was a major motivation for documenting donations in inscriptional form, although another reason was to ensure that the terms of the property transfer were permanently maintained. Inscribing records in highly visible locations on temple walls and columns or on separate slabs and pillars within the temple compound was a way of honoring the benefactors of the temple (Stein 1980: 132). The act of giving was itself a public event, often witnessed by local notables and performed in the presence of a deity (ARE 13 of 1941–42). Once having made valuable endowments, donors continued to be publicly recognized on important ritual occasions. Ceremonial presentation of various temple honors was a widespread method for acknowledging and rewarding an individual or group's status as a generous patron. The most popular temple honor in recent times is a silk cloth that has adorned the deity (Fuller 1992: 80).

During the Kakatiya period, epithets (*biruda*) proclaiming devotion to a particular deity were borne by some individuals, including the Kalapa Nayaka whose inscription was translated earlier (SII 6.602). Although Kalapa Nayaka was documenting his founding of a Vishnu temple, one of his titles is the epithet "worshiper of the divine and illustrious lotus feet of the god Malleshvara of Vijayavada" (*Bejavāḍa-Mallīśvara-dēvara-divya-śrī-pāda-padm=ārādhaka*). In this standard formulaic phrase, the name of other deities such as the god Mallikarjuna of Srisailam could be substituted (SII 10.339). Almost always, the deity alluded to is one of the famous gods enshrined in a major temple. Presumably, such titles were conferred as a form of temple honor, in return for conspicuous acts of generosity.

The names of major benefactors were incorporated into temple worship at times. For example, a daily ritual service or a periodic festival paid for by a particular donor might be named after that person (SII 10.464). Tanks, temples, and villages frequently bore the name of the person who was responsible for their establishment. They could also be named after someone else whom the donor designated, usually a relative. Naming of a deity was a widespread practice, occurring in slightly more than half of the newly founded temples of the Kakatiya era (62 out of 120 temples). As a rule, it is explicitly referred to in foundation inscriptions with the phrase "in the name of" (*pēranu*) so-and-so. When a *liṅga* was consecrated ca. 1203 by the Telangana chief Malyala Chaunda, its name was compounded from the donor's personal name Chaunda and the title Ishvara, which denoted a Shaiva deity (HAS 13.8). Technically, the term Chaundeshvara meant "Chaunda's Lord" or "Chaunda's

God," to indicate the favored deity of Chaunda rather than imply that Chaunda himself was a god. But the deity's name served as a constant reminder of Malyala Chaunda's piety and perpetuated his memory for future generations.

Fame is often depicted as accruing from religious beneficence in Sanskrit inscriptions of the period. It is said to be the consequence of having a tank built in HAS 13.51: "By the praise of the good, the fame (*yaśas*) of the constructor of this praiseworthy tank . . . rests in the ten quarters."[41] A pillar is referred to in the record inscribed on it as a *kīrti-stambha*—"a pillar of fame" because it recorded the donor's generosity in gift-giving (HAS 13.7). Temples and other monuments were themselves sometimes known as *kīrti* in the sense of being a fame-producing work (Sircar 1966: 158). In his study of early modern temples in Bengal, H. Sanyal notes that many small temples were built by individuals on or adjacent to their house-sites. Although private in that sense and in enshrining family deities, care was taken to assure that these Bengali temples were visible and accessible to other villagers. The temples not only enhanced the eminence of their founders but gave them more influence in village affairs (1976: 342–44).

The notion of fame in Kakatiya Andhra had religious connotations, in addition to its social dimensions. The religious gift-giving that led to fame also resulted in tremendous spiritual merit, sufficient perhaps to ensure safe arrival in heaven. That, in any case, seems to be the implication of the following verse in praise of Viryala Mailama, the wife of Malyala Chaunda: "There she, the one called Mailama, made a triad of temples, as if providing a pathway for her fame which yearns to ascend to heaven" (v. 10, HAS 19 Km.4). The Andhra scheme of the *sapta-santāna* (seven sons) also reflects the wish to leave something behind to perpetuate one's name while simultaneously enabling one to reach heaven. A son was important in Indian society not only to carry on the lineage but for the performance of funerary rituals without which the deceased could not find peace. Religious benefactions could be substituted for the *śrāddha* funeral rites, in the view of some medieval religious and legal texts (Kane 1953: 182–83, 265). Hence the various items included in the seven sons such as the building of a temple or tank could guarantee a life after death both in this world and in the other. The composition of a poem, one of the seven sons, was motivated by "the underlying belief . . . that a person lives in heaven as long as his/her name is remembered on earth" (Narayana Rao 1992: 143).

It seems likely that many donors also experienced tangible material benefits from their acts of endowment. I do not mean to diminish the importance of religious and social incentives for gift-giving in saying this. But a multiplicity of objectives could simultaneously be satisfied through a single incident of gift-giving, undoubtedly a strong part of its appeal. Some scholars have argued that temple endowments were a strategy for retaining or gaining control over resources both human and nonhuman. James Heitzman believes that many Tamil land grants of the Chola period were actually only assignments of revenues and not transfers of ownership over land. That is, only the share of produce that would have been appropriated by the state as tax revenue was endowed to the temple recipient. The rights of proprietorship would remain with the donor, who could keep what was known as the cultivator's share. Since he or she would have had to pay taxes in any case, assigning those revenues to the temple did not lead to an overall economic loss for the donor.

Meanwhile, the donor's status as the cultivator-proprietor of the land would be confirmed and protected by the temple, strengthening his control over agricultural labor and his rights vis-à-vis the state. Because the endowed temple was generally a local institution, donors might also be able to influence the allocation of other temple resources (Heitzman 1997: 58–59, 72–78).

Similar advantages may have been gained by some Kakatiya-period donors of land, although I do not believe that these grants were necessarily confined to the assignment of revenues from land, as Heitzman suggests. In the inscription of Chodaya Reddi mentioned twice previously (SII 5.131), he was portrayed as purchasing land for donation from a man who was probably a brahman. Chodaya Reddi retained the land he bought but vowed to give the temple specified units of produce daily from that land. Under the guise of religious gift-giving, this individual acquired rights over land that he might not have been able to attain outside the context of temple endowment. Because not all aspects of these transactions are recorded, it is quite possible that other donors of land retained cultivating rights. Certainly, we witness continued access to their livestock endowments in the case of herders. Vemana Bondu (a variant of the title Boya) and Nara Bondu documented an endowment of two flocks of sheep to the god Gopala for a perpetual lamp. By stating that they (and their descendants after them) would each supply, on a daily basis, butter in amounts that would fill half a lamp, it is made clear that these flocks physically remained with the two men who ostensibly donated them (SII 10.441). The shepherd-donors obtained religious merit, social prestige, and—if they successfully managed the flocks—a potential economic gain.

In her analysis of the Tirumala-Tirupati temple complex during the fifteenth and sixteenth centuries, Carol Breckenridge points out several benefits possible from temple endowments. They were a primary means used by immigrant groups to claim agrarian produce, she explains:

> In a context of uncertainty, religious gifts can be seen as a complex system for ensuring some subsistence for non-claimants on local (agrarian) goods. A gift entitled the donor (and specified others) to rights of call on a share of the agrarian produce. And, if the gift of land was preceded by purchase, to rights of call on a share of agrarian labor. A gift then could mobilize a constituency which was not necessarily coextensive with the donating group. (1985b: 59)

In the post-Kakatiya period, when the trade in sacred leftovers of the god (*prasāda*) became widespread at large Vaishnava temples, donors would get a return of about a quarter-share of the food offerings they had financed. They could consume it themselves, transfer it to others to form linkages, or lease it to contract-holders who would then sell it to pilgrims. Sociopolitical alliances and monetary gains were thus some of the benefits gained in addition to religious merit and prestige (Breckenridge 1986: 31–38).

In short, temple patronage was a means of accruing religious merit and social prestige and influence, and possibly led to greater control over economic resources including labor. It could provide an entry into social circles outside one's kinship or occupational networks and access to property and labor beyond one's immediate command. Economic rights and privileges already possessed might also be guaranteed through endowment. With this overview of the motives for patronage behind us, we can now return to the issue we began with:—Why would different types of donors be drawn to different types of institutions when making religious gifts? Obviously, an individual's social status and occupational background were important in determining which institution to endow, for the kinds of alliances and benefits to be gained from patronage would vary according to the nature of the temple.

Brenda Beck's ethnographic study of the modern Kongu region in Tamil Nadu aptly illustrates the way that religious worship varied according to occupation. She found that the religious life of castes who base their livelihood on agriculture (known as right-hand castes), was quite distinct from that of castes who pursue nonagricultural occupations such as trade, banking, or the crafts (known as left-hand castes). The right-hand section of the community is closely bound to the land on which it works and has elaborate clan and lineage groupings based on territorial divisions. The hierarchy of social units is mirrored in the extensive network of local temples, each associated exclusively with a specific clan or lineage. These local temples were the sites of periodic group worship by the various groupings of the right-hand castes. In contrast, castes of the left-hand section do not possess territorially based clan and lineage groupings and are much less locally oriented. Their work often involves them in travel and communication with caste members in other localities. The larger perspective of the left-hand castes is relevant not only in their economic and social lives but extends to their religious concerns. Members of the left-hand castes in Kongu prefer to worship at large pilgrimage temples, sacred centers used by all communities. Furthermore, the left-hand castes seldom undertake group worship (Beck 1972: 13–14, 61–62, 74, 99, 106).

Some of the unique characteristics of the modern left-hand Kongu castes can be extended to the merchants and artisans of thirteenth-century Andhra. *Seṭṭis* were more mobile individually and more dispersed as a group than their landed counterparts, who were bound to the specific localities from which they derived power and wealth. By patronizing the major temples, which were pilgrim sites drawing on an expansive circulatory network, Kakatiya-period merchants extended their own network of alliances over a larger territory and became participants in socially and geographically diverse communities. Temple patronage could allow merchants entry into the complex economic networks of large temples. The process of expanding commercial activities through religious gifting has been documented by David W. Rudner for the Tamil Nakarattar caste of salt traders. They established contacts outside their areas of residence through patronage of the famous Murugan temple at Palani during the seventeenth century (Rudner 1987: 365–68).

Herders (*bōyas*) were the other prominent group of male donors at coastal Andhra's large temples and comprise the social category most closely linked with patronage of these sites. While they are similar to merchants and artisans in being more mobile and less bound to specific territory, the extent of the herder preference for the major temples is rather surprising. Indeed, practically no herders figure in inscriptions from the interior as either donors or trustees of livestock grants. But there is every reason to suppose that raising animals was a more important livelihood in interior Andhra. Telangana, in particular, is ecologically well suited for pastoralism (Alam 1968: 293–94). Today, the interior districts possess high ratios of sheep and other livestock in comparison to the human population (Sopher 1975: 189). And it is in inland Andhra that remains from protohistoric pastoralists have been recovered.

David Sopher reminds us that there is a significant difference between animal herding as an economic activity and the same pursuit as a social designation. Only when there is a differentiation of lifestyles and livelihoods does the specific social category of herder emerge. It is a classification implicitly formulated in opposition to that of agriculturalist. To restate Sopher's point, a mixed economy of field cultivation and animal husbandry is required before pastoralism becomes a defined occupational specialization (Sopher 1975: 204–7). Where agriculturalists had yet to settle in large numbers or where a distinct agrarian mode of production had yet to crystallize, we would not hear about pastoralists even if they constituted the majority of the population.

Modern herding groups have forged symbiotic bonds with the agricultural communities surrounding them. Research on the Dhangar pastoralists of Maharashtra reveals that the farming villages near their seasonal camps rely on sheep manure to fertilize their fields (Sontheimer 1975: 166–69). By ensuring that peasants depend on them economically, these pastoralists have protected themselves and their lifestyle. In the more densely populated and long-settled coastal country of Kakatiya Andhra, herders would have been similarly compelled to come to terms with agriculturalists, if they were to retain any rights over grazing land and preserve their livelihood. The epigraphic evidence indicates that temple endowments were a significant method of assimilation and accommodation for this community of people who were marginal to wet rice production. By making gifts to religious institutions, herders, like merchant-traders, became part of a larger social unit and established linkages with other communities.

The third group of donors who patronized major temples in large numbers were women. Quite a few female donors were the wealthy and influential relatives of powerful kings and princes. Others (roughly 50 percent) were of humbler descent, being the wives or daughters of *reḍḍis*, *nāyakas*, *bōyas*, and *seṭṭis*. Their reasons for patronizing large temple cults are not entirely clear, although we might point to the greater sanctity and religious prestige of the major temple as one likely factor. Patronage of religious institutions was the main public activity in which the women of Kakatiya Andhra could participate, and thirteenth-century inscriptions eulogize women almost solely on the grounds of their religious beneficence while praising men mostly in terms of their military accomplishments. Since social norms restricted the opportunities for enhancing their fame, many women may have sought the largest public arenas possible for their religious patronage. This certainly was true of royal women in medieval South India, who often played a more prominent role as donors of temples than did the men in their families. As an example, the queens and princesses of the imperial Chola dynasty made far more direct gifts to temples than did the kings and princes (Heitzman 1987: 41–42; for more on donations by Chola women, see Spencer 1983b).

The minor temple of the thirteenth century was preeminently a local institution with a restricted transactional network. Its local nature most sharply differentiates it from the large major temple. Minor temples received the bulk of their support from prominent individuals who controlled land and its produce. These patrons were not the peasant leaders or village headmen themselves, since *reḍḍi* donors were not noticeably involved with minor temples, but *mahārāja* chiefs and *nāyaka* military leaders who occupied the intermediate strata between the overlord and landed peasants. Inasmuch as a state system could be said to have existed, it was this class of people who represented the state at the local level. *Nāyakas* and *mahārājas* had the authority to alienate land and its revenues for their own purposes; they appear in the sources as the primary extractors of agrarian surpluses. Religious gifting to temples within the territories over which they wielded military power and economic control enabled these individuals to affirm their ties with the locality and consolidate their power base. The small size of the minor or local temple's redistributive network and social community would not be a disadvantage for *nāyakas* and *mahārājas*, who sought above all to intensify their control over local agrarian resources.

This brings up an important aspect of temple patronage that I have not yet discussed. One of the primary effects of endowment was to establish hierarchical relations between various property-holding individuals and groups. True, the making of religious gifts to a common deity may have united many social categories into a single larger community of worship, but the community itself was clearly stratified. That is, temple patrons were not ranked equally but hierarchically, partially on the basis of their relative munificence. Festivals were particularly significant in this regard, for it was on such occasions of procession with the deity that prominent patrons were most publicly rewarded with temple honors (Appadurai and Breckenridge 1976). Textual prescriptions regarding entry into the temple grounds also imply that different social categories were accorded differing levels of access, and again one of the determining factors was the quantity of gifts they gave (Inden 1985: 62–70). The more lavish donors garnered greater social prestige and, we can assume, greater influence over the temple's assets and their allocation. The hierarchical function of temple patronage was especially crucial for political elites who derived considerable moral authority from gift-giving, supplementing and reinforcing their economic and military clout.

In the rapidly changing setting of Andhra's interior frontier zone, patronage of temples was crucial for political elites in the process of consolidation. It validated their social position and at the same time facilitated greater intrusion into local agricultural processes. Temple endowments and inscriptions were an additional important means for creating and affirming political ties. The embedding of political strategies in religious gift-giving is apparent in a variety of forms. One is the simple citation of the name of the overlord in an inscription. Unlike the Tamil country, where the reigning king is almost always mentioned, many Kakatiya-period inscriptions are silent on the matter. When the king or a lord is specified in Andhra, we can therefore interpret it as a sign of political affiliation. Donors might also express their allegiance through transferring the religious merit of their gift to a lord or overlord. Naming the deity of a newly founded temple after a political superior was another means of displaying political loyalties.

In all these respects, we witness a marked divergence between major and minor temples, with political relations figuring much more prominently in minor-temple inscriptions. Donors at minor temples were almost four times more likely to acknowledge their overlord's name. They also transferred merit to a lord at over four times the rate that major temple donors did (Talbot 1991: 332–33). The naming of deities was, of course, a phenomenon that occurred at newly founded temples, a category that includes some minor temples but no major ones. But minor temples were proportionately more frequent in interior districts, whereas the major temples were all situated in coastal Andhra. Of the 11 instances of naming a new temple deity after an overlord, only 4 occurred in the coastal districts.[42] Honoring an overlord in this manner was hence more common in interior Andhra. The existence of these various practices—citing the identity of an overlord, dedication of religious merit to the overlord, and establishing a deity in the overlord's name—suggests that the consolidation of political networks was one of the purposes behind the giving and recording of religious gifts. And their distributional pattern indicates that political objectives were more strongly pursued in Telangana and Rayalasima than in coastal Andhra.

The sociopolitical relations of Kakatiya Andhra can also be studied through a peculiar type of record I call the multiple-act inscription, which records a series of endowments made by different donors on the same day to the same deity. In format this inscription resembles the typical epigraph with its single documented endowment, but the donative core of the record is replicated more than once. Since only one introduction and one concluding set of benedictory-imprecatory verses frame the various donations, it is clear that these endowments were somehow associated, however. Multiple-act inscriptions do not appear at minor temples, since by definition a minor temple received only one endowment during this period. Although their geographical distribution does not correlate exactly with the distribution of minor temples, multiple-act inscriptions are more typical of the hinterland districts and less common at major temples, where they document only 8 percent of all donations.

Since we have 75 multiple-act inscriptions, we have evidence of 75 instances of donative action by affiliated people and groups.[43] They can be classified into three categories on the basis of the relationship between the donors. First of all, in 32 percent of these sets of grouped donations, the individuals are related by ties of kinship or bear the same status title and must have been neighbors or friends. These associations of relatives and friends appear mainly in the coastal region. Instead of such bonds, however, some multiple-act inscriptions uncover associations between people based on political ties. Typically, in this second category, the status of the two (or more) donors was dissimilar and one person was politically subordinate to the other. Many of these inscriptions include donations by collectives such as village organizations and merchant groups which fell under the jurisdiction of a local lord or official. Forty-nine percent of all the multiple-act inscriptions belong to this class. In other words, half the time people came together to engage in religious gifting, they did so not on the basis of shared occupational or kin allegiances but, rather, of some political affiliation. None of the records in this category are found at major temples, and most of them are located in Telangana or the southern coastal districts of Guntur and Prakasam. Very few occur in Vengi. In a third, miscellaneous category comprising 19 percent of the multiple-act inscriptions, the affiliations between donors cannot be identified.

Religious gifting by coalitions of political associates was not always initiated by the person of superior status. In slightly less than half of these cases, the first donor noted in the multiple-act inscription—the one who made the initial gift—was subordinate to another donor (commonly an individual with the title of *mahārāja*, *rāju*, or *nāyaka*). Often the primary donor had founded a new temple, which the overlord then endowed with lands. The overlord's financial support for the institution established by his subordinate was a public acknowledgment of their relationship, as well as a practical means to help the subordinate enhance his local position. When the first donor was superior in status, he was generally the chief of a region or an official in charge of supervising a town. In such instances we frequently find corporate bodies making donations, presumably in order to gain the favor of this official or chief by endowing his favored deity.

The political alliances revealed in Kakatiya-period inscriptions are vertically aligned factions of political superiors and subordinates, not horizontally aligned assemblies of equals from different locales. Participation in vertically structured coalitions of lords and subordinates was far more typical of inland and minor temple donors than of northern coastal and major temple donors and may reflect the greater importance of military associations or war-bands in interior society. A patron of a small local temple might therefore not only be enhancing his own prestige and legitimacy in the locality through an act of religious donation but concurrently be confirming his membership in a powerful political network, usually headed by the Kakatiyas of Warangal. It was the Kakatiya subordinates who engaged in religious gifting, not their overlords, and their interest was in solidifying their positions in the locality. These political motivations contributed to the high level of Kakatiya-period inscriptions noted in chapter 1.

We can now return to an issue raised in a previous section of this chapter—whether all temples were functionally equivalent or homologous. I would argue that this is not the case, for the minor temples are not merely smaller replicas of their more successful major temple counterparts. The social groups associated with the minor temple were distinct from those at major temples and the motives for patronage also diverged. Of the two, the major temple more closely approximates the standard model of the precolonial South Indian temple. Major temples were significant—and nonlanded groups chose to make religious donations to them—because they brought together all the important property-holding communities of the period. The intensity of donative activity at these sites created a pool of wealth drawn from many sectors of society that was parceled out to numerous individuals, pastoralists as well as agriculturalists. By integrating nonlandowning social groups with landed groups, the large pilgrimage temple was a significant channel for the establishment of linkages between various types of peoples. It enabled individuals from many walks of life to participate in a culturally meaningful and honored activity.

Many features of major temples are noticeably lacking when we turn to the smaller temples more characteristic of the Andhra hinterland. Surplus economic resources were contributed by only a small segment of the society of the interior regions and redistributed among a limited number and range of people. The economic networks established by temple patronage in inland Andhra thus involved fewer social groups than in coastal Andhra. Furthermore, the scale of temple economies was far more localized in inland Andhra, since resources were alienated to numerous institutions in a diffuse pattern of temple patronage, in contrast to the centralized foci where gifts accumulated in coastal Andhra. Religious endowments in inland Andhra created linkages mainly among members of local society and particularly among the social groups that controlled land. Unlike the major temple which effected the horizontal integration of socially and geographically diverse peoples, the minor temple integrated a local power structure vertically. Patronizing the two types of temples could lead to radically different effects—this is my chief rationale for insisting that they served different functions.

Because of the broad horizontal integration fostered by large temple complexes, there has been a tendency to view temples as beneficial institutions for the society as a whole. Indeed, the very concept of integration implies a positive force, one that acts to harmonize discordant elements. Yet conflicts in temples over issues of inclusion or precedence in temple rituals are often noted in the secondary literature on colonial India (Appadurai 1981). In the distant past, just as in the recent past, temple patronage was frequently an arena of contention because of the hierarchical sociopolitical relations established in temple worship. Economic redistribution also worked in an unequal manner, for resources were not allocated evenhandedly to all comers. The definition of redistributive exchange postulates a power center toward which goods flow and from which patronage is dispensed. Redistribution by its nature fosters patron-client ties or a hierarchical set of relationships.

Richard G. Fox has criticized the common depiction of the medieval South Indian temple as a "consensus and homeostatic model" and point outs that redistribution of resources is also a strategy for creating inequalities, both economically and politically (Fox and Zagarell 1982: 15–16). Temple patronage, particularly at smaller local temples, was a significant means of articulating the power structure and of suppressing alternate claims. It could lead to a greater stratification of society rather than initiate any form of inclusive and reciprocal interaction. In a recent revisitation of South Pacific exchange systems, Nicholas Thomas rejects many of the earlier romantic assessments of small-scale societies (for which we can substitute "premodern societies"), which are characterized as possessing solidarity, equality, and coherence. Regardless of the size or stage of development in an economy, he asserts that exchange is always implicitly a political process of negotiation (1991: 7, 10). Susan Bayly believes that temple patronage was a form of conquest for South Indian warriors and kings, a fundamentally violent and contentious transaction (1989: 58–61). Perhaps the most elegantly phrased criticism of the earlier model is the following paragraph, penned by V. Narayana Rao, David Shulman, and Sanjay Subrahmanyam to describe South India of the seventeenth century:

> This is not a system of orderly, reciprocal mutuality, or of redistribution rooted in reciprocity—as the political economy of medieval South India is sometimes described, in ideal terms, with the king regulating exchanges through the medium of court and temple—but of symbolic interdependence in a competitive mode which constantly enlarges the circles of political activity and pushes the major actors into new, more elaborate, and more risky exchanges. (1992: 19)

Temples were a public arena in which an ever-increasing number of Andhra people were active over the Kakatiya period. Seeking both to achieve religious goals and to articulate social and political identities, donors had a range of options for their patronage. It is tempting to create models of the institution which stress its homogeneous and harmonious character. But that would collapse the diversity of temple types and gloss over the competitive nature of endowment. Temples, like every other aspect of medieval life, were situated in a context of historical change and thus subject to processes of conflict, contention, and diversity.

Summary: Subregional Patterns of Endowment

Analysis of donative patterns in Kakatiya Andhra highlights the contrasts in the historical development of the coastal subregion as opposed to the interior. While the temple cult was already well-established in coastal Andhra by the beginning of the Kakatiya era, it had not yet spread far into the inland territories. The greater age and sanctity of coastal temples meant that they garnered the lion's share of the religious endowments. We witness a concentrated network of donative activities in coastal Andhra, centered on a relatively small number of temple sites that had established a reputation and built up a varied community of patrons over the centuries. The endowment patterns of the coast changed little over the Kakatiya period, for rates of donative activity remained relatively level and new temples were rarely founded. In contrast, the volume and frequency of religious donations in inland Andhra was rapidly accelerating during the Kakatiya period, as new temples sprang up throughout the landscape. Hence, this was a time of great vitality in the religious culture of inland Andhra, which was experiencing a dramatic expansion of the temple cult.

The dynamism of interior Andhra in terms of temple building and patronage is closely connected to its character as a frontier region. During the Kakatiya era, inland Andhra's economy underwent considerable growth due to the extension of agriculture into uncultivated territories, the boosting of agricultural productivity through the construction of irrigational facilities, and an overall rise in trade—all trends in which the temple as an institution was intimately intertwined. Meanwhile, the social and political systems of the inland territories were still very much in the formative stages. As land and the labor of the populace became more valuable, political stratification intensified with the appearance of local chiefs and military leaders who attempted to assert control over these newly emergent resources, and temple patronage was one means by which they could allocate surpluses to allied or sympathetic groups. Many members of the interior political elites had only recently risen to dominance and hence relied on temple patronage as a crucial source of social prestige and political legitimacy. The diffuse network of donative activities in Telangana and Rayalasima is therefore not only a result of the dispersed settlement patterns, when compared to coastal Andhra, but also of the greater fragmentation and instability of political power in this situation of flux.

Due to the varying ecological, social, and political contexts within which the temple operated, its role was different in coastal Andhra than in the hinterland.

The characteristic institution of the coast was the major pilgrimage temple, whose patronage was broadly based as a result of the well-diversified economy and more complex social organization of this long settled subregion. While political elites were included among the major temple patrons, they were not as prominent as in the interior, perhaps because their claims to lordship were older and more widely acknowledged, thus requiring less validation. Because coastal temples drew on patrons from a large geographical territory and a range of social categories, they functioned as a means of incorporating varied social communities over a wide area. The minor temple of the hinterland, in contrast, had a limited pool of patrons and served rather as a way of strengthening political alliances among social groups that wielded power and authority over land in a restricted, local geographic space.

While I have emphasized the divergences in temple patronage between the dry peninsular interior and the wet coastal zone, I should point out that, from a larger perspective, the expansion of the temple cult into Telangana and Rayalasima also acted as a unifying force. Just as they had done centuries before in coastal Andhra, the people of the inland territories now increasingly participated in forms of religious worship and practice that revolved around the temple and hence resembled practices found widely elsewhere in India. While the specific foci of temple devotion remained largely local, there was a greater commonality in the religious culture of Andhra after the Kakatiya period in that all subregions were now encompassed within the cult of temple worship. The growing popularity of temple patronage should therefore be regarded as one of the processes that contributed to the formation of Andhra as a regional society.

4

The Kakatiya Political Network

The rise and fall of the Kakatiya dynasty marks a distinctive epoch of Andhra's past, a time when much of the Telugu-speaking area was first politically unified and the society's consciousness of itself simultaneously took clearer shape. For an increasing number of people, Andhra was synonymous with the territory controlled by the Kakatiya overlords from their well-fortified capital at Warangal. The expansion of Kakatiya power exemplifies many of the dynamic trends of the late twelfth through early fourteenth centuries, for, as John F. Richards has observed, "the Kakatiya state was a political expression of the settlement of the interior by Telugu warriors" (1975: 4). The accelerating pace of agrarian development in Telangana fueled the rapid growth of a temple-building and inscription-making society. In the vigorous frontier zone of interior Andhra, opportunities for advancement proliferated for merchant-traders, warriors, and agrarian entrepreneurs. Telangana's fighting men were the most loyal supporters of the Kakatiya regime throughout its existence, and they are the ones who spearheaded the Kakatiya conquest of coastal Andhra.

As the influence of the Kakatiya rulers grew in the years between 1175 and 1325, they featured more and more prominently in the records of religious endowment issued in the Telugu linguistic region. Andhra inscriptions of this period abound in references to the names and exploits of the Kakatiya rulers and their allied lords, as well as to the various sorts of political relations that linked numerous donors into the Kakatiya network of power. Aside from the social identities of donors and the nature of their religious gifts, inscriptions are most informative on aspects of political ideology and practice. Indeed, inscriptions are virtually the only sources we have from Andhra before 1500 that allow us to reconstruct some of the actual workings of the political system. The primary material for this chapter, which examines the accomplishments and functioning of the Kakatiya political system, is a corpus of approximately 450 inscriptions. In addition to the two dozen records issued by the Kakatiyas rulers from 1175 onward, this body of inscriptions includes all others that recognize Kakatiya overlordship in one of three ways: by stating that they were governing, by situating the donor in relation to them, or by transferring the merit of a gift to them.

The Kakatiyas are specifically cited as the ruling dynasty in the beginning portion of many Andhra inscriptions. The reference to them often occurs in the phrase "while the Mahamandaleshvara Kakatiya X Maharaja was ruling the earth enjoying friendly interchanges" (*sukha-saṅkathā-vinōdambulam brithvi-rājyambu sēyucuṇḍaṅgān*). This formula, widely adopted in areas of the Deccan that had formerly come under the sway of the Kalyani Chalukyas, was typically inserted into an inscription immediately after the date. Kakatiya sovereignty was not universally alluded to, however, even within the core areas of dynastic power, for the majority of Andhra inscriptions say nothing whatsoever about who was ruling.[1] In this respect, Andhra inscriptions are quite different from those of Tamil Nadu, in which the name of the king is routinely provided because regnal dating systems are used. Regnal eras are seldom witnessed in the Deccan, where the normal practice was to express dates in terms of years in the Shaka era. Since this meant that the overlord's name did not have to be stated in Andhra inscriptions, any occurrence of a reference to the Kakatiyas can be understood as meaningful. That is, acknowledgment of Kakatiya sovereignty was not just a formal convention but also an indication that the person commissioning the inscription had some involvement or contact with the Kakatiya political network.

A second, and more explicit, way by which political relations with the Kakatiyas are often made manifest in inscriptions is in connection with the donor's social identity. A substantial number of donors describe themselves as the political subordinates of the Kakatiyas, either through official titles like general and minister or with phrases indicating personal subservience to the rulers. Because their association with the Kakatiyas was such an important element in the public selves whom they display in inscriptions, these individuals were undoubtedly active members of the Kakatiya ruling elite. A third manner in which the Kakatiyas frequently figure within Andhra inscriptions is as recipients of the merit accruing from a religious gift. Rather than retaining the spiritual benefit of a charitable endowment for themselves, in other words, many donors generously transferred it to the Kakatiya overlords, whose favor they were presumably seeking through this act. Political relations are hence integral to other aspects of social life that we have covered in chapters 2 and 3—inscriptional donors frequently expressed their public identities in terms of their ties to the king and had political objectives for donating religious gifts.

For the sake of convenience, all inscriptions that recognize the sovereignty of the Kakatiyas—whether simply by naming them as the ruling dynasty, through the more intimate connections implied by the transference of merit, or by the claim to hold a position of rank within their political network—will be referred to collectively as Kakatiya records, although only a fraction were the direct products of the dynasty. Several crucial aspects of Kakatiya polity are only tangentially illuminated by these sources, whose ostensible objective was to document religious endowments. The full range of a subordinate's obligations to his overlord, the exact workings of the revenue system, and the precise methods by which local communities were incorporated into the state are among the issues that remain obscure. But there are many insights on medieval polity that inscriptions can still be coaxed into yielding, if one only makes the effort. The processes of state-formation can be tracked through the mapping of inscriptional find-spots over time, for instance. We can also learn something about the structure of the political elite, by systematically analyzing the inscriptional donors who held titles of rank or office. Another untapped dimension of inscriptions as a historical resource is their ideological content—inscriptional eulogies and epithets are a rich mine of symbols, images, and conceptions concerning kingship and warriorhood. In the following pages, I employ these and other approaches to the Kakatiya corpus of inscriptions in a wide-ranging discussion of the Kakatiya rulers and their warrior-based network of power. The vexing question of how to categorize the medieval Indic state, which has consumed so much scholarly energy over the past few decades, is addressed at the conclusion of this chapter.

Expansion of Kakatiya Power

When the Kakatiyas first surface in the historical record, in the mid eleventh century, they are a minor family of chiefs entrenched in the town of Hanumakonda who rule its vicinity in Warangal District.[2] Inscriptional genealogies suggest that the Kakatiyas may have been active in Telangana as far back as the tenth century, but their earlier activities are obscure. By the eleventh century, however, the Kakatiyas were among the several Telangana chiefs who accepted the overlordship of the Kalyani Chalukyas and issued their inscriptions in Kannada, following the conventional format used throughout the sphere of Chalukya hegemony. Aside from fighting other petty chieftains in Telangana, the Kakatiyas also participated in the military campaigns launched by the powerful Chalukya emperors Someshvara I and Vikramaditya VI outside Andhra. Meanwhile, coastal Andhra was dominated by the imperial Cholas of the Tamil country, to whom the minor local chiefs paid their subservience. This situation persisted until the mid twelfth century, when both the Kalyani Chalukya and imperial Chola empires declined, which left behind a political vacuum in Andhra.

Kakatiya Rudradeva, who became head of the lineage in 1158, took advantage of the changed political circumstances to launch the dynasty on a rapid and aggressive program of expansion. Soon after he came to power, Rudradeva had the Thousand Pillared temple built in Hanumakonda, then the Kakatiya capital. The Sanskrit inscription recording its foundation in 1163 contains an elaborate genealogy of Rudradeva's ancestry as well as an extensive account of his military accomplishments (HAS 13.3). Since it was the earliest of Rudradeva's inscriptions to omit any mention of the Chalukya dynasty of Kalyani, we can assume that the construction of the temple was meant to mark Rudradeva's new status as an overlord in his own right. From this time on, the Kakatiyas are always portrayed in inscriptions as the paramount power, and so 1163 C.E. is generally understood as the beginning point of Kakatiya independence. Over the next thirty years, Rudradeva conducted a series of victorious military campaigns within Telangana, aimed primarily at other local chiefs who had also once been subordinate to the Kalyani Chalukyas. By the end of his reign, Kakatiya military supremacy within this subregion of Andhra was firmly established.

The enhanced stature of the Kakatiyas as a subregional power is reflected in the new fort constructed by Rudradeva at Warangal, which became the Kakatiya capital no later than 1195 (IAP-W.42). Warangal is located only four miles from the original Kakatiya stronghold of Hanumakonda. But whereas Hanumakonda fort is situated among hilly outcrops that both defended it and limited its growth, Warangal is on a relatively flat expanse of land with plenty of room to expand. Indeed, the outer fortifications were considerably extended by a later Kakatiya king, Ganapati, who added two sets of earthen ramparts surrounding the inner stone fort (Venkataramanayya and Somasekhara Sarma 1960: 595–615; Parabrahma Sastry 1978: 173). But the fort proper seems to have been laid out in Rudradeva's day, for its various neighborhoods were named after towns that Rudradeva had conquered on his way to success (EI 3.15, v. 9). At the heart of Rudradeva's new capital lay the temple of Svayambhudeva, of which nothing remains today but a group of pillars and the four gateways that stood at its entrances (Radhakrishna Sarma 1972: 109).[3] Inscriptions composed from 1172 onward frequently describe the Kakatiyas as devotees of this Shaiva god, whom a literary text of the early fourteenth century labels as the tutelary deity (*kulapatidēva*) of the lineage.[4] Hence the new and improved capital of the independent Kakatiya kings also housed a god who was closely associated with the dynasty.

Rudradeva's activities extended outside of Telangana as well. He is thought to have participated in the conflict in Guntur District that has been immortalized in *Palnāṭi Vīrula Katha* and to have conquered two princely families there, the Kotas and the Kondapadmatis. Rudradeva's own inscriptions prove that he visited the coastal territories, for he made an endowment at the Tripurantakam temple in Prakasam District in 1185 and one to Draksharama's Bhimeshvara temple in East Godavari District the following year.[5] But there is little evidence that Rudradeva's expeditions into the coastal Andhra districts of Guntur and East Godavari had a significant impact, since no other inscriptions in these localities cite Rudradeva subsequently.[6] Rudradeva was followed on the throne by his younger brother Mahadeva, whose brief reign of three years ended in 1199 during the course of a military campaign against the Yadava dynasty from the western Deccan. Mahadeva left behind only one inscription, which records a gift made at one of Srisailam's "gateway" temples, Umamaheshvaram (IAP–N 1.61).

Because their eventual control over both the interior and coastal subregions is such a critical aspect of the Kakatiyas' historical significance, any narrative of their political history should simultaneously track the geographic dimensions of their rise to power. The best way to determine the territory encompassed by a medieval South Indian state is by mapping the find-spots of inscriptions that refer to the dynasty, but this time-consuming approach is seldom pursued (Spencer and Hall 1974). It yields a far more accurate picture of the area controlled by a polity than does the standard methodology, which relies on the claims of conquest found in the *praśasti* portions of inscriptions or in later genealogies. Since *praśastis* are by definition eulogies, they are patently unreliable for the purpose of establishing the extent of a kingdom. Genealogies are even more prone to exaggerate the degree of military success enjoyed by a royal lineage. The materiality of inscriptions, on the other hand, provides irrefutable proof of a dynasty's influence in practice and enables us to accurately plot the vicissitudes of dynastic fortune.

The mapping of early Kakatiya inscriptions confirms that their sphere of influence was confined to Telangana. The shaded areas in map 10 indicate the taluks in which inscriptions citing the Kakatiyas were issued from 1175 through 1198. Aside from the two peripheral taluks where Rudradeva's endowments were made to the

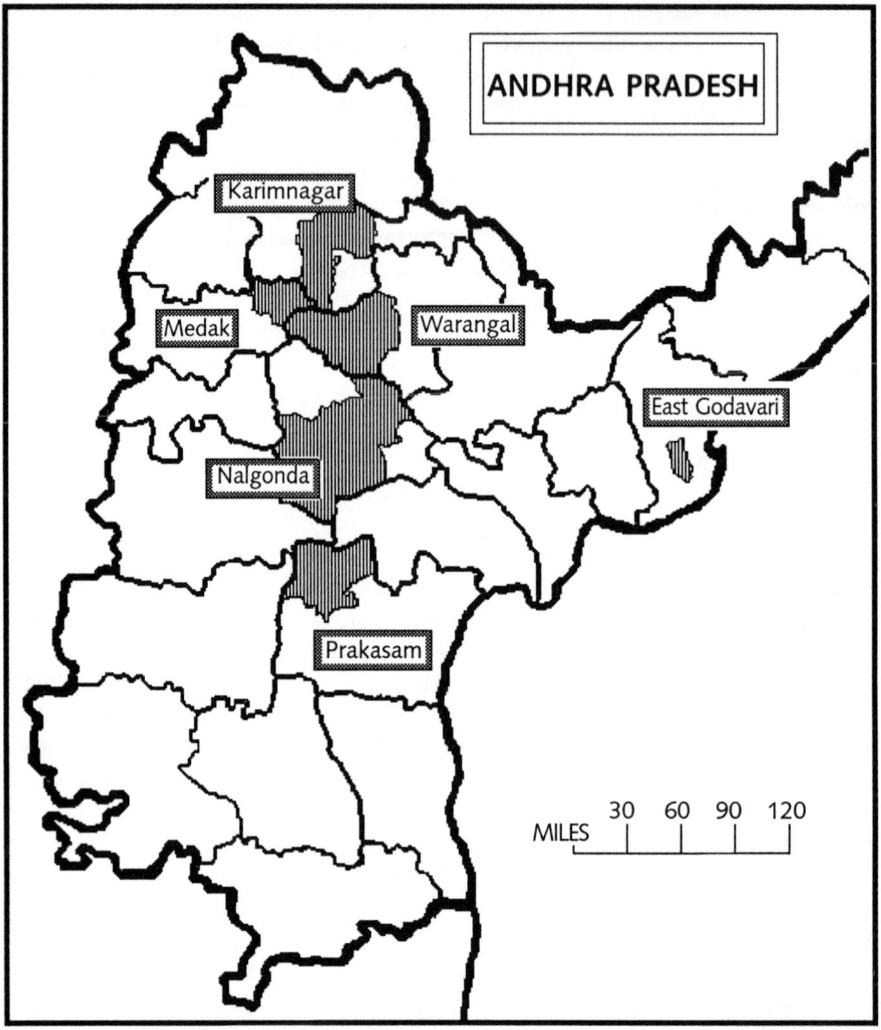

Map 10. Kakatiya Records, 1175–1198

Draksharama and Tripurantakam temples, the remaining taluks extend along a north-south axis from the Kakatiya capital in the western portion of Warangal District. Even within Telangana, only the central portion was firmly under Kakatiya control. If consolidated, Kakatiya territory from 1175 through 1198 would not comprise much more than the area of a modern district. But under Rudradeva and Mahadeva, the foundations had been laid for the rapid growth of the Kakatiya sphere of influence that would occur in the thirteenth century.

Only in the time of Mahadeva's son Ganapatideva do a sizable number of records that mention the Kakatiyas begin to appear outside of Telangana. Ganapati, the third independent sovereign, was the one responsible for making the Kakatiyas a statewide power during his long reign of over six decades (1199–1262). Soon after ascending the throne, he launched an attack on coastal Andhra. Within a decade Ganapati controlled the area around the mouth of the Krishna River (modern Divi Taluk) and the coastal territory immediately south of it. In the process, he displaced the Velanati Chodas, the most powerful lineage in the fertile deltaic area of the Krishna and Godavari Rivers known as Vengi. But the Eastern Ganga dynasty of Kalinga, who were firmly entrenched in Andhra northeast of the Godavari River, also sought to bring Vengi under their control. Frustrated in his ambitions in the northern direction by the presence of the Eastern Gangas, Ganapati turned his attention toward the south. His second southern campaign, launched in the late 1240s, succeeded in penetrating northern Tamil Nadu and, according to inscriptional eulogies, led to much territorial acquisition in southwestern Andhra. In the very last years of his reign, however, Ganapati suffered a serious reverse when a coalition of armies led by the Pandyas of the Tamil country wrested control of most of Andhra south of the Krishna River away from the Kakatiyas and their allies.

The geographic expansion of Kakatiya influence over the more than sixty years of Ganapati's rule is illustrated in map 11. To begin with, Ganapati considerably extended Kakatiya sway in the subregion of Telangana. Inscriptions issued in most taluks of Karimnagar, Warangal, and Nalgonda Districts now acknowledged Kakatiya overlordship, which also reached into Khammam and Mahbubnagar Districts for the first time. More important, Ganapati made major inroads into the central coastal districts of Guntur, Prakasam, and Krishna. This southern part of the deltaic area, along the Krishna River, yields the main concentration of Kakatiya records during Ganapati's time, since the northeastern sector was dominated by the Eastern Gangas. Ganapati's activities in southern Andhra are also reflected in the spread of Kakatiya inscriptions into Rayalasima, for parts of Kurnool and Cuddapah Districts were brought into the Kakatiya political network for the first time while he was king. All in all, Ganapati established the Kakatiyas as an important force throughout Andhra. From a small central Telangana realm in the late twelfth century, the Kakatiya dominion had grown to encompass roughly half of modern Andhra Pradesh by the mid thirteenth century.

Ganapati's greatest achievement was his establishment of a secondary center for the Kakatiyas in the coastal districts of Guntur and Prakasam. The importance of Guntur and Prakasam in Ganapati's geopolitical program is evidenced by the king's decision to make 10 of his own 13 religious beneficences in these two districts.[7] They include the only temple we know that Ganapati built, at Motupalli. Motupalli is the port in Prakasam District where Ganapati left behind a famous proclamation that promised safety and security to all traders arriving by sea (EI 12.22) and was clearly a flourishing trade center in this era. Although the inscription recording the founding of Ganapati's temple at Motupalli is undated, internal references suggest it was composed in 1249 (Venkatasubba Ayyar 1947–48: 193). The events described in the record relate mainly to Ganapati's campaigns in support of the Telugu Choda prince Manuma Siddhi II, who had been ousted from his kingdom in southern coastal Andhra. Ganapati personally went as far south as Nellore town, Manuma Siddhi's former capital, and sent an army further on into the Tamil country. This marked the greatest penetration of southern territory during Ganapati's reign. His Motupalli temple must have been built soon after his return from Nellore, where

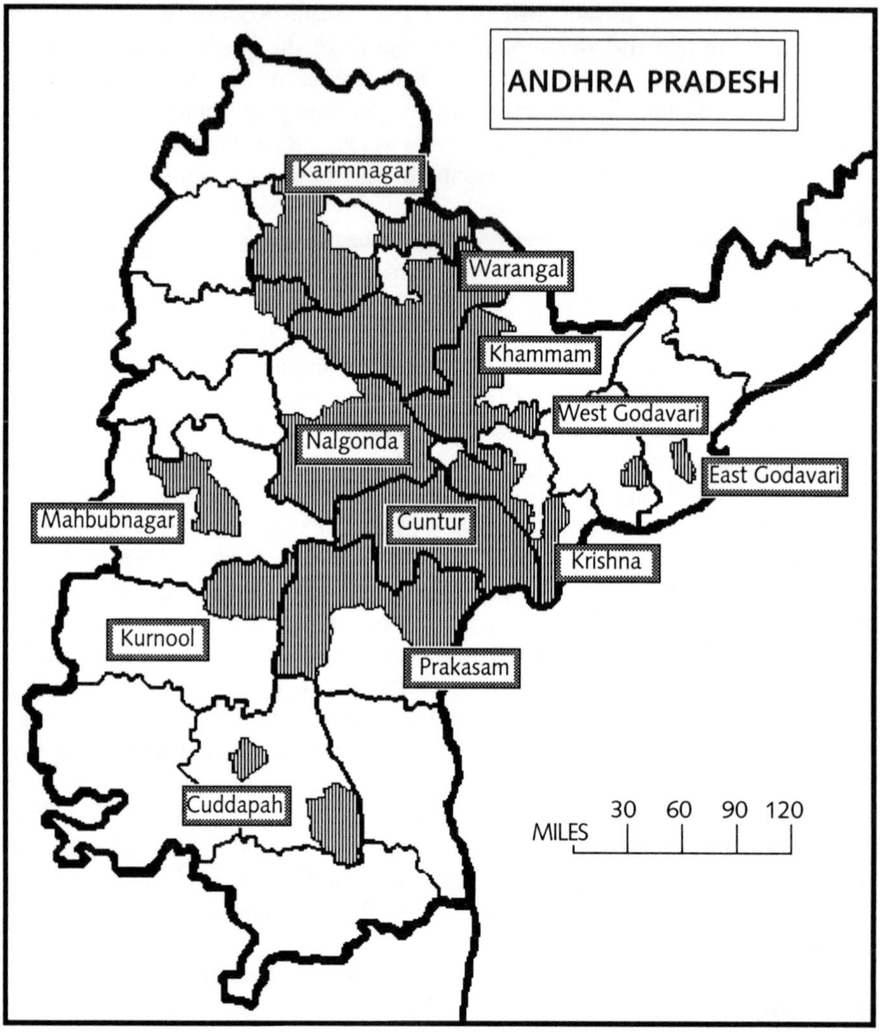

Map 11. Kakatiya Records from Ganapati's Reign, 1199–1262

he had reinstated Manuma Siddhi to the throne. But there are no other references in Kakatiya-period sources to Ganapati's temple, which appears to have quickly lapsed into obscurity.[8] If Ganapati was trying to create a royal religious center in the new Kakatiya territory along the coast, his attempt must be deemed a failure.

Ganapati followed in his uncle Rudradeva's footsteps not only in founding a new temple, but also in extending his patronage to several famous temples. Like Rudradeva, Ganapati personally made endowments to the deities at Tripurantakam and Yeleshvaram. He also had one of his generals make a gift of a village to the Ekamranatha temple at Kanchipuram, after a Kakatiya victory against the Telugu Choda king Vijayaganda Gopala in 1249 C.E. This gift after conquest was another typically royal gesture—a means of publicly proclaiming one's might and of redistributing newly acquired resources (in this instance, a village in Chingleput District, Tamil Nadu). Other major pilgrimage temples in Andhra were brought more indirectly into the Kakatiya sphere of influence through Ganapati's support of the leaders of the Golaki Matha, a Shaiva Siddhanta sectarian organization that originated in Madhya Pradesh. The prestige they acquired from serving as Ganapati's spiritual teachers (*rājaguru*) enabled two successive abbots of the Golaki Matha to set up a series of *maṭhas* (sectarian institutes) at important pilgrimage sites like Srisailam and its eastern "gateway" Tripurantakam in the mid thirteenth century (Talbot 1987). A village in Guntur District was also given to the second leader Vishveshvara-shiva as an *agrahāra* by Ganapati in a grant that he made jointly with his daughter Rudramadevi (SII 10.395). Because Golaki Matha ascendancy at well-known religious centers gave its leaders considerable control over temple resources, Kakatiya patronage of the Golaki Matha could be interpreted as a royal attempt to infiltrate temple networks indirectly. But it did not last much beyond Ganapati's reign, for his successors made no attempt to associate themselves with the Golaki Matha.

Of all the Kakatiya rulers, Ganapati was hence the most prominent patron of religion. He both made more endowments and directed them to a wider variety of recipients than did any other Kakatiya monarch. Ganapati's patronage of temples was particularly wide-ranging, for he founded his own institution in addition to endowing revered pilgrimage temples and making gifts to sectarian leaders. He was also the only Kakatiya ruler to grant *agrahāra* villages to brahmans and to record his patronage of brahmans on copper plates—both uniquely royal activities. There are other signs, besides his vigorous religious patronage, that Ganapati aspired to an imperial style of kingship. Only in some of Ganapati's inscriptions do we find an attempt to elevate the Kakatiya *varṇa* status from *śūdra* to *kṣatriya* by linking the family to the Puranic genealogy of the solar line of ancient Indian kings (e.g., EI 12.22; SII 10.395). Ganapati also occasionally assumed the imperial title *mahārājādhirāja* (king of kings; e.g., SII 10.407), whereas the other Kakatiyas were content with the title *mahāmaṇḍalēśvara* (great tributary lord), which they had borne since the days of their subservience to the Kalyani Chalukyas. Ganapati, who transformed the Kakatiya realm from a subregional power to the paramount polity of Andhra, thus tried to project a royal image that was commensurate with his newly enlarged territory. We witness the beginnings of a new style of kingship for the Kakatiyas under Ganapati, one that emulated the lofty imperial grandeur of the Chola and Chalukyas. The imperial formation in the making was never to achieve fruition, however, for his successors adopted radically different strategies in their bid for power, as the following discussion shows.

Ganapatideva was followed on the throne by his daughter Rudramadevi (r. 1263–1289).[9] She ascended the throne under difficult circumstances, since much of southern Andhra had just been lost to the Pandyas of Tamil Nadu and their allies. Further military threats confronted her soon after she became queen, from the Eastern Gangas of Kalinga (northeastern Andhra) and the Yadavas of the western Deccan. Rudramadevi dealt with both successfully: first she led an expedition into Yadava territory that extended Kakatiya influence in western Andhra, and later she repelled the Eastern Gangas to a position north of the Godavari River in the late 1270s. But internal opposition to her rule from the Kayastha chief Ambadeva

II was more difficult to overcome. Although both Rudrama and Ganapati had relied on earlier Kayastha family members in their military campaigns, Ambadeva began to challenge Kakatiya overlordship as soon as he took over as head of the Kayastha lineage in 1273. Ambadeva's power increased throughout Rudramadevi's reign until he eventually controlled much of southwestern Andhra as well as portions of Guntur District. Rudramadevi may have died fighting against him in 1289 and it was not until a few years later that Ambadeva was finally subdued.[10]

In short, Rudramadevi's reign was a period of setbacks for the Kakatiyas during which their sphere of influence shrank. The fairly compact distribution of inscriptions that cite Rudramadevi's name, found primarily in central Andhra, is revealed by the shaded area in map 12. Few localities either north of the Krishna River or in southern

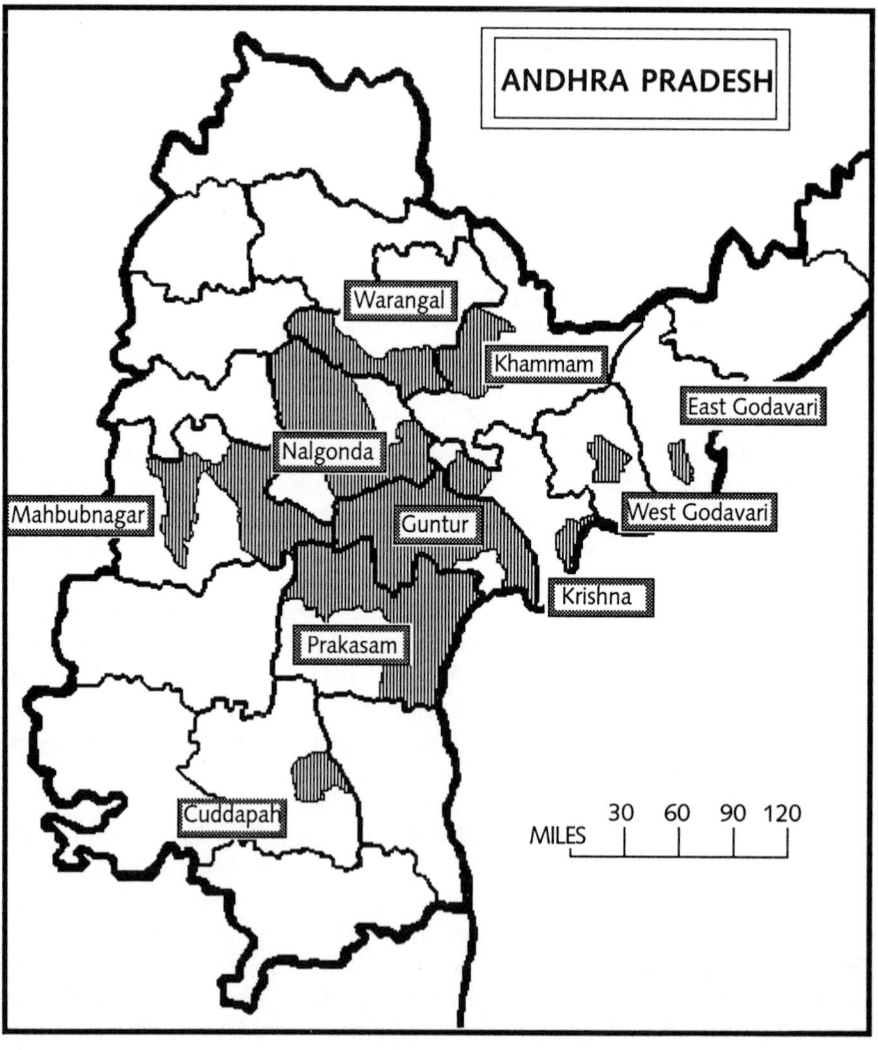

Map 12. Kakatiya Records from Rudramadevi's Reign, 1263–1289

Andhra acknowledged the Kakatiyas as sovereigns, and their control had diminished in northern Telangana as well. Rudramadevi herself is scarcely visible in the historical documentation, for she made only two charitable donations to temples, one directly and another through an intermediary (NDI Ongole 143; IAP-N 1.85). Rudramadevi also abandoned Ganapati's other efforts to enhance the Kakatiya royal prestige through the appropriation of imperial titles and genealogies. Instead, she concentrated on projecting an image of martial heroism, going so far as to adopt a masculine persona and, it would appear, leading her troops in battle (Talbot 1995b).

The Kakatiya fortunes were recouped under Rudramadevi's grandson, Prataparudra (r. 1290–1323), who gradually reasserted Kakatiya dominance in southern Andhra, conquering not only the Kayastha chief Ambadeva but also other chiefs who had been entrenched in Rayalasima in alliance with the Pandyas since the last years of Ganapati's reign. By around 1315, the Kakatiyas were strong enough to defeat a Pandya army near the town of Kanchipuram in Tamil Nadu. Meanwhile, however, Prataparudra was faced with a new military threat from northern India. He was first forced to pay tribute to Ala-ud-din Khalji, the Delhi sultan, after the successful siege of Warangal fort by the Khalji general Malik Kafur in 1310. Ritual submission to his new overlord was also required of Prataparudra, who had to accept a robe of honor from the Delhi sultan and agree to bow in his direction (Eaton 1997). The expedition against the Pandyas was another result of Prataparudra's defeat in 1310, for it was instigated by the Delhi sultan although largely fought by Prataparudra's own forces. Prataparudra apparently stopped remitting tribute to Delhi regularly, however, for another Khalji army was sent against Warangal in 1318 and he had once again to pay tribute and ritually acknowledge his subordination. Warangal was finally seized in 1323 after two more sieges within a year's time. Prataparudra died soon thereafter while in captivity, bringing about an abrupt end to both the Kakatiya dynasty and kingdom.

Although Prataparudra failed the ultimate test of kingship by losing his realm to an enemy, he was in some ways the greatest of the Kakatiya rulers. For one thing, Kakatiya inscriptions reached their maximum territorial extent during his reign. Records referring to Prataparudra appeared in more localities (map 13) than had been the case when Ganapati was king (map 11), despite the fact that Ganapati ruled almost twice as long. Particularly noteworthy are the inclusion of areas in southwestern and northwestern Andhra which had never before come under Kakatiya influence. Kakatiya Andhra in Prataparudra's time (map 13) is thus only slightly smaller than the territory covered by Telugu inscriptions during the entire Kakatiya period (see gray area on map 6 in chapter 1). The mapping of inscriptional distributions in space only tells us about a king's horizontal reach, however, and not about how pervasive his power was within the territory where it was exercised. The frequency with which a sovereign's name is cited, on the other hand, allows us to gauge the magnitude of Kakatiya authority. Prataparudra far exceeds his predecessors by this measure as well, for a much larger percentage of inscriptions from his era cite his name than was true earlier.

The statistics in table 11 clearly demonstrate the steady increase in the proportion of Telugu and/or Sanskrit inscriptions referring to the Kakatiyas from the time of Rudradeva and Mahadeva onward, within the fourteen districts of modern Andhra

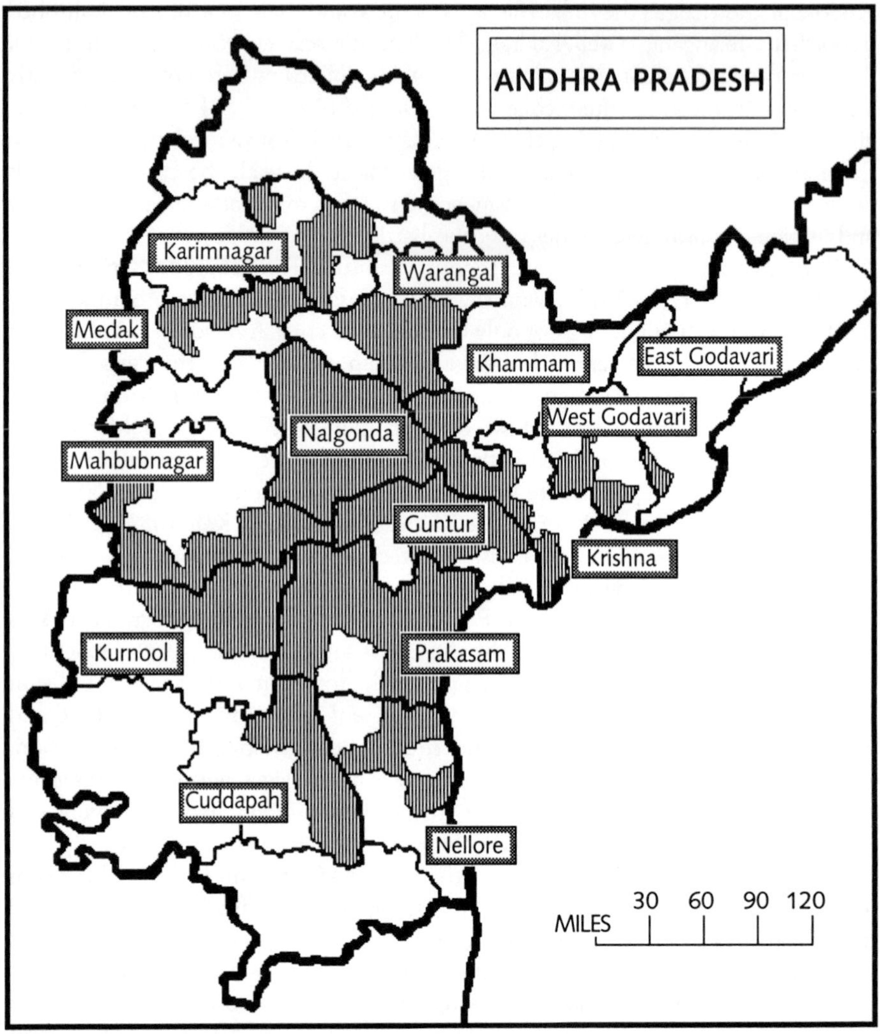

Map 13. Kakatiya Records from Prataparudra's Reign, 1290–1324

Pradesh that would eventually comprise the Kakatiya polity.[11] The 9 percent figure for Rudradeva and Mahadeva is not surprising, given how small a territory they controlled. It is more significant that Rudramadevi was mentioned by a larger percentage of donors than Ganapati, in spite of her restricted geographical sphere of operation. Even more dramatic is the situation while Prataparudra was king. Forty-four percent of all inscriptions issued during his reign allude to the Kakatiyas as compared to between 24 and 27 percent in Ganapati's time. The territory they ruled was roughly comparable in size, yet people commissioning inscriptions felt the need to link themselves publicly with Prataparudra considerably more often than they had with Ganapati. Moreover, Prataparudra attained widespread recognition as sovereign without engaging in the typical strategies for enhancing

Table 11. Allegiance to the Kakatiyas by Regnal Periods

Dates	Ruler	All Records No.	Kakatiya Records No.	Other Records No.	Kakatiya Records %
1175–1198	Rudradeva & Mahadeva	98	9	89	9
1199–1230	Ganapati	213	51	162	24
1231–1262	Ganapati	353	94	259	27
1263–1289	Rudramadevi	223	68	155	30
1290–1324	Prataparudra	292	128	164	44
All periods		1,179	350	829	30%

royal legitimacy.[12] He retained the humble title of *mahāmaṇḍalēśvara* used also by many of his professed subordinates and never pretended to have *kṣatriya* origins. Nor did he found a royal temple or patronize brahmans. Even his endowments to established temples were modest in scale, comprising two direct gifts and another two made by subordinates on his order.[13] Among them is a second Kakatiya example of a gift made after conquest, in that the granting of an Andhra village to the Sriranganatha temple in the Kaveri River delta of Tamil Nadu commemorated the Kakatiya victory against the Pandyas (EA 4.13; EI 27.48.).

This survey of the geographic expansion of Kakatiya power has shown how quickly the dynasty expanded from the late twelfth century onward. The ancestral lands of the Kakatiyas in Warangal District were an area of moderate rainfall as compared to the arid expanse of western Telangana or much of Rayalasima. Although the extension of irrigational facilities during the Kakatiya era further augmented the productive capacity of central Telangana, it could never offer the yields produced by the alluvial soils of the coast. The attempts by Kakatiya rulers from the time of Rudradeva onward to extend their control over the more fertile coastal territories were therefore motivated by a desire to augment their resource base. In achieving their aims, however, the Kakatiyas reversed the patterns of the previous millennium, for the paramount power in Andhra had previously always been based in the coastal delta formed by the Krishna and Godavari Rivers. Subsequently, there would be other polities based in the interior which too would gain dominion over the coast.

Although the Kakatiyas eventually became an all-Andhra power, the intensity of their control varied considerably from area to area. Throughout their existence, central Telangana continued to display the most consistent level of allegiance to the Kakatiyas. This is demonstrated in table 12, which displays the percentage of Kakatiya inscriptions in each district, in descending order.[14] Warangal, the Kakatiya homeland, ranks the highest, unsurprisingly, followed by the four districts adjacent to it—Karimnagar, Medak, Nalgonda, and Khammam. A secondary zone of control was established in the coastal districts of Guntur and Prakasam, which fall into the intermediate range with about 40 percent of all their inscriptions citing the Kakatiyas. Numerically, however, Guntur and Prakasam Districts yield the highest

Table 12. Allegiance to the Kakatiyas by District

	All Records	Kakatiya Records	
Districts	No.	No.	%
Warangal	34	29	85
Medak	6	5	83
Karimnagar	11	8	73
Nalgonda	74	49	66
Khammam	12	7	58
Kurnool	21	11	52
Mahbubnagar	39	19	49
Prakasam	207	83	40
Guntur	270	99	37
Cuddapah	47	9	19
Krishna	145	17	12
E. Godavari	94	8	9
Nellore	55	2	4
W. Godavari	164	4	2
Total/Average	1,179	350	30%

quantity of Kakatiya records, which reflects the vigorous scale of Kakatiya activity there. Elsewhere along the coast, the Kakatiya position was far weaker. But no other indigenous polity of the precolonial era made its presence felt throughout the Telugu linguistic area in the manner of the Kakatiyas.

Even at its peak under Prataparudra, however, the sphere of Kakatiya influence was considerably smaller than historical maps generally suggest. The *Historical Atlas of South Asia* (Schwartzberg 1978: 147), for instance, situates the boundaries of the Kakatiya state at its maximum extent much farther to the northeast, west, and south than is the case in map 13. To be sure, the Kakatiyas did send military expeditions into the territories of the Eastern Gangas, Yadavas, and Pandya kings and, in the course of their campaigns, Kakatiya armies left behind a handful of inscriptions in places such as Bidar (Karnataka) and Kanchipuram (Tamil Nadu). But the goal of their military expeditions was not the annexation of territory and there is no sign of long-lasting Kakatiya influence in these areas. Standard techniques of mapping political boundaries have inflated the size of the area controlled by the Kakatiyas, as well as by many other precolonial dynasties. They also ignore the reality that large expanses of medieval South India were never incorporated into a major polity.

Any attempt to delineate the boundaries of a medieval South Indian state is inherently misleading, of course, for it implies that borders were fixed and that a dynasty's control within the territory was absolute. At best, we can speak only of spheres of influence that constantly fluctuated in size and intensity. But maps based on the distributions of inscriptions show us where people who participated in a polity were based, and this network of people constituted the premodern state—not a geographic territory in and of itself. More mapping of this nature is imperative if we are ever to shed our tendency to regard premodern Indian polities as akin to modern nation-states with their clearly demarcated spatial dimensions and uniform degree of control.

Royal Religious Patronage and Dharmic Kingship

Over the past quarter century, Western scholars have identified royal patronage of religion as a critical element in medieval South Indian state formation. Since the nationalist model of a bureaucratic state that maintained control via a well-articulated administrative apparatus and a large standing army is now largely discredited, scholars look elsewhere for an explanation of how medieval polities gained their ascendance, and the abundance of religious activity attested to in inscriptions makes it a logical candidate. Consequently, scholars point to the increase in a king's symbolic resources which resulted from religious benefaction and allege that the legitimacy of a dynasty's right to rule was confirmed when sovereigns conspicuously followed normative injunctions to give generously. Kings could acquire some of the prestige of the brahmans and temples whom they patronized and thereby reinforce the precarious physical bases of their control. Religious patronage is thus seen as *a*, if not *the*, major means of enhancing royal authority (Spencer 1969; Appadurai and Breckenridge 1976).

Royal support of religion might take a variety of forms, as we saw in the case of Kakatiya Ganapati (Kulke 1978c: 131–37). The greatest scholarly attention has been paid to the founding of new temples in royal centers, as was done by Rajaraja I of the Chola dynasty at Tanjavur in the beginning of the eleventh century. The construction of an imperial temple not only glorified the royal dynasty but also created new redistributive networks directly under its control. The establishment of brahman villages was a second means of augmenting royal power. By seeding these settlements in the various parts of their kingdoms, rulers obtained loyal allies at the same time that they exhibited their own piety. The lavish endowment of pilgrimage sites renowned in the region was a third type of religious patronage, conferring great visibility on the king as patron. Last, late medieval lords often channeled their patronage to temples through the sectarian organizations that increasingly controlled temple administration (Appadurai 1977).[15]

Contrary to what one might expect from the secondary literature, we have seen that the religious patronage of the Kakatiyas was quite limited. Altogether, the five independent Kakatiya rulers left behind 26 inscriptions documenting their religious gifts, a paltry number indeed considering the 150-year span of their rule. Rudradeva made six of these grants, while Mahadeva made one. Ganapati was the closest to an exemplary royal donor with his twelve acts of religious patronage made on his own and another in conjunction with his successor Rudramadevi. He engaged in the full range of royal forms of religious patronage—the setting up of brahman villages, founding of a new temple, endowment of revered pilgrimage temples, and patronage of sectarian leaders. But subsequently, the Kakatiya rates of endowment declined precipitously, with Rudramadevi accounting for only two royal gifts and Prataparudra for four. Neither Rudrama nor Prataparudra ever commissioned a new temple, even though Prataparudra controlled at least as much territory as had Ganapati. Never munificent at its best, the extent of Kakatiya royal gifting apparently did not correspond to the size of the polity.

Despite the restricted volume of Kakatiya religious patronage, we can still discern a general pattern in the timing and placement of their gifts. This is most noticeable in relation to the founding of royal temples, which visibly marked important milestones in the dynasty's growth. The first was Rudradeva's assertion of independence from Chalukya overlordship, commemorated by the construction of the Thousand Pillared Temple in Hanumakonda. His attainment of military supremacy in Telangana was signified by the construction of a new capital, Warangal, in the center of which stood a temple to the Kakatiya tutelary deity Svayambhudeva.[16] Ganapati's temple at Motupalli similarly followed his greatest military feat, the deep penetration of Tamil territory, and it was situated in one of the more southerly localities under Ganapati's control at the time. Once a region was firmly under Kakatiya dominion, however, the rulers made little effort to patronize institutions or individuals within that area. No Kakatiya ruler after Rudradeva made any endowments to temples in the Warangal-Karimnagar home base. Indeed, only three subsequent gifts were made anywhere in Telangana (IAP-N 1.61 and 85; ARE 132 of 1954–55, all in Nalgonda District).[17] Having established their credentials as royal donors in Telangana with Rudradeva's initial gifts, the Kakatiya rulers obviously felt it was unnecessary to reinforce their status. Instead, Ganapati made almost all of his donations to brahmans and temples in Prakasam and Guntur Districts. He was the first Kakatiya king to permanently annex territory in this central coastal zone, which I describe as the secondary core of Kakatiya polity. Perhaps because Guntur and Prakasam Districts were not as staunchly under their control as Telangana, Rudramadevi and Prataparudra continued to patronize institutions there, albeit on a lesser scale.

Royal donations are similarly rare in other areas of the medieval South. James Heitzman's comprehensive examination of 2,400 inscriptions from five subregions of Tamil Nadu during the Chola era uncovered only 12 that recorded gifts from the Chola kings (1997: 145). Their wives and sisters were considerably more active in this respect. Yet even if we add in the gifts made by female family members, the total number of Chola donations is a mere 68. During the approximately 350 years from 849 to 1279 C.E. that Heitzman investigated, Chola royal family patronage never constituted more than 6 percent of all inscriptions in any of the roughly century-long subperiods (1997: 147). Heitzman also observes that the majority of royal donations were made in the first half of the Chola period, when the dynasty was still in the process of building up its power. In the same way, the early Kakatiya kings were the more vigorous donors, patronizing a variety of institutions and individuals as well as sponsoring the construction of Shiva temples in their capitals. But religious patronage was not essential to the maintenance of political power for either dynasty. The Cholas eventually resorted to more direct methods of consolidating their power (Heitzman 1997: 160–61), while the later Kakatiya rulers also adopted new strategies of political control (a point that will soon be elaborated).

Heitzman's analysis of Chola donations is particularly significant because these kings are the prototype for Burton Stein's influential model of ritual sovereignty (Stein 1980: 254–365). According to Stein, Chola sovereignty took two distinct forms. In their core area that consisted of the Kaveri River delta, the Cholas exercised direct mastery through military means. While actual physical control was restricted to the central portion of their polity, the Cholas possessed a ritual hegemony—a more intangible form of dominion—over a much larger area. Stein initially asserted that Chola ritual sovereignty was exercised via a royal Shiva cult emanating from the imperial temples founded by Rajaraja I and Rajendra I, which encompassed a loosely knit network of Shiva temples throughout the South Indian macroregion. It was a religiously based authority, in other words, and quite distinct from the typical political power obtained through military might. Stein has gone farther than any other scholar in asserting that religious patronage was *the* constitutive element in medieval sovereignty. In more recent publications, however, he retracted both his conception of ritual as necessarily religious in character and his differentiation of two separate ritual and political domains.[18]

Hermann Kulke is another scholar who has, along with Stein, stressed the importance of royal religious patronage in medieval state formation. Instead of trying to create new royal cults, however, the kings of Orissa whom Kulke studied won the allegiance of tribal peoples by appropriating the worship of their gods. The most successful religious policy was pursued by the medieval Eastern Ganga dynasty (Kulke 1978a), whose patronage of pilgrimage temples created vertical linkages that joined the various subregions within their kingdom. Unfortunately, Kulke is every bit as vague as Stein on how the linkages actually functioned in integrating the polity.[19] But Kulke then makes the important point that religious gifting by medieval kings also fostered a horizontal or external form of legitimacy. That is, ostentatious royal benefaction—and especially the construction of monumental temples—was a display of might intended to discourage the rival chiefs and kings who posed a potential threat (1978c: 136–37).

Because of a preoccupation with links between center and locality, and because of the assumption that religious gifting resulted in harmonious integration, we have largely overlooked the more aggressive connotations of royal patronage suggested in Kulke's concept of horizontal legitimacy—the ways in which it served as a highly visible demonstration of dynastic power. Once we interpret religious gift-giving as, among other things, a strategy for exhibiting a king's greatness, the reasons for uneven distribution of royal patronage over time and space become clear. The Kakatiyas directed the bulk of their benefactions to the newly acquired territory on the central coast, where they most needed to proclaim their might. The same pattern of patronage has been noticed in connection with other South Indian dynasties. Kulke's analysis of fourteen temples endowed by the great Vijayanagara king Krishnadeva Raya and his father reveals that they were all "located either in the northern border region, or in regions which had only recently been conquered (e.g., Srisailam), or in those regions in the southeast between Tirupati and Rameshvaram which had been invaded by the troops of the Gajapati and had since then been troubled by intrigues and rebellions" (Kulke and Rothermund 1990: 196). Heitzman has also pointed out that the most significant of the later Chola royal endowments were made to temples in the border regions, since the Chola role as patrons remained crucial at these sites (1997: 148). Endowments to existing temples thus sought to affirm the strength of a dynasty in places where its dominance was contested. Once dynastic power was well entrenched in a locality—which had often experienced the earlier establishment of a royal temple—repeated, lavish gift giving was no longer necessary.

Precisely because royal gifts signified a king's might, we very often find donative inscriptions issued by kings at major temple centers within a rival's realm.[20] Gifts of this sort testified to the king's penetration of enemy territory during the course of a rapid military incursion but could scarcely have been intended to result in any meaningful incorporation of the said temple or locality into the king's own domain. This is not to deny the beneficial consequences of religious gifting for a king's public image, given the widespread societal sanction for such generosity. Nor do I mean to suggest that royal gifts demonstrated no more than a king's command over material resources, for they also highlighted his proximity to divine favor. In that sense, religious patronage could only enhance the prestige of a king (Spencer 1969: 56). But I would argue that we have placed too much emphasis on royal support of religious institutions as an integrative mechanism for state building. Given both the paucity of royal endowments and their concentration in either capitals or the outermost territories, religious patronage cannot be regarded as a critical means by which medieval polities were constituted.

On the other hand, there is a definite correlation between heightened levels of religious patronage and large medieval polities, as noted in chapter 1. Rates of inscriptional production were considerably higher in Andhra during the Kakatiya and late imperial Vijayanagara periods than they were in the times of less political unity. A greater need to document the transference of property rights in larger, supralocal, polities might be a factor in the increased number of inscriptions under Kakatiya and imperial Vijayanagara rule. But it is likely that the actual quantities of endowments also rose in eras when vigorous state systems flourished. I have previously mentioned that people may have resorted to temple endowments to escape the burden of taxes while still retaining control over assets. The making and recording of religious gifts was also an esteemed way to publicly exhibit one's political affiliations by honoring overlords and/or rewarding followers. In addition, religious patronage was one of the few arenas for competition within a large polity, since direct conflict between subordinates of the same lord would be unacceptable. The fact that temple endowments provided an excellent point of entry into local communities of worship may also have proved attractive to Kakatiya associates who were moving into new territories. While all of these motives may have impelled members of large networks of power to make more endowments, the relevant issue here is that religious patronage was engaged in primarily by political subordinates rather than their superiors.

Recent scholarship has also emphasized the ideological link between kingship and divinity in medieval South India. Regardless of the extent of any individual king's donative activities, kingly authority is considered comparable or homologous to the authority of gods, in this view. Arjun Appadurai and Carol A. Breckenridge, for instance, cite a series of parallels in the conceptualization of the Tamil king and deity. Both are addressed as lord or master and dwell in an abode called *kōyil* where their needs are served by a retinue of attendants who use the same ritual paraphernalia and the same ritual forms (1976: 191–92). Appadurai and

Breckenridge conclude that kings who served deities, through gift-giving and temple protection, partook in some share of the "paradigmatic royalty" possessed by the gods (p. 207). In a related vein, Nicholas B. Dirks has argued that *pūjā* was the root metaphor for political relations in precolonial India (1987: 47, 289). He notes the correspondences in the relationship between an overlord and his underling, on the one hand, with that of a god and his devotee, on the other. In both cases, the relationship was highly hierarchical and the attitude of the inferior party toward the superior was one of worshipful submission. Just as a devotee could not compel the god to give him a boon, so too could the political subordinate not expect any automatic reward for the military service he offered his king (pp. 93–102). But both human and divine lords might extend their favor to supplicants in the form of material goods that embodied some of the lordly essence (e.g., temple food offerings and royal emblems).

In both these formulations, the basic point is that power was an attribute shared by both human and divine lords, although it might be possessed in differing measure. Medieval South Indians envisioned not two distinct spheres of political and religious dominion, but a continuum of lordship that extended from the highest gods down to the lowliest little king or "a scale of divine and human wills," in Ronald Inden's words (1990: 237). Political authority, by implication, was no different from religious authority. Moreover, the sovereignty of both kings and gods could be transmitted to their loyal subjects—kings could become even more kingly through serving the gods, according to Appadurai and Breckenridge, while Dirks believes that chiefs were transformed into little kings through their service to an overlord. Through sustained contact with a mightier lord, whether man or deity, a lesser being could thus partake of his superior's greatness.

The conceptually homologous position of kings and gods as lords who ranked high above other creatures accounts for the similarities in the ritual forms employed in revering them. During the famous Mahanavami festival held yearly in the Vijayanagara capital, both the ruler and the deity were ritually honored in comparable ways (Dirks 1987: 41). Both rulers and images routinely engaged in ceremonial processions through their domains, at which time they were accompanied by the same emblems of sovereign status like the umbrella, elephant, and fly whisk (Appadurai and Breckenridge 1976: 191). But some of these rituals were also found in other contexts—washing the image's feet or offering food during the daily *pūjā* worship in temples, for instance, were acts of respect extended to all honored elders and guests. Nor are the terms of address signifying "master" unique to gods and kings, for a husband was the only lord (*svāmi*, *īśvara*) that a wife was to acknowledge, at least in theory. Hierarchical relations of all sorts were therefore ritually expressed in similar forms, regardless of the identity of the superior being in the relationship. In stating that the deity was the paradigm or that *pūjā* was the root metaphor, however, Appadurai, Breckenridge, and Dirks accord an ontological priority to the realm of the divine. In turn, this implies that medieval South Indian kingship was somehow derivative and predicated on an association with the gods. But one could just as easily argue that the relationship between king and subject was the basis of the conception of the god-devotee relation or that royal ceremonial bore this same relationship to religious ritual.

The model of dharmic kingship proposed by Western scholars has admittedly been useful in overcoming the artificial distinction drawn between state and church in earlier interpretations of medieval South India. We can now view the temple as an institution embedded in a larger sociopolitical setting and appreciate the variety of intersections between religious and political interests. Having recognized the homologous aspects in indigenous constructions of human and divine lordship, we can better grasp the conceptual overlap between the worlds of humans and the gods. But the recent trend has also, perhaps unintentionally, deflected our gaze from the actual rhetoric of medieval South Indian kingship and, in doing so, has led us to exaggerate the importance of religious patronage, divine models, and moral behavior in constituting royal authority. The trait that is most insistently featured in inscriptional representations of kings is not their piety, righteousness, or godlike attributes but rather their forceful subjugation of others.

That political power has a physical basis in armed might is so obvious a point that it need not be belabored. But the significance of a martial ethos in medieval South India and the importance of its military networks should not be discounted simply because they are found widely in other societies and eras. To be sure, kingship in medieval South India was not just about being a good warrior, either in theory or in practice. But military action was a very substantial element in both the success of actual kings and in the ways people thought about kings, and, as such, merits far more consideration than it has hitherto received from historians of South India. Because a king's own martial skills and his ability to recruit and retain the loyalties of other fighting men were essential to his survival, the web of military associations underlying every state system should be prominent in our models of non-Muslim medieval polity. While divine legitimation and the support of institutionalized religion were important assets to royal authority, they could never constitute its fundamental ground. Even donative inscriptions, which by their nature as records of religious endowments magnify religious dimensions over other aspects of society, reveal the ideological premium placed on martial heroism as a royal attribute and highlight the bonds of military service uniting leading warriors. And so our next focus is the militaristic language of medieval Andhra inscriptions.

Warrior Prowess and Military Service

The epithets (*birudas*) associated with the Kakatiya rulers provide a convenient entry point into medieval Andhra constructions of the king. These *birudas* were not just bardic pleasantries meant to flatter a patron but were often physical objects in the form of an anklet or insignia—what we might consider a medal of honor—as well as titles announced in public appearances and enumerated in inscriptions. *Birudas* could not be adopted freely but had to be inherited from a predecessor, bestowed by an overlord, seized from an enemy, or justified by some deed. A list of *birudas* was a synopsis of a lineage's achievements, in effect, a summary of a person's claim to fame. The Kakatiya *birudas* are largely martial, as can be seen in this extract repeated in two Telugu inscriptions:[21]

While the illustrious Mahamandaleshvara Kakatiya Ganapatideva Maharaja who possesses all the praiseworthy titles such as the Mahamandaleshvara who has acquired the honors known as the five great sounds, lord of the excellent city Hanumakonda, ruler of the three kings, famous for his heroic character, exceedingly devoted to Shiva, the sole lord of the goddess of heroism, punisher of insolent men, ferocious in combat, the worshiper of the divine lotus feet of the illustrious god Svayambhudeva, the destroyer of the enemy army; was ruling the earth from his capital in Warangal . . . (HAS 13.52 and HAS 19 Mn.47)

Not all inscriptions give the same series of Kakatiya titles. But there was a fixed pool of possibilities, so to speak, from which the composer of an inscription could choose. The example just translated contains the four most widespread of the Kakatiya *birudas*:—*calamarti-gaṇḍa* (punisher of insolent men), *mūrurāya-jagadāḷa* (ruler of the three kings), *Anumakoṇḍa-pura-var=ādhīśvara* (lord of the excellent city of [H]anumakonda), and *śrīsvayambhūdēva-divya-śrīpādapadm=ārādhaka* (worshiper of the divine lotus feet of the illustrious god Svayambhudeva).[22] It is also representative in the relative weight placed on titles that acclaim martial prowess and political might as compared to religious devotion. As with *calamarti-gaṇḍa*, many Kakatiya-period *birudas* are Dravidian in linguistic origin and seem to draw on an ancient South Indian tradition of martial heroism.

Functionally equivalent to the list of *birudas* found in Telugu records is the genealogical portion of Sanskrit inscriptions, where a donor and his or her overlord's praiseworthy features are catalogued, although in far more elaborate terms than in Telugu records. Sanskrit inscriptions, which were usually composed by brahman poets, are more likely to highlight the moral goodness and generosity of a ruler for reasons that are easy to guess. Heroic references are prevalent even in lengthy Sanskrit compositions that commemorate the establishment of a temple, however, where one might expect piety to command the most attention. Whereas Telugu *birudas* were often unique to a specific individual or lineage, the language of Sanskrit eulogies is repetitive. Certain standard images and tropes appear repeatedly, in the overblown language of the Sanskrit *praśasti*.

The supremacy of an overlord is customarily expressed in *praśastis* by the image of a multitude of subservient kings kneeling at his feet. In one case, the edge of Kakatiya Mahadeva's golden footstool is said to have become sharpened into a whetting stone through constant pressure from the crowns of those who saluted his feet (HAS 13.15, v. 12). Another indirect way of conveying the same situation is the statement, "his commands always become intimate with the luster of the enemies' crown jewels," which means that the king's orders were obeyed by his enemies, who bowed down before him in submission (SII 10.334, v. 3). A king's greatness thus consisted in his forceful subjugation of other kings, in his literally becoming a king over other kings.

Many conventional tropes in medieval Sanskrit inscriptions deal directly with warfare. Fierce fighting between mounted horsemen is the main theme, for elite warriors were invariably found in the cavalry contingents. A battle scenario is nicely evoked in several verses relating to the Kakatiya ruler Ganapati, in an inscription from Ganapapuram village, Nalgonda District:

When the thundering of the war-drums of his victorious army on the march pervaded the far corners, it was as if the echoes reverberating off the towering houses of his enemies were telling them, "Escape to the forest quickly, for King Ganapati, a master in the battlefield, is approaching!"

Held up high on tall poles and waving vigorously in the wind, his army's battle colors seem to signal to the many rival kings from a distance with the threat, "Run far away at once!"

When the rays of the sun's light had been totally extinguished by the clouds of dust that rose up from the ground as the rows of sharp hooves of his throngs of horses tore it asunder, the astonished people thought the sun had gone away, observing the frightful heads of the hostile kings rise up (in the air) as they were cut off by his weapons and mistaking them for an army of Rahus.[23] (HAS 13.22, vv. 3–5)

The reference to the dust kicked up by the hooves of the warriors' horses, found in the last verse, is the most popular of all battle images in Kakatiya-period inscriptions.

A more gruesome image, of enemy heads rolling around on the battlefield, is also highly popular and figures in the eulogy of Ganapati just translated. Sometimes, the warrior is depicted as nonchalantly playing with those heads, as in this line from an inscription issued by Kayastha Ambadeva: "Having cut off Mallideva's head, Ambadeva then cast down his own weapon and because he repeatedly knocked the head around the ground with his feet, as if kicking a playing ball, he who was never tired finally grew weary" (SII 10.465, v. 10). The utter humiliation of an enemy was evidently the aim of the inscriptional poet, if not the warrior himself, for what could be more contemptuous than using a fallen foe's head as a soccer ball! A similar conceit is found in the Telugu title *Pṛthvīśvara-śiraḥ-kanduka-krīḍā-vinōda*, "he who amused himself in playing with the ball that was the head of Prithvishvara," a Velanati Choda king (Parabrahma Sastry 1978: 150, 168).

Perhaps the most charming of the standard motifs found in Kakatiya-period *praśastis* is that of the beautiful heavenly women (*apsarā*) who awaited a warrior dying in battle. It is generally enemies who are dispatched to the welcoming arms of these celestial maidens by some great hero (e.g., HAS 3.1, v. 20). But, occasionally, an ancestor who died while fighting is said to have met that happy fate. For instance, the death of Kakatiya Mahadeva, which probably occurred in combat with Yadava forces, is alluded to in this verse: "Having fallen asleep in a great battle on the two temples of a female elephant, this foremost among warriors awoke on the two breasts of a distinguished nymph of heaven" (translation from Sanskrit by E. Hultzsch [1894–95b: 101]). The idea of a warrior's heaven, little noticed in the secondary literature, is nonetheless widespread in medieval Sanskrit inscriptions.

The ethos of martial heroism was shared equally by kings and the many warriors who figure in medieval inscriptions. The king was paramount in that he stood above all others—or, more accurately, he sat above all others who prostrated themselves at his feet. Records commissioned by warriors subordinate to the Kakatiyas typically presented the Kakatiya genealogy or titles before those of the donor's own family, in a tacit acknowledgment of Kakatiya superiority. But the Kakatiya subordinates, often warriors themselves, are praised in ways quite comparable to the king. Inscriptions also sometimes specify that the warriors' commendable deeds occurred while they fought for the king. So, for instance, we are told that Recherla Nama Reddi, a Telangana chief with his own band of warriors, was part of Kakatiya Rudradeva's army:

> Nama—whose warriors became (as savage as) lions and tigers, whose horses became (as swift as) thoughts and winds, and whose elephant-troops became (as towering as) mountains and clouds when Rudradeva's army exhibited its fearsomeness in the extermination, dispersal, or capturing of (enemy) kings without effort—was renowned for his mighty prowess at arms. (HAS 13.38, v. 4)

In a world where martial heroism was highly esteemed and warfare was recurrent, military service was the primary way bonds were forged between overlord and subordinate. At least in the rhetoric of the medieval Sanskrit inscription, heroes fought for their lord and were recognized accordingly. The following passage well illustrates how military service could be central to a political relationship:

> The king welcomed and took into his service their younger brother, the handsome Jayana, who, in spite of his youth, commanded respect on account of the great modesty, wisdom, cleverness, firmness, profundity, and bravery, indicated by (his) face.
>
> Then, pleased by (his) deeds, the king joyfully granted to this Jayana the dignity of a general (and) of a commander of the elephant-troop, along with a palanquin, a parasol, and other emblems.
>
> Having been appointed general by his lord, surrounded by wise men, (and) full of power, young Jaya, the slayer of hostile warriors, resembles (the god) Kumara, who has been appointed general by (Indra) the lord of the gods, is surrounded by gods, (and) bears a spear.[24] (EI 3.15, vv. 37–39)

These verses come from a record issued by a man known as Jaya(na) Senapati, the son of a minor chief who had controlled Divi island in the mouth of the Krishna River. Kakatiya Ganapati defeated the chief in the early thirteenth century, married two of his daughters, and recruited his son Jaya as a general. The composer informs us that Jaya Senapati had all sorts of good qualities—he was handsome, modest, and clever.[25] Most important, however, he was a fierce fighter on behalf of his lord. He is compared to the war-god Kumara, who was the epitome of a warrior. But Kumara was subservient to the supreme lord of the gods, Indra, just as Jaya was subordinate to his overlord Kakatiya Ganapati.

The bond between a lord and his underling was cemented by the bestowal of honors. When Jaya was assigned the rank of *sēnāpati* (general), he received a number of objects from the king that signified his high status. In Jaya's case, the items named are a palanquin and an umbrella. Elsewhere, the Kakatiyas are known to have given jewels, fly whisks, ointments, and clothing to their subordinates (HAS 13.56; Parabrahma Sastry 1978: 144). These were all part of the paraphernalia of kingship. In giving such royal objects to others, the Kakatiya king was not only displaying his favor but simultaneously sharing the substance of his sovereignty with them. Jaya Senapati's inscription uses the word *cihna* for the items he was given, a term that is best glossed as "insignia." These items were coveted as emblems of lordship, rather than because of any intrinsic value.

Birudas were among the cherished insignia of high rank conferred by a king on a subordinate. New titles were sometimes invented to honor a warrior who had won a major victory for his sovereign, like "the conqueror of the Kota (chiefs)" (*Kōṭa-gelpāta*, HAS 13.8 and 9) and "the disperser in all directions of the army of the western king Damodara" (*paścima-rāya-Dāmōdara-sainya-diśāpaṭṭa*, SII 10.346). Some *birudas* were more widely circulated. Of these, the most noteworthy is *Kākatīya-*

rājya-sthāpan=ācārya, which literally translates as "a learned master (or, one who is skilled) at the maintenance of the Kakatiya kingdom," implying that the designated individual was a pillar of support in keeping the Kakatiya kingdom from collapsing. Several of Ganapati's favorites had the title *Gaṇapatidēva-dakṣiṇa-bhuja-daṇḍa*, which can loosely be rendered "he who embodied the force that was Ganapatideva's right arm" (e.g., SII 10.402; HAS 13.52; IAP-K.33). *Daṇḍa* literally means a "rod" or "staff" but symbolizes the armed might of a king and particularly the royal duty to forcibly quell disorder and punish the lawless. Titles like *Kākatīya-rājya-sthāpan=ācārya* or *Gaṇapatidēva-dakṣiṇa-bhuja-daṇḍa* highlighted the ruler's continuing reliance on the recipient and, by extension, the legitimacy of the latter's authority and activities.

The greatest sign of the ruler's favor must have been the bestowal of one of his own *birudas*, for this constituted an intimate sharing of the king's selfhood or substance. At least one of the Kakatiya subordinates, Gangaya Sahini of the Kayastha family, earned this great honor. An inscription dated 1251 from the Palnad area of Guntur District tells us that he gained Kakatiya Ganapati's favor, appeared before the king with all his armor on, and had been granted the *mūrurāya-jagadāḷa* banner (*paḍaga*) and *calamarti-gaṇḍa* title (SII 10.334, ll. 62–65). Both *calamarti-gaṇḍa* and *mūrurāya-jagadāḷa* were *birudas* closely associated with the Kakatiya dynasty. Subsequent leaders of the Kayastha family inherited the two *birudas* that Gangaya Sahini received from the Kakatiyas and continued to include them in their own inscriptions (e.g., NDI Darsi 1; SII 10.402). Ironically, this is true even of Kayastha Ambadeva, although he refused to recognize Kakatiya overlordship (SII 10.465).

The conferral of *birudas* and other insignia was a transaction initiated by the overlord in what was clearly a hierarchical relationship. The hierarchy is further underscored in the inscriptional rhetoric used by subordinates. Warriors who were part of the Kakatiya political network often called themselves the *bhṛtya* (servant) of the Kakatiya ruler (NDI Kandukur 1). The term "servant" implies total compliance with the wishes and commands of the superior being, the master (*svāmi*) (HAS 13.51). *Svāmi*, according to Robert Lingat, is "a word which can be applied equally to a proprietor as to a husband or a chief, and which denotes an immediate power over a thing or over a person" (1973: 212). The master-servant hierarchy is also indicated in a Telugu phrase based on the verb *ēlu*, meaning "to rule, govern, or master." *Tannēlina*, "(he who) rules over me," is typically prefixed to the name of a Kakatiya king like Prataparudra (NDI Darsi 12). Another way to express the dependent position of the subordinate was by use of two formulaic phrases, *tat-pāda-padm=ōpajīvi* (who subsists on the lotuses that are his [lord's] feet) and *tat-pāda-padm=ārādhaka* (who worships the lotuses that are his [lord's] feet). The underling offers verbal obeisance to the lord in these words, which invoke the image of a beelike servant hovering in anticipation over the lotus-feet of his master (e.g., CTI 35; SII 10.290).

However, Kakatiya subordinates were not merely passive recipients of honors from their king. They also took active measures to reciprocally honor their lords within the context of temple patronage, for instance by naming a new deity after the Kakatiya overlord. Jaya Senapati took this route, according to the inscription partially translated above (EI 3.15). It says that he founded a temple for a deity called Ganapeshvara in the name of the king Kakatiya Ganapati, in the town Dvipa (or Divi) that had been established by Jaya's grandfather. Through this act, Jaya Senapati not only conveyed his personal reverence for Ganapati but also displayed his overlord's greatness. The consecration of a god named after Ganapati by a member of a subjugated lineage was a potent sign of the submission of his ancestral territory to the superior force of Kakatiya might. Aside from temple deities, villages and tanks were also named after the Kakatiyas (HAS 4, HAS 13.51).

A more common method of showing high regard for the overlord was by transferring the merit accruing from a religious gift to him. When a temple endowment was made, donors frequently stated that it was done for the sake of the religious merit of someone else. Typically, the spiritual benefit that resulted from the gift was dedicated to the donor's parents or other family members. But the Kakatiya ruler is also specified, often in conjunction with the donor's parents, in over half of the recorded instances (107 out of 187). The prosperity of the Kakatiya kingdom is another reason given for the making of a religious gift by subordinates (SII 4.952). The practice of dedicating merit to the overlord can also be observed in many sixteenth-century Tamil inscriptions, and Noboru Karashima suggests that this was "an Indian way of expressing the fidelity of a subordinate to his lord" (1984: xxxii). Whether naming gods after their overlords or generously surrendering the fruits of their religious gifts, Kakatiya "servants" actively engaged in strategies that would elevate their superiors.

Nicholas B. Dirks's pioneering work on the late precolonial Tamil kingdom of Pudukkottai was the first to recognize the importance of ritual gifting in consolidating political ties. The gift of titles, emblems, and land by the overlord was, in Dirks's view, "the principal symbolic mechanism for the establishment of 'political' relations" (1982: 672). The family histories and genealogies of warrior lineages that Dirks studied describe not only the occasions when an ancestor received such honors from a king, but also the episodes of heroic action on the king's behalf that preceded them. But Dirks states that "though heroic action was a necessary prerequisite, genuine transformations only took place when the chief developed a relationship with a greater king who endowed him with these gifts" (1987: 52). And so for Dirks the critical event was the king's "gifts of limited sovereignty," even though the groundwork was laid by the subordinate's offering of military service (1987: 47). The underling could not expect or demand honors from his king, for he was to maintain an attitude of worshipful submission.

Kakatiya inscriptions conform to convention in casting political subordinates as devoted servants of the king. Yet the temple donors who had inscriptions commissioned also felt proud of what they had achieved, ostensibly on behalf of their lord. Subordinates are portrayed as eminently deserving of the honors proffered by the overlord, even if these were not culturally construed as rewards for their prior service. There is no contradiction in this, of course. The worthier the followers of a king, the greater a master of men he was, in theory at least. The author of the following verses cleverly praises both the Kakatiya overlord and the donor-chief and, in so doing, illustrates their interdependence:

> Thinking, "it is fitting that king Ganapati—profound (or deep), protecting the ally-kings (or liking the mountainsides), naturally superior in character (or situated in the best substances), and not transgressing the bounds of morality (or not crossing the shore line)—should also be the repository (or source) of jewels," the Malyala chief [Chaunda] presented him with a storehouse filled with jewels seized from the treasuries of other kings.[26]
>
> Then the wise king Ganapati bestowed the famous name "Looter of Divi" on General Chaunda. (HAS 13.8, vv. 54–55)

What is described is a fairly straightforward transaction—Malyala Chaunda gathered much plunder for the king during a military campaign (probably to the Divi region of the Krishna delta, where Jaya Senapati's forebears had flourished) and in return was given a heroic title. The two events are not presented as causally connected, but there is a chronological sequentiality, and the implication is that the one (military service) led to the other (gift of emblem). By proclaiming the king's excellence first, the composer suggests that Ganapati merited no less than the great treasure that Chaunda won for him in an act of homage. But whatever the spirit of this offering, the valuable goods Chaunda obtained were obviously beneficial for the king. Since plunder was a major source of revenue for medieval South Indian polities (Spencer 1983a), Chaunda's activities augmented the strength and prosperity of the kingdom. Clearly, the overlord needed the military service of his subordinates, just as much as the subordinates valued the honors they received as a consequence.[27]

I have tried to make two main points in the last few pages: that martial prowess was the most admired quality in the ideology of Kakatiya kingship and that shared action in military activities brought lords and subordinates together. Inscriptions represent the lord-subordinate relationship in very hierarchical terms, in which the underling voluntarily assumes what Dirks has called a stance of worshipful submission. At the same time, warrior-subordinates are themselves glorified in inscriptions—Jaya Senapati was compared to the war-god Kumara while Malyala Chaunda is said to have wrested treasure away from many kings. Although the conceptual inequality inherent in the lord-underling relationship is never forgotten in the rhetoric of inscriptions, it is clear that subordinates were active agents whose accomplishments were admired and who engaged in their own forms of honoring overlords. Royal gifts of titles and other emblems ritually incorporated the subordinate to the king, but other privileges such as land grants, which we have not yet discussed, also bound the warrior to him. In short, a series of transactions linked the lord and his subordinates, but the most essential of them was military service.

The myriad personal connections and interdependent interests forged through joint military objectives and actions were, in my opinion, the fundamental ligaments of the Kakatiya body politic which linked its various elements in one unified corpus. We have just examined the language of political loyalty that reaffirmed the bonds between warriors; in the remaining pages of this section, we turn to the actual components of the Kakatiya military complex. We can seldom see beyond the topmost layer of the warrior elite, for only the most successful men's exploits are illuminated in our epigraphic gaze. But the Kakatiya armies were composed of many more humble fighters, organized at the simplest level into a multitude of small war-bands—some attached directly to the Kakatiyas and others more obliquely.

Among the war-bands that were closely associated with the Kakatiyas, the retinue (*parivāra*) of Gundaya Nayaka figures in three different inscriptions from Magatala town in Mahbubnagar District, where it was apparently garrisoned (HAS 19 Mn.19, 20, 21). Gundaya Nayaka, a subordinate of Kakatiya Prataparudra who held the position of *gaja-sāhiṇi* (commander of elephant troops), had *nāyakas* under him who acted as officers (*pradhāni*). The bulk of his soldiers, however, were divided into the two basic ranks of *rautu* and *baṇṭu*. On two occasions when tithes were assessed, Gundaya Nayaka's *rautus* were assigned a far higher rate of contribution than were the *baṇṭus*. Since a second war-band associated with another Kakatiya *nāyaka* in Warangal District followed the same practice in their donation (*Bhārati* 54: 56), the division of men into a higher class of *rautu* and a lower-ranking category of *baṇṭu* must have been widespread. *Rautu* invariably meant "horse-riding warrior," so in these contexts *baṇṭu* may have signified "foot soldier."[28]

Although foot soldiers presumably constituted the bulk of the fighting force, we find few traces of them in literary sources. But visual representations of medieval Andhra warriors, found on hero-stones commemorating their death, typically show a standing figure armed with a sword and shield (Chandrasekhara Reddy 1994: 125). The non-Kakatiya *baṇṭus* who occasionally endowed perpetual lamps to coastal Andhra temples, a relatively modest form of religious gift, might also have been foot soldiers—particularly when they held the status titles of *reḍḍi* and *bōya* rather than the more lofty status of *nāyaka* (e.g., SII 10.437, SII 4.790). Some Kakatiya *baṇṭus* were not members of organized war-bands but instead seem to have been stationed in small numbers in the countryside. In that capacity they are included among a long list of varied donors who made endowments at the same time. For instance, *baṇṭus* joined brahmans, cultivators, village officials, and other residents in Palakavidu village of Nalgonda District on one occasion of religious gifting, while on another they acted in concert with weavers, merchants, artisans, and others in Kandukuru village of the same district (IAP-N 1.80 and 100). Because their contributions were limited, these men must have been common foot soldiers rather than mounted horsemen. They were perhaps subsidized by taxes like the *baṇṭela-āyamu* ("soldiers' income") mentioned in one inscription (SII 10.521).

We are on firmer ground with the term *rautu* since it was used to denote a horse-riding warrior throughout medieval North India, as well as in Andhra and Orissa (Prasad 1990: xxii; Subrahmanyam 1973a: xvi).[29] Like *baṇṭus*, however, *rautus* are sparsely documented in Kakatiya-period sources. The leading mounted horsemen who are typically visible in inscriptions adopted status titles other than *rautu*, as did Vishaveli Masake Sahini, whose inscription was translated in chapter 2 (SII 10.283). He, like several other men of the time (e.g., HAS 3.2, ll. 33–34), possessed a *biruda* that compared his riding ability to that of the consummate horseman of myth, Revanta. Vishaveli Masake Sahini even cites the name of the horse upon which he won victory in battle. There is no doubt, given the prevalence of horse-riding imagery in Sanskrit inscriptions combined with the references to horsemanship in Telugu *birudas*, that high-ranking warriors customarily fought on horseback.[30] But only common cavalrymen were called *rautu* in Kakatiya Andhra, while their superiors bore other designations.

There is reason to believe that the role of cavalry became more prominent in

South Indian warfare during the Kakatiya period. Jean Deloche's recent study (1989) of sculptural reliefs from twelfth- and thirteenth-century Hoysala temples in southern Karnataka clearly demonstrates the gradual adoption of a series of improvements in horse-riding equipment. These included better horse-harnesses and saddles, as well as foot stirrups and nailed horseshoes. Although no comparable sculptural data from Kakatiya sources corroborate Deloche's findings, it is likely that these improvements spread to Andhra as well, due to the frequent military conflicts between the Kakatiyas and the Yadavas of northern Karnataka. The greater efficiency of mounted horsemen that resulted from the new technology meant that the outcome of battles rested even more heavily on the fate of the cavalry charge (Deloche 1989: 48). The prestige of horse-riding warriors must have risen accordingly, as would also their numbers. Some testimony that mounted horsemen were more widespread and more important in Kakatiya Andhra than they had been previously is furnished by Chandrasekhara Reddy's observation that memorial sculptures from the Kakatiya period are unusual in regularly featuring warriors on horseback (1994: 119–24).

A war-band like Gundaya Nayaka's, which contained both infantry and cavalrymen (along with other specialized fighters such as camel riders), was in effect a miniature army, capable of engaging the enemy in a limited military conflict. Because Gundaya Nayaka was a professed officer of the Kakatiyas, presumably they could call on him and his men at any time to participate in a military campaign. The Kakatiyas also had armed followers who were members of their personal fighting force or bodyguard (known as *leṅka* and *aṅgarakṣa*), as well as entire villages in Telangana occupied by accomplished warriors sworn to them called *ekkaṭīlu*. Aside from those directly affiliated war-bands, however, the Kakatiyas must also have mustered forces from their principal subordinates. Raje Nayaka, for instance, was a warrior who fought in at least one engagement on the side of the Kakatiyas (SII 4.1117; HAS 3.2), although his main loyalty was to Recherla Rudra, a subordinate chief (*maṇḍalika*) and general (*camūpati*) of the Kakatiyas. Raje Nayaka's prominence and numerous military activities, coupled with his son's ability to generously endow a temple in Warangal District, suggest that this family itself controlled a band of warriors. Through its allied subordinate chiefs, therefore, the Kakatiyas could marshal numerous bands of fighters in addition to those commanded by their own officers.

The key to Kakatiya success was their ability to augment the limited coercive strength of their "standing" army—that is, the fighters personally beholden to them—with the manpower of other warrior lords. The more they could win the allegiance of important leaders like Raje Nayaka's lord Recherla Rudra, who could mobilize fighters on their behalf, the larger would be the size of the army they could field in battle and the greater their chance of victory. The largest coalitions must have been assembled during the major campaigns against enemies such as the Yadavas, Eastern Gangas, and Pandyas. Unfortunately we have no complete records of who participated in any given campaign. Since inscriptional eulogies aim at glorifying the individual patron, they typically ascribe a major victory entirely to his efforts. But at least four notable Kakatiya warriors possessed heroic titles related to the Kakatiya war against the Pandyas that took place around 1315 (Parabrahma Sastry 1978: 163, 165, 170–71). The armies of the Kakatiyas and their allies formed the bulk of the forces who marched into Tamil Nadu on this occasion, although they were joined by some contingents of the Khalji army (Venkataramanayya and Somasekhara Sarma 1960: 648–49). Another large coalition of warriors came together to fight the rebellious Kayastha chief Ambadeva, who boasted of confronting 75 kings in the battlefield and of besting all the lords of Andhra (SII 10.465, vv. 9 and 15). In his quest for independence, Ambadeva formed alliances with two dynasties outside Andhra, the Pandyas and Yadavas, as revealed by his epithets.

It is impossible to estimate accurately the size of the military forces assembled for battle in the Kakatiya era, although the Khalji army besieging Warangal fort in 1310 is said to have numbered 100,000 men (Habib 1931: 63). At the conclusion of that encounter, Kakatiya Prataparudra reportedly presented 20,000 horses and 100 elephants in tribute to Sultan Ala-ud-din Khalji. Indo-Islamic chronicles also tell us that Prataparudra was assessed an annual tribute in 1318 of 1,000 horses and 100 elephants (Digby 1971: 48, 61). Although these figures might be exaggerated in order to magnify the greatness of sultanate victories, they were noted down very close in time to the events described and might be given some credence on those grounds.[31] In any case, the implication is that the Kakatiyas possessed a formidable cavalry by contemporary standards.[32]

Another indication of the magnitude of the Kakatiya military effort is the scale of fortifications at Warangal. According to Indo-Muslim sources, large numbers of chiefs and warriors retreated into Warangal fort for refuge while the sultanate armies were advancing (Venkataramanayya 1942: 34). Muslim chroniclers speak of two "forts" or sets of walls at Warangal—the outer mud one being "very extensive" (Habib 1931: 116). The most detailed description comes from Amir Khusrau's account of the 1310 siege. At that time Warangal had a strong outer fortification of hardened mud with a deep ditch in front, which had to be filled with dirt before the Khalji army could surmount it. The inner fortress was built of stone and surrounded by a moat that the Muslim soldiers swam across. The forts described by Khusrau correspond to the two inner circles of fortifications that exist today at Warangal.[33] The innermost circle, consisting of stone walls over 30 feet high, has a diameter of three-quarters of a mile, while the second ring of (earthen) walls comprises a circle of approximately one and one-half miles in diameter and reaching up to 20 feet in height. Both sets of walls were once encircled by moats, and the stone one has regularly spaced bastions projecting outward (Michell 1992: 2–9). We know that Warangal's fortifications were formidable enough to keep the sultanate armies at bay for periods of up to six months, and it is quite feasible that many thousands of fighting men were housed inside during a siege.

Through their own personal charisma and capacity to attract the loyalty of leading warrior lords, the Kakatiyas were thus able to command a vast coalition of fighting men. These men constituted the backbone of Kakatiya polity—its coercive force—and were further bound to the Kakatiya cause by the bestowal of honors and economic resources. But all of this is rather abstract. I proceed to flesh out the picture in the following section with a closer look at the identity of the prominent Kakatiya subordinates and the changes in the composition of the political network over time.

Classifying Kakatiya Subordinates

Few systematic studies of political intermediaries, those individuals who occupied an intermediate position between the king at the top of the hierarchy and the villagers at the bottom, have been conducted despite the considerable energy expended debating the nature of the medieval south Indian state.[34] Because models of medieval polity differ drastically, these men have been variously regarded as the bureaucratic agents of a centralized administration, the vassal lords in a feudal structure, and local chiefs who represented communal groups such as tribes or castes. Close analysis of inscriptions will not resolve all issues, for many aspects of the relationship between kings and intermediary political figures are never mentioned in them. But inscriptions do shed light on the social background of political intermediaries, the extent of their autonomy from the king, and the degree of authority they wielded. This information is vital in determining the nature of the state system and the relative power of the center.

Kakatiya subordinates—that is, men who acknowledge Kakatiya overlordship and admit to some official or personal tie with the rulers—can be broadly differentiated into two groups: those with some claim to lordly status and those without such claims. I call members of the first category "nobles" because they had a distinct sense of belonging to a defined hereditary grouping, one that could be named. Individuals in the second category of Kakatiya subordinates tell us much less about their ancestry, probably because it was not illustrious. Since many of them bear "administrative" titles such as minister or general, I refer to them as "officers."[35] Nobles and officers are, of course, two ideal types and the reality is less clear-cut. Within the noble class, in particular, we find a wide spectrum of royal styles, ranging from a Sanskritic imperial mode to a regional "little king" mode. I am somewhat arbitrarily designating nobles who emulate a pan-Indic style of kingship as "princes" and those with less elevated aspirations as "chiefs." Despite the diversity within the noble class, however, there are sufficient differences between the way they represent their social identities and the way officers talk about themselves to warrant classifying nobles as a social group distinct from officers.

Inscriptions issued by nobles typically devote a good deal of attention to genealogies and inherited names and titles. Princely families often traced their ancestry back to a well-known South Indian dynasty who claimed *kṣatriya* rank such as the Chalukyas, Chodas (the Telugu version of the Tamil name Chola), or Pallavas. Through such assertions, princely families could connect their antecedents to the solar or lunar races of the ancient kings of North India.[36] The royal stature of the individuals I am calling princes is also reflected in the administrative title they possessed, *mahāmaṇḍalēśvara*. This title was based on the notion of a circle (*maṇḍala*) or domain of political influence and became widespread during the period of the Kalyani Chalukyas. At that time it was employed by numerous subordinate families in the Deccan including the Kakatiyas (Desai 1951: 310). Members of princely families also signified their high rank through the use of royal status titles following the personal name. Most common was *mahārāja*, followed by *rāju* (the Telugu equivalent of the Sanskrit *rāja*), and the imperial title *cakravarti*. Most of the princely families were situated in coastal Andhra.

Other noble lineages, located mainly in Telangana, made no claim to *kṣatriya* rank nor did they associate themselves with some great royal dynasty of the past. Members of these locally powerful families of chiefs usually prefixed the lineage name to their personal names. Often they possessed no administrative title, unlike the *mahāmaṇḍalēśvara* princes. When chiefs did have an administrative title, it was either *mahāsāmanta* or *maṇḍalika*, both of which signified a lord of inferior status (e.g., SII 10.508; HAS 19 Kn.16; IAP-W.55). Chiefs also usually lacked status titles, but occasionally used *mahārāja*, *rāju*, or even *reḍḍi*. However, they did generally have their own unique family *birudas* just as the princely lineages did. In the case of the Recherla Reddis of Warangal and Nalgonda Districts, the standard set of titles was as follows:[37]

> May all fare well! The illustrious Recheruvula Kami Reddi, son of Ayitambika, who possesses all the praiseworthy titles such as he who is ornamented with good qualities, distant from other men's women, the lord of the excellent city of Amaningallu, the sole lord of the goddess of valor, an ocean of truth, the terror of bad men, the sun of the Manuma clan, lauded by great warriors; like a Bhima to the opponent's strength, a Rama on the battlefield, a Karna in charity, a Garuda in valor, an Anjaneya [i.e., Hanuman] in serving his lord, a Bhishma in purity . . .

Because *birudas* were possessions that were passed on to each successive head of a lineage, they reinforced the strong sense of family found among all nobles.

Both nobles and officers were indispensable in the coalitions built up by the Kakatiyas from the mid twelfth century onward, but in differing proportions. In the initial stages of power building, the Kakatiyas relied mainly on the support of other chiefly lineages from Telangana. Examples of Kakatiya allies during the second half of the twelfth century are the Viryala and Natavadi families, who shared a similar past history of service under the Kalyani Chalukyas. Several other lineages of Telangana warriors joined forces with the Kakatiyas once their star began to rise under Rudradeva in the late twelfth century. The Recherla Reddis (with two branches located in Warangal and Nalgonda Districts), the Malyala chiefs of Warangal and Mahbubnagar, and the Cheraku chiefs of Mahbubnagar all participated in Kakatiya campaigns and continued to be staunch allies under Ganapati in the period from 1199 to 1230. As Ganapati's activities increasingly shifted to the coastal region after 1230, a growing number of princely lineages were incorporated into the Kakatiya coalition. While he still had supporters drawn from the Telangana chiefs, Ganapati was now also allying himself with coastal families such as the Kotas of Guntur District and the Chalukyas of Vengi. Other princely allies between 1231 and 1261 were the Yadavas of Addanki and the Telugu Chodas of southern Andhra.

A number of Kakatiya subordinates of noble background were from lineages that had been conquered by the Kakatiyas and then reinstated to power (Sundaram 1968: 9). Relations with these defeated families were often strengthened through the formation of marriage ties. Rudradeva, for example, is said to have won a victory over the Kanduri Choda lineage of Mahbubnagar early in his career. The former chief Bhima was replaced by Kanduri Odaya Choda, whose daughter Padma became Rudradeva's wife (Venkataramanayya and Somasekhara Sarma 1960: 588–89). Similarly, Rudradeva is thought to have conquered the Kota king Dodda Bhima and installed his son Keta II on the throne ca. 1183. Sometime in the next two decades, the relationship between the Kakatiyas and Kotas was solidified through the marriage of Ganapati's daughter Ganapamadevi to the grandson of Keta II. The marriage of Ganapati's other daughter, Rudramadevi, may also have been arranged with a subjugated princely lineage. Rudramadevi's marriage to Chalukya Virabhadra, a member of a minor Chalukya branch based in the Vengi area, probably occurred shortly after Ganapati's conquest of Vengi in 1240 (Parabrahma Sastry 1978: 112). Ganapati himself married the daughters of the chief of Divi island, whom he conquered in 1201. And, once again, he elevated the defeated chief's son Jaya Senapati, who continued to be prominent in the Divi area while simultaneously serving as one of Ganapati's generals.

The type of benevolent conquest practiced by the early Kakatiya kings Rudradeva and Ganapati—wherein subjugated chiefs and princes were allowed to remain as rulers within their own hereditary territories—was a hallowed technique for creating allies known as *dharma-vijaya* (Gopal 1963: 29–30). The marriage alliances established with several of the conquered lineages only served to solidify their ties with the Kakatiyas. The king received military assistance from his subsidiary nobles, as well as the acknowledgment of allegiance through epigraphic recognition of Kakatiya overlordship. Whether tribute and other forms of financial aid were also required is unclear. In any case, Kakatiya influence was exercised indirectly and can be described as a kind of formal hegemony. The early Kakatiya state should be envisioned as a loose federation with the Kakatiya ruler at the central nexus of a horizontal network of ostensibly subordinate substates. The paradigm of a king-of-kings heading a circle of subsidiary kings was found throughout India during the early medieval period (Inden 1982: 107–8).

As the Kakatiya political network grew in size and controlled an ever-larger expanse of territory, its composition underwent striking changes. The second broad group of Kakatiya subordinates, the officers, became increasingly important. The relative insignificance of family background is the primary feature that differentiates this class from nobles. Officers typically identified only one or two preceding generations at most, unlike chiefs and princes who traced their descent back for numerous generations to the lineage founder. Rarely do we find records from more than one member of an officer family, in contrast to chiefly and princely families, in which inscriptions were commonly issued by five or more individuals. We can surmise that hereditary privileges were considerably less important to the advancement of officers than to that of chiefs and princes.

Another area of contrast between nobles and officers is the number and range of their "administrative" titles. Unlike nobles, among whom only a handful of titles (i.e., *mahāmaṇḍalēśvara*, *mahāsāmanta*, and *maṇḍalika*) circulated, officers could possess one or more of approximately 25 different designations. The most widely held title of official ranking was *mahāpradhāni* and its variant *pradhāni* (minister, officer), followed by *gaja-sāhiṇi* (leader of the elephant corps). Broadly speaking, one can differentiate administrative titles with more clerical connotations—*karaṇam* (accountant or record-keeper), *suṅkādhikāri* (tax farmer or toll collector), and *bhaṇḍāru* (treasury supervisor)—from those implying military functions like *sēnāpati* (army commander), *sāhiṇi* (leader of cavalry), or *camūpati* (army commander). However, the majority of men in the officer class appear to have had military backgrounds. Whereas administrative titles denoting some kind of official rank typically precede the family and personal names, status titles like *nāyaka* or *reḍḍi* are the last component of a man's name. The most frequently found status title among officers was *nāyaka*. Also common was *leṅka*, which in medieval Karnataka and Andhra denoted a warrior in one of the personal contingents of a lord.

Although I am using the word "officer" to designate the lower echelon of Kakatiya subordinates, I do not mean to imply that a coherent administrative structure existed. It is impossible to sustain any notion of bureaucracy or of a structure of discrete official positions in view of the unsystematic distribution of the so-called administrative titles. For one thing, an individual could hold more than one title concurrently, as we find in the case of Bhaskaradeva who was both a *mahāpradhāni* and a *gaja-sāhiṇi* (SII 6.622). Furthermore, numerous men at any given point in time simultaneously possessed titles like *mahāpradhāni* (chief minister), *sakala-sēnāpati* (commander-in-chief), and *gaja-sāhiṇi* (commander of the elephant corps). Hence, we have to discard any notion of a rigid organizational setup in which a single individual occupied only one post at a time. *Mahāpradhāni*, in particular, should be understood as a signifier of rank rather than as an occupational designation. But unlike *mahāsāmanta* or *mahāmaṇḍalēśvara*, which also indicated rank, nowhere in the Kakatiya corpus is the title *mahāpradhāni* transmitted hereditarily from father to son. Therefore *mahāpradhāni* must have been an honorary status granted by an overlord to valued individual subordinates of the officer category.

Further evidence that officers largely had to achieve their statuses rather than inherit them is the absence of long lists of *birudas* from their inscriptions. When officers did possess *birudas*, they were often not unique to the person, as they were in the case of noble subordinates. For instance, *svāmi-drōhara-gaṇḍa* (a mighty fighter against those who harm the lord) was borne by at least three different Kakatiya officers within the fifteen-year period between 1298 and 1313 C.E. (HAS 19 Mn.18; ARE 307 of 1934–35; SII 10.505). Officers whose skills were more in the civilian realm possessed *birudas* that extolled their knowledge. A popular epithet among this group was *nīti-Cāṇakya*, "equal to (Chandragupta Maurya's minister) Chanakya in the grasp of politics" (SII 10.314, 343, 407).

At this point, I should clarify the fact that some people I have classified as officers were not directly associated with the Kakatiya rulers themselves. Instead they, or one of their family members, served either under another Kakatiya officer or under a noble allied with the Kakatiyas.[38] They comprised a third echelon of subordinates in the hierarchy of power. This situation is clearly illustrated in an inscription issued by Namadeva Pandita in 1251 C.E. from the Palnad region of Guntur District (SII 10.334). It is unusual among records from the officer class because of its long Sanskrit verse introduction. The Telugu portion begins with the following succinct sketch of contemporary political realities:

> While the illustrious Mahamandaleshvara Kakatiya Ganapatideva Maharaja—the Mahamandaleshvara who has acquired the honors known as the five great sounds, who is exceedingly devoted to Shiva, whose actions are for the good of his lord, one for whom modesty is an ornament, the lord of the excellent city [H]anumakonda—was ruling the earth from his capital city Orungallu [Warangal] enjoying friendly interchanges (with the overlord),[39] and

> While the illustrious Gangaya Sahini—who subsisted on the lotuses that were his [Kakatiya Ganapati's] feet and who possessed the hero's anklet[40]—was ruling the area from Panugallu to Marjavadi enjoying friendly interchanges (with the overlord),
>
> Namadeva Pandita—who subsisted on the lotuses that were his [Gangaya Sahini's] feet, savior of the entire kingdom, the chief financial officer, the moon that swells the ocean of the Kayastha clan—established the god Vankeshvara in the name of his father Vayi Pandita, in Dugya town of Palli-nadu.

As a token of his favor, Gangaya Sahini endowed the temple built by his officer Namadeva Pandita with a village. Much attention is devoted in the inscription to the insignia of honor that Gangaya Sahini himself had recently received from the overlord Kakatiya Ganapati. Thus, the Kakatiya political network comprised several layers of lord-subordinate relationships, loosely bound together through personal ties of allegiance and service.

During the reigns of Rudramadevi and Prataparudra, the number and proportion of Kakatiya subordinates who were officers jumped sharply. The difference in the composition of the Kakatiya political network between Ganapati and his successors' reigns is illustrated in table 13.[41] It displays the number of people from noble and officer families who were part of the Kakatiya system, including wives and siblings along with the actual chiefs, princes, and officers themselves.[42] The figures reveal that the importance of officer subordinates grew steadily over the span of time from 1199 to 1323, matched by a corresponding diminution of the role of allied chiefs and princes. Telangana chiefly families were the largest category of individuals professing allegiance to Ganapati in the first half of his reign. Several princely families of coastal Andhra joined them as Kakatiya allies between 1231 and 1261, but the number of officer subordinates also grew. The two categories of nobles and officers were equal in size during the second half of Ganapati's reign, each comprising 33 percent of the individuals recognizing Kakatiya overlordship. An even greater erosion in the position of allied chiefs and princes occurred while Rudramadevi was queen, because only 17 percent of her subordinates were of noble background. The trend continued under the rule of Prataparudra, when the officer class reached its maximum size and comprised 45 percent of all individual subordinates, in contrast to the 12 percent who were chiefs or princes. In other words, most of the noble families had disappeared from the historical record by the time of Prataparudra's reign.

An accompanying change during late Kakatiya rule is the frequency of titles

Table 13. Individuals Acknowledging Kakatiya Overlordship

		Chiefs/Princes		Officers	
Ruler	Total	No.	%	No.	%
Ganapati, early (1199–1230 C.E.)	34	16	47	9	26
Ganapati, late (1231–1262 C.E.)	60	20	33	20	33
Rudramadevi	63	11	17	24	38
Prataparudra	78	9	12	35	45
All periods	235	56	24	88	37%

indicating a personal attachment to the Kakatiya overlords. Officers known as *aṅgarakṣas* (bodyguards), most of whom were *nāyakas*, first appear in Rudramadevi's reign.[43] Although this designation virtually disappears in the time of Prataparudra, he had many warrior subordinates called *leṅkas*.[44] *Leṅka* resembles *aṅgarakṣa* in its connotations of personal military service and probably identifies a man who fought alongside the lord. Proven loyalty to the overlord was also underscored in the prevalence of the title *rājya-sthāpan=ācārya* (a pillar of support for the kingdom). At least six different men were entitled to this *biruda* during the last 60 years of Kakatiya rule.[45] The cultural emphasis on intimacy with the overlord can be seen in the reference to one of Prataparudra's subordinates, Juttayalenka Gonka Reddi, as his "beloved son" (*priya-kumārulu*; SII 10.536). The lord-warrior relationship was similarly cast in filial terms in the later Nayaka kingdom of Madurai (Dirks 1987: 102). Titles like *aṅgarakṣa*, *leṅka*, and *Kākatīya-rājya-sthāpan=ācārya* that highlighted the allegiance of an officer-subordinate seem to have been treasured more than any official rank during the late Kakatiya period. Devari Nayaka is a case in point. He was evidently one of the most prominent of Prataparudra's officers—he figures in six different inscriptions, was "protecting" the Macherla region of Palnad in Guntur District in 1313, and participated in the Pandya war of 1315.[46] Yet he did not possess an administrative title and his only significant *biruda* was "pillar of the Kakatiya kingdom." Instead, inscriptions foreground the bond of loyalty that tied him to the Kakatiyas by calling him a dependent on Prataparudra's lotus feet.

Since nobles all but disappear from the epigraphic record after Ganapati's reign, it is likely that chiefly and princely lineages were displaced from power in many localities in favor of nonaristocratic officers like Devari Nayaka. The best evidence for this thesis comes from Guntur and Prakasam Districts, the secondary core area established by the Kakatiyas in coastal Andhra. Rudramadevi and Prataparudra's officers were very active in these two districts, where they issued two-thirds (42 out of 67) of all their inscriptions. In the process, they appear to have taken the place of locally important chiefs and princes because nobles are no longer visible subsequently. One such noble lineage was the Kota family, who at one time controlled much of Guntur, Sattenapalli, and Narasaraopet Taluks in Guntur District. Between 1211 and 1269, the Kotas only occasionally recognized Kakatiya overlordship in their own inscriptions, while none of their direct subordinates ever referred to the Kakatiyas at all.[47] Even though the Kotas had been nominally subjugated to the Kakatiyas, the people in their territory clearly continued to view the Kotas as the traditional lords of the territory. Once the Kotas vanished from sight after 1269, however, the frequency of inscriptional acknowledgment of the Kakatiyas rises.[48] Some of those who professed their allegiance to the late Kakatiya rulers were themselves Kakatiya officers ruling in the former Kota territory, revealing the weakness of their position when compared to hereditary nobles who could ignore such niceties.[49] The increased reliance on subordinates of the officer category may thus have been a conscious policy on the part of the late Kakatiya rulers to break the entrenched power of the noble class.

A crucial question at this juncture is whether the men who became Kakatiya officers were already locally powerful or whether they were newly introduced into the localities as agents of the Kakatiyas. If the former was the case, then one set of local magnates was merely replaced by another. But if the Kakatiyas did indeed appoint new leaders brought in from outside, this would indicate the greater strength of Kakatiya polity in relation to the local communities. Once again, we must turn to the situation in Guntur and Prakasam Districts, which provides the greatest documentation. We can say with a fair degree of certainty that some Kakatiya officers were transferred into this area, with the best example being provided by Gundaya Nayaka (whose war-band was described in the preceding discussion). According to an inscription issued ca. 1297 C.E., Gundaya Nayaka was governing Magatala, the modern Makhtal Taluk in Mahbubnagar District, adjoining the border with Karnataka state (HAS 19 Mn.21). About two years later, Gundaya Nayaka is said to be ruling Gurindala and Pingala *sthalas* (small territorial units) in what is now Palnad Taluk, Guntur District (SII 10.488). These two areas are considerably removed from each other. That Gundaya Nayaka was relieved of his command over Magatala is corroborated by a record of 1298 which states that Gajasahini Madaya Reddi was then ruling it (HAS 19 Mn.18). By 1311 Gurindala *sthala*, described as comprising 60 villages, was under the jurisdiction of a third man, Rudradeva, the son of Maraya Sahini (ARE 307 of 1934–35). These particular inscriptions imply that officers could be uprooted from their home bases and sent to various places as the Kakatiya ruler deemed fit. So some officers, at least, were essentially warrior-agents embodying Kakatiya might in the localities over which they held sway. Yet we cannot discount the possibility that the Kakatiyas recruited other warriors who were already prominent in the places where their records are located. It is noteworthy in this respect, however, that hereditary association with a territory is rarely mentioned by Kakatiya officers, whereas chiefs and princes frequently stipulate a connection between a given locality and their families.

In summary, the Kakatiya political network incorporated several different types of subordinates who varied greatly in their family background, status, and relative autonomy. Some of the Kakatiya affiliates were themselves lords or kings with their own networks of power, who accepted Kakatiya claims to overlordship and acted in concert with them for military purposes. At the other end of the spectrum were men whose only claim to fame came from some form of linkage with the Kakatiyas. The increased participation of officers of humble origin in the Kakatiya political network during the reigns of the last two rulers, Rudramadevi and Prataparudra, was to have momentous sociological repercussions, for it led to the emergence of a new class of warrior lords. Their actual and putative descendants were, as discussed in chapter 5, the sector of the Andhra population who most cherished the memory of the Kakatiyas in later centuries. Furthermore, the greater reliance on officers rather than noble subordinates transformed the character of late Kakatiya rule in that its constituent elements were drawn into a more tightly knit web. I noted in the previous discussion that a far higher proportion of Andhra inscriptions cited the overlordship of Prataparudra than that of Ganapati. We can now understand the reasons for this trend—the political intermediaries of the Kakatiya state were largely semi-independent nobles in the time of Ganapati, whereas those of Prataparudra's reign lacked political legitimacy in their own right. As more and more of the intermediary strata of political authority were occupied by dependent officers, the Kakatiya presence in the countryside became more palpable, and as I argue in the section that follows, more intrusive at the locality level.

Political Economy of the Kakatiya Era

Although shared military objectives were the fundamental incentive for the bonding of Kakatiya-period lords and subordinates, these ties were overlaid and consolidated through a web of common economic interests. Unlike the situation today, where wealth is typically a prerequisite to political influence, the primary route to wealth in precolonial India was through political connections. The ability to forcibly seize resources gave kings and chiefs the undeniable right to requisition a portion of their subjects' economic production. Inclusion in a political network thus meant entry into a privileged nexus of surplus extraction. But, as a corollary, a polity could not expand without an increased ability to appropriate local resources to support the growing numbers of warriors and other subordinates who were recruited into it. Some basic aspects of the political economy of Kakatiya Andhra are surveyed in the following pages—issues such as the sources of revenue for the Kakatiya elite, the sociopolitical structure through which taxes were funneled, and signs of greater Kakatiya economic intrusion into the localities. Because of the sketchy nature of the data, however, we can only arrive at tentative conclusions.

One source of support for Kakatiya-era lords was land that was seemingly set aside for them by virtue of their position. The word *rāca*, a Telugu variant of *rāja*, appears in conjunction with several terms meaning "field" and denoted a category of land distinct from the normal wet and dry lands of a village (HAS 13.26; IAP-N 1.101). Agricultural enhancement was responsible for the creation of some of this land belonging to lords. For instance, the Vira Balanjya merchant Bairi Setti had a tank constructed in 1303 near a temple that he established (IAP-K.38). But only one-third of the newly irrigated land was given to the temple, while the remaining two-thirds was reserved for the lord (*rācādinamu*). Presumably the area had not previously been under cultivation and so was virgin territory. The lord who received a substantial portion of the now-valuable wet land was probably Chinna Rudradeva Maharaja, who also figures in the inscription as a secondary donor to Bairi Setti's temple.

Generally, however, lords possessed only rights over specified revenues from land, rather than the land itself. In 1246 Kakatiya Ganapati endowed a portion of the royal share (*rāja-pālu*) of produce from lands irrigated by two tanks to the god Yeleshvara in Nalgonda District (ARE 132 of 1954–55). When an *agrahāra* brahman village was established, the royal prerogatives to income were transferred to the brahman recipients. This is evident from two instances when existing villages were transformed into *agrahāras* (EI 38.16; EA 4.11). The inscriptions are explicit in stating that revenues previously paid by residents to the king, which included professional taxes on nonagriculturalists as well as taxes on agricultural production, should now be given to the brahman-proprietors. The lord's revenues from land might sometimes be demanded in cash rather than in kind. When the residents of two villages made a collective endowment to a newly established temple, the amount donated is described as one-sixteenth of the money paid for the *rāca-siddhāya* (IAP-N 1.80).[50] The lord (*rāca*) to whom the tax was due in this instance must have been one of the two Cheraku chiefs who also endowed land to the new temple, and not the Kakatiya ruler himself. When no other lord but the Kakatiya is mentioned in an inscription, on the other hand, we can assume that the king received the revenue (e.g., IAP-W.86; HAS 19 Km.7).

The revenue term *rāca-suṅkamu* reveals that commercial activities were also a source of income for kings and lords (ARE 295 of 1936–37). *Suṅkam* or *suṅkamu*, the Telugu version of the Sanskrit word *śuṅkam*, is the most frequently mentioned tax in Kakatiya-period inscriptions. *Suṅkam* can figure alone as a blanket term denoting an entire class of imposts, or it can refer to a specific tax when joined with a word like "shop" (*aṅgaḍi*) or "marketplace" (*aḍḍavaṭṭa*). Broadly speaking, it means the various tolls levied on commerce, particularly customs duties charged on merchandise in transit and taxes on the buying and selling of commodities. A range of miscellaneous taxes are also subsumed under the word *suṅkam*, some of which were levied on productive processes rather than on the goods themselves, like the tax on oil presses (*gānugu-suṅkamu*, ARE 324 of 1930–31) and on areca-nut orchards (SII 10.530). The intervention of kings in the setting of tariffs and customs duties is amply demonstrated by Kakatiya Ganapati's Motupalli inscription (EI 12.22), which assured sea traders that they would not be subject to extortionary tolls at Motupalli and itemized the exact rates on a number of items.

Kakatiya subordinates of the noble class undoubtedly had claims to all three forms of economic support: their own plots of lands, rights to a portion of income from the agricultural production of villages, and revenues from commercial activities. As the hereditary lords of their localities, chiefs and princes either already possessed these privileges when they joined the Kakatiya political network as subordinate allies or were reconfirmed in their possession when reinstated to power after the Kakatiya conquest. Because they held their economic rights largely independently of the Kakatiyas, noble donors, when making charitable endowments, often did not bother to acknowledge their subservience to the Kakatiyas. Their favored objects of religious gift, by an overwhelming majority, were villages and plots of land. But joining the Kakatiya political alliance must have ensured a greater security for their claims, as well as the added benefit of obtaining even more resources from successful military campaigns in conjunction with the Kakatiyas.

Kakatiya subordinates who were officers also had various economic assets, but how they acquired them is less clear. It is evident that individuals of non-noble status could also possess rights over land, for plots of land and villages frequently comprised their religious gifts, although not as often as with nobles. On numerous occasions, officer donors specify that their grant of land is coming out of their own *vritti*, a term most commonly applied to lands given to temples and brahmans. While some of these donors may themselves have been brahmans and obtained their plots of land in this capacity, that was not always the case (e.g., HAS 13.34; ARE 324 of 1930–31). Certain Kakatiya officers also mention their own proprietary rights over land—Pennama Nayaka, for example, gave land out of his own domain (*maṇḍalamu*, SII 4.978), and three *nāyaka* brothers who were *aṅgarakṣa* bodyguards gave lands that were partially purchased and partially came out of their own share (*pālu*, SII 10.425). References to land intended for their subsistence also appear in inscriptions issued by officer-like donors outside the Kakatiya political network who were nonbrahmans.[51] In post–Kakatiya Andhra, *jīvitamu* signified a land grant given to a warrior (Somasekhara Sarma 1948: 247).

One gets a sense that the kinds of rights over land possessed by officer-level subordinates differed from those held by nobles, in connection with whose land grants the word *vritti* is never used. *Vritti* connotes a control over land that one received from a superior, as when the Shaiva devotee Maheshvara specifies that he is endowing a temple with land from a *vritti* given to him by the lord Recherla Beti (ARE 55 of 1970–71). Most *vrittis* were assessed at reduced levels of taxation, since they were intended for the maintenance of religious institutions (*dēva[ra]-vritti*) and specialists (*brāhmaṇa-vritti*) and could be farmed by tenant cultivators or leased out to an individual contractor. The repeated use of the term "one's own" in reference to rights over land held by officers is also striking since it seldom appears otherwise. While these are but fragmentary clues, they raise the possibility that low-ranking subordinates were sometimes recompensed for their service to the Kakatiyas by a form of proprietorship over land that could be alienated independently. Their participation in the Kakatiya political network may have led to concrete gains in the form of land that they would not have controlled otherwise, contrary to the advantages enjoyed by hereditary chiefs and princes.

A sizable segment of the non-noble Kakatiya subordinate class was subsidized economically by the commercial taxes and tolls that were collected in the name of the state. That is, people with names indicating involvement in the actual process of revenue extraction were often able to waive a temple's obligation to pay certain sales taxes or customs duties or, alternatively, could divert an incoming revenue from one source to another recipient. Thus, men called *sarvādhikāri* (head superintendent) twice exempted the transit charges due on bullock-loads of goods brought into the temple town of Tripurantakam (SII 10.304 and 497). Similarly, a man with the word *aḍḍavaṭṭa*, "officially recognized marketplace," in front of his personal name waived taxes on the sale of a number of items including horses, bullocks, grain, and oil in Velpuru (ARE 328 of 1934–35). On the other hand, a tax superintendent (*suṅkādhikāri*) endowed three gold coins taken out of the annual king's share of commercial revenues (*rāca-suṅkamu*) in the market-town Bhattiprolu (ARE 295 of 1936–37). In either case, whether remitting a tax or redirecting a portion of it, these officers obviously had the right to collect specific levies on commerce and retain some of what they extracted.

The taxes that were granted or exempted by Kakatiya officers were not limited to the commercial sphere. Men with militaristic titles like *nāyaka*, *gaja-sāhiṇi*, and *leṅka* frequently transferred revenues arising from herding or agricultural activities, in addition to revenues from trade or manufacturing. At least a part of the produce of land was thus retained in the hands of Kakatiya military officers who functioned as local governors, in effect, for the Kakatiya state. One of their primary sources of income was the *pullari* grazing fee, which the prominent Kakatiya warrior Devari Nayaka waived on temple lands in Kocherlakota. At the same time, he ordered the town's merchants to hand over half of the sales taxes from their stores (*aṅgaḍi-suṅkam*) to the temple (NDI Darsi 35). Marayasahini Rudradeva, a *mahārāya-gaja-sāhiṇi* (king's commander of the elephant corps) and servant of Kakatiya Prataparudra, is said to have been ruling the territory of Gurindala when he too exempted a temple's livestock from the grazing fee (ARE 307 of 1934–35). Bol Nayaka, on his successful return from a campaign against the Pandyas, exempted all the lands of a temple from payment of the *paṅga(mu)* tax, a levy in kind on agricultural produce, for the merit of Kakatiya Prataparudra (SII 10.540; Parabrahma Sastry 1978: 214–15).

Although there is every reason to suppose that Kakatiya-era lords similarly received revenues from agriculture, herding, and commerce, they seldom made these the explicit objects of their religious gifts or issued tax remissions. When nobles made their generous benefactions of villages or land, many such revenues (constituting the king's or state's share of resources) evidently accompanied the endowment to a temple or brahman. But the characteristic donors of taxes, the people who expressly made taxes the objects of their charitable endowments, were rather individuals from the officer class. We can be sure of this in approximately half of the 48 Kakatiya instances, since the donors bear official designations such as *sarvādhikāri*, *mahāpradhāni*, or *aṅgarakṣa*.[52] Several others who lacked administrative titles expressed their allegiance to the Kakatiyas through the dedication of the gift's merit or the display of *biruda*s like "pillar of the Kakatiya kingdom." In contrast, only a handful of tax grants and remissions were ever made by either Kakatiya nobles or members of the royal family. We can surmise that many Kakatiya officers, both civilian and military, were given the privilege of appropriating certain revenues in return for their participation in the Kakatiya political network. Because of the correlation between this form of gift and the officer class of Kakatiya subordinates, gifts of taxes are disproportionately clustered in time toward the end of Kakatiya rule, when officers were numerically dominant in the political network.[53]

The greater number of tax grants and remissions in the late thirteenth and early fourteenth centuries may also reflect a conscious royal effort to tap commercial sources of revenue.[54] In the same manner, it is possible that the last two Kakatiya rulers tried to enhance the efficiency of their extraction of landed income by a more direct penetration of the countryside—that is, by eliminating hereditary nobles and using dependent officers instead to collect revenue. We have seen that renowned Kakatiya generals like Devari Nayaka and Marayasahini Rudradeva ruled localities and could dispense certain incomes that accrued from their territory. Such officials would siphon off a portion of the state's revenues that they gathered, but presumably this would be a much smaller amount than a traditional lord would retain. Clearly, the association between charitable tax grants and Kakatiya officers suggests that their economic rights were more circumscribed than were those of the nobility—they could exempt or give away a specific tax that was owed to them, but they could not so easily transfer proprietary rights over land, including all revenues, in the manner of noble lords. This lack of autonomy underlies their propensity to profess public allegiance to the Kakatiyas when making religious endowments, which led to the increased visibility of the Kakatiya network in the public eye as the officer class grew in number.

The introduction of a new type of tenurial right over territory known as *nāyaṅkaramu* (also *nāyaṅkaṟamu*, *nāyaṅkuṟamu*) further supports my suggestion that late Kakatiya polity increasingly intruded into the small centers of military power (forts), religious power (temples), and economic power (markets) that served the various localities. Though better known in relation to the Vijayanagara period, *nāyaṅkaramu* actually originated first in the Andhra country and was subsequently adopted and refined by the Vijayanagara empire.[55] *Nāyaṅkaramu* was unquestionably a Kakatiya innovation, for the dynasty is cited in all but three of the relevant records.[56] The earliest references come from 1269 C.E., in the era of Queen Rudramadevi (SII 10.423 and 424). Seven of the total number of 23 inscriptions pertaining to *nāyaṅkaramu* come from her reign, and the remaining 16 date to Prataparudra's time.[57]

The Kakatiya allusions to *nāyaṅkaramu* are of two kinds: either a gift is made in some individual's *nāyaṅkaramu* ("in the *nāyaṅkaramu* of X") or else a person is labeled the holder of a *nāyaṅkaramu* (*nāyaṅkapuvāru*). The consciousness of a locality as situated in someone's *nāyaṅkaramu* was strong enough to compel frequent identification of a gift as occurring within that person's territory by a third party. The area of a *nāyaṅkaramu* is sometimes equated with the territorial unit *sthala*, which comprised anywhere from 18 to 60 villages (SII 10.521; ARE 307 of 1934–35). Twenty different men are named in connection with *nāyaṅkaramu* tenure, most of whom were warriors bearing a variety of status titles in addition to *nāyaka*. With rare exceptions, *nāyaṅkaramu* was a prerogative of officers rather than of nobles.[58] The close personal bond between the Kakatiya ruler and these men is highlighted in several inscriptions, as in the following instance:

> May all fare well and prosper! In the 1,191th year of the Shaka era [1270 C.E.], on the 13th (day of the) bright (fortnight in the lunar month) Paushya, a Monday;
>
> On the occasion of the winter solstice, Bolli Nayaka, the Guardian of the Courtyard Gate for the illustrious Mahamandaleshvara Kakatiya Rudradeva Maharaja, gave 10 *kha[ṇḍugas]* of land to the temple servants of the lord Kalyana Keshava of Kranja (village) in his own *nāyaṅkaṟamu* (territory) for the religious benefit of his own master Rudradeva Maharaja.[59] (SII 4.705)

Bolli Nayaka not only identifies himself as a Kakatiya official but also transfers the religious benefit that arises from the act of gift-giving to his lord (*svāmi*), the Kakatiya ruler. He was one of four *aṅgarakṣas* (bodyguards) of Rudramadevi who held *nāyaṅkaramu* rights over territory.[60] *Aṅgarakṣa* was a new position instituted during her reign, designating warriors who were members of the queen's retinue. The awarding of *nāyaṅkaramu* to personal bodyguards is reminiscent of early European feudalism, which is thought to have developed from the practice of entrusting territories to members of the class of household retainers and troops (Bloch 1961: 151–56).

Nāyaṅkaramu holders controlled a small territory, that much is clear. What rights they possessed within the delegated territory is harder to determine. But they did have the authority to waive taxes in their localities. Four occurrences of tax remissions by people with *nāyaṅkaramu* rights or their associates are documented, plus two grants of income from a tax.[61] *Nāyaṅkaramu* must therefore have been some kind of revenue assignment over a fairly limited number of villages. Many *nāyakas* who figure in sixteenth-century Tamil inscriptions also had the power to remit taxes (Karashima 1992: 192–93). Since *nāyaṅkaramu* appears in concert with the new trend in Kakatiya polity of incorporating people of officer status into the networks of power, it was probably a means for recompensing warriors for their military service to the dynasty. Through *nāyaṅkaramu* assignments, officer subordinates without any resources of their own were provided with sustenance. At the same time, the Kakatiya rulers could be assured of a roster of faithful warriors who could be called on for assistance in time of military need. The presence of the *nāyaṅkaramu* holders—who were representatives of Kakatiya might—in diverse localities throughout Kakatiya territory must also have furthered the Kakatiya political and economic agenda. Whether the possessor of *nāyaṅkaramu* rights was expected to maintain a set number of troops and/or forward a portion of the revenues he received, however, we cannot say.[62]

Although *nāyaṅkaramu* may have provided warriors with economic privileges akin to those of aristocratic lords, warriors' power was restrained both by convention and by the need to retain the favor of the Kakatiyas. An illuminating illustration of the limitations they faced is found in one inscription documenting a tax remission:

> May all fare well and prosper! In the 1,236th year of the auspicious Shaka era [1314 C.E.], (corresponding to the cyclic) year Ananda, on the 6th (day of the) bright (fortnight of the lunar month) Ashadha, a Thursday;
>
> May all fare well! While the illustrious Mahamandaleshvara Kakatiya Prataparudradeva Maharaja is ruling the earth;
>
> (I), the Doorkeeper of his palace, Erraya Lenkangaru—because Doddapoti Peddingaru of Pinapadu protested about these (taxes being imposed on religious endowments)—in order to avoid (any) sinful error, poured water (and gave away) for the religious merit of Prataparudradeva Maharaja, as a tax-free tenure for as long as the sun and moon (endure):
>
> the *kānika* and *gaḍḍuga-māḍalu* (taxes) on the subsistence lands [*vritti*] of the temple complexes in the 22 villages of my *nāyaṅkaramu* territory—Penumbuluvu, Uppalapadu, Manchchekalapundi, Jupundi, . . . lapundi, Nandiveluvu, Katyavaramu, Prambarru, Telaprolu, Mallivelanturu, Pinapadu, Pinaravuru, Pulukantlamu, . . . puru, Potumbarru, Pundivada, Koduru, Lamu, Krolukondda, [Kro]llikondda, Gunddimada, and Singaramu—and the *avanāyālu* (taxes) including *puṭṭi-pahiṇḍi*, *puṭṭi-kolupu*, *upakṣiti*, and *suṅkamu*, as well as the grazing tax on animals and *kānika* on the existing subsistence lands of brahmans in these villages.
>
> I am having an inscription pillar (to this effect) set up in front of the temple of the illustrious lord Gaurishvara of Penumbuluvu. The witness to these voluntary religious contributions is the illustrious lord Svayambhunatha of Orungallu [Warangal]. (SII 10.509)

Erraya Lenka obviously possessed the right to retain the enumerated revenues from the twenty-two villages in his *nāyaṅkaramu* territory. But he had demanded them from brahman and temple lands as well as normal village lands, apparently in contravention of customary practice. When he received a complaint from Doddapoti Peddi, who was most probably a brahman, Erraya Lenka decided to waive certain taxes on lands that had been endowed to brahmans and temples. In this scenario, we witness how the strength of custom could curtail the greed of the powerful, for temple and brahman lands were traditionally exempt from the full complement of taxes. Erraya Lenka's anxiety that he may have committed a religious offense and his need to publicly atone for it come through clearly in this record, as does his desire to please the Kakatiyas, whose tutelary deity Svayambhudeva he invokes (unusually) in testimony to his good intentions.

One last piece of evidence to support the view that localities came to be more tightly integrated into the late Kakatiya polity comes from the chronological distribution of inscriptions issued by village groups. Some collective endowments were made by groups such as the *aṣṭādaśa-praja* ("the eighteen [kinds of] people," also called the eighteen *jātis*) or *samasta-praja* (all the people), who purportedly represented all village residents. Other endowments were made by one or more segments of a village population such as its brahmans (*mahājana*), land-controllers (*bhūmi-prabhu*), and peasants (*kāmpu*). The total of 31 records by village collectives are overwhelmingly correlated with late Kakatiya rule. Three inscriptions were issued by groups of villagers prior to 1263 but none of them mentions Ganapati, in contrast to the four from Rudramadevi's reign which all cite her as overlord. Then there is a marked surge in the number of endowments by village collectives in Prataparudra's era—24 in all, only one of which does not acknowledge Prataparudra.[63]

Groups of villagers making religious endowments were thus far more active during Prataparudra's reign and they almost invariably recognized his sovereignty in their inscriptions. Some of the village collectives that were closely affiliated with the Kakatiya state during its last decades of existence may even have owed their existence to Kakatiya instigation since those called *aṣṭādaśa-praja* flourished only in the areas that were the bases of Kakatiya power: central Telangana (especially Nalgonda District) and Guntur-Prakasam Districts. It is possible that the *aṣṭādaśa-praja* was an officially recognized local body with distinct responsibilities in reference to the Kakatiya state, for instance in the sphere of revenue. In any case the visibility of village collectives in the epigraphical record of the late Kakatiya period testifies to the growing incorporation of local communities into both the culture of temple worship and the political network of the Kakatiyas. The widespread presence of many officer-level subordinates, whose appropriation of economic resources was sanctioned by their association with the Kakatiyas, was surely a factor in the increased recognition of Kakatiya overlordship by local corporate bodies. Many, although not all, of these officers served the Kakatiyas at least occasionally in a military capacity. In this way the contours of physical power had a high degree of congruence with the networks of resource extraction.

Conceptualizing the Kakatiya State

Having closely examined several facets of Kakatiya political culture and rule through the prism of inscriptions, we must now consider the question of classification. How would we categorize a polity of the Kakatiya kind—one in which the power is conveyed through personal channels, concentrated in the hands of a horseback-riding martial elite, differentially distributed in a hierarchy of rank, and dispersed in a multiplicity of centers? The first label that comes to mind is feudalism, a term widely applied to premodern, militaristic states that are neither centralized nor unitary. There are indeed some broad similarities between Kakatiya Andhra and medieval Europe, which might justify use of the term "feudalism" if one defines it primarily as a political institution, in the manner of Marc Bloch (1961: 446). In the Indian context, however, a more Marxist definition of feudalism is generally employed by historians. Feudalism, in the sense that R. S. Sharma (1965) and others subscribing to the school of Indian feudalism use it, means not only personalized rule by a warrior elite but also a socio-economic formation marked by oppression of the peasantry, economic stagnation, and deurbanization. Although the model of feudalism represented an advance on earlier formulations of medieval India when it was first offered, since it at least recognized that India was subject to historical change like the rest of the world, it no longer has many adherents.[64] The image of an economically depressed land of isolated villages full of serfs is particularly inappropriate for medieval South India (Kumar 1985).

A popular alternative to the feudalistic interpretation of medieval Indian polities is the segmentary-state model developed by Burton Stein (1977; 1980: 254–365). A segmentary state, in Stein's definition, is composed of a multitude of largely autonomous local units. In Tamil Nadu the localized segments were known as *nāḍu*, a term that denoted a particular locality. But the *nāḍu* was not just a physical territory, it was also "an interactional region defined by relatively dense interrelations among social groups with common interests in some tract of cultivable land" (Stein 1980: 90). While others have regarded the *nāḍu* as either an administrative unit represented by an assembly (Nilakanta Sastri 1955: 503–4), a local marketing territory (Hall 1980: 187), or a cluster of peasant settlements formed around a common irrigation source (Subbarayalu 1982: 273), Stein viewed the *nāḍu* as a complete social and economic universe—an ethnically coherent territory within which peasants formed their marriage and kin relationships and carried out their economic activities and transactions. The *nāḍu* was at the same time the effective political unit of medieval Tamil Nadu, headed either by the *nāṭṭār* assembly representing peasant landholders or by a chief who belonged to the dominant peasant group (Stein 1980: 90–111).

According to Stein, the hundreds of *nāḍus* that comprised the Chola segmentary state were joined together in a pyramidal structure that converged on the king, "the moral center of society" (1980: 269). Unlike hierarchical political structures where the lower levels had qualitatively different kinds of power delegated to them, the various units in a pyramidal structure each had essentially the same kind of authority and control. The power exercised by a *nāḍu* chief or "little king" was no different in quality from that of the Chola king, but merely more limited in its territorial jurisdiction or quantity. Stein stated that the Chola state existed "only in the sense that all of the constituent territories recognized the single ritual sovereignty of the largest, wealthiest, and most powerful territorial unit, that of the Cholas in the Kaveri," since the Cholas neither exercised direct control over *nāḍus* outside their core area nor received any resource transfers from them (Stein 1977: 45). Although the segmentary-state model most accurately describes the political system of the Chola period, Stein believed that the segmentary state was the typical political form throughout the medieval era within the entire South Indian macroregion, defined as modern Tamil Nadu, southern Karnataka, and southern coastal Andhra (1980: 32–44). A variety of cultural, social, and political criteria were supposedly employed to delineate the macroregion, but Stein admitted that it "is almost coterminous with the maximal extent of the Chola overlordship" (1980: 34).

Stein's formulation of the segmentary state has been extensively criticized, on two basic grounds: that he exaggerated the weakness of the Chola state and drew an artificial differentiation between ritual and political methods of rule. In reacting to the previous depiction of Chola polity as a bureaucratized unitary state by K. Nilakanta Sastri and others, Stein went so far in the other direction that he almost denied the existence of a state. Specialists on the Chola period argue that Stein overlooked crucial evidence that the royal "center" did exert some measure of administrative control over the localities through the intervention of its officials and the extraction of tax revenues (Subbarayalu 1982: 299–300; Heitzman 1987). We need not say much here about the second main objection to Stein's model—the theoretical separation of ritual sovereignty and political control—since Stein subsequently abandoned this position.[65] A related charge is that Stein subordinated "the political and economic dimensions of the state structure to its ritual dimension" (Chattopadhyaya 1994: 215) or that he overemphasized gift-giving (Inden 1990: 208).

A third critique that can be leveled against Stein's segmentary model is its characterization of the peasant world of *nāḍus*, described as "relatively self-sufficient, enduring and often quite ancient localised societies" (1980: 275). While *nāḍus* are certainly larger than the villages that Orientalist constructions identified as the basic units of rural life, Stein's repeated use of the words "persistence" and "durability" in reference to these "ethnic" regions (e.g., 1980: 99–101, 104–5) reinforces earlier notions that India was composed of discrete social cells that had replicated themselves since time immemorial. Doubt has been cast on the accuracy of Stein's portrayal of the *nāḍu* even for the Tamil country and there are no grounds whatsoever for imputing such a neat compartmentalization of peasant society into territorially based divisions in medieval Andhra.[66] The named localities in Kakatiya-period inscriptions are generally larger than the Chola-era *nāḍu* (encompassing at least one or two modern taluks whereas most *nāḍus* were between 8 and 40 square miles in size) and few were more than 200 years old.[67] Nor were Andhra territorial units arranged in a systematic hierarchy, as they were in Tamil Nadu.[68] Even the designations used in medieval Andhra for the same territory were subject to considerable fluctuation.

Stein himself excluded inland Andhra from the South Indian macroregion characterized by the segmentary state and ritual sovereignty, calling Telangana a shatter region on the borders of South India proper (1980: 59). Several aspects of Stein's treatment of Kakatiya Andhra are flawed, for he implied that the Kakatiyas were restricted primarily to Telangana and achieved an "operating state" only during the later part of Ganapati's reign. He also felt that Telangana culture lacked the balance of Sanskritic and non-Sanskritic elements found elsewhere in the macroregion, apparently because he believed (wrongly) that most Telangana inscriptions were composed in Sanskrit. Thus, in Stein's opinion, a "self-conscious Telugu culture" was to be found only in Vengi, the Krishna-Godavari region of coastal Andhra. But even though Stein may have been misled by incomplete or erroneous information, I fully concur with his view that Telangana lay outside the segmentary-state system. Indeed, I would go much farther and assert that no place within Kakatiya Andhra matches the model Stein presents for the Tamil country of the Chola era. The discrepancy between my account of medieval Andhra—with its stress on social and physical mobility, military activity, and rapid demographic and economic expansion—and Stein's depiction of a stable and orderly Tamil world confined to local networks is too large to reconcile.

One explanation for this discrepancy between Stein's and my reconstructions may simply be chronological. Stein derived his ideas principally from Tamil Nadu in the tenth and eleventh centuries when Chola power was at its height, whereas my temporal parameters have focused on the years from 1175 to 1325. Stein acknowledged that the Tamil country was undergoing considerable transformation during the late twelfth and thirteenth centuries when the Kakatiyas were concurrently flourishing in Andhra (1980: 216–53). Supralocal activity emerged in a number of different spheres in the Tamil society and polity of the post-Chola period—leaders of peasant origin operating in a realm larger than the *nāḍu* formed new supralocal assemblies while corporate bodies of merchants and artisans came together to articulate distinct group identities that transcended the *nāḍu*. Moreover, the growth of temples fostered the rise of new urban centers in the Tamil Nadu of the Kakatiya era. Noboru Karashima has similarly described the thirteenth century as a period of change, and even "turmoil," in the Tamil country. Private landholding first became widespread then, he believes, which led to the transference of much landed property through sale and donation in the lower Kaveri valley (Karashima 1984: 1–35). Several of the elements of dynamism I have noted in Kakatiya Andhra—the presence of large-scale organizations, allegiances, and identities as well as the considerable movement of peoples—therefore seem more characteristic of Tamil Nadu in the thirteenth century than in earlier times.

Also relevant to our discussion of why Stein's and my interpretations are so divergent is the changing balance of geopolitical power in the thirteenth-century peninsula. We have already observed that the Kakatiyas were the first dynasty from interior Andhra to successfully annex some of the coastal region. A similar development transpired in neighboring Karnataka, where a second dynasty based in an upland area—the Hoysalas of Dorasamudra—became politically dominant. Thirteenth-century sources reflect the growing influence and power of warriors from the semiarid regions of the peninsular interior, whose society differed markedly from that of the longer-settled expanses of wet rice cultivation.[69] In the case of Tamil Nadu, the social world of inland zones (Stein's intermediate *nāḍus*) was seemingly far less stratified than that of the wet zones populated by brahmans, dominant peasants, and landless cultivators. And political power was exercised in the dry uplands by local strongmen or chieftains wielding coercive force rather than by peasant assemblies conjoined in an overarching system of ritual sovereignty. Kakatiya Andhra thus more closely resembles the medieval Tamil hinterland than it does Stein's paradigmatic fertile Kaveri River delta. The militaristic culture of upland warriors permeated much of Andhra, with its large expanse of arid and semiarid territory, and this led to greater social fluidity and opportunity than was possible in the more hierarchical societies of the wet zones.

But differing time spans and ecological characteristics do not account for all the disparities between my Kakatiya Andhra and Stein's Chola Tamil Nadu. A major factor in the gap between our reconstructions is our fundamental disagreement over the nature of political intermediaries. Stein believed that all political power in Chola Tamil Nadu was exercised by representatives of the dominant peasantry acting on behalf of local interests. Regardless of whether governance was controlled by the corporate body of peasant landholders or by chiefs who belonged to the dominant peasant group, Stein insisted that political leaders were locally based and owed none of their power to the Chola kings. Supralocal chiefs who were "increasingly divorced from the locality peasantry" (1980: 223) did emerge in the twelfth and thirteenth centuries and subsequently "this stratum of powerful men was to become merged in the new and highly martial power system of the Vijayanagara period" (1980: 253). Yet even the Vijayanagara kings could not destroy the strength of local communities, because "very localised affinities, sentiments and, especially, entitlements—and the cultural, social, and political means for defending them—continued to persist" (1995: 136). At least until the seventeenth century, Stein asserted that "no intermediate statuses of offices stood between powerful peasant chieftains and kings; none ceased to identify themselves with the peasant lineages from which they came and through which they exercised their local authority" (1985: 85).

Stein rightly refuted the interpretations of earlier scholars who read every inscriptional title as standing for a discrete administrative position in a highly bureaucratized state apparatus. But current specialists on Chola inscriptions agree that some titles denote an official state function, particularly in relation to revenue collection, whereas others simply signify high rank (Subbarayalu 1982: 278–85; Heitzman 1997: 148–61). Stein's blanket refusal to acknowledge that locality leaders could ever constitute a different class than the peasantry they ruled was a serious flaw in his thinking, as was his inability to conceive of subordinate chiefs as individuals who were simultaneously active in local and state-level networks. Since Stein could not accept the existence of intermediaries—people who straddled the divide between the locality and the state—he was unable to present a convincing explanation of the mechanism of political integration. Local chieftains accepted Chola ritual sovereignty, according to Stein, because it gave them legitimacy (1977: 46–47), but in other respects they acted as fully independent rulers rooted in their localities. One wonders why chiefs needed royal legitimacy if they were indeed so closely bound, by origin, to the local communities whose power they embodied. In this respect, it is noteworthy that Stein consistently portrayed agrarian relations as highly harmonious.

I have argued, in contrast, that there were numerous motives for the relationships that developed between kings and lower-level power holders, some of whom depended on the kings at least partially for their authority and positions. Joint military action was an especially strong incentive, leading both to enhanced martial prestige and the practical benefits of greater control over territory. Through military service, numerous Kakatiya subordinates of the officer class must have elevated their social status for they often came from obscure families. That officers are rarely identified in relation to an ancestral village or locality, could sometimes be transferred from place to place, and regularly cited Kakatiya overlordship proves their dependent status—that they could never have been the "natural" leaders of a local peasant constituency. Nor can the more aristocratic Kakatiya subordinates have represented a local peasant or ethnic group, even if they possessed a power base of their own forged through generations of rule and fortified by command over a corps of military and civilian followers. Since military entrepreneurship could lead to migration into a new region, many lordly families of the Kakatiya era were undoubtedly not indigenous to the territories they ruled. And given the large percentage of herding and hunting peoples in the Andhra population, it is extremely unlikely that all political leaders were of peasant origin. In brief, I emphatically reject Stein's claim that political power was inherently collective and originated solely from local peasant or ethnic communities. I attribute far more variety and individuality to the intermediary strata of political power, as well as agency—for even lowly officers could actively choose to form strategic alliances with the more powerful to further their own interests.

The Kakatiya "state" is best understood as a fluctuating political network composed in large part of a multitude of personal ties between lords and underlings. Some of the fibers in the fabric of Kakatiya polity united the rulers directly to their primary subordinates; others led from these subordinates to different tiers of associates in a densely ramified pattern. Connections extended horizontally, integrating localities spread over a wide territory, as well as vertically, reaching down into the villages and towns. Several scholars have considered political systems of this sort—in which multiple foci of power (i.e., lords of differing status) are conjoined through common affiliation to a single overlord—to typify early medieval India (Chattopadhyaya 1994: 183–222; Kulke 1995a; Inden 1982). The paradigm of the "*sāmanta* system" or "a hierarchy of kings" is particularly well suited to early Kakatiya rule, when the Kakatiya overlords governed through a loose alliance of numerous hereditary chiefs and princes. Yet many features of the late Kakatiya period more closely approximate a patrimonial model of the state. In Max Weber's definition, patrimonialism was characterized by the personalized authority wielded by a ruler through a class of dependent officials. Rulers of patrimonial states typically attempted to extend their control at the expense of local authorities and often relied heavily on levies on trade and other forms of additional surplus extraction (Stein 1985: 76, 81–82; Kulke 1995b: 5, 36–37). The promotion of a class of humble officer-warriors to positions of power in the late Kakatiya period, the virtual disappearance of entrenched hereditary lordships, and the increased mention of commercial revenues all reveal a patrimonial trend.[70]

A similar fluctuation in the balance of power between a king and his affiliates has been observed in relation to the Chola state. Chiefs were highly visible in Chola inscriptions prior to 1000 C.E. but virtually vanished from the records between approximately 1000 (the reign of Rajaraja I) to 1133 (the reign of Kulottunga II; Subbarayalu 1982: 270). Whereas the Kakatiya political network was abruptly terminated at this stage of its evolution by an enemy with superior military capabilities, the Chola pendulum continued to its full cycle with the reappearance of chiefs after 1133. During the rule of the most powerful Chola kings, in other words, chiefs were either displaced or turned into officials, but as the royal dynasty waned chiefs once again flourished. Perhaps the rise of officer subordinates in the late Kakatiya polity would have followed the Chola example in a cyclic progression back to a phase of chiefly efflorescence if its internal development had not been interrupted by an outside force. One could argue that medieval South Indian polities regularly oscillated between two poles: from one (where hereditary nobles were ascendant) to the other (where intermediaries were largely dependent officers) according to the strength of the central dynastic power.

While future research must be more sensitive to changes in the membership of ruling elites over time so as to elucidate the developmental trajectories of medieval polities, what happened during the late Kakatiya period appears to be more than just a periodic episode in a rhythmic swing. During its last few decades, the Kakatiya polity exhibited several new and distinctive features, most notably the incorporation of large numbers of lowly warriors with status titles like *nāyaka* and *reḍḍi*. Andhra political elites of subsequent centuries retained the titles and militaristic ethos that evolved in the Kakatiya period along with the *nāyaṅkaramu* revenue assignments that subsidized the warrior class. The accelerating pace of agrarian development partially explains the growing militarization of Andhra society, since it led to the absorption of upland peoples with a strong martial tradition. The prevalence of martial skills made it easy for the Kakatiyas to recruit armed men but may also have forced this recruitment in order to forestall the emergence of secondary centers of power. But larger trends throughout the subcontinent were also encouraging militarization. With the diffusion of improved horse-riding technology, the coercive capability of the state was considerably enhanced but also increasingly confined to a specialized class of trained horsemen (Deloche 1989: 48; Wink 1997: 90). Rulers who could attract and retain the services of professional fighters were able to exert greater power over local communities than in the past, which accounts for the more pronounced patrimonialism of the late Kakatiya period. The growing incorporation of the subcontinent into a broader Indian Ocean system of trade may also have contributed to an expansion of commerce, another change that fostered a break from the early medieval system of indirect rule through a circle of kings to a more intrusive and personalized form of political power.

In conclusion, many of the developments of the late Kakatiya period—its growing militarism, the disappearance of ancient lineages of chiefs, the migration of warriors into areas outside their places of origin, the emphasis on personal ties between lord and subordinate, *nāyaṅkaramu* revenue assignments, and the greater control over distant localities exercised by kings through their delegated officers—are specified in the secondary literature as innovations of the Vijayanagara period. The reason is that South Indian scholarship has focused so heavily on Tamil Nadu, where these changes were not introduced until the late-fifteenth-century takeover of much of the region by Vijayanagara. The conventional periodization of South Indian history, which interprets Vijayanagara as a response to the new Muslim "threat" and hence sees a sharp disruption in historical continuity, has also obscured the many sociopolitical patterns that unite the centuries before and after 1336 C.E., the traditional date of Vijayanagara's founding. My analysis of Kakatiya Andhra has instead shown that the critical period of political transition was the thirteenth century. As more research is conducted, I suspect we will increasingly regard the thirteenth century as the beginning of the early modern period since the seeds of so much of South India's later development originated in that era.

5

The Kakatiyas in Telugu Historical Memory

Many aspects of the Kakatiya period's significance have been covered in the previous pages. It was the first era in Andhra's history when the two widely disparate zones of the wet coastal territory and drier upland area were integrated into one polity. This political integration is reflected in the displacement of Kannada as an epigraphic language in western Andhra in favor of Telugu. Telangana, the nucleus of Kakatiya power, was henceforth indisputably part of a united Telugu cultural sphere. The twin processes of demographic and agrarian growth pushed settlement farther into the hinterland throughout the Kakatiya period. The dynamism of interior Andhra is revealed not only by the building of new temples and tanks but also by the appearance of inscriptions for the first time in many localities.

As agricultural technologies intensified and more land was settled and cultivated, tribal and pastoral peoples who had formerly followed nonagricultural lifestyles and/or had engaged in shifting cultivation were absorbed by the growing Telugu society and transformed into peasants. The vibrant society of frontier Andhra also included migrants from long-settled areas as well as long-distance traders. In the resulting social mix, there was ample room for advancement of individual status and for altering social identities. The prevalence of military skills heightened the possibilities for social mobility in this era when military loyalties and service formed the backbone of the political system. As the military-political coalition built by the Kakatiyas grew over time, it destroyed the vestiges of older principalities and chiefdoms. By incorporating scores of local warrior-peasants into its network, Kakatiya polity penetrated more deeply into the localities at the same time that it created a new ruling elite of Telugu warriors.

This interpretation of Kakatiya Andhra has been derived largely from contemporary inscriptions. But it is, of course, also influenced by a considerable body of recent scholarship on medieval South India and shaped by my own personal views. In attempting to escape the distortions caused by colonial knowledge and anachronistic projection of present-day realities back into the past, I have adopted a somewhat Protestant insistence on returning to the original sources in my reconstruction of medieval Andhra. But an alternative perspective can be contrasted to the evidence of inscriptions—the ways in which the Kakatiyas were remembered by Andhra society in subsequent times. Rather than analyzing Kakatiya-era documentation in order to extract its significance, we can instead ask what the significance of the Kakatiyas was for later generations in the Andhra region. Because historical constructions are often produced by a small set of patrons and only circulate within a limited circle, we can assume that many historical writings of the late medieval and early modern eras are no longer available to us. But even those conceptions of the past that survive up to the present day are sufficient to demonstrate the continuing role played by the Kakatiyas in Andhra's understanding of its history.

Social memories are admittedly not accurate reflections of what actually happened, even aside from the inevitable losses and errors that occur over time. Historical memories do not preserve the past as much as create meaning for the present by supplying it with a vision of what came before. In the process, the degree of continuity between past and present is often exaggerated, so as to bring the two into alignment. Present-day arrangements or beliefs can be legitimized by portraying them as ancient, since once they are naturalized as inherent to society they become regarded as inviolable. Conversely, aspects of the past that do not conform with present conditions may be omitted from future transmission or transformed to be made more comprehensible. Memories of the past are therefore generally revised in ways that make them appropriate to the present, with its own realities and issues.[1]

Because constructions of the past must resonate with present concerns, only those aspects that are meaningful to the present are transmitted in social memory. In that sense, what a society "remembers" is not a matter of random chance and is not based on illogical principles. The very existence of traditions relating to the Kakatiyas attests to the ability of succeeding generations to derive significance from constructions of the Andhra past in which the Kakatiyas were important. Why and how the Kakatiyas should have remained so meaningful for centuries afterward is the main question addressed in this chapter. Understanding the import of the Kakatiyas in Andhra conceptions of the past adds another dimension to our reconstruction of their place in Andhra history derived from inscriptions, one that not so much corrects the epigraphic analysis as reminds us that historical significance is multilayered. Because the various historical memories of the Kakatiyas are themselves the cultural products of specific times and places, they must be viewed within the context of the sociopolitical milieus in which they were composed. Hence, I begin this chapter with an account of the fall of the Kakatiya kingdom and its immediate aftermath.

Reviving Past Glory: Warrior Appropriations of the Kakatiyas

Kakatiya Successors in the Fourteenth Century

The era of Kakatiya greatness came to an abrupt end in 1323, the year that the capital Warangal was seized by an army sent by the Tughluq ruler of Delhi. The conflict between the Kakatiyas and the Delhi sultanate had begun twenty years earlier, when the earliest expedition sent against Andhra ended in utter failure. Subsequent sultanate campaigns into Kakatiya territory, far more successful, have been documented in several Indo-Muslim chronicles.[2] Warangal was first attacked in 1310 by the general Malik Kafur on the orders of the sultan Ala-ud-din Khalji. After a four-month siege of the Kakatiya capital, the sultanate forces obtained much booty and a promise of tribute in the years to come. Following this defeat, Prataparudra even cooperated with the sultanate militarily, sending his forces far into the Tamil country.[3] But Prataparudra did not remit his payments to Delhi as previously agreed, and this led to another Khalji expedition in 1318 under the command of Khusrau Khan. It too resulted in the extraction of tribute from the Kakatiya kingdom.[4]

The Kakatiya political network seems to have survived intact through these encounters with the armies of the Khalji sultans. But under the military assaults of the next dynasty, that of the Tughluqs, the Kakatiya kingdom was to collapse entirely. Ghiyas-ud-din Tughluq, who proclaimed himself sultan in 1320, sent an expedition against Telangana the following year, with his eldest son, Ulugh Khan, in charge. When a half-year siege of Warangal fort still did not compel the Kakatiyas to sue for peace, Ulugh Khan was forced to retreat to Devagiri in modern Maharashtra. Devagiri, the former capital of the Yadava kingdom, had been the first peninsular political center captured by Delhi forces and now served as a launching point for attacks against the remaining kingdoms of the Deccan. Reinforced by additional troops sent from Delhi, Ulugh Khan soon returned to Warangal for a second siege. This time Warangal held out only five months before surrendering. Prataparudra was captured and dispatched to Delhi—according to most accounts, he died en route.

The seizure of the Kakatiya capital and king in 1323 had a devastating effect, for nothing of the Kakatiya political system survived, at least in recognizable form. There were no subsequent claimants to the Kakatiya throne nor do any attested Kakatiya subordinates figure in later epigraphic records (although any former Kakatiya warrior who had switched allegiance to the sultanate would certainly not have advertised his previous affiliation).[5] With the fall of the kingdom, political conditions in Andhra immediately became highly unstable and turbulent. Ulugh Khan did not remain long in Warangal, for he appears to have quickly led a military force into Orissa and possibly to Tamil Nadu as well. He was then recalled to Delhi, where he assumed the position of sultan in 1325 under the name Muhammad bin Tughluq. By that time, coastal Andhra between the Krishna and Godavari Rivers was no longer under sultanate control and the same was true of the rest of the coastal region within a few years. While the martial abilities of local Telugu warriors are generally cited as the reason for their rapid resurgence, internal problems within the Delhi sultanate were also a major factor. Muhammad bin Tughluq's attempt to stabilize his Deccan conquests by setting up a second capital at Devagiri (renamed Daulatabad) failed in the face of continued revolts by his generals, which culminated in the establishment of an independent Muslim state in Gulbarga (Karnataka) by the Bahman Shah. By the time of the Bahmani sultanate's founding in 1347, Telangana had largely slipped out of Muslim control.[6]

Little is known about the local warriors credited with expelling the Muslim forces from Andhra. Both along the coast and in the interior, the dominant Telugu chiefs of the 1330s and 1340s belonged to an obscure lineage called Musunuri. Prolaya Nayaka is the first member of the Musunuri family visible in the historical sources, followed by his cousin (father's brother's son) Kapaya Nayaka. Repeated armed conflicts between Musunuri Kapaya Nayaka and the Bahmani sultanate based in Gulbarga eventually led to a treaty, around 1364, in which the border between the two was set at the edge of western Andhra, at Golkonda in modern Hyderabad District. Thus the Bahmani sphere of influence was quite restricted on the east, reaching only into the Telangana borderlands of Hyderabad, Medak, and Nizamabad Districts. These boundaries were maintained even after Musunuri Kapaya Nayaka was killed in battle around 1367 and his place was taken by Anapota Nayaka, a chieftain of another Telugu warrior lineage, the Recherlas. The Recherla Nayakas (not to be confused with the Recherla clan of the early Kakatiya period who used the status title *reḍḍi*), like the Musunuris, were a group that moved into the limelight only after the fall of the Kakatiyas.[7] Upon Musunuri Kapaya Nayaka's death, the Recherla Nayakas became the leading power in Telangana, where they built two fortified strongholds: Rachakonda (also known as Rajukonda) and Devarakonda, both in Nalgonda District.

While first the Musunuris and then the Recherlas were entrenching themselves in Telangana, coastal Andhra witnessed the rise of a third new warrior lineage. The power of the Reddis of the Panta clan was established about 1325 by (Prolaya) Vema Reddi, alias Komati Vema. He seems to have controlled the coastal territory as far south as Nellore and as far west as Srisailam, from a base in Addanki (the modern taluk headquarters in Prakasam District). His successor Anavota Reddi (r. 1353-64) is credited with both consolidating the kingdom and moving its capital to Kondavidu in Guntur District. By approximately 1395, a second Reddi kingdom was set up by a junior branch of the family, with its capital in Rajahmundry, East Godavari District. At the dawn of the fifteenth century, the Recherla Nayakas and the Panta clan Reddis dominated Telangana and coastal Andhra, respectively.[8]

The newly emergent Telugu warrior lineages of the immediate post-Kakatiya period—the Musunuris, Recherla Nayakas, and Panta Reddis—share several characteristics. Although none of them is known from any Kakatiya-era sources, either epigraphic or literary, they all seem to have emerged out of the late Kakatiya military milieu. That is, the style of their inscriptions, the types of heroic epithets they adopted, their modest genealogies—all of these suggest continuity with the Telugu warrior culture and society that had evolved by the end of the Kakatiya period. Despite the radical change in political circumstances, the martial ethos and social origins of the Telugu political elite remained largely unaffected. What was lacking, what differentiated them from the earlier warriors of the Telugu country, was the absence of a common focal point—the king who had created an overarching coalition and mobilized these men in unified large-scale action. Without such a king to whom the warrior class as a whole could swear allegiance, post-Kakatiya leaders instead consciously utilized the still symbolically potent memory of the Kakatiyas.

One way a warrior could assume the Kakatiya aura was through simple juxtaposition of his exploits with those of the Kakatiyas in the introductory portion of an inscription. We find this strategy employed in the Vilasa grant of Prolaya Nayaka, the Musunuri chief.[9] The Vilasa grant, a copper-plate inscription composed about 1330, begins its narrative with an account of the greatness of the Kakatiya dynasty. Despite Prataparudra's military strength and skill in diplomacy, however, he was eventually defeated by the Lord of the Turks, Ahmad Sultan, in their eighth conflict. Evil (*adharma*) now reigned unchecked, once Prataparudra had died on the banks of the Narmada River while being taken to Delhi. The great suffering of the Andhra people and the wicked behavior of the conquering Turkic warriors are then described with great gusto. The figure of the Musunuri chief Prolaya Nayaka is finally introduced more than halfway through the grant. According to the composer, the king Prola was like one of Vishnu's incarnations who descended to earth out of compassion for the people. Through the strength of his arm, he was able to overthrow the Turkic warriors and revive dharma by restoring order to a disordered world, says the inscription. Hence, Prolaya Nayaka was a righteous king, just as Kakatiya Prataparudra had been. This righteousness in itself gave him legitimacy. The Vilasa grant's narrative sequence also clearly implies that Prolaya Nayaka was the rightful successor to the Kakatiyas. By presenting a chronology that led from the Kakatiyas to Prolaya Nayaka, the inscription links the two in a single genealogy of royal power.

The unbroken transmission of kingship from the Kakatiyas to later Telugu warrior chiefs is the message of a second inscription, the Kaluvacheru grant of 1423.[10] This record issued by Anitalli, a female member of the Panta Reddi clan, carries the process of association with the Kakatiyas much further than Prolaya Nayaka's Vilasa grant a century earlier. The Kaluvacheru grant also begins with a description of Kakatiya greatness. After Prataparudra went to heaven of his own will, it tells us that the world was overrun by Yavanas (i.e., Turks). But due to Prolaya Nayaka, who lifted up the earth that was submerged in the ocean of Yavanas, just as (the boar-avatar of Vishnu) Varaha had done, the world was set back firmly on its foundations.[11] Kapaya Nayaka took over the protection of the realm upon Prolaya Nayaka's death, assisted by 75 subordinate *nāyakas*, including Vema Reddi of the Panta clan. Among Kapaya Nayaka's notable activities was the restoration of brahman villages that had been seized by the Turks. When he died, the subordinate *nāyakas* dispersed to their own towns and protected their respective lands. The chain of command, according to this inscription, thus passed from Kakatiya Prataparudra to the Musunuri cousins, Prolaya Nayaka and Kapaya Nayaka, and thence to their subordinate Vema Reddi.

The narrative technique of first praising the Kakatiyas and then describing the exploits of later warriors, seen in the Vilasa and Kaluvacheru grants, was effective in implying a smooth and legitimate succession of power. Other inscriptions employ the simpler strategy of comparing the described chief with a Kakatiya ruler, generally Prataparudra. In the Prolavaram grant dated 1346 C.E., Kapaya Nayaka is said to be as majestic as Prataparudra (*pratāparudra-pratima-prabhāva*), whom he further emulated by choosing to reside in Warangal.[12] Kapaya Nayaka's qualitative resemblance to Kakatiya Prataparudra was the justification here for his wielding of power. Vema Reddi likewise refers to Prataparudra in his Madras Museum Plates of 1345, when he claims to have restored all the endowed villages that had been appropriated from brahmans by the wicked barbarian (i.e., Muslim) kings since the time of Kakatiya Prataparudra (EI 8.3, v. 12).

While the evoking of past Kakatiya glory is a common motif in the inscriptions described above, they resemble each other in a number of other ways as well. The Vilasa grant of Prolaya Nayaka, Kapaya Nayaka's Prolavaram inscription, Vema Reddi's Madras Museum Plates, and the Kaluvacheru grant of queen Anitalli are all Sanskrit inscriptions written on copper plates and all record the gift of a village to a brahman. In other words, these inscriptions document the most paradigmatically royal gift (the grant of an *agrahāra*) in the most kingly medium—the Sanskrit language inscribed on copper plates.[13] The attempts to derive prestige though association with the Kakatiyas in these inscriptions must be viewed within this larger context. In the aftermath of the catastrophic events of the early fourteenth century, a number of minor Telugu warrior chiefs were striving to set themselves up as authentic kings using every means possible. Part of this effort to appear kingly entailed appropriating the memory of Kakatiya Prataparudra, but it was only one among several strategies in the quest for royal status. The depiction of Muslims as demonic barbarians in these inscriptions served the same purpose (Talbot 1995a). By portraying themselves as kings who subdued the enemies of the gods and brahmans, Telugu warriors who came after the Kakatiyas sought to live up to the classical Indian prototype of a king. In the classical tradition, the obligation of maintaining order justified the existence of the royal class.

The figure of Prataparudra was even more central to the status claims of the Recherla Nayakas. The earliest inscription of the Recherla clan was issued in 1369 by Anapota Nayaka, who gained control of Telangana after the death of the Musunuri chief Kapaya Nayaka (IAP-W.103). It states that Anapota's family of Recherla Nayakas had been honored in past times by the Kakatiya kings. More specifically, the inscription tells us that Kakatiya Prataparudra conferred the heroic epithet *Pāṇḍya-rāya-gaja-kēsari* (a lion against the elephant who was the Pandya king) on Anapota Nayaka's grandfather, Dachaya. This was presumably in recognition of Dachaya's military service in the Tamil campaigns during Prataparudra's last years as king.[14] Through such acts, the former royal dynasty had already publicly attested to the character and ability of the Recherla Nayakas. Furthermore, the Recherlas had contributed to the greatness of the Kakatiyas by participating in their military campaigns. Unlike the Musunuris and Panta Reddis who merely compared themselves to the Kakatiyas, the Recherla Nayaka chiefs of fourteenth-century Andhra claimed a direct link with the now-defunct Kakatiya rulers. Throughout subsequent centuries, the Recherlas and warrior groups descended from them continued to assert their prior military association with the Kakatiyas. For once a South Indian warrior lineage received sanction from a king through a relationship of service, its legitimacy was established for posterity.

While it is possible that early members of the Recherla clan served in Kakatiya armies as warriors, there is no independent testimony to their importance in the Kakatiya political network despite the traditional claims. The meteoric rise to power of the Musunuris, Recherlas, and Panta clan Reddis in the decades after 1323 was certainly based on military ability, and we can assume that these chiefs came from families with previous martial experience. But the limited reach of their genealogies as presented in the inscriptions—which commence at the earliest in the late Kakatiya period—is evidence that these chiefs could not plausibly posit an illustrious ancestry. They had few competitors in the social arena, for there are no credible traces of the famous Kakatiya-era warriors or their descendants. The main Kakatiya generals must have all been killed, dispossessed, or co-opted in the waning days of the kingdom.[15] An almost complete disruption of previous political networks occurred elsewhere in the peninsula as well, as a result of the Khalji and Tughluq armed incursions that toppled the Kakatiya polity. The three other major regional kingdoms that had flourished in the beginning of the fourteenth century—those of the Yadavas in Maharashtra, the Hoysalas in southern Karnataka, and the Pandyas in Tamil Nadu—all vanished soon after this show of Muslim military might. As one political elite after another succumbed to the ravages of changing political fortunes, new elites emerged on the scene to take their place. But the upwardly mobile are under the greatest pressure to justify their new positions, and thus the parvenu Telugu warrior lineages of the Kakatiya aftermath continued to invoke the Kakatiya name in their quest for authoritative status.

The Persistence of Kakatiya Memories in Telangana

Although political conditions in Andhra stabilized for a brief period during the late fourteenth and early fifteenth centuries, this situation did not last long. The two main Telugu warrior lineages, the Recherla Nayakas of central Telangana and the Panta Reddis of coastal Andhra, were not the only powerful groups in the region. The Bahmani sultanate of Gulbarga maintained a presence in western Telangana, while the Eastern Gangas of Kalinga controlled modern Andhra Pradesh's two northeastern districts (Srikakulam and Visakhapatnam) largely undisturbed by Muslim incursions. Meanwhile, much of southern Andhra had been taken over by Vijayanagara, a powerful new state established in Karnataka from the ruins of the Hoysala kingdom. By the mid fourteenth century, the Vijayanagara kings had established a fort in Udayagiri, Nellore District, from which they exercised an active role in Andhra political affairs. Several Vijayanagara princes were appointed as governors of Udayagiri province from the late fourteenth century on, with some future kings including Devaraya I serving in this capacity. Despite the fragmentation of Andhra's political scene, a balance of power was maintained for decades through the formation of coalitions. On one side were the Recherla Nayakas and the Bahmanis, while the two Panta Reddi branches generally cooperated militarily with Vijayanagara.

Once the fragile equilibrium established between the various power-holders of northwestern Andhra and those of southeastern Andhra was disturbed, however, political conditions quickly deteriorated. The exact sequence of events is not entirely clear, but conflict appears to have been triggered by rivalry between the two Reddi branches at Kondavidu and Rajahmundry. The senior Kondavidu Reddis switched their allegiance from Vijayanagara to the Bahmanis, in a reaction against Vijayanagara support for the Rajahmundry Reddis. This in turn angered the Recherla Nayakas, who had long been allied with the Bahmanis in opposition to the Reddis. Hence, the Recherlas also shifted their allegiance, but from the Bahmanis to

Vijayanagara. A major battle fought at Panugal (Nalgonda District) in 1419 led to victory for the new Vijayanagara-Rajahmundry Reddi-Recherla Nayaka coalition.

The consequences were to prove disastrous not only for the Kondavidu Reddis but for the other main Telugu warrior lineages as well. While the Kondavidu Reddis rapidly declined and were taken over entirely by Vijayanagara in the 1430s, the Rajahmundry Reddis also disappeared from the historical record by 1437. The Recherla Nayakas, having defected to the Vijayanagara side, now had to face the wrath of the Bahmani sultanate, which began attacking them in the 1420s. By 1435 the Bahmanis had conquered Warangal and seized one of the Recherla capitals, Rachakonda. Individual Recherla chiefs remained scattered throughout Telangana but were henceforth only minor players, leaving Andhra with no political networks headed by indigenous warriors. This was a far cry from the situation at the height of Kakatiya might, when almost all of the Telugu-speaking area was incorporated into one political network, for the first and last time until the mid twentieth century.

In the vacuum resulting from the elimination of Telugu warrior power, fifteenth-century Andhra was fought over by polities based outside of it. A new player in the Andhra political arena was the Suryavamshi Gajapati dynasty of Orissa, which took over from the Eastern Gangas around 1434. The Gajapatis conquered Rajahmundry in northern coastal Andhra by 1448 and continued to advance southward down the coast into what was now Vijayanagara territory, taking Kondavidu by 1454 and Udayagiri in 1460. The Gajapatis also turned inward into Telangana and joined the Recherla chief of Devarakonda in wresting several major forts such as Khammamet, Rachakonda, and Warangal away from the Bahmanis. The rapid Gajapati expansion was stopped only by a succession dispute that followed King Kapileshvara's abdication of the throne in 1466. The internal conflict among the Gajapatis allowed Vijayanagara to recover control of the Andhra coast south of the Krishna River by about 1475. The Bahmanis were also temporarily able to regain some localities in Telangana, as well as Rajahmundry itself, as a result. But the Gajapatis rebounded during the 1480s, as their Bahmani and Vijayanagara rivals both underwent problems of their own, and Gajapati hegemony was re-established over large portions of the coast.[16] Meanwhile, much of Telangana was in the hands of small local chieftains.[17]

Because of Andhra's political fragmentation and instability in the fifteenth century, there were no indigenous royal figures with prestige and charisma comparable to Kakatiya Prataparudra. Telugu warriors of southern Andhra, many of whom were absorbed into the Vijayanagara system in this period, had an alternate focal point for their loyalties. But Telugu warriors in Telangana had no such royal banner, nor did any of the powerful Telugu warrior families left in Telangana hold sway over more than a small expanse. Thus the paucity of symbolic resources was particularly acute in Telangana, which had no kings to emulate or serve as sources of authority. Occasional references to the Kakatiyas continue to surface in fifteenth-century Telangana as a consequence. Possession of the hallowed epithet *Kākatīya-rājya-sthāpan=ācārya* (a master at upholding the Kakatiya kingdom) was proclaimed in a record issued by a minor Recherla chief from Warangal District in 1464, for instance (IAP-W.110). Another inscription probably from the same century, on the wall of Khammam fort, attests to the enduring popularity of this Kakatiya-period *biruda* even at such a late date (HAS 19 Km.8).[18]

While the absence of other royal paradigms meant that the Kakatiyas continued to be symbolically important throughout fifteenth-century Telangana, memories of them were most intense in their former capital Warangal. This can be seen in an inscription commissioned by the Telugu warrior Shitab Khan or Chittapa Khana (Sastri 1932). Since Indo-Muslim chronicles clearly indicate that Shitab Khan was not a Muslim, his Persianized name reveals the extent of acculturation already accomplished in Telangana by this era. Although Perso-Arabic sources state that he had at one time been a Bahmani subordinate, Shitab Khan is characterized as a Gajapati ally in a later Telugu text and may have been a local Telangana chief who switched his allegiance as the political winds dictated (Sastri 1932: 3; Wagoner 1993: 145–46). Whatever his former political allegiance may have been, at the time he issued his only inscription in 1504 Shitab Khan was an independent ruler ensconced in Warangal. Once again, as in the case of the Musunuri Nayakas and Vema Reddi of the Panta clan, we find a relatively minor chief commissioning a long inscription in Sanskrit verse, the better to sustain his pretensions to royal status. Despite the long gap of almost two centuries since the collapse of the Kakatiyas, Shitab Khan's inscription is replete with references to this former dynasty. After all, he *was* in command of Warangal, the very center of past Kakatiya might. And under Shitab Khan, his inscription suggests, Warangal would once more experience an era of greatness.

Shitab Khan tells us that he captured Warangal, "which was formerly ruled by a number of virtuous kings belonging to the family of Kakati," in order to ensure "the worship of the gods and the brahmans." His attempts to revive the glory that had been Warangal included the restoration of the images of Krishna, "who was removed from his place by the strength of the wicked," and of the Goddess who "was the Lakshmi of the throne of the Kakati kingdom" but "had been removed from her place by the wicked Turushkas."[19] Commemoration of these pious acts was the overt purpose of Shitab Khan's stone record inscribed on a pillar in a minor shrine within the fort. But Shitab Khan was not only acting in a righteous manner that resembled the Kakatiyas, he was also, through his restoration of divine images from the Kakatiya period, symbolically recreating Kakatiya power. And so the record ends with a vision of him engaged in the daily worship of the Shaiva deity at Warangal who was the protector of the Kakatiya dynasty. The Kakatiyas were now not merely a former dynasty of considerable renown, but an archetype for all future Telangana kings.

Although Shitab Khan saw himself as the reviver of Warangal's former glory, the city was no longer the nucleus of a regional polity but merely an important fortress within the subregion of Telangana. It is not surprising that subsequent rulers of Warangal would attempt to evoke images of Kakatiya might, for the Kakatiya era had been the heyday of Warangal's greatness. Furthermore, the city owed its very existence to the Kakatiyas, who had built it from scratch as their second capital, and several neighborhoods within the city were named after towns conquered by Warangal's founder, Kakatiya Rudradeva (EI 3.15, v. 9). This notion of the capital city as a microcosm representing the larger territory of the Kakatiya kingdom is repeated in the sixteenth-century Telugu text, *Pratāparudra Caritramu*, which depicts the fortress of Kakatiya Warangal as possessing 77 bastions, each guarded by the man in charge of one of the kingdom's 77 territorial divisions (Wagoner 1992: 17–18).[20] The association between Warangal city and the Kakatiya dynasty was so strong in Andhra culture that the Kakatiyas were generally referred to in later times as the kings of Warangal rather than by their dynastic label.[21] Since Kakatiya times, the importance of Warangal in regional affairs had steadily declined. So, even more than residents of other places in Telangana, the people of fifteenth- and sixteenth-century Warangal must have looked back at the Kakatiya period with nostalgia. Hence, from a situation immediately after the fall of the Kakatiyas, when upstart chiefs represented themselves as successors to the Kakatiya legacy of greatness, we have now reached a stage where the Kakatiyas were viewed as exemplars of the Golden Age past.

Memories of the Kakatiyas continued to be preserved and transmitted in Warangal up until the early colonial period, when a number of historical traditions were collected under the auspices of Colin Mackenzie. Mackenzie began his project of gathering information on South India's past in the last decade of the eighteenth century while he was surveying the area of Mysore and its adjoining territories.[22] Although his official work was cartographic, Mackenzie believed that the mapping of the physical world of South India needed to be supplemented by a similar mapping of its social universe. In 1796 the Telugu brahman Kaveli Venkata Boria became his chief assistant in the massive endeavor of collecting every conceivable type of data that might provide historical insights, including literary texts, inscriptions, oral accounts, and artifacts. Upon Boria's death in 1803, his brother Lakshmayya took over the supervision of a growing Indian staff, who scoured the countryside in their search for material until 1817, when Mackenzie left South India. As early as 1794, one rendition of Kakatiya history was passed on to Mackenzie by an English officer encamped near Warangal.[23] He received another written account from Hyderabad in 1798 (Johnston n.d.: 73). A third version was derived from an oral narrative collected by one of Mackenzie's assistants from an aged brahman living in Hanumakonda.[24] Histories of the Kakatiyas, although not unknown elsewhere, thus seem to have been most prevalent in the vicinity of their former capital.

With one minor exception,[25] the various accounts of the Kakatiyas preserved in the Mackenzie Collections closely resemble the more lengthy narratives found in two Telugu literary texts, the *Pratāparudra Caritramu* and the *Siddhēśvara Caritramu*.[26] Internal evidence in these two texts suggests that they were both composed in the vicinity of Warangal.[27] The *Pratāparudra Caritramu* is presumably the earlier of the two, since the *Siddhēśvara Caritramu* explicitly cites its author Ekamranatha as a source and closely follows its story line (Lakshmiranjanam 1960: ii–iii). How the meaning of the Kakatiyas was construed in this extended Telangana version of the past is the focus of the next section.

Pratāparudra Caritramu, a Telangana Chronicle

The Text and Its History

The *Pratāparudra Caritramu* is an unusual text. The fact that it is written in the regional language of Andhra, Telugu, sets it apart from the Sanskrit genre of historical biography known as *carita*, although both *carita* and *caritramu* mean the same thing: the deeds or life of someone. Biographies of kings written in Sanskrit were typically composed by court poets about their living patrons. This is true of the famous biography of the king Harsha (Bana's *Harṣa Carita*), who lived in North India during the early seventh century, and also of the eleventh-century biography of Vikramaditya VI, the Kalyani Chalukya king (Bilhana's *Vikramāṅkadēva Carita*). In contrast, Ekamranatha was probably not a court poet since he does not acknowledge any patron, nor was his hero still alive. The title of his work is also misleading: although labeled as "The Life of Prataparudra," about half of the *Pratāparudra Caritramu* deals with Prataparudra's predecessors. Not only is the *Pratāparudra Caritramu* a distinctly non-Sanskritic type of work, but it is most probably the first historical biography in Telugu (Lakshmiranjanam 1974: 164–65; Ramachandra Rao 1984: 4). Its unsophisticated language further differentiates it from the bulk of medieval Telugu literature.

The work can be divided into three main segments, with each successive section progressively more detailed in its discussion of the various individuals. First is an elaborate genealogy of the dynasty's beginnings, traced all the way back through Parikshit and the *Mahābhārata* heroes as far as the moon (eleven pages). Several legendary local kings are also incorporated into the family's past. The most important of these was Madhavavarman. By winning the goddess Padmakshi's favor, Madhavavarman ensured the good fortune of his descendants and the success of the Kakatiya dynasty. In the second part of the *Pratāparudra Caritramu*, we find an account of the "historic" Kakatiya rulers prior to Prataparudra (twenty-three pages). Considerable emphasis is placed on Prola II (r. 1116–1157). The text attributes the founding of Warangal to him and explains why the city is called "One-rock" (Orugallu in Telugu, Ekashilanagara in Sanskrit). The name comes from a magical *liṅga* that was found buried, a so-called touchstone (*parusa-vēdi*, from Sanskrit *sparśa-vēdhi)* that could turn any base metal into gold. Rather than trying to move the touchstone *liṅga*, Prola had a new town built around it which became the capital in place of the adjacent Hanumakonda.

The last portion of the text is devoted to the life of Prataparudra (36 pages). The final 11 pages cover Prataparudra's prolonged conflict with the sultanate of Delhi and his ultimate defeat at its hands. Interspersed in the second and third sections of the work are several stories that have no relation to the main plot. These stories are religious in theme, extolling the virtues of devotion to Shaivism. The work as a whole is not a consistent, tightly woven narrative. On first reading, especially, it strikes one as unfocused and full of abrupt transitions. Only when we get to the last segment on Prataparudra does the narrative settle down and achieve consistency.

We know frustratingly little about the conditions under which the *Pratāparudra Caritramu* was produced, including its date of composition. In fact, we cannot even state with absolute certainty that the existing text was composed entirely at one time by a single author, although the coherency of style would suggest so. The lack of a fixed date for the chronicle's compilation prevents us from placing this historical construct in a clear time framework. The modern editors of the *Pratāparudra Caritramu* and its verse rendition, the *Siddhēśvara Caritramu*, have tried to determine their dates using two methods (Lakshmiranjanam 1960: iii–vi; Ramachandra Rao 1984: 6–12). One approach is to date these texts relative to each other and to two presumably later works.[28] According to this line of reasoning, the *Pratāparudra Caritramu* is the earlier and was composed prior to 1600. The other method for determining the date is through the *Pratāparudra Caritramu* references to historic figures. Individuals who lived as late as the mid sixteenth century are mentioned in the text. But there are no allusions to the most famous Vijayanagara king, Krishnadeva Raya. On the grounds that such an eminent person would never have been ignored by the author, Ramachandra Rao places the *Pratāparudra Caritramu's* composition shortly before Krishnadeva Raya's reign (1509–1529 C.E.), which would date the text sometime between ca. 1490 and 1510. Lakshmiranjanam is less decisive, giving the first half of the sixteenth century as the probable era of its creation.

An analysis of the anachronistic geopolitical worldview in the text also reveals that it was composed in the first half of the sixteenth century, as suggested by Ramachandra Rao and Lakshmiranjanam. Historical anachronisms have often been regarded in the past as grounds for discrediting the validity of a historiographic work. In today's climate, with its greater sensitivity to the constructed nature of historical narrative and the diversity of historical consciousness, anachronisms can be viewed as central to a decipherment of the social context of historical writings. This is because scholars no longer believe that alterations in social memory of the past occur at random. To make the past more meaningful to the present—partly so that it can act as a paradigm for future action—historical memories are often changed to make sense within the present society. In the words of a recent work: "The natural tendency of social memory is to suppress what is not meaningful or intuitively satisfying in the collective memories of the past and interpolate or substitute what seems more appropriate or more in keeping with their particular conception of the world" (Fentress and Wickham 1992: 58). The inclusion of anachronisms, as with other types of transformations, is a logical attempt to order the social universe, in this view, not a manifestation of disorderly or irrational thought processes. Anachronisms are an especially clear illustration of the effort to bridge gaps between the present and the past, to create greater continuity between them. As such, anachronisms are a flag marking the areas of most acute concern to the later society. "It is the deformed aspects of the past, then, that hold the greatest interest for us, since they point most clearly to the issues that medieval authors and audiences sensed as problematic," says Gabrielle Spiegel about medieval French historiography (1993: 106).

The most glaring of the historical "errors" in the *Pratāparudra Caritramu* is the repeated motif of a Kakatiya alliance with the Vijayanagara kings.[29] This is manifestly impossible since it was not until *after* the fall of the Kakatiyas in 1323 that the Vijayanagara kingdom was established, most probably a few years later than the conventional date of 1336 that is usually put forth for the founding of the Vijayanagara capital (Kulke 1985: 126). In the *Pratāparudra Caritramu*'s version of the past, good relations between the Kakatiyas and Vijayanagara were initiated by a marriage exchange generations before the conflict with the Delhi sultanate began. Kakatiya Prataparudra is also said to have visited Vijayanagara city during his conquest of the four quarters in the early part of his reign. Vijayanagara's most consequential role in the *Pratāparudra Caritramu*, however, consists of its loyal military aid to Prataparudra in the prolonged hostilities against the Delhi sultanate. Four main periods of conflict are narrated in the account, during each of which the Vijayanagara king deploys his army in defense of Warangal's northeastern sector. On every occasion the primary opponent of Vijayanagara is the ruler known as the Lord of Cuttack, who is one of the Delhi sultan's main allies. This is another anachronism. Although the Orissa town Cuttack became an important political center under the Eastern Gangas of the twelfth century, the Eastern Gangas were never major contenders for power against the Kakatiyas (Ramachandra Rao 1976: 30 and 75). But the subsequent Orissa dynasty of the Suryavamshi Gajapatis, who were also based in Cuttack, did pose a serious threat to Vijayanagara control of southern Andhra in the late fifteenth and early sixteenth centuries.

A further intimation that the geopolitical perspective of the *Pratāparudra Caritramu* is much later than the fourteenth-century events it purports to describe comes from its division of the Muslim enemy into two segments. On the one hand, the chronicle presents the Delhi sultan, whose army repeatedly confronts Prataparudra's main forces to the north of Warangal. But it also specifies a second Muslim army, which belonged to the (Turkic) Western king who naturally attacks Warangal from a westerly direction and against whom the subordinate Kakatiya contingents (led by the Padmanayakas) are dispatched over and over again. Until the establishment of the Bahmani sultanate to the west of Andhra in 1347, however, there was no separate Muslim polity in the Deccan.

If the actual protagonists of the fourteenth-century conflict, the Kakatiyas and the Delhi sultanate, are eliminated from the picture, three actors remain in the chronicle's geopolitical struggle: the Orissa polity in the northeast, a western Deccan polity, and Vijayanagara to the south. This is a fairly accurate picture of the balance of power within the Deccan from about the mid fifteenth century to the mid sixteenth century, the approximate parameters of Gajapati expansion outside of Orissa. The true situation was even more complex, for the Bahmani sultanate had splintered into several autonomous polities by the early sixteenth century (Sherwani 1973a: 194-201). But enmity between the Gajapatis, Vijayanagara, and the various Deccan sultanates was fierce in the hundred years or so from 1450 onward. The second half of the fifteenth century was an especially intense era of strife in the Deccan, exacerbated by internal contests over succession to the thrones in each area. One consequence of the prolonged violence was a significant decline in inscriptional production. As noted in chapter 1, the time span from 1325 to 1499 (Period 3) yields the smallest quantity of inscriptions of any of the four periods from 1000 to 1650 C.E. The drop in numbers was especially acute from 1450 to 1500. In contrast, the Kakatiya period extending from 1175 through 1324 had the highest level of epigraphic production.

The worldview we observe in the *Pratāparudra Caritramu* consists of a double vision. That is, the *Pratāparudra Caritramu* collapses two sets of conflicts by superimposing a scenario from ca. 1500 onto the events of ca. 1320. The struggle between the Vijayanagara kingdom of the southern peninsula, the Gajapati dynasty of the northeastern peninsula, and the Muslim power(s) in the western part of the peninsula, which is such a major theme in the last pages of the text, is indeed anachronistic and therefore inaccurate as a description of the late Kakatiya period.

But the conflation of two time periods, and two different conflicts, was not a result of faulty memory but an active attempt to situate the events of the early fourteenth century in meaningful terms. This anachronism reveals to us that major military struggles in the Deccan, such as those during the collapse of the Kakatiya kingdom, could not be understood at the time the *Pratāparudra Caritramu* was composed without recourse to a conception of a tripartite geopolitical configuration that included the Vijayanagara and Orissa polities. It is therefore unlikely that the work was composed much later than the mid sixteenth century, since dramatic changes in the peninsula's balance of power occurred subsequently.

The Padmanayaka Heroes

Although we can be fairly confident in situating the *Pratāparudra Caritramu*'s production in Warangal during the sixteenth century, the text is silent on the reasons for its creation and the nature of its audience, unusually so in fact. Most Telugu literature of the period was composed either by a temple poet, who proclaims the greatness of his deity in the work, or by a court poet (Narayana Rao 1992). Court poets not only identify the patron and his family but generally also provide details concerning their own ancestry. The *Pratāparudra Caritramu*'s Ekamranatha fits neither mold. He is unlike a court poet in having no named patron and in omitting a personal genealogy. Nor does his composition resemble a temple poet's, for there is no effort to eulogize a specific god or goddess. All we have left is indirect evidence, in determining who might have supported or appreciated Ekamranatha's literary efforts. Although the text does not specifically name a patron, it did have an audience that was ultimately responsible for its transmission and preservation up until the present. We can assume that the *Pratāparudra Caritramu* was designed to please this audience, who therefore shaped the final form of the chronicle.[30] The contents suggest a possible source of patronage, in other words, even though nothing is made explicit. I believe the text was aimed at the Padmanayakas, a social group that is consistently cast in a positive light in the text's final pages.

The Padmanayakas are first introduced into the narrative soon after two calamitous events. Some evil *nāyakas* residing in the capital had plotted to steal the touchstone *liṅga*—literally the source of the kingdom's fortune—and attacked the temple in which it was housed. Only Prataparudra's quick action, and his use of the divine sword and shield granted to Madhavavarman in order to kill the miscreants, saved the kingdom from this terrible offense. The next evening, another group of wicked *nāyakas* stabbed a brahman and stole all his household valuables. Hearing about the seriously hurt brahman, the king feared he would incur the sin of killing a brahman (for whatever happens in his realm is ultimately the king's responsibility). But the virtuous wife of the wounded brahman pleaded with the goddess Lakshmi and was able to get her husband restored to health (Ramachandra Rao 1984: 38).

Faced with these dire threats to the well-being of his kingdom, Prataparudra summons the members of his court and says:

> Because King Ganapati conferred *nāyaka* status on people of diverse castes, today there are many types of leaders. There must be a better strategy than this. But brahmans

are not meant to be *nāyakas* and others are not worthy. The Padmanayakas—rich in honor, exceedingly trustworthy, embued with discernment, like an ocean in profundity, very judicious, afraid of sin, acting in the lord's best interests—are respectable *śūdras*. They are suited for leadership!" When the assembled courtiers heard these words of Prataparudra, they praised him highly for his political acumen and said: "We fully agree. You should make it so."

Prataparudra summoned the Padmanayakas, greeted them, and declared their worthiness for leadership. He appointed one man to each bastion [*kottaḍamu*] and, so that they would possess all the (appropriate) signs (of their status), gave them wealth, gold, vehicles, palanquins, Chinese porcelains, and Chinese silks. In addition, he gave them umbrellas, fly whisks, processional banners, and insignia [*biruda*] commemorating their heroic deeds. Rewarding the 77 men of the 77 Padmanayaka clans in this manner, Prataparudra had 77 bastions made in the stone wall of Ekashilanagara [Warangal]. He appointed their relatives as assistant *nāyakas* and had bastions built for them as well. Furthermore, Prataparudra distributed one portion of his kingdom among these 77 *nāyakas*. Another portion was allotted to the relatives, one to his own standing army, and one to the brahmans. The remainder of the kingdom was assigned to his treasury. (Ramachandra Rao 1984: 39)

In this episode, we learn that the composition of the *nāyaka* class was consciously altered by Prataparudra. During his predecessor Ganapati's rule, *nāyakas* had been appointed from a number of different social categories, due to an incident narrated earlier in the text, in which Ganapati tried to commission a brahman as a *nāyaka*. But the brahman declined with the words, "The way of a warrior (*kṣātra-dharma*) is not fitting for me." Ganapati then selected his *nāyaka* leaders from a variety of nonbrahman groups instead. In the process, he earned the epithet "hero of the diverse assembly" (*nānā-maṇḍalīkara-gaṇḍa*; Ramachandra Rao 1984: 34). Because Ganapati's decision had not proved wise in the long run, Prataparudra had to find more satisfactory candidates for the trusted post of *nāyaka*. These are the so-called Padmanayakas, to whom the security of the capital was now handed over.

The Padmanayakas resurface in the last pages of the text, as staunch defenders of Warangal against the recurring assaults by sultanate armies. In three consecutive attacks, the Padmanayakas are successful in protecting the western approaches to the capital. At this point the disgruntled former *nāyakas*, who had lost their positions to the Padmanayakas, decide to avenge the shame of their dismissal by Prataparudra. They accept a bribe of 50 lakh gold coins from the commander-in-chief of the sultanate forces, Ulugh Khan—25 lakhs in advance and the remainder to be paid at a later date. The former *nāyakas* of various castes then return to Warangal, where they beseech Prataparudra to give them another chance in battle. He consents and assigns a large contingent of infantry to their command (Ramachandra Rao 1984: 59–62).

In the ensuing battle, the Padmanayakas are sent forth as usual to do battle against a subsidiary contingent of the Muslim forces. But the former *nāyakas* accompany Prataparudra and his standing army in combat against the main army of the sultanate. These *nāyakas* of various castes fight for a short while, then retreat to the rear. Seeing this, the Kakatiya contingent led by the warrior Terala Bhoju Reddi also leaves the battlefield under the mistaken notion that a general retreat has been called. The remaining Kakatiya forces fight valiantly but are inevitably overwhelmed now that they are so vastly outnumbered. Several allied kings perish on the battlefield and Prataparudra is himself captured while mounted on an elephant (Ramachandra Rao 1984: 63).

At nightfall the treacherous former *nāyakas* demand payment of the remaining 25 lakh gold coins in their bribe from Ulugh Khan. The victorious Ulugh Khan refuses and taunts them instead, saying that they should return the 25 lakhs he had already paid them. Apparently feeling responsible for the conduct of his former subordinates, the captive Prataparudra then reimburses Ulugh Khan for the amount he had already dispensed to the *nāyakas* of various castes. This noble gesture shames the former *nāyakas*, who vow to secure the release of Prataparudra. They intercept the army that is taking Prataparudra to Delhi and fight furiously for six hours, inflicting many casualties on the sultanate forces. Eventually, however, they are completely annihilated. The Padmanayakas and other surviving members of the Kakatiya alliance also rally in an effort to free Prataparudra. Although they kill the sultanate's main ally, the Lord of Cuttack, and slay many of the sultanate soldiers, Prataparudra has already been sent on to Delhi secretly (Ramachandra Rao 1984: 63–66).

Meanwhile, the sultan greets Prataparudra in Delhi and soon gives him permission to leave. Prataparudra goes first to the holy city Kashi, where he bathes in the Ganga River, worships the deity Vishveshvara, and distributes many alms. Upon his return to Andhra, Prataparudra summons his warriors and friends. He rewards them appropriately for their service, arranging marriages and distributing money from the treasury. To the Padmanayakas, Prataparudra entrusts an important charge. He orders: "You have served your master on the lion throne loyally. Now become independent and continue on as the kings and chiefs of the countries given to you!" (Ramachandra Rao 1984: 69). Released from their oath of allegiance to the Kakatiyas, the Padmanayakas go back to their various localities. They manage on their own, some becoming kings and others becoming subordinates of the Gajapati or Vijayanagara kings. Prataparudra dies soon thereafter.

Of all the different warrior groups who appear in the *Pratāparudra Caritramu* account of the Kakatiya kingdom's last days, the Padmanayakas are portrayed most favorably. Their stellar qualities are highlighted through the dramatic contrast drawn between their faithfulness to the Kakatiya cause down to the bitter end and the betrayal of the Kakatiyas by the former *nāyakas*. The Padmanayakas do everything in their power to secure victory for their side but are undermined by the treachery of the other *nāyakas*, who are directly responsible for the capture of Prataparudra and, ultimately, the collapse of the kingdom. Because of their loyalty, Prataparudra publicly rewards the Padmanayakas in his last days. He does more than acknowledge their service by rewarding them financially for their help. He also confers the status of king on his Padmanayaka subordinates when he commands them to disperse and become the lords of their assigned territories. Having amply demonstrated their worthy attributes, the Padmanayakas are henceforth authorized to exercise independent power.

Identity of the Padmanayakas

We are now in a position to grasp the significance of the *Pratāparudra Caritramu* version of the past for later generations. In effect, the chronicle constitutes a charter of legitimacy for certain Telugu warriors of subsequent times. The last great Telugu dynasty, according to this work, had elevated the Padmanayakas to the position of leaders in their own right. In the absence of any other royal authority, this Kakatiya sanctioning of kingship continued to be valid into the sixteenth century. The importance accorded to the Padmanayakas in the final few pages of the chronicle suggests that claimants to this status were the ones who transmitted the text.

But which of the many warrior lineages of post-Kakatiya Andhra was included in the rubric Padmanayaka? The earliest epigraphic occurrences of the designation Padmanayaka are later than the likely date of composition of *Pratāparudra Caritramu*. The first example comes from approximately 1586 C.E. (NDI Darsi 73), and another eight individuals figuring in inscriptions bear the label between that time and 1650.[31] The people called Padmanayakas in these inscriptions generally either issued their records in Telangana or came from Telangana to the localities where the inscriptions are situated. But the epigraphic Padmanayakas do not share the same clan affiliations. In some inscriptions, a person who calls himself a Padmanayaka also states that his clan (*gōtra*) name was Vipparla.[32] In other cases, the clan of the Padmanayaka man is given as Inigela (NDI Darsi 73) or Recherla (NDI Atmakur 3). The slim epigraphic evidence suggests that Padmanayaka was a social classification found among warriors of Telangana origin who were members of several different lineages and clans.

Twentieth-century historians have identified the Padmanayakas of the *Pratāparudra Caritramu* as Velamas, the name of an important landowning caste-cluster in modern Andhra (e.g., Parabrahma Sastry 1978: 164–66). The primary reason for this equation of Padmanayakas with Velamas is the evidence of the *Velugōṭivāri Vaṃśāvaḷi*, "the family history of the Velugotis." The text as it now exists, collected in the early nineteenth century by Colin Mackenzie's assistants, represents the historical traditions of the chiefs of Venkatagiri, a major town in modern Nellore District (Venkataramanayya 1939). Before moving to Venkatagiri, the family had resided in the town of Velugodu in Kurnool District, from which the lineage name was derived. Because the *vaṃśāvaḷi* is a collection of stylistically disparate verses arranged in chronological order by generation, it was probably composed over a long period by different family bards (Venkataramanayya 1939: 1; Somasekhara Sarma 1948: 11). While portions of it may date back as far as the fourteenth century, we should not treat it as contemporary to the events it relates.

The family genealogy laid out in the *Velugōṭivāri Vaṃśāvaḷi* begins with the eponymous ancestor Chevvi Reddi, who is the first to assume the lineage name Recherla and is said to have attracted the attention of Kakatiya Ganapati and been raised to warrior status. The main warrior of the next generation was Prasaditya, who allegedly served under the successive Kakatiya monarchs Ganapati, Rudramadevi, and Prataparudra as one of their 77 *nāyakas* and earned a great many honorific titles in the process (Venkataramanayya 1939: 2–4). When we reach the sixth generation, we arrive at the figure of Anapota Nayaka, the first in the genealogy whose existence can be verified through epigraphic sources. This is the same Anapota Nayaka who defeated the Musunuri chief Kapaya Nayaka around 1367 and succeeded him as paramount lord of central Telangana. It was Anapota Nayaka and his brother who, according to Velugoti family tradition, established the forts of Devarakonda and Rachakonda in Nalgonda District, the main centers of the Recherla Nayaka chiefs. The Velugotis are represented in the *vaṃśāvaḷi* as a junior branch of the Recherla clan, a branch that originated in the sixteenth generation of descent from the founder Chevvi Reddi (Rama Row 1875: 19, 29). Aside from belonging to the Recherla *gōtra*, the Velugoti family also belonged to the larger Padmanayaka *kula* grouping and the even broader Velama *vaṃśa* (Venkataramanayya 1939: 5).

The *Velugōṭivāri Vaṃśāvaḷi* therefore defines the Padmanayakas as a subset of the larger Velama group. Because the later Velugoti family claim descent from the Recherla chiefs of Rachakonda and Devarakonda, modern historians have consistently used the term Velama in describing the Recherla Nayakas of fourteenth- and fifteenth-century Telangana. If Anapota Nayaka and his Recherla kinsmen were Velamas, then they must also have been Padmanayakas, following this line of reasoning. The Padmanayakas of the *Pratāparudra Caritramu* can therefore be identified as Anapota Nayaka's immediate ancestors.[33] In brief, modern historians have unquestioningly accepted the Velugoti conception of themselves as descended from worthy warriors of the Kakatiya period. The problem with this formulation is that neither Velama nor Padmanayaka were meaningful terms for Telugu warriors of the thirteenth or fourteenth centuries.

I argue in chapter 2 that even names now widely understood to be caste labels, like *reḍḍi* and *seṭṭi*, should be viewed not as denoting closed kin categories in the Kakatiya period but rather as open occupational classes. It is all too easy to project the castes of modern ethnography back into the medieval period on the basis of resemblances in terminology. In the case of the Velamas, however, even this excuse does not stand because the name Velama appears only once in source material from Kakatiya Andhra. On that occasion it identifies a collective body, the Thousand Velamas, who act in concert with collectives of weavers and herders in assessing religious levies on their own communities (HAS 13.26). Here the Thousand Velamas represent an organization of agriculturists, not a hereditarily circumscribed set of people.[34] Nor did the chiefs of fourteenth- and fifteenth-century Telangana who are referred to as Velama today ever use that designation themselves. The critical social affiliation in the inscriptions of Anapota Nayaka and his direct descendants was membership in the Recherla clan. The earliest post-Kakatiya occurrence of Velama in an inscription dates from mid-sixteenth-century Nellore District (NDI Nellore 112), shortly before we get the first epigraphic reference to Padmanayaka. The Velama situation is thus a particularly apt illustration of my earlier point that the social divisions of modern-day Andhra developed very late in its history, certainly well after the Kakatiya period.

Twentieth-century Andhra historians have been as anachronistic in their writing of history as the composer of *Pratāparudra Caritramu*—both viewing the past through the lens of the present. For while Velamas and Padmanayakas were clearly not existing social categories in Kakatiya Andhra, they do emerge subsequently. Originally, however, Velama and Padmanayaka were not synonymous, for a Telangana record of 1613 (IAP-K.48) dubs one man a Padmanayaka while ascribing Velama clan status to another. Padmanayakas and Velamas are listed as separate *śūdra* communities in the *Bhīmēśvara Purāṇamu* (Somasekhara Sarma 1948: 50n.2

and 528).[35] Nor does the sixteenth-century *Pratāparudra Caritramu* ever use the name Velama for the Padmanayakas in its narrative. Thus it was not until at least the seventeenth century that the Padmanayaka label was appropriated by people who also called themselves Velamas.

In short, Padmanayaka was a social identity that appeared only two or more centuries after the fall of Warangal in 1323. It must have been closely associated with the Kakatiyas from the beginning and, as such, it connoted martial valor, loyalty, and the sanction to rule. These positive attributes were so appealing that Padmanayaka status was adopted by disparate warrior lineages from Telangana who had, up until this time, for the most part only identified themselves in terms of their lineage and/or clan affiliations. In this manner, a specific construction of Andhra's past (that is, a "history" of the Kakatiyas that included Padmanayaka warriors) generated a new social reality in the form of the community of Padmanayakas. Thus historical memories are not only shaped by present conditions but also themselves shape the contours of the future. As larger social groupings gradually developed from the sixteenth century onward, some warriors of Telangana origin, including the prominent Velugoti family of the Recherla clan, became classified broadly as Velamas. One of their late traditions says that Padmanayakas were formerly just agriculturalists (*kāpus*), then became Velamas, and were finally transformed into Padmanayakas because of their military service for Kakatiyas (Subba Rao 1930–31). In this last stage of development, therefore, the meaning of Padmanayaka was absorbed into the social identity of the Velama and eventually became established as historical truth. Earlier, however, Padmanayaka was a status that could be claimed by Telangana warriors of different backgrounds.

To return to the main topic of this section—the question of the audience of *Pratāparudra Caritramu*—we can conclude that it was an amorphous group of Telangana warriors who cannot be equated with any modern community. By self-definition the Padmanayakas were a social unit whose boundaries were determined by alleged past association with the Kakatiyas. As my discussion in chapter 4 demonstrated, the structure of Kakatiya polity changed considerably during the reigns of the last two rulers. From an initial reliance on loose alliances with entrenched aristocratic families, the Kakatiya state under Rudramadevi and Prataparudra instead established direct relations with large numbers of nonaristocratic warriors. Through their military service to the late Kakatiya rulers, many previously obscure fighting men attained positions of power and respect for the first time. While it is unlikely that many, if indeed any, of the post-Kakatiya Telugu warrior lineages actually originated with Prataparudra, it is evident that Prataparudra was remembered in later times as the legitimator of Telugu warriors as a class. The roots of post-Kakatiya Andhra society, dominated by *śūdra* warriors ensconced in local fortresses, were thought to lie in Prataparudra's reign. Hence, the identity of Padmanayaka was appropriated by a variety of individuals and families in late medieval times, who sought to establish a historical link with Kakatiya royalty.

Because the Kakatiyas came to symbolize the very origins of the Telugu warrior class, political elites continued to allege prior affiliation with the Kakatiyas well into the era of British colonial rule. In addition to the Velugotis, other Velama lords of Bobbili, Pithapuram, and Jatpole traced their antecedents to the Kakatiya period (Parabrahma Sastry 1978: 166). This was true as well of the chiefs of Paloncha in Khammam District and the Vipparla family of Nuzvid (Richards 1975: 33). The Damarla chiefs of southern Andhra contributed a genealogy to the early-nineteenth-century Mackenzie Collection which similarly asserts that an ancestor served Kakatiya Prataparudra (Mack. Transl. 7.49), a very unlikely scenario given that the Damarlas hardly figure in historical sources prior to the beginning of the early seventeenth century.

Another example demonstrates that even Telugu warriors who did not claim Padmanayaka status were familiar with Telangana historical traditions relevant to the Kakatiyas. In the early twentieth century, the ruling family of Bastar, a former princely state in what is now Madhya Pradesh, still proudly asserted their descent from the Kakatiya royal dynasty. We can trace this allegation of Kakatiya descent as far back as 1703, when an inscription containing the family genealogy was issued (Lal 1907–8: 164–66). It names the successive heads of the family continuously from Annamaraja, supposedly the brother of Kakatiya Prataparudra. Annamaraja presumably fled the destruction of the Kakatiya kingdom to resettle in Bastar, just north of Telangana across the Godavari River. Again this is unlikely, for only eight generations are listed between Annamaraja and the ruling prince of 1703, a thin genealogy for a purported descent line spanning close to four centuries. But an individual by the name of Annamadeva does figure in the *Pratāparudra Caritramu* as Prataparudra's brother. He is said to have left Warangal for the northeast after anointing Prataparudra's son as king. Thus, the founder of the family fortunes in Bastar may very well have been a Telugu warrior from Telangana who was familiar with the prevalent legends about the Kakatiyas.[36]

In many ways Andhra social memories of Prataparudra can be compared to medieval European memories of the king Charlemagne. In twelfth- and thirteenth-century western Europe, Charlemagne was similarly regarded as the originator of a wide variety of medieval political and religious structures. Just as the name of Prataparudra continued to surface in a multitude of contexts, so too did Charlemagne "soon become a symbol, a legitimation device for all sorts of subsequent activities" (Fentress and Wickham 1992: 171). Memories of the military conflicts during Charlemagne's reign were transformed to better agree with later conceptions of the world. Thus, in the age of the Crusades, Charlemagne was remembered as having fought the Saracens at the battle of Roncevaux (commemorated in *The Song of Roland*), whereas earlier chronicles from the ninth century tell us that his enemies on this occasion were the Basques (Fentress and Wickham 1992: 58–59). The substitution of the Saracens for the Basques can be compared to the imposition of a later geopolitical framework on Kakatiya history in the *Pratāparudra Caritramu.*

In another parallel, the concentration on Charlemagne in European social memory largely blotted out remembrances of earlier kings—Charlemagne's own Carolingian ancestors as well as Clovis and other Merovingian kings (Fentress and Wickham 1992: 156–57). Prataparudra likewise dominates Andhra social memory to the detriment of his grandfather Ganapati, a far more likely candidate for acclamation. For Telugu warriors of later centuries, it was Prataparudra, and not Ganapati, who stood at the center of the dramatic change that had refashioned subsequent society. Prataparudra was credited with the elevation of humble fighters to a higher status and with the consequent later dominance of *śūdra* warrior elites. Furthermore, during his reign Muslim military strength first became a reality for Andhra, which irrevocably altered the political landscape of the region. The contemporary world could be said to have begun with Prataparudra, from the perspective of later centuries. This is Prataparudra's meaning for subsequent generations of warriors. In turn, the circulation of historical constructions leading back to Prataparudra united warriors of Telangana origin, who now held in common a view of their own past.

The Vijayanagara Connection

Vijayanagara Rule in Andhra

A world without the Vijayanagara presence was clearly inconceivable to the sixteenth-century composer of the *Pratāparudra Caritramu*. Since the past only has meaning for the present if the two resemble each other, the past is often represented as a replica of the present in historical memories (Spiegel 1993: 105). And so the *Pratāparudra Caritramu* casts the Vijayanagara kingdom as a central actor on the stage of the fourteenth century. While portions of Andhra had indeed come under the sway of Vijayanagara since the mid fourteenth century, Vijayanagara's position there was seriously undermined by the expansion of the Gajapati dynasty during the second half of the fifteenth century. It was further damaged when Saluva Narasimha, the main Vijayanagara general in Andhra in the 1480s, turned his energies to the usurpation of the Vijayanagara throne. Narasa Nayaka, another Vijayanagara general whose military activities in Andhra led him to fame, succeeded to the throne in 1491 but had to spend the remainder of the decade consolidating his power both in the capital and in the Tamil region. Large portions of coastal Andhra, including the principal Vijayanagara fort Udayagiri, hence remained in Gajapati hands.

Vijayanagara reestablished its ascendancy in southern Andhra under the great king Krishnadeva Raya. He launched a sustained campaign against the Gajapatis from 1513 to 1519, recapturing Udayagiri and Kondavidu in the process. Krishnadeva Raya's army pressed as far northeast as Cuttack, the Gajapati capital in Orissa. The treaty signed subsequently confirmed Vijayanagara hegemony over Andhra south of the Krishna River. Southern Andhra remained firmly under Vijayanagara authority for the next few decades. Vijayanagara's chief rival in Andhra was now the Qutb Shah state, a product of the Bahmani sultanate's disintegration. From their center in Golkonda at the western edge of Telangana, the Qutb Shahs gradually reduced Gajapati influence in both the interior and coastal sectors of northern Andhra. By the 1530s, the Qutb Shahs were entrenched in the central Telangana district of Nalgonda and had made inroads into the Vengi area, pushing the Gajapatis north of the Godavari River.

Vijayanagara thus achieved its largest territorial extent within Andhra during the first half of the sixteenth century. That this was the apex of Vijayanagara influence and power is corroborated by epigraphic distributions. Beginning in the mid fourteenth century (IAP-C 2.5 from 1347 C.E.), inscriptions that acknowledged

Vijayanagara overlordship appear with fair regularity for the next 100 years. After a lull during the late fifteenth century, when the overall number of inscriptions issued in the region drops precipitously, there is a sharp increase from Krishnadeva Raya's reign in the early sixteenth century onward until the late 1560s. Of the total of 785 Andhra records associated with Vijayanagara during the three centuries before 1650, 574 (72 percent) come from the 65-year period between 1500 and 1565.[37] In other words, about three-quarters of all Vijayanagara-related inscriptions originated within a period that constituted less than one-quarter of the time span. Most of these inscriptions were issued not by the Vijayanagara kings themselves, but by various Telugu chiefs, warriors, and officials affiliated with Vijayanagara in some fashion.

The *Pratāparudra Caritramu*'s casting of Vijayanagara backward in time into the Kakatiya era is more comprehensible when we realize how many Telugu men were incorporated into the Vijayanagara network by the early sixteenth century. The presence of Vijayanagara was a tangible political reality for numerous Telugu warrior lineages, particularly in southern Andhra. With the increased assimilation of Andhra territory and people, the Vijayanagara court itself took on an increasingly Telugu character. That is, the cultural influence of Telugu language and Telugu places was far greater during the sixteenth century than previously. The prolonged residence in Andhra of members of the royal dynasties that usurped the Vijayanagara throne in the late fifteenth and early sixteenth centuries may have contributed to this trend (Rama Rao 1971: 7). Under these Saluva and Tuluva kings, royal patronage of Telugu literature and Andhra religious sites expanded greatly. The best-known examples come from the reign of Krishnadeva Raya, who himself wrote a highly regarded Telugu work called *Āmuktamālyada*. A story contained within the *Āmuktamālyada* explains that the king was told in a divine dream while traveling in Andhra that he should compose a work in Telugu, the best of all languages (Narayana Rao 1995: 24). Several Telugu poets, including the famous Allasani Peddana, resided in the court of Krishnadeva Raya, who is popularly credited with the patronage of numerous other Telugu literary figures (Raju 1944: 35).

Along with greater patronage of Telugu literature, the number of royal endowments to Andhra temples rose remarkably from the late fifteenth century onward. The most famous of the patronized sites is the Venkateshvara temple in the Tirumala-Tirupati complex, first endowed generously by Saluva Narasimha and then again by Krishnadeva Raya. Subordinates of the succeeding Tuluva rulers, Achyutadeva and Sadashiva, continued to extend patronage to this temple (Subrahmanya Sastry 1930: 35–40). Tirupati is somewhat exceptional, however, in being situated in a border zone where the Telugu, Tamil, and Kannada cultural spheres overlapped. The inter-regional character of Tirupati may explain its popularity rather than any specific attraction to Andhra temples. A second site, the Narasimha temple at Ahobilam, is a less ambiguous case, in that it had only regional appeal. Ahobilam's god Narasimha was originally a folk deity of tribal and pastoral groups, and one of his consorts is thought to have come from the local Chenchu tribe (Sontheimer 1985: 144–47). The temple was the recipient of numerous gifts from Vijayanagara political subordinates and was visited by the king Krishnadeva Raya himself.[38]

The increasingly Telugu nature of Vijayanagara political culture may explain the *Pratāparudra Caritramu*'s insistence on the close ties between the Kakatiya dynasty and the kings of Vijayanagara. Not only had this bond been sustained over many generations, according to the chronicle, but Vijayanagara came to the aid of the Kakatiya kingdom at the time of its greatest need, when confronting the Delhi sultanate. The depiction of Vijayanagara as a steadfast Kakatiya ally suggests that Vijayanagara was regarded as akin to the Kakatiyas, as possessing some qualities in common with the Kakatiyas. Even those Telugu warriors who were not directly affiliated with Vijayanagara during the sixteenth century must have felt that Vijayanagara was in essence a Telugu polity. Why else would the *Pratāparudra Caritramu*, a work produced and transmitted in Telangana, portray Vijayanagara so favorably?

The text's final episodes become more meaningful, once we understand that Vijayanagara's cooperation with the Kakatiyas in the chronicle resulted from the perception that Vijayanagara also was fundamentally a network of Telugu warriors. For in the *Pratāparudra Caritramu*'s version of the past, the Kakatiya kingdom does not end immediately with the death of Prataparudra. His son Virabhadra becomes the next king. When the Vijayanagara king leaves Warangal to protect his own kingdom, Kakatiya Virabhadra is unable to stave off the sultanate armies by himself and loses some territory to them. Meanwhile, vigorous resistance by Vijayanagara maintains the Krishna River as the border between it and the sultanate. The sultan builds the city Bidar in the region during the many years of war against Vijayanagara.[39] Eventually the sultan is too weak to continue, and having lost his capital Delhi in a rebellion, he remains in the Deccan as a tributary of Vijayanagara. But he is still strong enough to capture Warangal and oppress its residents. At the very end of the chronicle, Warangal is in Muslim hands while Vijayanagara triumphs in its paramount position (Ramachandra Rao 1984: 70–71). We are left with the implication that all was not totally lost, for a remnant of the former Kakatiya greatness lived on in Vijayanagara.[40]

In fact, Vijayanagara was not invincible. Its power collapsed dramatically after defeat in the 1565 battle of Talikota (or Rakshasa-Tangadi) at the hands of a confederacy of Muslim armies. The capital city was sacked soon thereafter, and much of the kingdom's original base in Karnataka was abandoned. The leaders of Vijayanagara's last dynasty, the Aravidus, retrenched as well as they could in southern Andhra and began using the title "sultan of Warangal," even though Telangana was not under their control (e.g., v. 34 of EI 16.18; v. 30 of NDI copper plate 6). This gesture can only be understood as a bid by the Aravidus to evoke the legacy of Andhra's last great indigenous dynasty, the Kakatiyas of Warangal, now that they too were exclusively operating within Andhra. The new Vijayanagara center in Penugonda (Anantapur District) soon came under attack from the Adil Shahs of Bijapur, a Bahmani successor state to the northwest, and the capital was shifted to Chandragiri in Andhra Pradesh's southernmost district, Chittoor. The Qutb Shah kingdom, a second polity that arose out of the earlier Bahmani sultanate, was to become an even greater threat to the now truncated Vijayanagara kingdom. From 1579 onward Qutb Shah armies started moving down the coast from Vengi, which had been seized in the 1530s, and soon gained control of the major fort of

Kondavidu and other towns in Guntur District. Vijayanagara decline was temporarily halted under Venkata II, possibly the greatest of the Aravidu kings, who ruled from 1584 to 1614. But what was left of the kingdom was lost rapidly after his death. The area of Kurnool was seized by Adil Shah forces in the 1620s, while the Qutb Shahs made major advances down the coast during the early 1640s. By the mid sixteenth century, the last Vijayanagara king had to flee Andhra, all of which was now under the nominal hegemony of Muslim polities.[41]

Migration and Transmission of Kakatiya Memories

During the heyday of Vijayanagara influence in Andhra, Telugu inscriptions were issued in more localities of southern and southwestern Rayalasima than ever before. In fact, Telugu inscriptions could be found even beyond the confines of the modern state, whose borders were demarcated in 1956 on the basis of linguistic distributions.[42] A good number of Telugu records are found in bordering regions like Bellary District of Karnataka or North and South Arcot Districts in Tamil Nadu.[43] But they were also inscribed far to the south in Tiruchirappalli and Tirunelveli Districts, long-established agrarian areas of the Tamil country.[44] The cosmopolitan nature of the Vijayanagara kingdom is one reason Telugu records appeared in such far-flung locales. For example, Krishnadeva Raya often recorded his own benefactions in four languages (Telugu, Tamil, Kannada, and Sanskrit) so that they could be widely understood. But the migration of Telugu speakers to other linguistic areas of the Vijayanagara realm better explains the appearance of Telugu inscriptions outside of Andhra.

When and how emigrants from Andhra moved to Karnataka and Tamil Nadu is unknown in most instances. One set of Telugu migrants to the Tamil country may have accompanied the victorious armies of the Vijayanagara general Kumara Kampana in his Tamil campaigns of the late fourteenth century. This explains the presence of the Telugu warrior Gandaragulu Marayya Nayaka in the South Arcot region of Tamil Nadu toward the end of the 1300s (Narayana Rao, Shulman, and Subrahmanyam 1992: 29). But many Telugu émigrés seem to have moved as independent figures rather than as part of larger military movements. Ettapa Nayaka of Chandragiri in Chittoor District, for example, left in 1423 because of disturbed conditions in his home locale. Accompanying him were over a thousand people, most of whom were his soldiers and retainers. This war-band settled in the vicinity of Madurai for some decades. In the 1560s their descendants constructed Ettaiyapuram fort in Tirunelveli District (Ludden 1985: 51). A major community of peasants in the northern Mysore region is thought to have migrated there from Andhra in the fourteenth century (Stein 1989: 82). Besides warrior-peasants, large numbers of Telugu artisans and merchants also emigrated over the centuries. The peak phase of large-scale migratory movement probably occurred between 1400 and 1550 (Subrahmanyam 1990: 357).

Although the exact historical circumstances are murky, the end result was a substantial movement of Telugu peoples into other areas. This is particularly evident in the case of Tamil Nadu. British census figures from the late nineteenth century reveal substantial Telugu-speaking minorities in the Tamil districts of Coimbatore,

Madurai, Salem, Tirunelveli, Chingleput, and Tiruchirappalli (Narayana Rao, Shulman, and Subrahmanyam 1992: 33). Telugu migrants settled primarily in areas that were elevated, dry, and often on black soils (Stein 1980: 394–96).[45] The political impact of Telugu speakers on the Tamil country is best evidenced by the establishment of the Nayaka kingdoms of Senji, Tanjavur, and Madurai during the 1520s and 1530s. Nominally subservient to the Vijayanagara kings until 1565, the Telugu warrior leaders of these states subsequently became autonomous (Narayana Rao, Shulman, and Subrahmanyam 1992: 38–44). It is likely that there was a second wave of Telugu migrants into the Tamil country in the turbulent years after 1565 (Breckenridge 1985b: 43). The physical (and social) mobility that were prominent aspects of Kakatiya Andhra thus continued to characterize Telugu society long afterward.

The Kakatiyas continue to figure in historical constructions produced by Telugu warrior émigrés of the post-1565 era. One such piece of historical writing is the *Rāyavācakamu*, a Telugu prose text composed about 1600 in the Madurai Nayaka kingdom. Although actually written decades later, it purports to be a contemporary account of events in the reign of the greatest Vijayanagara king, Krishnadeva Raya (r. 1509–29). At one point in the *Rāyavācakamu* narrative, the king inquires about the earlier history of the Deccan. He is told that long ago there was a war between the sultan of Delhi and Prataparudra of Warangal during which the latter was captured. The *Rāyavācakamu* continues that when Prataparudra was brought to Delhi, the sultan's mother desired to see this famous king and observed him as he slept. What she saw was not a human form, however, but an emanation of Shiva complete with trident and drum. The next night, the sultan's mother witnessed her own son as he lay asleep and realized that he, on the other hand, was an emanation of the god Vishnu. Since they shared this divine element, she asked that the sultan release Prataparudra and the sultan acceded to her request (Wagoner 1993: 122–23).

This episode closely resembles one in the *Pratāparudra Caritramu*, even though the *Rāyavācakamu* was written a half century or so later and in a place distant from Telangana, as recognized by its translator, Phillip B. Wagoner (1993: 206). In the comparable story from the *Pratāparudra Caritramu*, the sultan recognizes Prataparudra's divinity when a third eye suddenly appears on the latter's forehead. The sultan is smitten with guilt at having treated a deity so badly and informs his mother. The mother requests that he and Prataparudra sleep next to each other on a bed, so that she might judge their relative worth. That night she witnesses a blaze of radiance arising from their two sleeping bodies, the physical manifestation of their fundamental identity as Vishnu and Shiva. The mother urges the two to resolve their differences, whereupon the sultan promptly frees Prataparudra and provides him with an escort home (Ramachandra Rao 1984: 66–67). Aside from this similarity, the *Rāyavācakamu* and the *Pratāparudra Caritramu* agree that Prataparudra survived the journey to Delhi, contrary to other sources that allege he died on the way there.[46]

The *Rāyavācakamu*'s familiarity with historical traditions contained in the *Pratāparudra Caritramu* reveals that Telugu warriors shared a vision of the past in which the Kakatiyas played an important part.[47] Even Telugu warrior groups who had acquired positions of power under the Vijayanagara aegis and moved outside of the home territory retained some historical consciousness of the Kakatiyas. For these warriors the Vijayanagara association was the most significant in legitimating their position, and so the vast bulk of the *Rāyavācakamu* is devoted to Krishnadeva Raya. Krishnadeva Raya was responsible, according to other traditions, for sending the founder of the kingdom to Madurai (Narayana Rao, Shulman, and Subrahmanyam 1992: 44–56; Dirks 1987: 96–106). By concentrating on Krishnadeva Raya's reign, the *Rāyavācakamu* highlights the era of Vijayanagara's greatness, whence the Madurai Nayakas originated. Regardless of this difference in emphasis, the *Rāyavācakamu* echoes the *Pratāparudra Caritramu* in implying that the Kakatiyas were actually the lineal predecessors of the Vijayanagara kings. Only one place in the text reconstructs events prior to the establishment of Vijayanagara city, and it deals with the conflict between Kakatiya Prataparudra and the Delhi sultanate. By default, as the sole non-Muslim dynasty of earlier times mentioned, the Kakatiyas can only be construed as the forerunners of the Vijayanagara rulers (Wagoner 1993: 122–24, 205–6).[48]

Other historical writings that originated outside of Andhra are even more explicit in linking the Kakatiya and Vijayanagara kings. These are a set of Sanskrit traditions relating to the foundation of Vijayanagara city, supposedly built by the Shaiva saint Vidyaranya, who acted as the guru of the first two Vijayanagara kings of the Sangama dynasty, Harihara and Bukka.[49] The simplest rendition of the story is given in the *Vidyāraṇya Kṛti* (Vidyaranya's Creation).[50] It asserts that Harihara and Bukka were originally treasury guards at Warangal under Kakatiya Prataparudra, prior to their contact with Vidyaranya. After Warangal fell to the Delhi sultanate, the two Sangama brothers left for Kampili, near the site of the future Vijayanagara capital at Hampi, where they took service under the chief Ramanatha. They later tried unsuccessfully to conquer Ballala, the Hoysala king. Once they met Vidyaranya, however, and had the benefits of the sage's advice and blessings, Harihara and Bukka were finally able to defeat the Hoysalas and acquire their own territory (Wagoner 1993: 165–69).

Another version of the story found in the *Vidyāraṇya Vṛttānta* similarly situates the Sangama brothers at the Kakatiya capital but omits any mention of their subsequent service at Kampili:

> In the city of Mangalanilaya there ruled a Yadava chief of the name of Sangaraya. He had five sons who were known by the names of Harihararaya, Kamparaya, Bukkaraya, Madapparaya and Muddapparaya . . . . Harihara and Bukka went to the city of Orugallu [Warangal] where they entered into the service of its king, Prataparudra. In course of time, the Ashvapati Sultan, who was the king of Delhi, having invaded Telingana, Prataparudra, the ruler of Ekashila [Warangal], was defeated in battle. Harihara and Bukka, who were the superintendents of his treasury, were carried away as prisoners to the Sultan's camp. All the sentries that were guarding the camp fled in panic one evening owing to the outburst of a thunder-storm. Nevertheless, Harihara and Bukka sat in obedience to the orders within the prison. The Sultan saw them and, being convinced of their uprightness, took them into his service and retained them at the court.
>
> At that time, the Nava Ballalas, having gathered strength, rebelled against the Sultan in Karnataka. The Sultan dispatched Harihara and Bukka to Karnataka at the

> head of a large army to subdue the rebels; but being defeated in battle by the Ballalas, the brothers, who were exhausted, took rest at the foot of a tree. Harihara fell into a deep sleep. During the sleep, Revana Siddha appeared to him in a dream, gave him a linga of Chandramaulishvara and said, "You will have an interview with the yogi, Vidyaranya, the benefactor of the world. By the grace of the sage, you will obtain sovereignty." (Nilakanta Sastri and Venkataramanayya 1946, 3: 10–11)

N. Venkataramanayya used these historical traditions as the primary basis of his claim that Vijayanagara's first royal dynasty was Telugu in origin (Nilakanta Sastri and Venkataramanayya 1946, 1: 22–34). In his view, it was this actual firsthand experience with the Kakatiyas on the part of Vijayanagara's founders that accounted for the similarities in the administrative structures of the Kakatiya and Vijayanagara states (Venkataramanayya 1990: 102–11).

The allegation that the first kings of Vijayanagara had been warriors in the service of Kakatiya Prataparudra is thus found in several literary sources originating in Karnataka, but all of these works continue by narrating the story of the capital city's founding by the sage Vidyaranya. The historicity of Vidyaranya's central role is seemingly corroborated by a set of early inscriptions that likewise emphasize his part in the establishment of the kingdom. However, many scholars now believe that these inscriptions are spurious. Although they purport to be products of the early fourteenth century, the records citing Vidyaranya were most probably fabricated in the sixteenth century at the famous Shaiva monastery (*maṭha*) in Sringeri, Karnataka. Hermann Kulke has pointed out that the textual traditions relating to Vidyaranya—the same ones in which Harihara and Bukka are said to have been Kakatiya subordinates—are similarly of late origin and may also have been propagated by the Sringeri *maṭha* (1985: 123–27). In the late fourteenth century, there was indeed a religious leader called Vidyaranya who was abbot of the *maṭha* and received many benefactions from the Vijayanagara kings, although he was certainly not involved in the founding of the capital several decades earlier. But by the early sixteenth century, royal patronage had shifted away from the Shaiva site of Sringeri in Karnataka to the Vaishnava center at Tirupati in Andhra. Hence, the claims of direct connection with Vijayanagara's origins must be construed as later attempts to bolster Sringeri's sagging fortunes. Kulke's argument is supported by the late date of the Vidyaranya manuscripts, which can be placed no earlier than 1580.[51]

It is not hard to fathom why a religious institution might seek to win back royal favor through the fiction that one of its early abbots was the source of Vijayanagara's greatness. But the reasons why Harihara and Bukka were purported to have been Kakatiya subordinates are less readily apparent. The effect of this fiction is to supply the first kings of Vijayanagara with a respectable past history, a pedigree of military service, in the Andhra region. It probably resulted from a desire to directly link the state's origin with Andhra, since the Vijayanagara kingdom was more Telugu in personnel and culture during the sixteenth century than in earlier times. For Sringeri, a Shaiva site in Karnataka eclipsed by the greater popularity of Vaishnava establishments in Andhra, a Telugu association of some kind might have appeared politic. But to represent the early leader Vidyaranya as being from Andhra would have detracted from Sringeri's fame and Karnataka base and, in any case, the institution's potential patrons were the targeted audience of the new historical construction.[52] Therefore Vidyaranya's supposed disciples (and subsequent patrons), the Vijayanagara kings Harihara and Bukka, are described as having begun their military careers in Kakatiya Warangal. The extent to which sixteenth-century conceptions of being Telugu, even in Karnataka, revolved around an ancestral affiliation with the Kakatiyas is demonstrated in this ploy.

To recapitulate, the Kakatiyas were not forgotten among Telugu warriors who resided in the Tamil and Kannada Regions centuries after the fall of Kakatiya Warangal. The *Rāyavācakamu* narrates the story of Kakatiya Prataparudra's conflict with the Delhi sultan in such a way that the composer's acquaintance with the *Pratāparudra Caritramu* account is confirmed. Sanskrit literary works from Karnataka expand on the *Rāyavācakamu*'s inference that the Kakatiya and Vijayanagara kingdoms were united in a single continuum of power. By portraying the Kakatiyas as the forerunners of the Vijayanagara kings, a smooth transition from one dynasty to the other could be contrived and the distant past take on a comforting aura of conformity with the recent past. The allusions to the Kakatiyas outside the Andhra region show us that a history derived from the Kakatiyas was part of a Telugu warrior culture that spanned geographic borders and the passing of time. Nor did it matter whether the warrior's ancestors had more recently been in Vijayanagara employ. In the cosmopolitan atmosphere of early modern South India, one element of being Telugu was the shared conception of a past that began with the Kakatiyas.

Aside from memories of the Kakatiyas, Telugu warriors of later centuries had in common the notion of prior service to a king with a fixed number of warrior subordinates—either 72, 75, or 77. The version found in the *Pratāparudra Caritramu* has already been described, with its 77 Padmanayaka subordinates. One bastion of Warangal's fortifications was assigned to each of the 77 men who were, as a group, a metonym for the entirety of the Kakatiya warrior subordinate class. Modern historians have interpreted the story of the 77 Padmanayakas as a faithful reflection of the workings of the *nāyaṅkaramu* system during Prataparudra's reign, *nāyaṅkaramu* being a type of revenue assignment over territory that was awarded in exchange for military service.[53] Ambadeva's Tripurantakam inscription of 1290, wherein Ambadeva recounts a victory in battle against 75 kings, is often cited as further evidence of the chronicle's veracity (SII 10.465). Since Ambadeva is known to have rebelled against the Kakatiyas, the 75 kings mentioned in his inscription are taken to be the 75 Padmanayakas.

However, the conception of a warrior order composed of some 70 subordinates was not restricted to the *Pratāparudra Caritramu*, nor did it apply only to the Kakatiya kingdom. The mid-fourteenth-century political network headed by the Musunuri chiefs Prolaya Nayaka and Kapaya Nayaka is likewise said to have included 75 *nāyakas*, according to the Kaluvacheru grant of 1423 (Somasekhara Sarma 1945: 111–12). We have already discussed this inscription, in connection with its portrayal of the Musunuris as legitimate successors to the Kakatiyas. It states that after Kapaya Nayaka's death his 75 subordinate *nāyakas* dispersed to their own towns and protected their respective lands. This scenario is strikingly reminiscent of the *Pratāparudra Caritramu* account of Prataparudra's last days, during which he releases the Padmanayakas from their vows of service and enjoins them to become rulers of their own territories. Since the Kaluvacheru predates the chronicle by a century, the author of the Kaluvacheru grant may have appropriated an existing tradition about the Kakatiyas that was not recorded at length until the *Pratāparudra Caritramu*.[54]

Just as likely, however, is the possibility that the paradigm of 70-odd subordinates was a convention among Telugu elites in the post-Kakatiya period. Historical traditions from the Kondavidu area (Guntur District) collected in the last two centuries repeat the motif of a king with over 70 allied chiefs. One story describes events after the death of the last Kondavidu Reddi king, whose 72 warrior subordinates could not agree upon a successor. Krishnadeva Raya of Vijayanagara (who actually lived almost a century later) decided to turn this situation to his advantage and had a brahman invite the 72 chiefs to the consecration of an image at Kondavidu fort. The assembled chiefs were all assassinated and Krishnadeva Raya was then able to capture the fort easily (Luders 1900: 110). Other accounts say that Krishnadeva Raya's successor Achyutadeva defeated the 72 chiefs of Kondavidu (Mack. Gen. Coll. 7.2). In addition to having 72 chiefs, the Kondavidu Reddi kingdom allegedly also had 72 forts (Mack. Gen. Coll. 7.6).

Similar traditions from the Tamil country are described by Nicholas B. Dirks. Vishvanatha Nayaka, the Telugu founder of the Madurai Nayaka kingdom, is said to have selected 72 warrior lords to become his subordinates and assigned one of the 72 bastions of Madurai fort to each of them, in what Dirks calls "a classic rhetorical formulation of political-symbolic incorporation" (1987: 49). Of all our examples, this most closely replicates the *Pratāparudra Caritramu* story of the origin of the 77 Padmanayakas. Dirks reports that the family histories of many local Tamil chiefs in the eighteenth century highlighted this episode of incorporation into the Madurai Nayaka polity, because of the political recognition it conferred. The Telugu warrior conception of a kingdom as consisting essentially of an overlord with some 70 underlings was thus transferred outside the Andhra region. It was transmitted by the Madurai Nayakas to at least one non-Telugu line of chiefs, the later rulers of Ramnad. They too were said to have had a political network of 72 subordinates (Dirks 1987: 50, 68).[55] The conception of a kingdom where a ruler shared sovereignty with his carefully selected set of subordinates, a paradigm that was associated with the Kakatiyas if not actually derived from their example, was evidently disseminated by Telugu warriors as they migrated into other areas of South India. The widespread presence of this feature, as well as the shared belief in a past when ancestors had been legitimized through contact with the Kakatiyas, is testimony to the emergence of an elite Telugu warrior culture that transcended geographic borders.

Village Accounts and Popular Traditions

The memories of the Kakatiyas discussed in the previous pages all emanated from the warrior class. But Telugu warriors were not alone in remembering the Kakatiyas. Other segments of the population had a similar sense of the past in which the Kakatiyas figured. The most complete of the nonwarrior memories are contained in the village histories known as *kaifiyats* collected as part of the Mackenzie project from the last years of the 1700s into the second decade of the 1800s.[56] *Kaifiyats* typically trace the history of a village or locality back to its founding, recording memorable events along the way. They vary considerably in length and quality, with some agreeing closely with our understanding of this history and others quite fanciful by our standards. Out of the hundreds of village histories obtained, 68 mention the Kakatiyas in some fashion.[57] They are concentrated in eastern Kurnool District and the neighboring Cuddapah District, a pattern that corresponds with the distribution of inscriptions in Rayalasima during the Kakatiya period.[58] That is, memories of the Kakatiyas persisted most strongly in areas of southern interior Andhra which had once been strongholds of Kakatiya political influence.

The circumstances surrounding the production of the *kaifiyats* was not fully documented, although the names of the informants are sometimes recorded. In many cases local *karaṇams* (village accountants) seem to have provided the histories, in either oral or written form.[59] Because they were village-level officials responsible for details relating to land assessments and other administrative requirements, they may have been viewed as the best sources of information due to their occupation. The fact that Mackenzie's assistants, who did the actual collecting of data, were brahmans (supervised by two Telugu brahman brothers in succession) was probably another factor in the choice of the predominantly brahman *karaṇams* as informants. The quasi-official nature of the data collection, sponsored by a British administrator and supported by his fellow British officials in the various localities, must be considered in evaluating the results. One consequence of the context within which the Mackenzie *kaifiyats* were gathered is that a number of them seek to justify the position of the current brahman communities in the villages (Mack. Transl. 7.6; Parthasarathy 1982: 13). So, for example, the *kaifiyat* from Kammamur tells us that brahmans were appointed as *karaṇams* in the area by a Gajapati king, displacing the craftsmen who had formerly occupied these posts (Mack. Transl. 7.5). Overall, the *kaifiyats* document those past events that explain the privileged position of local temples and notables. The *kaifiyats* are thus evidently the products of village leaders, many of whom were brahman.

In close to half of the *kaifiyat* references to the Kakatiyas (44 percent), the Kakatiyas appear as part of the general chronological framework for the village's past or in connection with a military conflict in the vicinity. Memorable events like the founding of the village, redrawing of village boundaries, or building of tanks are said to have taken place during the reign of a specific Kakatiya monarch in roughly one-quarter of the accounts. But most interesting are the cases where a Kakatiya ruler or prominent Kakatiya subordinate is represented as having been directly involved with the village's past in some manner. A Kakatiya ruler or subordinate allegedly either founded the village, granted it as a brahman *agrahāra*, constructed a temple in the village, or made a major endowment to the village temple in slightly over one-third of the *kaifiyats* (35 percent).

The following account collected in 1811 from Mutyalapadu, a village in Kurnool District, represents this group of *kaifiyats*:

> During the days when Prataparudra governed from Warangal as the lord of the gem-covered throne, he once went on pilgrimage to Rameshvaram. On the way, he stopped

> at a thickly forested spot located about 10 miles southwest of Ahobilam. From the time he left his capital, he had a tank or well dug and temples to Shiva and Vishnu erected at every place he halted. He would march on after having consecrated and worshiped the gods. Following this custom, when he halted here he had a small tank constructed and to the west of it he had two temples built.
>
> One day during this time, some of his retinue found a pearl inside a piece of bamboo that they had just cut down. Seeing that, the king decided to establish a village on the site. He then recruited settlers by offering a contract [*kaulu*] that guaranteed 10 years without taxes.[60] He appointed Bhuci Raju as karnam [accountant] and assigned Boma Reddi and Bhima Reddi to the position of village reddi [headman]. The village founded after clearing of the thick forest was named Mutyalapadu.
>
> After the stipulated 10 years had elapsed, the king summoned the reddis and karnam to Warangal. They had been granted favorable terms for 10 years, he told them, but would henceforth have to collect revenues from the village. The king assigned an annual levy of 50 Kaveri-paka gold coins on the village which the reddis and karnam agreed to in writing. Afterward he presented them with cloths suitable to their rank. The reddis and karnam returned to the village and remitted the amount promised to the government. When another 3 years had passed, the king raised the levy by another 100 gold coins, bringing the total sum he received from the villagers annually to 150 gold coins. This state of affairs continued during the rest of Prataparudra's reign.[61]

The details on the tax levies give the account an air of authenticity. That Prataparudra may have visited the area around Ahobilam is quite plausible. The *kaifiyat* of Ahobilam, a nearby Vaishnava temple in Kurnool District that was popular during the Vijayanagara period, claims that Prataparudra donated the festival images of the main Ahobilam deity, Narasimha, as well as contributing to the buildings at the site (Sitapati 1982a: 13). Another *kaifiyat* states that the stones for renovating the main Ahobilam shrine were obtained by the king from its village (Mahalingam 1976: 108–9).

The only Kakatiya ruler described in the Mutyalapadu account is Prataparudra. The dominance of Prataparudra in later Andhra traditions related to the Kakatiyas is marked, as mentioned in the preceding discussion on other references to the dynasty. He is the sole Kakatiya remembered in two-thirds of the *kaifiyat* instances and in several other cases appears along with another Kakatiya ruler. This preoccupation with Prataparudra, which was also found in the *Pratāparudra Caritramu*, may derive from the sociopolitical changes he and his predecessor initiated. But Prataparudra is not always remembered with any specificity. In some *kaifiyats* he is presented merely as an important king of antiquity. This can be witnessed in the *kaifiyat* obtained in 1802 from Ongole, today a taluk headquarters in the southern coastal district of Prakasam:

> During the reign of Prataparuḍra Maharaja, which was prior to Shaka 1100 [1178–79 C.E.], his son Haripalaka argued with him and left the capital for the Addanki region. One day while he was governing this heavily forested district, Haripalaka went out in the woods with his army. Riding on horseback, he soon outdistanced the troops and found himself alone at sunset in the spot where Addanki town would later be established. During the night, the goddess Palairamma appeared to the prince and told him to erect a fort there after clearing the trees. She prescribed a particular method: the prince was to take mud from a basket on his head and throw it over his shoulder without ever looking backward. The prince followed these instructions until

the fort was three-quarters done. After he could no longer curb his curiosity and glanced back, divine assistance ceased and the remainder of the fort had to be built by regular means.

While Haripalaka was ruling from Addanki fort, Vijaya Ramudu, a brahman who had accompanied him there from Warangal, was given permission to clear the forest southeast of Addanki at some distance and establish a village. Having cleared the land, Vijaya Ramudu spent the night at that place. In his dreams, various gods told him that they approved of his possession of the site and had accompanied him from Warangal for that purpose. He was instructed to dig a tank called Devatala Bavi in their honor, erect a temple for the deity Gopala, and label the new town he would build Ongole. All of this Vijaya Ramudu did as ordered.[62]

Apart from the reference to Warangal, the Ongole *kaifiyat* could substitute the name of any king for Prataparudra. Here, as in most of the *kaifiyats* from coastal Andhra, Prataparudra is not a distinct personality easily identifiable with the Kakatiya king whose exploits we know from inscriptions. Instead, the Kakatiya ruler Prataparudra has been conflated with other kings who at some time ruled over the coastal territory. A number of accounts state that Prataparudra began his rule in Dharanikota, an ancient town in Guntur District, before moving to Warangal (e.g., Mack. Gen. Coll. 8.7). The memories of Kakatiya Prataparudra were probably intermixed with those of a second Prataparudra, who belonged to the Gajapati family of coastal Orissa and Andhra, in these instances. The name Mukkanti (three-eyed) also sometimes appears as a synonym for Prataparudra in traditions from Guntur District. Mukkanti Kaduvetti or Trilochana Pallava is a legendary figure famed for clearing the forests of the lower Krishna valley and settling it with immigrants from the north (Venkataramanayya 1929: 71–72).[63]

The difference in the quality of *kaifiyat* memories of Kakatiya Prataparudra between the coastal districts and Rayalasima is striking. In Rayalasima accounts such as the one from Mutyalapadu, Prataparudra is explicitly said to be from Warangal. His family name Kakatiya and/or details of his ancestry are often offered. The dates assigned to his reign tend to be quite accurate, and inscriptions issued by him or his subordinates are sometimes cited in detail. There is little doubt in the Rayalasima references that the king being remembered is actually Kakatiya Prataparudra. The rise in inscriptional production in central Rayalasima, and specifically in Cuddapah District, indicates that agricultural settlement in that subregion did expand considerably during the Kakatiya period. The historical memories contained in Rayalasima *kaifiyats* may therefore have a basis in factual events. But the greater importance of Prataparudra in Rayalasima may also be due to the relative paucity of royal figures there as compared to the coast. With the exception of the Vijayanagara rulers who are also prominent in Rayalasima *kaifiyats*, there were few kings of note in the southern interior aside from Kakatiya Prataparudra. Historical traditions from the coast, on the other hand, extend much further back in time and are therefore full of references to a plethora of former kings. In coastal Andhra's construction of the past, Prataparudra was therefore both less unique and less significant.

Whether distinct or hazy, however, the salient point for us is that Kakatiya Prataparudra's memory was transmitted by people other than warriors in both the interior and coastal territories of southern Andhra. Important village-level individuals, many of whom were brahmans, remembered the Kakatiyas as notable kings of the past. Quite often, important transitional moments in the village's past—its founding, change in revenue status, the building of a temple or tank, a shift in village boundaries—were associated in their minds with the rule of the Kakatiyas. Like the political elites of Andhra origin, therefore, early colonial village officials also had a vision of the past in which the Kakatiyas were prominently featured.

That the Kakatiyas were a royal dynasty at the very threshold of contemporary society was an idea shared also by landholding peasants. Hence we find references to Kakatiya Prataparudra in stories about the origins of the primary Telugu agriculturalist groups, which were recorded by Edgar Thurston in his early twentieth-century work *Castes and Tribes of Southern India*.[64] The major cultivating caste-clusters—the Kapus or Reddis, the Kammas, and the Velamas—are said to have a common ancestry in these legends. The Kapus were the first caste, *kāpu* (earlier, *kāmpu*) being the normal Telugu term for "cultivator" (Thurston 1975, 3: 227). The Kammas and Velamas evolved out of the Kapus, according to these traditions, because of an incident involving Kakatiya Prataparudra.

Typical of the several variants gathered by Thurston is the following tale that he recounts when describing the Kapus:

> During the reign of Pratapa Rudra, the wife of one Belthi Reddi secured by severe penance a brilliant ear ornament (*kamma*) from the sun. This was stolen by the King's minister, as the King was very anxious to secure it for his wife. Belthi Reddi's wife told her sons to recover it, but her eldest son refused to have anything to do with the matter, as the King was involved in it. The second son likewise refused and used foul language. The third son promised to secure it, and, hearing this, one of his brothers ran away. Finally the ornament was recovered by the youngest son. The Panta Kapus are said to be descended from the eldest son, the Pakanatis from the second, the Velamas from the son who ran away, and the Kammas from the son who secured the jewel. (Thurston 1975, 3: 231–32)

The story tells us that four different groups—the Panta Kapus, the Pakanatis, the Velamas, and the Kammas—were descended from the same family. Pakanati simply means "of the eastern region" and serves as a name for subdivisions within several Telugu caste-clusters today, but here it refers to the Pakanati Kapus who are also called Pakanati Reddis. They are one of the main divisions within the Reddis along with the Panta Reddis (or Panta Kapus). The story narrated above clearly owes much to folk etymology, for *kamma* means "female ear-ornament" while the assertion that the Velamas ran away comes from the word *veli*, "away" (Thurston 1975, 5: 469 and 3: 96). It also reveals that the various prominent cultivator caste-clusters of modern Andhra were all regarded as having developed from the same stock—an interesting conception given the social fluidity among nonbrahman status categories that was noted in the analysis of Kakatiya society in chapter 2.

More relevant to this context, however, is the fact that social memory traced the schism of the Andhra peasant community to an event involving Kakatiya Prataparudra. The principal units of the agrarian social order—its main groups of land controllers—were thought to have emerged during his reign. Even more significantly, Prataparudra is himself indirectly enmeshed in the seminal events. The stories are vague enough that the figure of the ruler is indistinct—any king could have served the narrative function, and so Prataparudra may have been specified for no other reason than the general familiarity with his name. Nonetheless Thurston's stories reveal that Prataparudra was a meaningful figure to a broad sector of the population, the dominant peasant castes, up until the twentieth century. Even the segment of Andhra society charged specifically with the preservation of historical information believed they owed their own presence in Andhra to the Kakatiyas. According to the traditions of the Bhatraju bardic community, who recited genealogies and lauded ancestral exploits for their landed patrons, they emigrated to Warangal from North India upon the invitation of Prataparudra (Thurston 1975, 1: 225). The very embodiment of the Telugu historical imagination—the bardic class itself—hence originated with the Kakatiyas, the ground zero of the Andhra vision of its roots.

The diverse array of contexts in which he was remembered in Andhra historical constructions implies that Prataparudra was a potent symbol for Telugu-speaking peoples from a wide variety of social backgrounds. But the importance of the Kakatiyas for Telugu people of later generations varied tremendously. For some Telangana chiefs, the Kakatiyas were the great kings responsible for transforming their ancestors into little kings. For certain Telugu subordinates of the Vijayanagara empire, the Kakatiyas were the direct precursors of their current overlords. In other histories the Vijayanagara kings themselves resembled the many Andhra warrior lineages who claimed they had bonds of military service to the Kakatiyas. The recollections of the Kakatiyas among some village notables, on the other hand, were dim and confused. But there was a widespread perception in Andhra social memory that crucial junctures of history had occurred in the period of Kakatiya rule, a conclusion we had also reached from our reconstruction of the Kakatiya era based on inscriptional sources. Today we may attribute the significance of the period to a different set of reasons than did earlier Andhra conceptions of history, which focused on the Kakatiya kings as the primary causal factors rather than on large-scale processes of development. But in both my interpretation and Andhra historical memory, the Kakatiya period is regarded as the seminal phase in Andhra's evolution.

Conclusion

Toward a New Model of Medieval India

The inscribing on stone of records relating to religious endowments is one of the few cultural practices of precolonial India for which the surviving evidence is both copious and measurable. Due to the large number of tangible objects produced as a result, we can more easily witness the growing momentum and eventual waning of the impulse to make stone inscriptions than we can in the case of many other contemporary trends. Precisely because studying a corpus of inscriptions clearly conveys a sense of historical change and progression, I began my analysis with an examination of their shifting spatial and temporal distributions. What inscriptions tell us most immediately is that the people of Andhra increasingly desired to document religious gifts in an enduring fashion. Inscriptions also provide indirect testimony to the spread of a pan-Indic complex—of religious values and practices revolving around the worship of images in temples—in a regional variant that developed its own sacred geography for the Andhra area. Through the medium of inscriptions, we can also glean the existence of a host of interconnected developments that accompanied the expansion of temple worship.

One process concurrent with the rise of the temple cult was the extension of agricultural cultivation, most particularly of intensive agrarian techniques involving irrigation. Temples were both a symptom of the growing agricultural base and a stimulus for further growth—the founding of new temples resulted from the forward movement of the agrarian frontier, but in turn their material needs accelerated the pace of economic development. Tanks and other water resources provided better sustenance for the deity and his staff, the services of artisans and craftsmen were employed to better honor the god, and merchants congregated for the periodic fairs that took place in many temple towns. The patronage of temples became so popular because a multiplicity of social and political objectives could be subsumed within that act, along with the undoubtedly powerful incentive of providing spiritual solace for oneself and one's family. A temple donor might enhance his stature as a lord, express solidarity with colleagues in commerce or in war, achieve tax reductions on property still under his control, make new contacts in an established community of worship, or advance any number of other ambitions. The public nature of temple endowment surely accounted for much of its appeal to individuals seeking to establish themselves within the rapidly changing milieu of medieval Andhra.

Indeed, much of what we can grasp from inscriptions about the social and political dimensions of Kakatiya Andhra is intelligible only within the context of a dynamic and expansionistic world. The primacy placed on occupation as a way of classifying people, the porous boundaries between social groups who were neither brahmans nor merchants, the possibility of earning a title of status—all of these suggest the fluidity of a society that was very much evolving. The rigid and hierarchical social universe that scholars have inferred from literary texts (if indeed textual analysis warrants such an inference) is a construction of the upper echelons of social actors observed in inscriptions. It was the kind of society—orderly, peaceful, and reverent—that learned brahmans and great kings may have wished to witness and perhaps had managed to create to some degree in the longer-settled nuclear zones of peninsular India. But it was not the world being formed in the upland portions of the peninsula, where the many isolated pockets of settlement were gradually coalescing through the migration of agriculturalists from the coastal territories and the acculturation of others who had formerly concentrated on herding, hunting, and/or shifting cultivation. As the landscape filled in, new overland routes were forged to convey an accelerating quantity of goods and people more expeditiously as well as to connect temple complexes in an ever-widening circuit of pilgrimage. In this scenario of physical movement and social transformation, the kinds of territorially based subcastes described in later ethnographic literature were conspicuously absent.

The prevalence of martial skills and values is another aspect of medieval Andhra found in inscriptions that seems surprising at first sight. Here is yet another instance where we have obviously placed too much credence on the hegemony of brahman ideology in the non-Muslim societies of medieval India. Historians do, of course, give token recognition to the military basis of South India's non-Muslim polities but generally prefer to invoke ritual sovereignty or a symbolically incorporative strategy as their main source of power. In a revealing contrast, the military apparatus and militaristic ethos of Muslim polities are typically treated at considerable length. But there were plenty of occasions when non-Muslims displayed martial prowess to advantage in the recently settled territories of inland Andhra, as numerous newly emergent warrior lineages sought to carve out niches for themselves. Each chief or lord needed a coterie of warrior followers, who were recruited from a variety of backgrounds. Because the widespread existence of military skills has largely been overlooked, we have seriously underestimated the extent to which military careers provided opportunities for social mobility. To be sure, it has long been recognized that the founders of royal dynasties often had humble origins, but kings were few and far between when compared to the large number of fighting men whose fortunes could rise, or fall, as a result of their own actions.

Our models of the Indian past are flawed in part because we have ignored the large expanses of uncultivated land that existed well into the early modern era. The very antiquity of India's history is deceptive in this regard, since the very early emergence of some centers of civilization can easily suggest that a similar situation prevailed elsewhere in the subcontinent. Standard accounts of precolonial Indian history compound the problem by moving straight from one historic center to another in their narrative, with little consideration of conditions outside the core zones. While the expansion of settled agriculture certainly commenced extremely early in India, we tend to forget that the process was ongoing and has not entirely subsided even today. A striking example of the relatively late date of agrarian settlement in some parts of the subcontinent is offered by eastern Bengal (today Bangladesh), which was still only sparsely inhabited by peasant cultivators in the thirteenth century. Moreover, the Bengal delta experienced a significant ecological metamorphosis as recently as the sixteenth and seventeenth centuries, when the main river courses shifted substantially toward the east (Eaton 1993: 17–21, 194–98). Similarly, there is considerable evidence that uncultivated, unclaimed land was available for settlement even in the peninsular India of the fifteenth and sixteenth centuries—new villages were regularly being founded in the interior and there was ample room for people to get away from oppressive taxation or other unfavorable circumstances.

A failure to take into account the vast sociological expanses ignored by the historical sources also contributed to the distorted depiction of precolonial India. The scope of our historiographic vision is limited to the "civilized" sector, that part of India's population instrumental in the production of the monumental structures and literary texts that comprise the main remnants of the past. While we can obviously infer the presence of less privileged people like agricultural laborers or domestic servants within the social spheres of these elites, there were also numerous individuals and communities operating outside the confines of the state societies and settled agrarian economies of the medieval peninsula. When I say that much territory was uncultivated, I do not mean that it was entirely uninhabited—the emptiness of the historical record for some areas should not be construed as the absence of people per se but only of the kinds of people who collectively constitute what we call civilization. Both the high degree of movement within supposedly settled societies and the existence of social groups like pastoralists who had no sedentary base are effaced in the constructions of society passed down to us. Since "civilization in South Asia is defined inside the locations of sedentary life: village, town, city, kingdom, and empire," David Ludden concludes that "the perspective provided by Sanskrit texts, brahman experience, and elite culture in mediaeval states has attained a privilege in the framework of civilization that it does not deserve in history" (1994: 6–7, 11).

Inscriptions, both because they record a multiplicity of acts and because they were generated in a larger social circle, provide more glimpses of the physical and social mobility that was intrinsic to medieval India than do the more conservative literary texts of the upper elites. Even inscriptions have to be interpreted within the larger context of the world beyond their purview, however, since they too are the cultural products of a restricted set of people. Once we accept that many elements of dynamism are missing from or repressed in the source materials at our disposal, it is not difficult to envision a medieval India in which individuals could move around and change their social identity or political allegiance, although the possibility might not always, or even routinely, have been actualized. India would then be comparable to other medieval societies like those of western Europe or

Japan, where hereditary privilege and ascribed status were more commanding in theory than in practice, especially along the moving frontier of agrarian development.

Elite representations of society are valuable to historians not as actual descriptions of society, but due to their significance in shaping constructions of community that spanned large spaces and long times. In situating their patrons firmly within a town and territory, texts commissioned by the political elites fostered the notion of lordship as something that extended over a specific area of land and the citizenry within it—and, in that respect, created an "imagined" community. We witness the association drawn between sovereign, kingdom, and region in a Sanskrit copper-plate inscription issued by one of the son-in-laws of the ruling Kakatiya queen Rudramadevi in 1290, to cite but one of many examples. It tells us that among the many splendid countries (*dēśa*) like Anga, Vanga, Kalinga, Karnata, and Magadha, the Andhra realm (*maṇḍala*) is the most pleasing. The city of Warangal, which allegedly outshone the other hundred or so great towns there, is next praised in several verses. We move from there to the figure of the monarch in Warangal, the prowess of whose swinging arms supported the burden of the Kakatiya kingdom (*rājya*; EI 38.16, vv. 6–10). The praise of capitals is not uncommon in long Sanskrit inscriptions, while epithets like "overlord of the best of cities, Hanumakonda" appear regularly in Telugu records. In coastal Andhra, where some localities had a long history of settlement, aristocrats were often called the lords of a named locality.

Through their patronage of regional languages, political elites fostered the growing differentiation of literary cultures in peninsular India and thereby helped constitute these languages as significant boundaries between communities. Sheldon Pollock notes that the turning points in regional literary histories—the composition of authoritative texts or the initiation of new genres—occurred when strong expansionistic polities were flourishing (1996: 243–44). As he explains, "regional language writing often appears to develop . . . [in order] to demonstrate the capacity of vernacular elites and their language for playing the game of elite cultural politics" (1995: 130–31). The concept of a region was, of course, nothing new in medieval India but, largely due to the impetus of political elites, it increasingly came to signify a linguistic sphere as well as a geographic area. This is why the words Andhra and Telugu were interchangeable, as when a Kondavidu Reddi king is praised in a late-fourteenth-century inscription for commissioning an Andhra version of the *Rāmāyaṇa*, i.e., one composed in Telugu (NDI Kandukur 35, v. 3). Just as Andhra could mean the Telugu language, so too could Telugu stand for the Andhra region. A Marathi text of the Mahanubhava sect from the late thirteenth or early fourteenth century therefore enjoins devotees to stay in Maharashtra and not go to the Telugu or Kannada countries (Feldhaus 1986: 534–35).

The linkage between kingdom, region, and linguistic community in peninsular India was heightened during the twelfth through early fourteenth centuries, when political boundaries corresponded by and large with linguistic ones. The Yadavas of Devagiri, for instance, were the first major dynasty to use the fairly young language Marathi for official purposes in their inscriptions. Hemadri, the well-known brahman author and minister to the Yadavas, not only composed works in Sanskrit but also "is supposed to have made vigorous efforts to formalize Marathi with Sanskritic expressions and bolster its image as a court language" (Deshpande 1993a: 117). Prior to the Yadavas, both Marathi and Kannada had been used in Maharashtra; subsequently, at least partly due to their efforts, Marathi became dominant. The Kakatiyas likewise made a political statement when their inscriptions switched from the Kannada of their erstwhile Karnataka overlords to Telugu, the language prevalent where they now ruled independently. The relationship of kingdom to language was so close in this era that the North Indian writer Amir Khusrau called the Kannada language Dhur-Samundri after the name of the Hoysala capital (Dorasamudra) in his 1318 list of Indian languages (Nath and Gwaliari 1981: 75).[1] Even after the age of the regional kingdoms had ended, lords and polities were conceptualized largely in terms of their affiliations with a specific linguistic region. Many fifteenth- and sixteenth-century inscriptions from Andhra append phrases at the end stating that "if an Odda [i.e., Orissi-speaking] king, a Turkic king, a Karnata king, a Telugu king, or anyone who works for these kings should appropriate these (donated) cows, they will incur the sin of cow-killing and of brahman-killing" (SII 4.659). All but the Turkic king are designated by a name that denotes a linguistic realm in these lines; the Turk, or Muslim, instead bears an ethnic label.

Over time, linguistic markers were therefore increasingly employed to designate the separate cultural communities of peninsular India. Even members of the Muslim elites in the Deccan, who themselves identified with the Persian language and its tradition, classified the inhabitants on the basis of their regional languages. Muhammad Qasim Firishta, a scholar at the Bijapur court in the early seventeenth century, wrote that "the Deccan had three sons, who make up the Kingdom (*mulk*) of the Deccan. Their names are Marhat, Kanhar, and Tiling. Presently these three races (*qaum*) reside in the Deccan."[2] The Deccan peoples categorized as speakers of Marathi, Kannada, or Telugu were related but distinct species in this formulation. Language also serves as the chief method of differentiating communities (as well as geographic regions) in an account collected in 1802 by Mackenzie's assistants. Its anonymous author, conscious that the text would wind up in foreign hands, helpfully explains that there were 56 countries in India and then goes on to state:

> The people in these countries, though they profess different religions have different family names and customs yet are known or specified according to the language they speak; as Tamils, Telugus, etc. Languages are pertinent with countries in which they are spoken but not with the religion that their speakers profess. Sanskrit is known as the language of the Devas. Karnata (Kannada) is derived from karna (ears) atati (rolls) that is, what rolls in the ears (of every one) which is the language of the Karnata country. Similarly, other languages take their names from the country. (Mahalingam 1976: 320)

In the mind of this local official in the early colonial era, people belonged first and foremost to the community demarcated by a linguistic region.

Political elites also helped bring about conceptions of community that spanned large areas and incorporated many people through their formulation and transmission of historical memories. For who one is at any given point in time is determined to a large extent by perceptions of who one once was, among communities just as much as individuals. If their pasts were thought to be intertwined, then disparate social groups also had an element of commonality—that is, a joint cultural genealogy.

The vision of a shared history that was propagated by political elites often revolved around the central figure of a particular king or dynasty, and, in this way, political leaders came to symbolically represent a larger social group—a development that has been almost entirely overlooked by scholars of precolonial Indian history. Constructions of the past produced by political elites could gradually gain circulation among other social strata and thus lead to a growing sense of membership in the same community of people.

My analysis of Telugu historical memories has demonstrated how the Kakatiyas were quickly appropriated by powerful but parvenu warrior lineages as a source of legitimation in the unstable conditions of post-Kakatiya Andhra. Within less than two centuries, the Kakatiyas had advanced, in Andhra social conceptions, from merely being great kings of the past to becoming exemplars of Telugu kingship who had created Andhra's bygone Golden Age. Traditions relating to the Kakatiyas persisted most forcefully in Telangana, the former base of their political network, as illustrated in the chronicle *Pratāparudra Caritramu*. But memories of the Kakatiyas were spread to other areas of Andhra as well as to other regions of South India. Much of this later transmission occurred as a result of the growing influence of Andhra warriors within the Vijayanagara political network and the simultaneous emigration of Telugu-speaking peoples out of Andhra. It was among Telugu warriors, wherever they resided, that the Kakatiyas were most intensely remembered, but even village elites and dominant peasants in Andhra came to view the Kakatiyas as an integral part of their cultural roots.

The "remembering" of a past in which the Kakatiyas assumed a prominent role simultaneously reflected and generated new social realities. The fact that Telugu warriors throughout South India projected their origins into the Kakatiya era reveals the growth of a common warrior culture that existed apart from territorial loyalties—by Telugu, I thus mean a common culture, not just a common language. In turn, the belief in a joint past further strengthened the feeling of unity among disparate warrior families and lineages—it could even, as we saw with the Padmanayakas, create a new social grouping where none had existed before. The idea of solidarity derived from a joint set of past experiences extended beyond the ruling warriors over time to include village-level brahman officials and dominant peasants. Whatever else the Kakatiyas may have done, their greatest significance may be this contribution to Andhra's later culture. For, throughout the subsequent centuries, reimaginings of the Kakatiya past provided a shared history from which an evolving sense of Telugu community could be formulated.[3]

Medieval South Indian polities additionally had an important role in stimulating cultural practices like religious gifting and the making of inscriptions, which were strategies for consolidating social ties and articulating social identities. The religious donors commemorated in the inscribed records were aligning themselves with certain groups of people rather than with others, both in their self-portrayals and in their resource allocations. Religious patronage, and the related act of having a record inscribed, was therefore one of the primary strategies in medieval India for creating and affirming bonds that linked individuals and groups. The communities thus constituted existed on a smaller scale than their broadly based counterparts formed by a shared language or territorial association, but were probably even more significant to the social actors involved. And people living in the midst of a vigorous polity evidently felt a greater need to establish their social identities in a clear and public manner, for the largest numbers of inscriptions were made at the times when strong states held sway.

The reasons that powerful polities inspired an increase in inscriptional production, and presumably in religious patronage as well, are not altogether clear. I have argued that some of the affiliations expressed in inscriptions were essentially political in nature: between overlord and subordinate lord, between a leading warrior and his retinue, and between the man in charge of a locality and prominent mercantile groups there. Political networks were thus extended and reinforced through the public rituals of endowment in which relationships were ceremoniously enacted. Religious gift-giving also served as a sanctioned arena wherein lords, warriors, and their followers could openly compete with each other. Rivalries among peers must have been intense in large states and had few other outlets, since they could not be enacted in combat. But not all of the people appearing in the inscriptions of the Kakatiya or Vijayanagara periods played important roles in the political arena. Many of the donors, maybe even the majority, were members of the political elite during the half century when Vijayanagara was at its peak of power in southern Andhra (ca. 1510–1565 C. E.); this is less true of the Kakatiya era, since many of the inscriptions issued then do not cite an overlord.

A possible factor in the rising number of inscriptions may simply be the greater importance of having an official record of rights over land and income. Whereas property rights might be well known and undisputed within a small autonomous realm, in the complex world of a major kingdom it would have been prudent to spell out the exact terms of an endowment or protect assets in this manner As polities grew in size, there was also more justification for public records of other economic and legal transactions—such as the remission of taxes, the sale of land, or the settling of boundary disputes. More funds may have been available for religious purposes, in this era of relative prosperity. We could continue to speculate about the correlation between numbers of inscriptions and political unity, but the explanations are unquestionably complex and multiple. What I am most concerned with here, however, is the outcome: polities were catalysts in the processes of supralocal identity formation and community building. The cultural practices of the political elites fostered constructions of community that extended far beyond the locality and the family and also forged new networks and associations among people.

In conclusion, this study of Andhra highlights a last area where our ideas about medieval India need reevaluation: the impact of polities on the shaping of regional societies. We can no longer agree with Burton Stein's dismissive attitude toward medieval states, which he considered inconsequential when compared to local communities. In an assessment of Vijayanagara, arguably the greatest of medieval South Indian polities, Stein remarked, "It is difficult to identify the ways in which Vijayanagara *as a state* made a difference. It is perhaps strange, and it may appear trivial, that one way in which Vijayanagara influence may be seen to have mattered was in changes of architectural styles of temples" (1989: 110; italics in original). For Stein, the alleged inability of Vijayanagara to extract economic resources from the localities meant that it had no real power, but he overlooked the important ways in which it shaped ideas of community and fashioned social networks. At the opposite extreme are the views of Nicholas B. Dirks, to whom the king "was a central ordering factor in the social organisation of caste" (1989: 59). It is doubtful, however, for reasons I have already mentioned, that the early colonial Pudukkottai analyzed by Dirks represented conditions in earlier centuries. Not only was Pudukkottai a very small kingdom that emerged at the culmination of a long era of agrarian expansion, but also its political system had been frozen in time and place by the colonial overlords. No elements of dynamism remain in the static colonial society Dirks describes, where the orderly political and social hierarchies were almost congruent and determined largely by the degree of proximity to the king. Although kings, polities, and political elites were surely tremendously influential in the regional societies of medieval India, let us not go from one immoderate stance to another and attribute all generative force to the state.

It is time to reenvision medieval India as a complex kaleidoscope of diverse regions and cultures, where a multiplicity of historical processes, cultural practices, and powerful agents impinged upon each other to produce a continually changing material and conceptual world. We scholars of precolonial India have been too prone to seize upon a single explanatory framework, as opposed to the more intricate scenarios offered by historians of medieval Europe or East Asia. There must be a place in the historiography of a medieval past—whether we are speaking of India or another region of the globe—for historical contingency, the particularity of circumstance, and the agency of the individual as well as for commonalities of experience or shared ordering principles. For a history of transition demands no less than a historiography that constructs its patterns out of the shifting threads of the singular and the transitory.

Appendix A

Andhra Inscriptions, 1000–1649

The inscriptions are arranged according to the categories used in table 1, differentiated both by language and by period. Unpublished inscriptions noted in the *Andhra Pradesh Reports on Epigraphy* (APRE) and *Annual Reports on Epigraphy* (ARE) are cited first by year of the report followed by the number of the record. In most cases they are found in section B ("Stone Inscriptions") of the relevant year's report; otherwise the appropriate section is given before the number (e.g., D 13). Duplicates of published inscriptions are indicated by equal signs in parentheses except in the case of *Temple Inscriptions of Andhra Pradesh* (TIAP), since the details on prior publication are already noted there.

Part 1: Telugu and Sanskrit Inscriptions from Period I (1000–1174 C.E.)

APAS—31.13 (= IAP-N 1.60), 31.23 (= IAP-N 1.123), 31.24 (= IAP-N 1.125), 31.25 (= IAP-N 1.124), 38.8, 38.9, 38.10.

ARE—1893/414, 1893/415, 1897/213, 1908/7, 1908/8, 1912/39, 1915/342, 1915/363, 1915/364, 1915/396, 1915/404, 1917/855, 1919/294, 1920/632, 1920/707, 1920/709, 1922/831, 1925/571, 1927–28/1, 1929–30/2, 1929–30/4, 1929–30/66, 1929–30/71, 1930–31/290, 1930–31/316, 1930–31/334, 1932–33/263, 1932–33/265, 1932–33/270, 1932–33/271, 1932–33/285, 1932–33/286, 1932–33/289, 1932–33/290, 1932–33/291, 1932–33/292, 1932–33/294, 1932–33/295, 1932–33/298, 1932–33/299, 1932–33/300, 1932–33/305, 1932–33/306, 1932–33/307, 1932–33/308, 1932–33/314, 1932–33/315, 1932–33/317, 1932–33/320, 1932–33/325, 1932–33/327, 1932–33/334, 1932–33/336, 1932–33/337, 1932–33/342, 1932–33/343, 1932–33/396, 1932–33/400, 1934–35/300, 1934–35/322, 1934–35/323, 1934–35/341, 1934–35/344, 1934–35/360, 1934–35/361, 1934–35/362, 1934–35/371, 1935–36/204, 1935–36/213, 1935–36/217, 1935–36/219, 1935–36/221, 1935–36/239, 1935–36/243, 1936–37/299, 1936–37/302, 1936–37/303, 1936–37/309, 1936–37/348, 1937–38/344, 1937–38/348, 1938–39/E 2, 1938–39/E 3, 1938–39/E 7, 1938–39/E 23, 1938–39/448, 1938–39/449, 1939–40/62, 1939–40/67, 1939–40/73, 1939–40/E 17, 1939–40/E 18, 1939–40/E 20, 1940–41/459, 1941–42/2, 1941–42/43, 1941–42/E 30, 1941–42/E 31, 1941–42/E 33, 1942–43/59, 1943–44/32, 1947–48/142 ,1947–48/143, 1947–48/144, 1947–48/146, 1949–50/222, 1949–50/224, 1949–50/244, 1949–50/287, 1953–54/91, 1954–55/158, 1956–57/9, 1956–57/11, 1956–57/

16, 1956–57/20, 1956–57/25, 1958–59/108, 1958–59/126, 1959–60/103, 1959–60/114, 1959–60/161, 1959–60/164, 1960–61/106, 1960–61/109, 1969–70/9, 1969–70/10, 1973–74/18, 1973–74/41, 1973–74/46, 1973–74/47, 1973–74/48, 1976–77/47, 1976–77/49, 1978–79/28, 1978–79/29, 1978–79/39, 1978–79/40.

EA—4.10 (= IAP-N 1.40), 4.8, 5.7

EI—6.20, 6.21-A, 6.26, 39.38-B.

HAS—13.03 (= IAP-W.36), 13.32 (= CTI 39), 13.36 (= HAS 19 Ng.7, IAP-N 1.58), 19 Mn.10, 19 Mn.11, 19 Mn.12, 19 Mn.13, 19 Mn.45.

IAP—C 1.121, C 1.128, K.14, K.23, K.25 (= HAS 13.56), K.42, K.74, N.20, N.21, N.27, N.35, N.47, N.48, N.50, N.55, N.126, N.127, W.13 (= HAS 13.6), W.16, W.21, W.24 (= HAS 19 Km.13), W.25 (= HAS 19 Km.12), W.26, W.37.

NDI—Darsi 5, Darsi 38, Darsi 39, Darsi 40, Darsi 43, Darsi 48, Darsi 49, Darsi 68, Kavali 3, Ongole 18, Ongole 19, Ongole 28-A, Ongole 50, Ongole 51, Ongole 59, Ongole 60, Ongole 79, Ongole 128, Ongole 142, Podili 38.

SII 4—662, 664–67, 672–78, 680–83, 685, 687–89, 691, 692, 704, 717, 719, 722, 744, 749, 753, 754, 762, 778, 804, 806–8, 920, 927, 929, 930, 943, 944, 967, 974, 990–96, 1000, 1006–17, 1020, 1029, 1031, 1035, 1036, 1039, 1041, 1042, 1044, 1046, 1050–53, 1055, 1057, 1058, 1061, 1063, 1066–69, 1071, 1073, 1075, 1077, 1080, 1082, 1083, 1086, 1090, 1091, 1094–1096, 1098, 1099, 1102, 1104, 1107– 9, 1111–16, 1120–22, 1127, 1128, 1130–34, 1137–40, 1142, 1146–51, 1154, 1156–58, 1160, 1161, 1165–67, 1170, 1171, 1173, 1175, 1176-A, 1177, 1179, 1182, 1185, 1186, 1190, 1191, 1193–96, 1198, 1199, 1203, 1205, 1208–10, 1212, 1213, 1216, 1217, 1220, 1224, 1228, 1233, 1235, 1238, 1239 (= EI 22.23), 1241, 1242, 1244, 1248, 1250, 1251, 1253, 1254, 1256, 1258, 1263, 1264, 1276, 1280, 1282, 1287, 1293, 1295, 1300, 1305, 1306, 1308, 1310, 1314, 1316, 1317, 1323–25, 1327, 1330, 1339, 1339-B, 1339-C, 1357, 1358, 1361, 1363, 1364.

SII 5—62, 63, 92, 105, 160, 162–164, 207, 208, 1005, 1007, 1008, 1012, 1015–20, 1022, 1024–36, 1038–40, 1042–46, 1048, 1051, 1052, 1054–56, 1058, 1061, 1062, 1064–68, 1070–75, 1077, 1079–84, 1088–91, 1093, 1094, 1096–99, 1101, 1102, 1105–12, 1114–18, 1120, 1123, 1125, 1126, 1131, 1136–41, 1143, 1144, 1146–48, 1270, 1277–81, 1316, 1322, 1323, 1326–28, 1330–36, 1339–45, 1347–50.

SII 6—87, 88, 91, 98, 101–3, 108, 109, 116, 117, 121, 123–25, 127–29, 131–37, 139–43, 147, 148, 150–56, 159, 160, 163, 168–70, 172–74, 176–78, 181, 183, 185, 186, 189–193, 195, 198, 199, 210–12, 217, 218, 238, 239, 247, 586, 598, 599–601, 605–13, 617, 624–27, 630, 634, 636, 637, 639, 640, 641, 644–49, 651, 756, 1173, 1174, 1189.

SII 10—6–10, 27, 57–74, 77–97, 99, 100–2, 104–14, 116–21, 123–52, 155–64, 166–92, 195, 235, 651–55, 658–74, 676–709, 716.

SII 26—619.

TIAP—4, 9, 19, 33, 35, 50, 51, 52, 59, 89, 95, 96, 98, 101, 110, 121, 154, 157, 184, 196, 206, 213, 218, 223, 352, 411, 412, 417, 420, 421–23, 426, 427.

Part 2: Additional Telugu and Sanskrit Inscriptions from Period II (1175–1324 C.E.)

Note: Period II inscriptions from the 14 districts encompassed by the Kakatiya state are marked in columns D and E of Appendix B, Part 1. The following list covers inscriptions that were issued in the remaining districts of Adilabad, Anantapur, Chittoor, Hyderabad, Nizamabad, Srikakulam, and Visakhapatnam.

ARE—1905/380, 1926/635, 1929–30/5, 1958–59/111, 1964–65/31, 1964–65/76, 1964–65/77, 1970–71/2, 1973–74/49, 1980–81/7, 1980–81/8b (= IAP-N 2.45), 1980–81/9 (= IAP-N 2.41).

EI— 5.4-A, 5.4-B, 5.4-C, 5.4-D, 6.25, 6.25 postscript 1, 6.25 postscript 4, 6.25 postscript 5, 41.25.

SII 5—1078, 1085, 1086, 1113, 1129, 1130, 1135, 1142, 1150, 1151, 1163, 1166, 1168, 1173, 1177–79, 1183, 1185–88, 1195, 1197, 1204, 1205, 1209, 1216, 1217, 1219, 1222, 1231–33, 1235, 1236, 1238, 1245, 1252, 1258, 1259, 1261, 1263, 1264, 1265, 1267–69, 1271, 1272–75, 1282–84, 1287–99, 1302–4, 1307, 1308, 1310, 1314, 1317, 1320, 1324, 1325, 1329, 1337, 1338.

SII 6—692, 693, 704, 706, 712–14, 719, 726, 728, 824, 845, 868, 885, 886, 896, 897, 904, 912, 928, 934–38, 941, 943, 947–49, 952, 957, 965, 967, 969, 975, 976, 982, 992, 995, 998, 1000, 1002, 1118, 1137–43, 1166, 1167, 1176–83, 1186–88, 1193–95, 1197–99, 1201, 1203, 1204, 1208, 1209, 1213.

SII 10—211, 710–15, 717–19.

TIAP—215, 233, 240, 241, 243, 249, 261, 266, 272, 298, 325, 327, 329, 336, 353, 356, 357, 359, 361, 365, 371.

Part 3: Telugu and Sanskrit Inscriptions from Period III (1325–1499 C.E.)

APAS—31.22, 31.27.

ARE—1904/251, 1904/252, 1905/254, 1905/275, 1905/280, 1905/281, 1905/310, 1905/312, 1906/468, 1906/505, 1906/509, 1906/527, 1906/530, 1906/531, 1906/538, 1912/43, 1912/45, 1912/46, 1912/49, 1912/50, 1912/55, 1912/92, 1912/312, 1913/155, 1913/173, 1913/527, 1913/528, 1915/26, 1915/33, 1915/39, 1915/40, 1915/47, 1915/52, 1915/306, 1915/317, 1915/322, 1915/339, 1915/371, 1915/373, 1915/374, 1915/385, 1915/399, 1915/408, 1915/413, 1915/418, 1915/426, 1915/430, 1915/434, 1915/435, 1915/447, 1915/448, 1915/449, 1915/450, 1915/451, 1915/452, 1915/453, 1915/467, 1915/468, 1915/472, 1915/473, 1915/474, 1915/476, 1917/67, 1917/74, 1917/75, 1917/84, 1917/85, 1917/110, 1917/150, 1917/814, 1919/292, 1919/293, 1920/654, 1920/668, 1920/680, 1920/706, 1922/340, 1922/668, 1922/758, 1922/771, 1922/778, 1922/781, 1922/790, 1922/842, 1923/425, 1924/248, 1924/299, 1924/306, 1924/307, 1924/308, 1924/323, 1926/306, 1926/381, 1926/384, 1926/388, 1926/390, 1926/694, 1927–28/26, 1929–30/7, 1929–30/8, 1929–30/9, 1929–30/65, 1929–30/95, 1929–30/96, 1929–30/100, 1930–31/262, 1930–31/263, 1930–31/264, 1930–31/265, 1930–31/266, 1930–31/267, 1930–31/268, 1930–31/269, 1930–31/270, 1930–31/271, 1930–31/272, 1930–31/305, 1930–31/311, 1932–33/259, 1932–33/264, 1932–33/282-A, 1932–33/312, 1932–33/331, 1932–33/339, 1932–33/348, 1932–33/356, 1932–33/367, 1934–35/316, 1934–35/319, 1935–36/205, 1935–36/226, 1935–36/242, 1935–36/255, 1935–36/264, 1935–36/300, 1935–36/301, 1935–36/327, 1936–37/318, 1936–37/327, 1936–37/328, 1936–37/354, 1937–38/193, 1937–38/281, 1938–39/365, 1938–39/384, 1938–39/385, 1938–39/E 15, 1938–39/E 26, 1939–40/45, 1939–40/E 9, 1939–40/E 13, 1939–40/E 14, 1940–41/329, 1940–41/336, 1941–42/60, 1941–42/61, 1941–42/E 48, 1942–43/43, 1942–43/45, 1943–44/3, 1943–44/15, 1943–44/52, 1945–46/143, 1945–46/150, 1945–46/151, 1949–50/252, 1949–50/278, 1953–54/2, 1953–54/20, 1953–54/55, 1953–54/85, 1955–56/5, 1955–56/6, 1956–57/7, 1956–57/49, 1956–57/60, 1957–58/27, 1958–59/30, 1958–59/32, 1958–59/72, 1959–60/19, 1959–60/158, 1960–61/29, 1960–61/33, 1961–62/14, 1961–62/15, 1961–62/16, 1961–62/18, 1961–62/21, 1961–62/103, 1962–63/1, 1962–63/2, 1962–63/10, 1962–63/148, 1962–63/208, 1964–65/60, 1965–

66/13, 1965–66/14, 1967–68/19, 1970–71/42, 1970–71/54, 1971–72/1, 1971–72/2, 1973–74/44, 1973–74/54, 1976–77/50, 1977–78/12, 1977–78/13, 1977–78/15, 1977–78/18.

CTI—49.

EI— 4.47-A, 4.47-B, 4.47-C, 11.33-A, 11.33-C (= SII 10.582), 14.4 (= IAP-C 2.11), 36.10, 36.24 (= IAP-K.45), 37.10.

HAS—13.40, 19 Mn.7, 19 Mn.28, 19 Mn.30, 19 Mn.35.

IAP-C—2.5, 2.6, 2.7 (= SII 16.1), 2.8, 2.10, 2.12, 2.13, 2.15, 2.17–22, 2.24–26, 2.28 (= SII 16.016), 2.29–32, 2.34, 2.36, 2.39–42, 2.44, 2.45, 2.47–49, 2.53, 2.54.

IAP-N— 1.108–13.

IAP-W—103 (= HAS 19 Wg. 1), 104 (= HAS 19 Km.3), 107–9, 110 (= CTI 50).

NDI—Atmakur 39, Atmakur 47, Darsi 9, Darsi 13, Darsi 19, Darsi 20, Darsi 23, Darsi 33, Darsi 46, Darsi 47, Darsi 56, Darsi 63, Darsi 67, Kandukur 12, Kandukur 16, Kandukur 17, Kandukur 18, Kandukur 19, Kandukur 21, Kandukur 35, Kandukur 43, Kandukur 68, Kandukur 75, Kanigiri 4, Kanigiri 10, Kanigiri 23, Kanigiri 34, Kavali 14, Kavali 18, Kavali 33, Nellore 28, Nellore 78, Ongole 2, Ongole 30, Ongole 35, Ongole 55, Ongole 56, Ongole 72, Ongole 73, Ongole 78, Ongole 83, Ongole 85, Ongole 97, Ongole 104, Ongole 105, Ongole 109, Ongole 115, Ongole 132, Podili 12, Podili 18, Podili 21, Podili 26, Podili 39, Podili 42, Rapur 27, Rapur 78, Udayagiri 17, Udayagiri 28, Udayagiri 29, Udayagiri 46.

SII 4—659, 660, 694–97, 761, 772, 774, 776, 796, 940, 975, 988, 1347, 1352, 1353, 1374, 1375, 1378, 1379, 1383.

SII 5—1, 2, 4, 5–7, 10, 14, 26–31, 34–40, 44, 46–49, 52, 53, 57, 86, 87, 94, 102–4, 109, 113–15, 118, 129, 133, 134, 149, 154–56, 1011, 1104, 1153–55, 1157, 1160, 1162, 1165, 1167, 1170, 1174, 1175, 1180–82, 1184, 1189–91, 1193, 1194, 1196, 1198–1201, 1207, 1208, 1210, 1211, 1218, 1220, 1223–27, 1229, 1237, 1239, 1240, 1242, 1243, 1246–48, 1250, 1313.

SII 6—118, 119, 219, 226, 226b, 242, 243, 589, 655, 656, 657 (= EI 19.25), 660–64, 665 (= EI 19.26), 666–68, 676, 677, 705, 707–11, 715–18, 721–25, 727, 730–36, 738–47, 750–55, 757–77, 779–86, 788–92, 794–98, 800–21, 823, 825, 827–30, 832–44, 846–53, 855–67, 869–84, 887–94, 898, 900–2, 905–7, 910, 911, 913–19, 921–25, 929–33, 939, 944–46, 950, 951, 954–56, 958–64, 966, 968, 970–74, 977–79, 981, 983–89, 991, 993, 994, 996, 997, 999, 1001, 1003–17, 1019–25, 1027, 1028, 1030–48, 1050, 1052–77, 1079–88, 1090–98, 1100–17, 1119–36, 1168, 1171.

SII 10—547–59, 563–66, 568–73, 574 (= IAP-C 2.33), 575–77, 579 (= IAP-C 2.35), 580, 581, 583–87, 720, 730, 731, 745.

SII 16—2–5, 6 (= IAP-C 2.16), 7–12, 14, 15, 17–24, 26, 27, 28 (= IAP-C 2.37), 29 (= IAP-C 2.9), 30, 31 (= IAP-C 2.38), 32, 33, 35, 36 (= IAP-C 2.51), 37 (= IAP-C 2.52), 38, 39 (= IAP-C 2.55).

SII 26—586, 587 and 588, 622.

TIAP—322, 431.

TTD—1.179, 1.192, 1.209, 2.30.

Part 4: Telugu and Sanskrit Inscriptions from Period IV (1500–1649 C.E.)

APAS—31.28.

ARE—1904/402, 1904/407, 1905/284, 1905/311, 1905/376, 1905/379, 1906/470, 1906/529, 1907/589, 1909/592, 1911/376, 1912/58, 1912/62, 1912/65, 1912/66, 1913/137, 1913/143, 1913/172, 1915/12, 1915/13, 1915/16, 1915/34, 1915/35, 1915/44, 1915/46, 1915/

296, 1915/302, 1915/328, 1915/337, 1915/354, 1915/355, 1915/356, 1915/368, 1915/388, 1915/400, 1915/411, 1915/423, 1915/425, 1915/436, 1917/61, 1917/69, 1917/112, 1917/126, 1917/142, 1917/143, 1917/144, 1917/149, 1917/168, 1917/685, 1917/688, 1917/695, 1917/704, 1917/801, 1917/839, 1919/333, 1919/683, 1920/305, 1920/347, 1920/350, 1920/363, 1920/367, 1920/370, 1920/383, 1920/431, 1920/436 , 1920/662, 1922/297, 1922/667, 1922/754, 1922/755, 1922/756, 1922/800, 1923/431, 1923/432, 1924/178, 1924/243, 1924/278, 1924/285, 1924/290, 1924/293, 1924/294, 1924/310, 1924/321, 1924/322, 1924/329, 1926/287, 1926/297, 1926/300, 1926/325, 1926/327, 1926/332, 1926/369, 1926/374, 1926/386, 1926/394, 1926/410, 1926/412, 1926/416, 1926/417, 1926/710, 1926/713, 1927–28/21, 1928–29/430, 1928–29/431, 1928–29/435, 1928–29/540, 1928–29/541, 1929–30/15, 1929–30/20, 1929–30/22, 1929–30/52, 1929–30/57, 1929–30/59, 1929–30/64, 1929–30/84, 1929–30/88, 1929–30/89, 1929–30/92, 1930–31/273, 1930–31/283, 1930–31/284, 1930–31/291, 1930–31/295, 1930–31/296, 1930–31/297, 1930–31/302, 1930–31/313, 1932–33/260, 1932–33/262, 1932–33/277, 1932–33/282, 1932–33/283, 1932–33/284, 1932–33/310, 1932–33/322, 1932–33/332, 1932–33/340, 1932–33/341, 1932–33/344, 1932–33/345, 1932–33/347, 1932–33/350, 1932–33/351, 1932–33/352, 1932–33/360, 1932–33/361, 1932–33/370, 1932–33/371, 1932–33/373, 1932–33/374, 1932–33/375, 1932–33/378, 1932–33/382, 1933–34/187, 1934–35/271, 1934–35/273, 1934–35/280, 1934–35/288, 1934–35/289, 1934–35/291, 1934–35/292, 1934–35/295, 1934–35/296, 1934–35/297, 1934–35/298, 1934–35/309, 1934–35/312, 1934–35/314, 1934–35/315, 1934–35/330, 1934–35/336, 1935–36/206, 1935–36/208, 1935–36/212, 1935–36/223, 1935–36/238, 1935–36/258, 1935–36/259, 1935–36/265, 1935–36/267, 1935–36/269, 1935–36/270, 1935–36/271, 1935–36/272, 1935–36/274, 1935–36/275, 1935–36/289, 1935–36/292, 1935–36/293, 1935–36/303, 1935–36/318, 1935–36/320, 1935–36/321, 1935–36/325, 1935–36/335, 1936–37/304, 1936–37/311, 1936–37/316, 1936–37/321, 1936–37/323, 1936–37/368, 1936–37/372, 1937–38/195, 1937–38/211, 1937–38/216, 1937–38/223, 1937–38/227, 1937–38/234, 1937–38/239, 1937–38/248, 1937–38/249, 1937–38/253, 1937–38/254, 1937–38/257, 1937–38/271, 1937–38/285, 1937–38/289, 1937–38/294, 1937–38/295, 1937–38/296, 1937–38/300, 1937–38/301, 1937–38/311, 1937–38/313, 1937–38/314, 1937–38/316, 1937–38/325, 1938–39/20, 1938–39/334, 1938–39/335, 1938–39/341, 1938–39/342, 1938–39/367, 1938–39/375, 1938–39/377, 1938–39/383, 1938–39/392, 1938–39/404, 1938–39/416, 1938–39/E 24, 1938–39/E 76, 1938–39/E 81, 1939–40/2, 1939–40/25, 1939–40/34, 1939–40/39, 1939–40/40, 1939–40/358, 1939–40/359, 1939–40/361, 1939–40/363, 1940–41/347, 1940–41/369, 1940–41/397, 1940–41/404, 1940–41/408, 1940–41/416, 1940–41/430, 1940–41/437, 1940–41/446, 1940–41/480, 1941–42/4, 1941–42/6, 1941–42/15, 1941–42/57, 1941–42/58, 1941–42/67, 1941–42/68, 1941–42/E 19, 1941–42/E 20, 1941–42/E 53, 1941–42/E 54, 1941–42/E 56, 1942–43/3, 1942–43/4, 1942–43/6, 1942–43/7, 1942–43/8, 1942–43/10, 1942–43/11, 1942–43/12, 1942–43/16, 1942–43/19, 1942–43/23, 1942–43/24, 1942–43/25, 1942–43/26, 1942–43/28, 1942–43/39, 1942–43/50, 1942–43/51, 1942–43/58, 1942–43/65, 1942–43/66, 1942–43/67, 1943–44/4, 1943–44/5, 1943–44/6, 1943–44/9, 1943–44/10, 1943–44/17, 1943–44/20, 1943–44/22, 1943–44/24, 1943–44/28, 1943–44/30, 1943–44/33, 1943–44/39, 1943–44/40, 1943–44/51, 1943–44/57, 1943–44/64, 1943–44/148, 1943–44/152, 1945–46/94, 1945–46/115, 1945–46/124, 1945–46/137,1946–47/3, 1947–48/8, 1947–48/9, 1947–48/10, 1947–48/11, 1947–48/13, 1947–48/15, 1947–48/17, 1947–48/18, 1947–48/19, 1947–48/20, 1947–48/22, 1947–48/23, 1947–48/24, 1947–48/25, 1947–48/26, 1947–48/29, 1947–48/31, 1949–50/230, 1949–50/231, 1949–50/235, 1949–50/237, 1949–50/238, 1949–50/243, 1949–50/248, 1949–50/250, 1949–50/258, 1949–50/259, 1949–50/270, 1949–50/271, 1949–50/276, 1950–51/188, 1950–51/189,

1950–51/191, 1950–51/192, 1950–51/193, 1950–51/195, 1950–51/201, 1950–51/204, 1950–51/205, 1952–53/285, 1952–53/286, 1952–53/291, 1952–53/296, 1953–54/21, 1953–54/22, 1953–54/23, 1953–54/24, 1953–54/36, 1953–54/37, 1953–54/38, 1953–54/39, 1953–54/47, 1953–54/53, 1953–54/66, 1953–54/82, 1954–55/42, 1955–56/3, 1955–56/15, 1956–57/24, 1956–57/47, 1956–57/52, 1958–59/24, 1958–59/25, 1958–59/45, 1958–59/63, 1958–59/96, 1958–59/105, 1959–60/6, 1959–60/11, 1959–60/14, 1959–60/105, 1959–60/108, 1959–60/109, 1960–61/24, 1960–61/26, 1960–61/30, 1960–61/35, 1960–61/36, 1960–61/37, 1961–62/38, 1961–62/55, 1961–62/110, 1962–63/3, 1962–63/4, 1962–63/6, 1962–63/8, 1962–63/9, 1962–63/11, 1962–63/13, 1962–63/14, 1962–63/18, 1962–63/19, 1962–63/21, 1962–63/151, 1962–63/152, 1962–63/168, 1963–64/20, 1963–64/43, 1964–65/2, 1964–65/3, 1964–65/4, 1964–65/5, 1964–65/12, 1964–65/13, 1964–65/15, 1964–65/17, 1964–65/20, 1964–65/23, 1964–65/29, 1964–65/33, 1964–65/38, 1964–65/39, 1964–65/40, 1964–65/54, 1964–65/56, 1964–65/58, 1965–66/1, 1965–66/10, 1965–66/12, 1965–66/16, 1965–66/19, 1965–66/21, 1970–71/3, 1970–71/4, 1970–71/7, 1970–71/8, 1970–71/48, 1973–74/17, 1976–77/45, 1976–77/53, 1976–77/54, 1976–77/55, 1977–78/9, 1978–79/24.

CTI—51, 60.

EI—6.12-A, 6.12-B, 6.22, 7.3, 37.18 (= SII 16.309 and IAP-C 3.244), 38.9-B (= IAP-C 2.103).

HAS—19 Mn.15, 19 Ng.6.

IAP-C 2—46, 56–63, 66–72, 74–77, 79, 81, 82, 84, 90–93, 95–98, 100, 101, 104, 106–16, 118, 119, 122–27, 129–34, 136–39, 143, 153, 154, 158–60, 162–69, 171, 172, 174–77, 179–81, 183–93, 196–206, 208–17, 219–23, 225, 226, 228–37, 239–44, 246, 249–52, 254–59, 261–64, 266, 267, 271, 273, 278, 282, 284.

IAP-C 3—1, 15, 19, 52, 62, 72, 73, 96, 97, 100, 104, 112, 114, 133, 150, 157, 205, 206, 215, 242.

IAP-K—46-49.

IAP-N—1.116, 1.154.

IAP-W—112.

NDI—Atmakur 1, Atmakur 3, Atmakur 5, Atmakur 6, Atmakur 16, Atmakur 17, Atmakur 28, Atmakur 35, Atmakur 40, Atmakur 48, Atmakur 53, Atmakur 54, Darsi 15, Darsi 22, Darsi 34, Darsi 37, Darsi 50, Darsi 52, Darsi 53, Darsi 65, Darsi 66, Darsi 73, Gudur 46, Gudur 82, Gudur 108, Gudur 109, Gudur 110, Gudur 111, Gudur 112, Gudur 113, Gudur 114, Kandukur 3, Kandukur 4, Kandukur 12, Kandukur 14, Kandukur 20, Kandukur 25, Kandukur 27, Kandukur 28, Kandukur 30, Kandukur 71, Kandukur 74, Kandukur 76, Kandukur 77, Kandukur 78, Kandukur 80, Kandukur 82, Kandukur 83, Kandukur 85, Kandukur 86, Kanigiri 5, Kanigiri 15, Kanigiri 17, Kanigiri 20, Kanigiri 21, Kanigiri 22, Kanigiri 33, Kanigiri 38, Kavali 1, Kavali 46, Kavali 49, Kavali 50, Nellore 1, Nellore 2, Nellore 4, Nellore 6, Nellore 7, Nellore 9, Nellore 10, Nellore 11, Nellore 13, Nellore 26, Nellore 46, Nellore 47, Nellore 52, Nellore 54, Nellore 99, Nellore 104, Nellore 105, Nellore 112, Nellore 114, Nellore 115, Nellore 116, Nellore 117, Nellore 122, Nellore 124, Ongole 4, Ongole 15, Ongole 21, Ongole 23, Ongole 29, Ongole 31, Ongole 32, Ongole 41, Ongole 46, Ongole 47, Ongole 52, Ongole 62, Ongole 68, Ongole 71, Ongole 77, Ongole 111, Ongole 141, Podili 4, Podili 5, Podili 13, Podili 14, Podili 19, Podili 24, Podili 25, Podili 27, Podili 29, Podili 30, Podili 34, Podili 35, Podili 36, Rapur 3, Rapur 5, Rapur 6, Rapur 7, Rapur 11, Rapur 18, Rapur 22, Rapur 24, Rapur 25, Rapur 28, Rapur 30, Rapur 33, Rapur 34, Rapur 35, Rapur 40, Rapur 41, Rapur 43, Rapur 49, Rapur 50, Rapur 51, Rapur 53, Rapur 54, Rapur 60, Rapur 63, Rapur 74, Rapur 79, Sulurpet 16, Udayagiri 1, Udayagiri 2, Udayagiri 4, Udayagiri 19, Udayagiri 22, Udayagiri 23, Udayagiri 24, Udayagiri 30, Udayagiri 40, Udayagiri 42.

SII 4—686, 698, 699, 702, 709, 711, 789, 793, 794, 797, 800–3, 810, 936, 981.
SII 5—25, 120, 165, 166, 1164, 1215, 1228, 1260, 1312.
SII 6—122, 146, 203, 227, 248, 659, 669, 671, 694, 695, 696, 698, 699, 926, 1170, 1184, 1190, 1191, 1210.
SII 7—554–57, 559–61, 563, 564, 569, 731 (= IAP-W.111).
SII 8—495.
SII 10—732–37, 739, 743, 744, 746–49, 751–57.
SII 16—40–44, 45 (= IAP-C 2.65), 46, 47 (= IAP-C 2.73), 48–50, 52–55, 59–64, 65 (= IAP-C 2.78), 66 (= IAP-C 2.80), 67, 69 (= IAP-C 2.83), 70 (= IAP-C 2.85), 72–75, 77 (= IAP-C 2.87), 78 (= IAP-C 2.89), 79 (= IAP-C 2.88), 81 (= IAP-C 2.94), 82 , 83, 84 (= IAP-C 2.102), 85–87, 89, 90, 91 (= IAP-C 2.105), 92–96, 98, 101, 103–7, 108 (= IAP-C 2.117), 109, 110 (= IAP-C 2.120), 111, 112 (= IAP-C 2.121), 113–17, 121, 122, 123 (= IAP-C 2.135), 124–26, 127 (= IAP-C 2.161), 128 (= IAP-C 2.275), 129–38, 139 (= IAP-C 2.170), 140, 142, 144 (= IAP-C 2.173), 145–47, 148 (= IAP-C 2.178), 149 (= IAP-C 2.182), 150–52, 153 (= IAP-C 2.218), 154–61, 162 (= IAP-C 2.195), 163 (= IAP-C 2.194), 165–71, 173 (= IAP-C 2.207), 174–76, 178, 179 (= IAP-C 2.224), 180–84, 185 (= IAP-C 2.227), 186–94, 195 (= IAP-C 2.238), 196–209, 214, 215, 219 (= IAP-C 2.245), 220 (= IAP-C 2.247), 221, 222 (= IAP-C 2.248), 223, 224 (= IAP-C 2.253), 225–41, 243–46, 248–50, 252, 253, 255, 256 (= IAP-C 2.260), 257–69, 278–81, 283–93, 296, 297, 299, 300 (= IAP-C 3.128), 301, 302, 304, 305 (= IAP-C 3.117), 306 (= IAP-C 3.193), 308, 310, 311, 313–24, 326, 327, 330, 331 (= NDI Nellore 33), 332.
SII 26—583, 597, 598, 612, 614, 618, 621, 627, 630, 631.
TIAP—399, 432.
TTD—3.32, 3.38, 3.41, 3.49, 3.51, 3.59, 3.60, 3.65, 3.68, 3.71, 3.74, 3.76, 3.80, 4.8, 4.20, 4.144, 5.44, 6.1, 6.5, 6.33.

Part 5: Inscriptions in Other Languages from Period I (1000–1174 C.E.)

APAS—3.54
ARE—1903/84, 1904/273, 1905/316, 1905/317, 1906/534, 1907/579, 1907/583, 1909/100, 1917/15, 1917/733, 1917/734, 1917/758, 1920/325, 1920/392, 1920/416, 1920/451, 1920/453, 1922/677, 1922/819, 1923/430, 1927–28/9, 1927–28/11, 1929–30/3, 1935–36/323, 1936–37/317, 1937–38/318, 1942–43/38, 1947–48/5, 1950–51/240, 1952–53/287, 1952–53/288, 1953–54/65, 1954–55/154, 1956–57/45, 1956–57/46, 1957–58/44, 1957–58/45, 1958–59/12, 1958–59/110 1959–60/107, 1959–60/111, 1959–60/112, 1959–60/115, 1959–60/116, 1959–60/117, 1959–60/119, 1959–60/120, 1959–60/123, 1959–60/124, 1959–60/126, 1959–60/127, 1959–60/134, 1959–60/135, 1959–60/138, 1959–60/139, 1959–60/142, 1959–60/153, 1960–61/41, 1960–61/72, 1960–61/73, 1960–61/82, 1960–61/83, 1960–61/84, 1960–61/86, 1960–61/87, 1960–61/88, 1960–61/91, 1960–61/94, 1960–61/100, 1961–62/26, 1961–62/57, 1961–62/60, 1961–62/61, 1961–62/62, 1961–62/63, 1961–62/65, 1961–62/68, 1961–62/69, 1961–62/71, 1961–62/90, 1961–62/92, 1961–62/93, 1961–62/99, 1961–62/113, 1961–62/114, 1962–63/174, 1962–63/176, 1962–63/182, 1962–63/186, 1962–63/189, 1962–63/191, 1962–63/192, 1962–63/207, 1962–63/209, 1962–63/217, 1962–63/236, 1962–63/238, 1963–64/58, 1963–64/62, 1964–65/73, 1965–66/28, 1965–66/30, 1968–69/10, 1968–69/21, 1968–69/25, 1968–69/A 5, 1970–71/41, 1973–74/15, 1973–74/22, 1978–79/21, 1978–79/22, 1980–81/6.

APAS—3 Mn.42, 3 Mn.45, 3 Mn.46, 3 Mn.47, 3 Mn.49, 3 Ng.44, 3 Ng.45; 31.3, 31.4, 31.5, 31.6, 31.7, 31.8, 31.9, 31.10, 31.11, 31.29, 38.3.
CTI—6, 8, 12 (= APAS 38.4), 13.
EA—4.7
EI—35.35, 36.9, 36.19, 39.38-A, 39.38-C, 40.27-A, 40.27-B.
HAS—13.23 and 24 (= IAP-W.27).
IAP— C 1.123, C 1.128, K.10, K.11, K.12, K.13, K.14 (= EA 4.9 pt. 1), K.15, K.16, K.18, K.19, K.20, K.21, K.22 (= EA 4.9 pt. 4), K.24, K.74 (= HAS 19 Kn.3), K.75, K.77, W.8, W.9, W.10, W.14 (= EA 1.10), W.15 (= HAS 13.7), W.17, W.18, W.22 (= EI 9.35), W.23.
SII—6.182, 6.1144.

Part 6: Inscriptions in Other Languages from Period II (1175–1324 C.E.)

ARE—1903/215, 1903/231, 1903/233, 1905/327, 1906/483, 1907/597, 1907/598, 1907/599, 1907/610, 1907/618, 1907/621, 1907/622, 1909/98, 1909/603, 1911/399, 1911/400, 1911/401, 1911/402, 1911/403, 1911/404, 1911/408, 1911/416, 1911/427, 1911/428, 1911/437, 1911/440, 1911/446, 1912/83, 1912/95, 1913/238, 1913/239, 1913/240, 1917/28, 1917/34, 1917/738, 1917/771, 1917/772, 1917/773, 1917/796, 1920/345, 1922/324, 1925–26/425, 1926/298, 1927/104, 1933–34/159, 1937–38/315, 1939–40/33, 1949–50/288, 1949–50/289, 1949–50/290, 1953–54/15, 1953–54/18, 1953–54/19, 1953–54/75, 1953–54/83, 1953–54/C 77, 1954–55/23, 1954–55/25, 1955–56/18, 1956–57/73, 1958–59/71, 1959–60/157, 1960–61/3, 1960–61/4, 1960–61/5, 1961–62/4, 1963–64/70, 1963–64/71, 1963–64/72, 1964–65/1, 1964–65/59, 1966–67/D 1, 1966–67/D 3, 1971–72/17, 1976–77/D 12.
EA— 5.8.
EI— 30.8 (= IAP-C 1.138).
IAP—C 1.129.
NDI—Atmakur 14, Atmakur 18, Gudur 9, Gudur 11, Gudur 17, Gudur 27, Gudur 29, Gudur 39, Gudur 45, Gudur 50, Gudur 64, Gudur 66, Gudur 85, Gudur 90, Gudur 115, Kandukur 57, Kandukur 58, Nellore 12, Nellore 16, Nellore 21, Nellore 31, Nellore 40, Nellore 60, Nellore 71, Nellore 74, Nellore 97, Nellore 109, Nellore 111, Nellore 121, Rapur 8, Rapur 39, Rapur 65 , Rapur 70, Sulurpet 3, Sulurpet 4 and 8, Sulurpet 5, Sulurpet 6, Sulurpet 7, Sulurpet 9, Venkatagiri 1 and 10, Venkatagiri 2, Venkatagiri 3, Venkatagiri 4, Venkatagiri 5, Venkatagiri 6, Venkatagiri 7 and 13, Venkatagiri 8 and 18, Venkatagiri 15.
SII— 4.798, 5.493 (= NDI Nellore 62), 5.496 (= NDI Nellore 55 and 57), 5.498 (= NDI Nellore 73), 5.1244.
TTD—1.34

Part 7: Inscriptions in Other Languages from Period III (1325–1499 C.E.)

ARE—1901/338, 1901/339, 1903/174, 1903/185, 1903/190, 1903/192, 1903/193, 1903/194, 1904/243, 1904/249, 1904/250, 1904/253, 1904/254, 1904/255, 1904/258, 1906/523, 1907/603, 1912/81, 1912/584, 1915/22, 1915/24, 1915/25, 1916/734, 1916/762, 1917/27, 1917/33, 1917/681, 1917/710, 1917/711, 1917/715, 1917/765, 1917/774, 1917/778, 1917/779, 1917/780, 1917/791, 1917/803, 1917/804, 1917/818, 1920/401, 1920/404, 1921/106, 1922/336, 1924/246, 1926/346, 1927/102, 1931–32/203, 1931–32/226,

1931–32/227, 1931–32/232, 1933–34/156, 1933–34/172, 1933–34/173, 1940–41/341, 1952–53/196, 1953–54/43, 1953–54/56, 1953–54/57, 1958–59/69, 1960–61/32, 1961–62/37, 1963–64/45, 1963–64/D 1, 1963–64/D 2, 1968–69/D 150, 1970–71/15, 1978–79/5.

EI— 33.23.

NDI—Gudur 42, Nellore 76.

SII— 5.1176, 5.1213, 26.635.

Part 8: Inscriptions in Other Languages from Period IV (1500–1649 C.E.)

APAS—9.3, 9.4.

ARE—1901/340, 1903/83, 1903/92, 1903/177, 1903/180, 1903/186, 1903/187, 1904/244, 1904/246, 1904/247, 1904/301, 1904/302, 1904/385, 1905/309, 1905/330, 1912/47, 1912/68, 1912/69, 1912/70, 1912/71, 1912/72, 1912/73, 1912/76, 1912/84, 1912/87, 1912/88, 1912/89, 1912/90, 1912/585, 1913/153, 1913/179, 1913/531, 1915/19, 1915/21, 1915/32, 1915/558, 1915/559, 1916/729, 1916/732, 1916/733, 1916/737, 1916/739, 1916/740, 1916/742, 1916/745, 1917/1, 1917/29, 1917/32, 1917/38, 1917/49, 1917/57, 1917/717, 1917/720, 1917/728, 1917/730, 1917/736, 1917/757, 1917/769, 1917/770, 1917/775, 1917/781, 1917/782, 1917/785, 1917/789, 1917/794, 1917/800, 1920/329, 1920/340, 1920/360, 1920/381, 1920/384, 1920/387, 1920/391, 1920/402, 1920/407, 1920/409, 1920/412, 1920/423, 1920/425, 1920/433, 1920/446, 1920/449, 1920/450, 1921/105, 1922/350, 1924/150, 1924/151, 1924/152, 1924/153, 1924/154, 1924/155, 1924/156, 1924/157, 1924/159, 1924/160, 1924/161, 1924/163, 1924/164, 1924/165, 1924/166, 1924/167, 1924/168, 1924/170, 1924/171, 1924/172, 1924/173, 1924/174, 1924/175, 1924/176, 1924/177, 1924/179, 1924/180, 1924/181, 1924/182, 1924/183, 1924/184, 1925/548, 1925/550, 1926/294, 1926/320, 1926/339, 1926/358, 1927/23, 1927/98, 1927/108, 1929–30/84, 1931–32/212, 1933–34/158, 1936–37/313, 1936–37/314, 1937–38/183, 1939–40/355, 1939–40/356, 1939–40/357, 1939–40/360, 1939–40/364, 1939–40/365, 1942–43/60, 1946–47/27, 1946–47/29, 1952–53/C 77, 1952–53/C 78, 1952–53/C 79, 1953–54/17, 1953–54/C 27, 1953–54/C 28, 1953–54/C 29, 1953–54/C 30, 1953–54/C 31, 1953–54/C 42, 1953–54/C 59, 1953–54/C 60, 1953–54/C 70, 1953–54/C 71, 1953–54/C 78, 1955–56/D 1, 1956–57/D 1, 1956–57/D 2, 1957–58/1, 1958–59/70, 1958–59/D 1, 1958–59/D 20, 1958–59/D 21, 1961–62/2, 1961–62/38, 1961–62/D 1, 1962–63/183, 1962–63/184, 1962–63/D 8, 1962–63/D 15, 1963–64/22, 1963–64/30, 1963–64/31, 1963–64/D 5, 1963–64/D 6, 1963–64/D 11, 1963–64/D 12, 1963–64/D 13, 1963–64/D 14, 1963–64/D 20–D 22, 1963–64/D 29, 1963–64/D 30, 1964–65/D 1, 1964–65/D 2, 1964–65/D 4, 1964–64/D 13, 1966–67/D 26, 1966–67/D 27, 1966–67/D 29, 1966–67/D 31–D 33, 1966–67/D 37, 1966–67/D 38, 1966–67/D 39, 1966–67/D 41, 1966–67/D 42, 1967–68/D 2, 1967–68/D 8, 1967–68/D 12, 1967–68/D 14 and 15, 1967–68/D 16, 1967–68/D 17, 1967–68/D 21, 1967–68/D 24, 1967–68/D 25, 1967–68/D 28, 1967–68/D 33, 1967–68/D 34, 1967–68/D 38, 1967–68/D 39, 1967–68/D 64, 1967–68/D 68, 1967–68/D 76, 1967–68/D 80, 1967–68/D 82, 1967–68/D 87, 1968–69/D 8, 1968–69/D 9, 1968–69/D 10, 1968–69/D 11, 1968–69/D 18, 1968–69/D 21, 1968–69/D 24, 1968–69/D 37, 1968–69/D 40, 1968–69/D 47, 1968–69/D 49, 1968–69/D 50, 1968–69/D 53, 1968–69/D 55, 1968–69/D 60, 1968–69/D 61, 1968–69/D 62, 1968–69/D 63, 1968–69/D 68, 1968–69/D 70, 1968–69/D 72, 1968–69/D 73, 1968–69/D 74, 1968–69/D 77, 1968–69/D 78, 1968–69/D 103, 1968–69/D 106, 1968–69/D 118, 1968–69/D 147 and 148, 1968–69/D 153, 1968–69/D 156, 1968–69/D 157, 1969–70/D 3, 1970–71/48, 1973–74/D 1, 1975–76/D 2,

1975–76/D 18, 1975–76/D 20, 1975–76/D 21, 1975–76/D 22, 1975–76/D 32, 1975–76/D 34, 1975–76/D 37, 1975–76/D 42, 1975–76/D 49, 1975–76/D 55, 1976–77/D 2, 1976–77/D 14, 1976–77/D 26, 1976–77/D 36, 1977–78/D 4, 1977–78/D 5, 1977–78/D 12, 1977–78/D 21, 1977–78/D 22, 1977–78/D 26, 1977–78/D 38, 1977–78/D 41, 1978–79/23, 1978–79/D 7, 1979–80/C 2, 1981–82/C 4, 1982–83/C 9, 1982–83/C 14.

NDI—Gudur 110, Rapur 5, Sulurpet 11.

SII— 8.497.

TL— 465, 468, 486, 489, 493, 639, 641, 643, 644, 668, 674, 683, 684, 697, 1303, 1630.

Appendix B

Kakatiya Andhra Inscriptions

I read the texts of all inscriptions contained in this appendix, which was not true for every case in Appendix A. Duplicates of published inscriptions are indicated by equal signs in parentheses; when readings differed I relied on the one contained in the first version noted. Inscriptions are occasionally listed under their unpublished version, even when a published version exists, either because that was the first one I obtained or because it is more complete and/or accurate.

Part 1: Inscriptions used in Tables 4–13 (Chaps. 2, 3, and 4)

Note: "X" indicates that the inscription in the left-hand column was included in the specific table(s) represented by columns A through F, as follows:

column A = table 4 (individual donors and endowments)
column B = table 5 (status titles held by father-son pairs)
column C = temple corpus used in compiling tables 6–10
column D = Kakatiya inscriptions enumerated in tables 11 and 12
column E = non-Kakatiya inscriptions enumerated in tables 11 and 12
column F = table 13 (individual Kakatiya subordinates)

Inscription	A	B	C	D	E	F
APAS 31.15 (= IAP-N 1.56)	X				X	
APAS 31.26 (= IAP-N 1.137)	X	X			X	
APAS 31.30	X		X		X	
APAS 31.33			X		X	
APAS 38.11	X	X		X		X
APAS 38.12	X		X	X		X
APAS 38.13			X	X		
APRE 1965/113 (= IAP-N 1.62)	X		X	X		X
APRE 1965/167	X		X		X	

Inscription	A	B	C	D	E	F
APRE 1965/193	X		X			
APRE 1965/194	X					
APRE 1965/197	X					
APRE 1965/198	X		X			
APRE 1965/248	X	X	X	X		X
APRE 1966/133	X			X		X
APRE 1966/184	X	X			X	
APRE 1966/192			X			
APRE 1966/244	X	X		X		X
APRE 1966/286	X		X		X	
APRE 1966/358-A	X	X	X		X	
APRE 1966/358-B (= SII 7.737)	X	X	X		X	
APRE 1967/407			X	X		
APRE 1967/408	X	X	X	X		X
ARE 1905/182					X	
ARE 1905/186					X	
ARE 1905/188					X	
ARE 1905/218					X	
ARE 1905/279					X	
ARE 1905/344					X	
ARE 1906/509-A					X	
ARE 1909/608					X	
ARE 1909/611					X	
ARE 1911/410					X	
ARE 1911/414					X	
ARE 1913/535					X	
ARE 1915/41					X	
ARE 1915/357					X	
ARE 1915/366	X	X	X		X	
ARE 1915/367				X		
ARE 1915/375					X	
ARE 1915/410				X		
ARE 1917/77					X	
ARE 1917/80					X	
ARE 1917/154				X		
ARE 1917/157					X	
ARE 1917/158					X	
ARE 1917/167				X		
ARE 1917/702					X	
ARE 1920/295	X	X	X		X	
ARE 1920/296	X		X		X	

Inscription	A	B	C	D	E	F
ARE 1920/297	X		X		X	
ARE 1920/298	X		X		X	
ARE 1920/299	X		X		X	
ARE 1920/300					X	
ARE 1920/302					X	
ARE 1920/667					X	
ARE 1920/688					X	
ARE 1920/725	X	X	X		X	
ARE 1920/729					X	
ARE 1920/741	X		X		X	
ARE 1920/752	X	X	X		X	
ARE 1922/292					X	
ARE 1922/293					X	
ARE 1922/773				X		
ARE 1922/775			X	X		
ARE 1922/776					X	
ARE 1922/805	X		X	X		X
ARE 1924/260					X	
ARE 1924/277					X	
ARE 1924/281					X	
ARE 1924/291					X	
ARE 1924/315	X		X		X	
ARE 1924/317					X	
ARE 1924/319	X	X	X		X	
ARE 1924/330			X		X	
ARE 1925/524	X		X		X	
ARE 1925/525	X	X	X		X	
ARE 1925/526	X		X		X	
ARE 1925/527					X	
ARE 1925/570					X	
ARE 1925/585				X		
ARE 1925/593					X	
ARE 1926/704	X		X		X	
ARE 1926/705					X	
ARE 1926/706					X	
ARE 1927–28/2					X	
ARE 1927–28/5	X		X		X	
ARE 1928–29/535					X	
ARE 1928–29/536					X	
ARE 1928–29/537					X	
ARE 1928–29/538					X	

Inscription	A	B	C	D	E	F
ARE 1929–30/16					X	
ARE 1929–30/21	X		X	X		X
ARE 1929–30/24	X		X	X		X
ARE 1929–30/26	X	X	X	X		X
ARE 1929–30/29					X	
ARE 1929–30/30	X	X	X			
ARE 1929–30/31					X	
ARE 1929–30/39				X		
ARE 1929–30/39a	X		X		X	
ARE 1929–30/43	X		X		X	
ARE 1929–30/44	X		X		X	
ARE 1929–30/45	X	X	X		X	
ARE 1929–30/47			X		X	
ARE 1929–30/51				X		
ARE 1929–30/55	X	X	X	X		X
ARE 1929–30/67	X	X	X		X	
ARE 1929–30/68	X				X	
ARE 1929–30/69	X		X		X	
ARE 1929–30/70	X				X	
ARE 1929–30/72	X		X	X		X
ARE 1929–30/77					X	
ARE 1929–30/87				X		
ARE 1929–30/87a					X	
ARE 1929–30/91					X	
ARE 1929–30/93				X		
ARE 1930–31/275					X	
ARE 1930–31/276					X	
ARE 1930–31/277					X	
ARE 1930–31/278					X	
ARE 1930–31/279					X	
ARE 1930–31/280	X	X	X		X	
ARE 1930–31/281	X		X	X		X
ARE 1930–31/287	X		X		X	
ARE 1930–31/289	X			X		X
ARE 1930–31/301	X	X	X		X	
ARE 1930–31/310	X	X				
ARE 1930–31/312			X		X	
ARE 1930–31/314	X		X	X		X
ARE 1930–31/317				X		
ARE 1930–31/319	X		X	X		X
ARE 1930–31/321	X		X	X		X

Inscription	A	B	C	D	E	F
ARE 1930–31/322	X				X	
ARE 1930–31/323	X	X	X	X		X
ARE 1930–31/324	X		X	X		X
ARE 1930–31/332	X		X	X		X
ARE 1932–33/261	X		X		X	
ARE 1932–33/268				X		
ARE 1932–33/293	X		X		X	
ARE 1932–33/301					X	
ARE 1932–33/302	X		X		X	
ARE 1932–33/303	X		X	X		X
ARE 1932–33/304	X		X		X	
ARE 1932–33/309					X	
ARE 1932–33/311					X	
ARE 1932–33/313			X	X		
ARE 1932–33/316					X	
ARE 1932–33/319	X		X		X	
ARE 1932–33/329	X		X		X	
ARE 1932–33/397	X				X	
ARE 1932–33/398	X				X	
ARE 1932–33/399			X		X	
ARE 1934–35/277					X	
ARE 1934–35/299			X		X	
ARE 1934–35/301			X		X	
ARE 1934–35/307	X	X	X	X		X
ARE 1934–35/317					X	
ARE 1934–35/318			X		X	
ARE 1934–35/325	X		X		X	
ARE 1934–35/326	X		X	X		X
ARE 1934–35/328	X		X	X		X
ARE 1934–35/337					X	
ARE 1934–35/338	X		X		X	
ARE 1934–35/346					X	
ARE 1934–35/347					X	
ARE 1935–36/207					X	
ARE 1935–36/224	X				X	
ARE 1935–36/235				X		
ARE 1935–36/240	X		X	X		X
ARE 1935–36/244					X	
ARE 1935–36/246	X		X		X	
ARE 1935–36/247	X		X		X	
ARE 1935–36/248	X		X		X	

Inscription	A	B	C	D	E	F
ARE 1935–36/249	X		X		X	
ARE 1935–36/250					X	
ARE 1935–36/251	X	X	X		X	
ARE 1935–36/252			X		X	
ARE 1935–36/253	X		X		X	
ARE 1935–36/254					X	
ARE 1935–36/260				X		
ARE 1935–36/278	X		X	X		X
ARE 1935–36/304					X	
ARE 1936–37/289	X		X		X	
ARE 1936–37/291					X	
ARE 1936–37/292					X	
ARE 1936–37/293	X		X	X		X
ARE 1936–37/294	X		X	X		X
ARE 1936–37/295	X	X	X	X		X
ARE 1936–37/297			X		X	
ARE 1936–37/298					X	
ARE 1936–37/300			X		X	
ARE 1936–37/301	X		X	X		X
ARE 1936–37/305				X		
ARE 1936–37/307	X			X		X
ARE 1936–37/322					X	
ARE 1937–38/269			X		X	
ARE 1937–38/320	X				X	
ARE 1937–38/321	X	X		X		X
ARE 1937–38/322	X		X		X	
ARE 1937–38/323	X		X		X	
ARE 1937–38/345	X	X	X		X	
ARE 1937–38/346			X		X	
ARE 1937–38/347	X		X		X	
ARE 1937–38/349	X	X	X		X	
ARE 1937–38/352				X		
ARE 1938–39/391	X	X	X		X	
ARE 1938–39/E 8					X	
ARE 1938–39/E 9					X	
ARE 1938–39/E 10					X	
ARE 1938–39/E 11				X		
ARE 1938–39/E 12					X	
ARE 1938–39/E 13					X	
ARE 1939–40/49			X			
ARE 1939–40/71					X	

Inscription	A	B	C	D	E	F
ARE 1940–41/327					X	
ARE 1940–41/328					X	
ARE 1940–41/472					X	
ARE 1940–41/473					X	
ARE 1940–41/475	X	X	X		X	
ARE 1940–41/477					X	
ARE 1940–41/479					X	
ARE 1941–42/7	X	X	X		X	
ARE 1941–42/8					X	
ARE 1941–42/10	X					
ARE 1941–42/13	X	X	X	X		X
ARE 1941–42/25				X		
ARE 1941–42/50 (= IAP-C 1.140)	X				X	
ARE 1941–42/56					X	
ARE 1941–42/E 32				X		
ARE 1942–43/22	X	X	X	X		X
ARE 1942–43/40	X		X	X		X
ARE 1942–43/44					X	
ARE 1943–44/2	X	X		X		X
ARE 1943–44/7					X	
ARE 1943–44/16	X	X		X		X
ARE 1943–44/44				X		
ARE 1949–50/223	X		X		X	
ARE 1949–50/267 (= APRE 1965/205)				X		
ARE 1949–50/274	X		X		X	
ARE 1949–50/285	X	X	X		X	
ARE 1950–51/241					X	
ARE 1951–52/130			X		X	
ARE 1951–52/131	X	X			X	
ARE 1952–53/268			X	X		
ARE 1952–53/269	X		X		X	
ARE 1952–53/270	X	X	X		X	
ARE 1952–53/272					X	
ARE 1952–53/273			X		X	
ARE 1952–53/277	X				X	
ARE 1953–54/26	X	X			X	
ARE 1953–54/28	X	X	X		X	
ARE 1953–54/29					X	
ARE 1953–54/30	X				X	
ARE 1953–54/34					X	
ARE 1954–55/17	X	X			X	

Inscription	A	B	C	D	E	F
ARE 1954–55/132 (= IAP-N 2.40)	X	X	X	X		
ARE 1954–55/147	X		X		X	
ARE 1955–56/11	X		X		X	
ARE 1956–57/4					X	
ARE 1956–57/10	X				X	
ARE 1956–57/18					X	
ARE 1957–58/9					X	
ARE 1957–58/20	X	X	X	X		X
ARE 1958–59/75			X		X	
ARE 1958–59/76	X		X		X	
ARE 1958–59/89 (= IAP-K.32)	X	X	X			
ARE 1958–59/94 (= IAP-K.34)	X		X			
ARE 1961–62/28	X	X	X	X		X
ARE 1961–62/29	X		X		X	
ARE 1961–62/108					X	
ARE 1961–62/109					X	
ARE 1962–63/161					X	
ARE 1962–63/180	X			X		X
ARE 1962–63/210					X	
ARE 1962–63/211					X	
ARE 1963–64/61	X	X			X	
ARE 1965–66/15					X	
ARE 1968–69/18	X	X			X	
ARE 1969–70/12	X	X	X		X	
ARE 1969–70/13					X	
ARE 1969–70/15	X	X	X		X	
ARE 1969–70/16	X	X	X		X	
ARE 1969–70/17	X	X	X		X	
ARE 1969–70/18					X	
ARE 1970–71/26	X				X	
ARE 1970–71/28	X	X	X			
ARE 1970–71/55	X	X	X		X	
ARE 1971–72/7					X	
ARE 1971–72/8					X	
ARE 1971–72/19	X		X		X	
ARE 1973–74/3	X			X		X
ARE 1973–74/4 (= IAP-N 2.44)	X	X	X	X		X
ARE 1973–74/6	X	X	X		X	
ARE 1973–74/13 (= IAP-N 2.35)	X	X	X	X		X
ARE 1975–76/27					X	
ARE 1975–76/33					X	

Inscription	A	B	C	D	E	F
ARE 1975–76/37				X		
ARE 1975–76/38				X		
ARE 1976–77/51					X	
ARE 1976–77/52					X	
ARE 1977–78/16			X		X	
ARE 1977–78/38	X		X	X		X
Bhārati 15:555	X	X				
Bhārati 29:260	X					
Bhārati 37:35	X	X				
Bhārati 37:6	X	X				
Bhārati 54:56	X	X	X	X		X
Bhārati 55:40 (= IAP-N 1.89)	X		X	X		X
CPIHM 1.10	X	X				X
CPIHM 1.11	X	X				X
CTI 22 (= IAP-N 1.72)	X	X		X		X
CTI 26 (= SS: 223-31, IAP-N 2.29)	X	X	X			
CTI 29	X		X			
CTI 30 (= IAP-N 2.42)	X		X	X		X
CTI 35	X		X	X		X
CTI 41 (= APAS 38.6)	X		X			
CTI 46	X	X	X		X	
CTI 47	X				X	
EA 1.7	X					
EA 4.11	X					X
EA 4.12—A	X	X				X
EA 4.12—B	X	X				
EA 4.13	X	X		X		X
EA 4.14 (= IAP-N 1.96)			X	X		
EI 3.15	X	X	X	X		X
EI 3.16	X		X	X		X
EI 4.4	X		X		X	
EI 4.10			X		X	
EI 4.33	X		X		X	
EI 5.17	X	X	X	X		X
EI 6.5	X	X	X	X		X
EI 6.15-A	X	X	X		X	
EI 6.15-B	X		X	X		X
EI 6.15 postscript	X	X	X	X		X
EI 7.18		X				
EI 12.22				X		
EI 18.41	X	X				X

Inscription	A	B	C	D	E	F
EI 25.27	X	X			X	
EI 27.35 (= SII 10.376)	X	X				
EI 34.13 (= IAP-K.28)	X			X		X
EI 38.16	X	X				X
HAS 3.1 (= IAP-W.50)	X	X	X	X		X
HAS 3.2 (= IAP-K.30)	X	X	X	X		X
HAS 4 (= IAP-W.67)	X	X				
HAS 6		X				
HAS 13.1 (= IAP-W.74)	X	X				
HAS 13.2	X	X	X	X		X
HAS 13.4 (= IAP-W.94)	X		X			
HAS 13.8 (= IAP-W.48)	X	X	X	X		X
HAS 13.9 (= IAP-W.64)	X		X	X		X
HAS 13.11			X			
HAS 13.13 (= IAP-W.70)	X	X	X			
HAS 13.14 (= IAP-W.63)			X	X		
HAS 13.16 (= IAP-W.89 and SII 7.732)			X	X		
HAS 13.17 (= IAP-N 2.47)	X				X	
HAS 13.18	X	X	X	X		X
HAS 13.22 (= IAP-N 1.64)				X		
HAS 13.25 (= IAP-N 1.82)	X	X	X	X		X
HAS 13.26 (= IAP-N 1.98)			X	X		
HAS 13.27 (= IAP-N 2.36)	X	X	X	X		X
HAS 13.28 (= IAP-N 2.46)	X			X		X
HAS 13.29					X	
HAS 13.30			X	X		
HAS 13.31-A (= IAP-N 2.49)		X	X		X	
HAS 13.31-B (= IAP-N 2.49)	X	X	X		X	
HAS 13.31-C (= IAP-N 2.49)	X	X	X		X	
HAS 13.33	X		X			
HAS 13.34	X	X	X	X		X
HAS 13.35	X	X	X	X		X
HAS 13.37	X	X	X			
HAS 13.38 (= IAP-N 2.30)	X	X	X	X		X
HAS 13.41 (= IAP-N 2.31)	X	X	X	X		X
HAS 13.42-A (= IAP-N 2.32)	X		X	X		X
HAS 13.42-B (= IAP-N 2.32)	X		X		X	
HAS 13.43 (= IAP-N 2.34)	X		X		X	
HAS 13.44				X		X
HAS 13.45 (= IAP-N 2.71)	X		X			
HAS 13.46 (= IAP-N 2.39)				X		

Inscription	A	B	C	D	E	F
HAS 13.48 (= IAP-N 2.37)	X	X	X		X	
HAS 13.49 (= IAP-N 2.33)			X	X		
HAS 13.50	X		X	X		X
HAS 13.51	X	X		X		X
HAS 13.52	X	X	X	X		X
HAS 13.53			X	X		
HAS 13.54	X		X	X		X
HAS 13.55			X	X		
HAS 19 Km.1			X	X		
HAS 19 Km.2			X	X		
HAS 19 Km.5				X		
HAS 19 Km.6			X	X		
HAS 19 Km.7			X	X		
HAS 19 Km.9	X		X		X	
HAS 19 Km.14				X		
HAS 19 Km.15	X		X		X	
HAS 19 Km.16-A			X	X		
HAS 19 Kn.4				X		
HAS 19 Mn.4	X	X	X		X	
HAS 19 Mn.5	X	X	X		X	
HAS 19 Mn.6	X	X	X		X	
HAS 19 Mn.8	X		X		X	
HAS 19 Mn.17	X	X			X	
HAS 19 Mn.18	X	X	X	X		X
HAS 19 Mn.19			X	X		
HAS 19 Mn.20			X		X	
HAS 19 Mn.21			X	X		
HAS 19 Mn.22	X		X			
HAS 19 Mn.25	X	X	X		X	
HAS 19 Mn.26			X		X	
HAS 19 Mn.27-B	X		X		X	
HAS 19 Mn.32	X		X	X		X
HAS 19 Mn.33	X		X	X		X
HAS 19 Mn.34	X	X			X	
HAS 19 Mn.38				X		
HAS 19 Mn.41	X		X	X		X
HAS 19 Mn.46-A	X		X	X		X
HAS 19 Mn.46-B	X	X	X		X	
HAS 19 Mn.47	X	X	X	X		X
HAS 19 Ng.1 (= IAP-N 1.63)	X		X		X	
HAS 19 Ng.2 (= IAP-N 1.81)	X		X	X		X

Inscription	A	B	C	D	E	F
HAS 19 Ng.3 (= IAP-N 1.73)	X	X	X		X	
HAS 19 Ng.4 (= IAP-N 1.90)				X		
HAS 19 Ng.5 (= IAP-N 1.136)	X	X	X		X	
IAP-C 1.107			X		X	
IAP-C 1.109	X				X	
IAP-C 1.111	X		X		X	
IAP-C 1.127					X	
IAP-C 1.130					X	
IAP-C 1.131	X		X		X	
IAP-C 1.134			X		X	
IAP-C 1.136					X	
IAP-C 1.137	X		X		X	
IAP-C 1.139	X		X		X	
IAP-C 1.141	X			X		X
IAP-C 1.142	X			X		X
IAP-C 1.143				X		
IAP-C 1.144	X		X		X	
IAP-C 1.145					X	
IAP-C 1.146	X	X			X	
IAP-C 1.147					X	
IAP-C 1.148					X	
IAP-C 1.149					X	
IAP-C 1.150					X	
IAP-C 1.151					X	
IAP-C 1.153	X	X	X		X	
IAP-C 1.156	X	X	X	X		X
IAP-C 1.157	X			X		X
IAP-C 1.159	X	X			X	
IAP-C 2.3					X	
IAP-C 2.4					X	
IAP-K.26	X		X		X	
IAP-K.27				X		
IAP-K.29 (= HAS 19 Km.4)	X		X	X		X
IAP-K.31				X		
IAP-K.35	X	X	X	X		X
IAP-K.36			X			
IAP-K.37	X		X	X		
IAP-K.38	X		X	X		X
IAP-K.43					X	
IAP-K.69					X	
IAP-N 1.61				X		

Inscription	A	B	C	D	E	F
IAP-N 1.65					X	
IAP-N 1.66				X		
IAP-N 1.67					X	
IAP-N 1.68				X		X
IAP-N 1.69					X	
IAP-N 1.70	X			X		X
IAP-N 1.71	X			X		X
IAP-N 1.80				X		X
IAP-N 1.83				X		
IAP-N 1.91				X		X
IAP-N 1.92				X		X
IAP-N 1.93				X		X
IAP-N 1.95				X		
IAP-N 1.100				X		
IAP-N 1.101				X		X
IAP-N 1.102				X		X
IAP-W.38	X		X	X		X
IAP-W.39	X		X		X	
IAP-W.40	X	X	X		X	
IAP-W.41	X	X		X		
IAP-W.42	X		X	X		X
IAP-W.43	X					
IAP-W.46	X		X			
IAP-W.49	X	X	X	X		X
IAP-W.51	X	X				
IAP-W.52	X	X		X		X
IAP-W.53	X	X	X		X	
IAP-W.54	X	X	X	X		X
IAP-W.55	X	X		X		X
IAP-W.56	X	X	X			X
IAP-W.57	X		X	X		
IAP-W.58 (= CTI 27)	X			X		
IAP-W.59	X		X	X		
IAP-W.60	X					
IAP-W.61			X	X		
IAP-W.65	X		X	X		X
IAP-W.66 (= HAS 19 Wg.17)	X			X		
IAP-W.69	X	X	X			
IAP-W.73	X	X	X			
IAP-W.75 (= CTI 58)					X	
IAP-W.76				X		

Inscription	A	B	C	D	E	F
IAP-W.83	X				X	
IAP-W.84	X	X	X	X		X
IAP-W.85	X	X	X	X		X
IAP-W.86			X	X		
IAP-W.87	X	X	X	X		X
IAP-W.90				X		
IAP-W.91	X		X			
IAP-W.92	X					
NDI copper plate 17	X	X				X
NDI Atmakur 7	X		X		X	
NDI Atmakur 11					X	
NDI Atmakur 13					X	
NDI Atmakur 24	X		X		X	
NDI Atmakur 25			X		X	
NDI Atmakur 29	X				X	
NDI Atmakur 38	X		X		X	
NDI Atmakur 51	X				X	
NDI Atmakur 55	X	X	X		X	
NDI Atmakur 56	X	X	X			
NDI Atmakur 57	X				X	
NDI Darsi 1	X			X		X
NDI Darsi 6	X		X	X		X
NDI Darsi 10	X	X	X	X		X
NDI Darsi 12	X			X		X
NDI Darsi 24	X		X		X	
NDI Darsi 25	X			X		X
NDI Darsi 27	X	X				
NDI Darsi 28	X				X	
NDI Darsi 35	X	X	X	X		X
NDI Darsi 57	X			X		X
NDI Darsi 60					X	
NDI Darsi 69	X		X		X	
NDI Darsi 70	X	X	X		X	
NDI Darsi 72	X		X	X		X
NDI Darsi 74	X				X	
NDI Kandukur 1	X	X	X	X		X
NDI Kandukur 22					X	
NDI Kandukur 23	X	X	X			
NDI Kandukur 26					X	
NDI Kandukur 29	X	X			X	
NDI Kandukur 40	X		X	X		X

Inscription	A	B	C	D	E	F
NDI Kandukur 50	X		X	X		X
NDI Kandukur 52					X	
NDI Kandukur 53	X		X		X	
NDI Kandukur 54				X		
NDI Kandukur 55	X	X		X		X
NDI Kandukur 60	X				X	
NDI Kandukur 61	X	X			X	
NDI Kandukur 62	X				X	
NDI Kandukur 63	X	X	X		X	
NDI Kandukur 64	X	X	X		X	
NDI Kandukur 65	X	X	X		X	
NDI Kandukur 66	X	X	X		X	
NDI Kandukur 84	X			X		X
NDI Kanigiri 11	X		X		X	
NDI Kanigiri 24	X	X	X		X	
NDI Kanigiri 31					X	
NDI Kavali 8	X	X	X		X	
NDI Kavali 10	X		X		X	
NDI Kavali 11	X		X		X	
NDI Kavali 13	X	X			X	
NDI Kavali 19					X	
NDI Kavali 21	X	X	X		X	
NDI Kavali 22			X		X	
NDI Kavali 23	X	X	X		X	
NDI Kavali 24					X	
NDI Kavali 25	X		X		X	
NDI Kavali 26	X	X	X		X	
NDI Kavali 27					X	
NDI Kavali 28	X		X		X	
NDI Kavali 29	X		X		X	
NDI Kavali 30	X		X		X	
NDI Kavali 31	X	X	X		X	
NDI Kavali 35	X				X	
NDI Kavali 36	X			X		X
NDI Kavali 37					X	
NDI Kavali 38	X		X		X	
NDI Kavali 39	X	X			X	
NDI Kavali 43					X	
NDI Kavali 45			X		X	
NDI Kavali 47	X				X	
NDI Kavali 48					X	

Inscription	A	B	C	D	E	F
NDI Kavali 51	X		X		X	
NDI Nellore 30					X	
NDI Nellore 32					X	
NDI Nellore 80				X		
NDI Nellore 102	X				X	
NDI Nellore 103			X		X	
NDI Nellore 106			X		X	
NDI Nellore 118					X	
NDI Ongole 6					X	
NDI Ongole 7	X		X	X		X
NDI Ongole 8	X		X	X		X
NDI Ongole 9	X		X	X		X
NDI Ongole 10	X		X	X		X
NDI Ongole 16	X		X		X	
NDI Ongole 17-A	X	X		X		
NDI Ongole 17-B	X				X	
NDI Ongole 27	X		X		X	
NDI Ongole 28	X		X	X		X
NDI Ongole 34	X		X		X	
NDI Ongole 45	X			X		X
NDI Ongole 49	X	X		X		X
NDI Ongole 53	X		X	X		X
NDI Ongole 54	X		X		X	
NDI Ongole 58			X	X		
NDI Ongole 67		X	X		X	
NDI Ongole 70				X		
NDI Ongole 75	X		X	X		X
NDI Ongole 76	X		X		X	
NDI Ongole 82	X		X		X	
NDI Ongole 86	X		X	X		X
NDI Ongole 87	X	X	X	X		X
NDI Ongole 88-A	X		X	X		X
NDI Ongole 89	X	X	X	X		X
NDI Ongole 90	X		X		X	
NDI Ongole 96				X		
NDI Ongole 98	X	X			X	
NDI Ongole 99	X		X		X	
NDI Ongole 101	X				X	
NDI Ongole 103	X				X	
NDI Ongole 110	X		X		X	
NDI Ongole 120	X				X	

Inscription	A	B	C	D	E	F
NDI Ongole 123					X	
NDI Ongole 125					X	
NDI Ongole 129	X		X	X		X
NDI Ongole 130	X		X		X	
NDI Ongole 136	X		X		X	
NDI Ongole 138	X		X		X	
NDI Ongole 139	X	X	X	X		X
NDI Ongole 143	X		X	X		
NDI Ongole 149				X		
NDI Ongole 150	X	X	X	X		X
NDI Ongole 151	X		X		X	
NDI Podili 6	X	X	X	X		X
NDI Podili 9	X				X	
NDI Podili 10				X		
NDI Podili 32	X				X	
NDI Rapur 20	X	X			X	
NDI Rapur 36			X		X	
NDI Rapur 47			X		X	
NDI Udayagiri 3					X	
NDI Udayagiri 14					X	
NDI Udayagiri 48	X				X	
SII 4.661	X	X		X		X
SII 4.679	X		X		X	
SII 4.700	X		X		X	
SII 4.705	X		X	X		X
SII 4.707	X		X	X		X
SII 4.712	X	X	X		X	
SII 4.713	X	X	X		X	
SII 4.714	X		X		X	
SII 4.715	X	X	X		X	
SII 4.718	X	X	X		X	
SII 4.720	X	X	X		X	
SII 4.721	X	X	X		X	
SII 4.723	X	X	X		X	
SII 4.724	X	X	X		X	
SII 4.725			X		X	
SII 4.726	X	X	X		X	
SII 4.727	X	X	X		X	
SII 4.728	X		X		X	
SII 4.729	X	X	X		X	
SII 4.730			X		X	

Inscription	A	B	C	D	E	F
SII 4.732	X	X	X		X	
SII 4.733	X	X	X		X	
SII 4.735	X	X	X		X	
SII 4.739	X	X	X		X	
SII 4.740	X	X	X		X	
SII 4.741	X	X	X		X	
SII 4.742	X		X		X	
SII 4.743	X		X		X	
SII 4.745					X	
SII 4.746	X	X	X		X	
SII 4.747	X		X		X	
SII 4.748	X	X	X		X	
SII 4.750	X	X	X		X	
SII 4.751	X		X		X	
SII 4.752	X	X	X		X	
SII 4.755	X	X	X		X	
SII 4.756	X		X		X	
SII 4.759	X			X		
SII 4.763	X	X	X		X	
SII 4.764					X	
SII 4.765			X		X	
SII 4.766			X		X	
SII 4.767	X	X			X	
SII 4.768	X	X	X		X	
SII 4.769	X		X		X	
SII 4.770	X	X	X		X	
SII 4.771	X		X		X	
SII 4.780	X		X		X	
SII 4.781-A	X		X		X	
SII 4.782	X		X		X	
SII 4.783	X		X		X	
SII 4.785	X		X		X	
SII 4.786	X	X	X		X	
SII 4.788	X		X		X	
SII 4.790	X	X	X		X	
SII 4.791	X	X	X		X	
SII 4.792	X		X		X	
SII 4.795	X	X	X		X	
SII 4.809	X		X		X	
SII 4.932	X				X	
SII 4.933	X		X		X	

Inscription	A	B	C	D	E	F
SII 4.934			X		X	
SII 4.935			X		X	
SII 4.937					X	
SII 4.939	X		X		X	
SII 4.941					X	
SII 4.952	X	X	X	X		X
SII 4.954	X		X		X	
SII 4.957	X		X		X	
SII 4.958	X	X			X	
SII 4.959	X		X		X	
SII 4.960	X		X		X	
SII 4.964	X		X		X	
SII 4.966					X	
SII 4.969	X	X	X		X	
SII 4.976	X		X			
SII 4.978	X		X			
SII 4.979	X		X			
SII 4.983	X	X	X		X	
SII 4.984	X		X		X	
SII 4.985	X	X	X		X	
SII 4.986	X	X				
SII 4.1001	X		X		X	
SII 4.1019	X	X	X		X	
SII 4.1022	X	X			X	
SII 4.1025	X	X	X		X	
SII 4.1032-A					X	
SII 4.1033					X	
SII 4.1037	X	X	X		X	
SII 4.1038	X	X	X		X	
SII 4.1043			X		X	
SII 4.1045	X		X	X		X
SII 4.1047	X	X	X		X	
SII 4.1056	X		X	X		X
SII 4.1074					X	
SII 4.1084			X		X	
SII 4.1085	X	X	X		X	
SII 4.1092	X		X		X	
SII 4.1100	X	X	X		X	
SII 4.1110	X	X	X		X	
SII 4.1117	X		X	X		X
SII 4.1118	X	X	X		X	

Inscription	A	B	C	D	E	F
SII 4.1119			X		X	
SII 4.1125	X		X		X	
SII 4.1145			X		X	
SII 4.1152	X	X	X	X		X
SII 4.1155	X	X	X	X		
SII 4.1162	X	X	X		X	
SII 4.1163	X	X	X		X	
SII 4.1168	X		X		X	
SII 4.1178	X	X			X	
SII 4.1200	X	X	X		X	
SII 4.1201	X		X		X	
SII 4.1206	X		X		X	
SII 4.1215	X	X	X		X	
SII 4.1218	X		X		X	
SII 4.1221	X		X		X	
SII 4.1223			X		X	
SII 4.1230					X	
SII 4.1231					X	
SII 4.1234	X				X	
SII 4.1245			X		X	
SII 4.1257	X		X		X	
SII 4.1259	X		X		X	
SII 4.1261	X		X		X	
SII 4.1275-B	X	X			X	
SII 4.1278	X	X	X		X	
SII 4.1279	X	X	X		X	
SII 4.1286	X		X		X	
SII 4.1307	X	X	X		X	
SII 4.1313	X		X		X	
SII 4.1315	X	X	X		X	
SII 4.1318	X		X		X	
SII 4.1333	X		X	X		X
SII 4.1335					X	
SII 4.1341	X		X	X		X
SII 4.1360	X		X		X	
SII 4.1365	X		X		X	
SII 4.1366	X		X		X	
SII 4.1367	X	X			X	
SII 4.1368	X		X		X	
SII 4.1369	X	X	X		X	
SII 4.1370			X		X	

Inscription	A	B	C	D	E	F
SII 4.1371	X	X	X		X	
SII 4.1372	X		X		X	
SII 4.1373	X		X		X	
SII 5.8	X	X	X		X	
SII 5.32	X	X	X		X	
SII 5.54	X				X	
SII 5.55	X	X	X		X	
SII 5.56			X		X	
SII 5.61	X	X	X		X	
SII 5.67	X		X		X	
SII 5.70	X	X	X		X	
SII 5.84					X	
SII 5.85			X		X	
SII 5.89	X		X		X	
SII 5.90	X		X		X	
SII 5.91	X		X		X	
SII 5.110	X	X	X	X		X
SII 5.111	X	X	X		X	
SII 5.112	X	X			X	
SII 5.116	X		X		X	
SII 5.121	X		X		X	
SII 5.122	X		X		X	
SII 5.123	X	X	X		X	
SII 5.124	X		X		X	
SII 5.125	X		X		X	
SII 5.126	X	X	X		X	
SII 5.127	X		X		X	
SII 5.128	X	X	X		X	
SII 5.130	X	X	X		X	
SII 5.131	X	X	X		X	
SII 5.132	X	X	X		X	
SII 5.136	X	X	X		X	
SII 5.137	X	X	X		X	
SII 5.138	X	X	X		X	
SII 5.139	X	X	X		X	
SII 5.140	X		X		X	
SII 5.141	X	X	X		X	
SII 5.142	X	X	X		X	
SII 5.143	X	X	X		X	
SII 5.144	X	X	X		X	
SII 5.146	X	X	X		X	

Inscription	A	B	C	D	E	F
SII 5.147	X	X	X		X	
SII 5.148	X	X	X		X	
SII 5.150	X	X	X		X	
SII 5.151	X	X	X		X	
SII 5.152	X	X	X		X	
SII 5.153	X		X		X	
SII 5.157	X		X		X	
SII 5.159	X	X	X		X	
SII 5.161	X				X	
SII 5.167	X		X		X	
SII 5.168	X	X			X	
SII 5.169	X				X	
SII 5.170	X				X	
SII 5.171	X	X	X		X	
SII 5.172	X		X		X	
SII 5.173	X				X	
SII 5.175	X		X		X	
SII 5.176					X	
SII 5.177	X	X			X	
SII 5.179	X	X	X		X	
SII 5.180	X	X			X	
SII 5.181	X		X		X	
SII 5.182	X	X	X		X	
SII 5.183	X				X	
SII 5.184	X	X			X	
SII 5.185	X				X	
SII 5.186	X				X	
SII 5.187	X				X	
SII 5.188	X		X		X	
SII 5.189	X	X	X		X	
SII 5.190	X	X	X		X	
SII 5.192	X				X	
SII 5.194	X	X	X		X	
SII 5.195	X		X		X	
SII 5.196	X		X		X	
SII 5.197	X	X	X		X	
SII 5.199	X		X		X	
SII 5.200			X		X	
SII 5.201					X	
SII 5.202	X	X	X			
SII 5.203	X		X		X	

Inscription	A	B	C	D	E	F
SII 5.204	X				X	
SII 5.205	X		X		X	
SII 5.206	X		X		X	
SII 5.209	X	X			X	
SII 5.210	X				X	
SII 5.211-A	X	X	X	X		X
SII 5.211-B	X	X		X		X
SII 5.213	X	X	X		X	
SII 5.214	X					
SII 5.215	X		X		X	
SII 5.216			X	X		
SII 5.217	X	X	X	X		X
SII 5.218			X		X	
SII 5.219	X	X	X	X		X
SII 5.505	X		X			
SII 6.81	X		X	X		X
SII 6.84	X		X		X	
SII 6.85			X		X	
SII 6.86	X		X		X	
SII 6.89	X		X		X	
SII 6.90			X		X	
SII 6.92	X		X		X	
SII 6.93	X		X		X	
SII 6.94	X				X	
SII 6.95	X	X			X	
SII 6.96	X	X	X		X	
SII 6.97	X				X	
SII 6.99	X	X	X		X	
SII 6.110					X	
SII 6.120	X		X		X	
SII 6.130					X	
SII 6.144	X	X	X		X	
SII 6.145	X	X	X		X	
SII 6.158	X	X			X	
SII 6.161			X		X	
SII 6.162	X	X	X		X	
SII 6.164	X		X		X	
SII 6.165	X		X		X	
SII 6.204	X	X		X		
SII 6.205	X		X		X	
SII 6.206	X		X			

Inscription	A	B	C	D	E	F
SII 6.207	X		X		X	
SII 6.209					X	
SII 6.214	X	X	X			
SII 6.215	X		X		X	
SII 6.216	X				X	
SII 6.221	X		X		X	
SII 6.224	X	X	X		X	
SII 6.225					X	
SII 6.228	X		X		X	
SII 6.229	X					
SII 6.236	X	X			X	
SII 6.237				X		
SII 6.249	X		X			
SII 6.587	X		X		X	
SII 6.588	X		X		X	
SII 6.591			X	X		
SII 6.592	X		X	X		X
SII 6.597					X	
SII 6.602	X		X	X		X
SII 6.603	X		X			
SII 6.618	X			X		X
SII 6.621	X	X	X		X	
SII 6.622					X	
SII 6.623	X	X	X	X		X
SII 6.628	X		X	X		X
SII 6.631	X	X	X		X	
SII 6.633	X	X	X	X		X
SII 6.650	X	X	X	X		X
SII 6.652	X	X				
SII 7.735			X		X	
SII 10.193	X				X	
SII 10.194	X				X	
SII 10.196	X				X	
SII 10.197	X	X	X		X	
SII 10.198	X	X	X		X	
SII 10.199 (= SII 6.236)	X	X			X	
SII 10.200	X	X	X		X	
SII 10.202	X	X	X		X	
SII 10.203					X	
SII 10.204					X	
SII 10.205	X	X	X		X	

Inscription	A	B	C	D	E	F
SII 10.206	X		X		X	
SII 10.207	X		X		X	
SII 10.208					X	
SII 10.209					X	
SII 10.210	X		X		X	
SII 10.231	X	X	X			
SII 10.241	X	X	X	X		
SII 10.242	X	X	X		X	
SII 10.243	X	X			X	
SII 10.244	X	X	X		X	
SII 10.245	X				X	
SII 10.246	X	X	X		X	
SII 10.247			X		X	
SII 10.248	X	X		X		
SII 10.249	X		X		X	
SII 10.250	X		X		X	
SII 10.251	X		X		X	
SII 10.252	X		X		X	
SII 10.253	X		X			
SII 10.254	X		X	X		
SII 10.256	X		X	X		X
SII 10.257	X				X	
SII 10.258	X	X	X		X	
SII 10.259	X	X	X		X	
SII 10.260			X		X	
SII 10.261				X		
SII 10.262	X	X	X		X	
SII 10.263				X		
SII 10.264	X	X	X		X	
SII 10.265	X		X		X	
SII 10.266	X		X		X	
SII 10.267					X	
SII 10.268	X	X	X		X	
SII 10.269	X		X		X	
SII 10.270	X			X		X
SII 10.271				X		
SII 10.272			X		X	
SII 10.273					X	
SII 10.274-A	X	X	X		X	
SII 10.274-B	X		X		X	
SII 10.275	X	X	X		X	

Inscription	A	B	C	D	E	F
SII 10.276	X	X	X		X	
SII 10.277			X	X		
SII 10.278	X	X	X	X		X
SII 10.279	X	X			X	
SII 10.280					X	
SII 10.281	X				X	
SII 10.282	X	X	X		X	
SII 10.283	X	X	X		X	
SII 10.284	X	X	X		X	
SII 10.285	X					
SII 10.286					X	
SII 10.287	X		X		X	
SII 10.288	X	X	X		X	
SII 10.289	X	X	X		X	
SII 10.290	X		X	X		X
SII 10.291	X	X	X		X	
SII 10.292	X		X		X	
SII 10.293	X	X	X		X	
SII 10.294					X	
SII 10.295	X		X		X	
SII 10.296	X		X		X	
SII 10.297	X		X		X	
SII 10.298	X		X		X	
SII 10.299	X	X	X		X	
SII 10.300	X	X	X		X	
SII 10.301	X	X			X	
SII 10.302	X	X	X		X	
SII 10.303	X		X	X		X
SII 10.304	X	X	X	X		X
SII 10.305	X		X		X	
SII 10.306	X		X		X	
SII 10.307	X	X	X		X	
SII 10.308	X	X	X		X	
SII 10.309	X		X	X		X
SII 10.310					X	
SII 10.311	X		X		X	
SII 10.312	X		X		X	
SII 10.313	X	X	X		X	
SII 10.314	X	X	X	X		X
SII 10.315	X		X		X	
SII 10.316	X		X		X	

Inscription	A	B	C	D	E	F
SII 10.317	X		X	X		X
SII 10.318	X	X	X		X	
SII 10.319	X	X	X		X	
SII 10.320	X	X		X		X
SII 10.321	X	X	X		X	
SII 10.322	X	X	X		X	
SII 10.323	X	X	X		X	
SII 10.324	X	X	X		X	
SII 10.325	X	X	X		X	
SII 10.326	X	X	X		X	
SII 10.327	X		X		X	
SII 10.328	X		X	X		X
SII 10.329	X		X		X	
SII 10.330	X	X			X	
SII 10.331	X	X	X		X	
SII 10.332	X		X	X		X
SII 10.333	X	X	X		X	
SII 10.334	X		X	X		X
SII 10.335	X	X	X		X	
SII 10.336	X	X	X		X	
SII 10.337	X	X	X	X		X
SII 10.338				X		
SII 10.339	X	X	X		X	
SII 10.340	X		X	X		X
SII 10.341	X		X		X	
SII 10.342	X	X	X		X	
SII 10.343	X		X	X		X
SII 10.344	X		X		X	
SII 10.345	X		X	X		X
SII 10.346	X		X	X		X
SII 10.347			X		X	
SII 10.348			X		X	
SII 10.349-A			X		X	
SII 10.349-B	X	X	X			
SII 10.350	X		X		X	
SII 10.351	X		X		X	
SII 10.352	X		X		X	
SII 10.353	X		X		X	
SII 10.354	X		X		X	
SII 10.355	X	X	X		X	
SII 10.356	X	X	X		X	

Inscription	A	B	C	D	E	F
SII 10.357	X	X	X		X	
SII 10.358	X		X		X	
SII 10.359	X	X	X		X	
SII 10.360	X			X		X
SII 10.361	X	X	X		X	
SII 10.362	X		X		X	
SII 10.363	X		X		X	
SII 10.364			X		X	
SII 10.365	X	X	X		X	
SII 10.367	X	X	X	X		X
SII 10.368	X		X	X		X
SII 10.369	X	X	X	X		X
SII 10.370	X		X	X		X
SII 10.371	X	X	X	X		
SII 10.372					X	
SII 10.373	X		X		X	
SII 10.375	X		X			
SII 10.377			X			
SII 10.380	X	X	X			
SII 10.381	X					
SII 10.386	X		X			
SII 10.393			X			
SII 10.394	X	X	X		X	
SII 10.395				X		
SII 10.396	X		X			
SII 10.397	X	X	X		X	
SII 10.398	X		X	X		X
SII 10.399	X				X	
SII 10.400	X	X	X		X	
SII 10.401				X		
SII 10.402	X		X	X		X
SII 10.403	X	X	X	X		X
SII 10.404					X	
SII 10.405	X		X		X	
SII 10.406	X	X	X		X	
SII 10.407	X		X	X		X
SII 10.408			X		X	
SII 10.409	X	X	X		X	
SII 10.410	X		X		X	
SII 10.411					X	
SII 10.412	X		X		X	

Inscription	A	B	C	D	E	F
SII 10.413			X	X		
SII 10.414	X	X	X		X	
SII 10.415	X	X	X		X	
SII 10.416	X	X			X	
SII 10.417	X		X		X	
SII 10.418	X					
SII 10.419	X	X	X		X	
SII 10.420	X	X	X		X	
SII 10.421	X		X	X		X
SII 10.422-A	X	X	X	X		X
SII 10.422-B		X	X		X	
SII 10.422-C	X	X	X		X	
SII 10.423	X		X	X		X
SII 10.424	X		X	X		X
SII 10.425			X	X		
SII 10.426	X		X		X	
SII 10.427	X	X	X	X		
SII 10.428	X			X		
SII 10.429			X		X	
SII 10.430	X		X		X	
SII 10.431	X		X		X	
SII 10.432	X	X	X		X	
SII 10.433	X				X	
SII 10.434				X		
SII 10.435			X		X	
SII 10.436					X	
SII 10.437	X	X	X		X	
SII 10.438				X		
SII 10.439	X	X	X		X	
SII 10.440	X			X		X
SII 10.441			X		X	
SII 10.442	X		X	X		X
SII 10.443	X		X	X		X
SII 10.444			X	X		
SII 10.445	X		X	X		X
SII 10.446	X	X	X		X	
SII 10.447	X		X	X		X
SII 10.448	X		X		X	
SII 10.449	X		X		X	
SII 10.450	X		X		X	
SII 10.451	X	X	X	X		X

Inscription	A	B	C	D	E	F
SII 10.452	X	X	X		X	
SII 10.453	X	X	X		X	
SII 10.454	X		X		X	
SII 10.455	X			X		X
SII 10.456	X	X	X		X	
SII 10.457	X		X		X	
SII 10.458	X	X	X		X	
SII 10.459			X	X		
SII 10.460	X	X	X		X	
SII 10.461					X	
SII 10.462	X		X	X		X
SII 10.464	X	X			X	
SII 10.465	X	X	X		X	
SII 10.466	X	X			X	
SII 10.467	X	X	X		X	
SII 10.468			X	X		
SII 10.469	X	X	X	X		X
SII 10.470					X	
SII 10.471	X	X	X		X	
SII 10.472	X	X	X	X		X
SII 10.473			X		X	
SII 10.474	X		X		X	
SII 10.475	X		X		X	
SII 10.476	X		X		X	
SII 10.477	X		X		X	
SII 10.478	X		X		X	
SII 10.479	X		X	X		X
SII 10.480			X	X		
SII 10.481	X	X	X		X	
SII 10.482	X		X		X	
SII 10.483-A	X		X		X	
SII 10.483-B	X	X	X		X	
SII 10.484					X	
SII 10.485	X	X	X		X	
SII 10.486	X	X	X		X	
SII 10.487	X	X	X		X	
SII 10.488				X		
SII 10.489 (= IAP-N 1.94)	X		X	X		X
SII 10.490					X	
SII 10.491	X	X	X	X		X
SII 10.492	X		X	X		X

Inscription	A	B	C	D	E	F
SII 10.493	X		X	X		X
SII 10.494 (= IAP-N 1.97)	X		X		X	
SII 10.495			X	X		
SII 10.496	X			X		
SII 10.497	X		X	X		X
SII 10.498 (= IAP-C 1.154)	X		X		X	
SII 10.499	X	X	X		X	
SII 10.500				X		
SII 10.501	X			X		X
SII 10.502				X		
SII 10.503	X		X	X		X
SII 10.504				X		
SII 10.505	X	X	X	X		X
SII 10.506				X		
SII 10.507				X		
SII 10.508 (= IAP-N 1.99)	X		X	X		X
SII 10.509	X		X	X		X
SII 10.510	X	X	X		X	
SII 10.511	X	X	X		X	
SII 10.512	X		X		X	
SII 10.513	X	X	X		X	
SII 10.514	X	X	X		X	
SII 10.515	X		X		X	
SII 10.516	X	X	X		X	
SII 10.517					X	
SII 10.518	X	X	X		X	
SII 10.519				X		
SII 10.520	X		X	X		X
SII 10.521	X		X	X		X
SII 10.522	X	X	X	X		X
SII 10.523	X	X	X	X		X
SII 10.524			X		X	
SII 10.525				X		
SII 10.526	X	X	X	X		X
SII 10.527	X			X		
SII 10.528	X		X	X		X
SII 10.529	X		X	X		X
SII 10.530	X	X	X	X		X
SII 10.531	X	X	X		X	
SII 10.532	X		X	X		X
SII 10.533			X	X		

Inscription	A	B	C	D	E	F
SII 10.534			X		X	
SII 10.535	X		X			X
SII 10.536	X	X				
SII 10.537	X		X			
SII 10.538	X		X			
SII 10.539			X			
SII 10.540	X		X			
SII 10.543			X			
SII 10.544	X		X			
SII 26.589					X	
SII 26.591	X	X	X		X	
SII 26.617	X	X	X	X		X
SII 26.626					X	
SII 26.645	X	X	X		X	
SS: 162-3 (= IAP-N 2.38)	X				X	
SS: 167-8 (= IAP-N 1.57)	X	X			X	
SS: 169-70 (= IAP-N 1.74)	X					
SS: 171-8 (= IAP-N 1.4)	X	X	X	X		X
SS: 232-7	X		X	X		X
SS: 239-43 (= IAP-N 1.78)			X	X		
SS: 258-64			X	X		
SS: 284-5 side 1 (= IAP-N 1.77)	X					
SS: 284-5 side 2 (= IAP-N 1.139)	X		X			
Studies in Indian Epigraphy 1.9	X		X	X		X
TS.1 Kakatiya 15	X	X	X		X	
TS.1 misc. 16	X	X	X		X	
TS.2 Kakatiya 11				X		

Part 2: Other Inscriptions from the Kakatiya Region

This list covers undated Telugu and Sanskrit records issued within the fourteen districts encompassed by the Kakatiya state. A few undated inscriptions are also noted in column A of the preceding table.

ARE—1902/103, 1907/619, 1913/139, 1913/159, 1915/319, 1920/307, 1922/767, 1922/772, 1922/774, 1924/258, 1924/289, 1925/590, 1925/591, 1926/419, 1929–30/76, 1929–30/94, 1930–31/304, 1930–31/306, 1930–31/315, 1932–33/328, 1934–35/278, 1934–35/284, 1935–36/282, 1935–36/309, 1936–37/337, 1939–40/48, 1941–42/E 42, 1942–43/36, 1952–53/274, 1953–54/70, 1954–55/136, 1954–55/142, 1954–55/144, 1954–55/145, 1954–55/150, 1955–56/4, 1957–58/33, 1957–58/58, 1958–59/13, 1959–60/432, 1960–61/112, 1961–62/33, 1961–62/74 (= IAP-N 2.50), 1965–66/18, 1967–68/3, 1969–70/6, 1969–70/7, 1976–77/27, 1977–78/11, 1980–81/8a.

APAS—38.14, 38.15.
CTI—40, 42, 45.
EI— 36.27 (= IAP-W.101), 41.26 (= IAP-W.100).
HAS—13.15 (= IAP-W.47), 13.23 (= IAP-W.27), 13.39, 13. 47 (= IAP-N 2.70), 19 Km.10 (= IAP-N 2.48), 19 Mn.44, 19 Wg.21.
IAP— C 1.158, C 1.161, K.32, K.33, K.34, K.39, N 1.54, N 1.75, N 1.79, N 1.85, N 1.86, N 1.87, N 1.103, N 1.147, W.44 (= HAS 19 Wg.3), W.71, W.72, W.78, W.79, W.81, W.82, W.93, W.95, W.97, W.98, W.99.
NDI—Darsi 26 and 59, Podili 7.
SII—4.968, 4.999, 6.629, 10.201, 10.218, 10.220, 10.233, 10.255, 10.366, 10.374, 10.378, 10.379, 10.384, 10.388, 10.390, 10.392, 10.418, 10.541, 10.542, 10.545, 10.589.
SS—pp. 284–85 side one (= IAP-N 1.77).

Notes

Introduction

1. For a critique of James Mill, see Guha 1989: 284–90; Inden 1990: 45, 56–58, 90–93, 165–72; and Trautmann 1997: 117–24.

2. Several statements to this effect can by found in the second edition of Hugh Tinker's survey of Indian history, including, "Although, no doubt, it is trite to describe society and government in South Asia before the entry of the West as static, still it is true to suggest that the great tradition held to the same course through the centuries" (1990: xvii). Another example from the same work is, "The great cycle of history in South Asia demonstrates an extraordinary continuity. There was ebb and flow, as we have seen, but at no time was there any great break with the past . . . or any great challenge to the past" (p. 27). See also the remarks of Madeleine Biardeau as quoted in Chattopadhyaya 1994: 3.

3. Vincent Smith's portrayal of medieval decline is discussed in Inden 1990: 7–12, 182–88; while Kulke 1995b: 6–18 summarizes the main debates on Indian feudalism.

4. Numerous works have expanded on these points in the past few years. Among them are Chatterjee 1992, which looks at how nationalist historiography blamed the Muslim, and Anderson 1974, which surveys the long history of the related notions of Oriental despotism and the Asiatic mode of production. The construction of caste as the essence of Indian society is the subject of Inden 1990: 49–84 and the alleged decline in sculptural forms is treated in Desai 1993. Also see Ludden 1993.

5. Some of the important studies challenging earlier representations of India include Appadurai 1988, Bayly 1989, Dirks 1987, Fuller 1977, Irschick 1994, and Washbrook 1988. I agree generally with this literature in its claims that many dynamic elements of the precolonial era were suppressed or eliminated during the colonial period. On the other hand, I differ from some recent perspectives in my belief that some continuities spanned the precolonial and colonial eras, particularly in the area of symbolic culture and identity formation.

6. Relevant publications on Indian merchants and Indian Ocean trade include Abraham 1988, Abu-Lughod 1989, Chaudhuri 1985, Habib 1990, Subrahmanyam 1990, and Wink 1990.

7. E.g., Abraham 1988, Breckenridge 1986, Hall 1980, Heitzman 1997, Karashima 1984, Ramaswamy 1985, Spencer 1983a, and Stein 1980.

8. Andhra is actually a bit smaller than Italy (116,000 sq. miles), but its population is

somewhat larger than Italy's (57 million in 1995). It is closest in size to Colorado, among the United States of America, but with more than 20 times the population.

9. Andhra Pradesh was first established as a state in 1953, but the Telugu-speaking districts of the former Hyderabad princely state were added to it in 1956.

10. The geographer B. Subbarao may have been the first to argue that the period from 700 to 1300 was not one of decay, however. He noted that the politically centrifugal forces of the period (as he called them) corresponded with a flowering of regional culture and language (1958: 25–31).

11. This argument was first laid out by R. S. Sharma in his book *Indian Feudalism* (1965) and elaborated in a number of his subsequent works (e.g., 1985), as well in those of his cohort. A brief sketch of the ideas and publications of this school of thought can be found in Kulke 1995b: 6–18.

12. Changing interpretations of the Mauryan period are briefly summarized in Thapar 1995: 123–26 and Kulke and Rothermund 1990: 67–70. Even these may still exaggerate the centralized character of Mauryan rule, in my opinion. One problem is the continuing reliance on the *Arthaśāstra* as a documentary source for the Mauryan period, even though it has been shown to be much later in date (Trautmann 1971) and is clearly prescriptive rather than descriptive. A more empirically grounded approach to the period is found in Fussman 1987.

13. Other aspects of the feudalism model have also been refuted. On the early medieval economy, see Deyell 1990; on urbanization, see Chattopadhyaya 1994: 130–82; also Kumar 1985 and Mukhia 1981.

14. S. Nagaraju dates the earliest Telugu inscriptions with poetic qualities to the mid ninth century (1995: 16). Their Kannada counterparts appear in the mid tenth century, while eleventh-century Chola inscriptions may be the first comparable Tamil records (Pollock 1996: 215–16). Judging from the secondary literature, it appears that Marathi inscriptions of this type were first composed in the twelfth- and thirteenth-century Yadava kingdom (Deshpande 1993a: 117).

15. The situation in North India differs in that Sanskrit continues to be the primary epigraphic language, joined later by Arabic and Persian. Literary production in the vernaculars also commences later in the North, beginning with what is called Old Western Rajasthani (or Gujarati) in the thirteenth century.

16. I thank Phillip B. Wagoner for providing me with a translation of the relevant passages. See also Narayana Rao 1995: 24–27.

17. I say more about the medieval conception of Andhra as the area inhabited by Telugu-speakers in chapter 1 and return again to the issue in the conclusion to the book. My main point here is that linguistic regions existed in medieval India not only as physical territories demarcated by linguistic practice but also as conceptual spaces.

18. I borrow the term "post-Orientalist" from an article by John D. Rogers (1994).

19. This aspect of post-Orientalist scholarship is coming under increasing criticism; see Duara 1995: 51, Ludden 1994: 21, Pollock 1995: 114, Rogers 1994: 20, and van der Veer 1994: 20.

20. While the names of many literary texts composed during the Kakatiya period have been preserved, very few of the texts themselves survive, as can be noted from a careful examination of Venkataramanayya and Somasekhara Sarma 1960: 689–703.

21. This is my translation of the words *svasti śrī* typically placed at the beginning of inscriptions in this period. Literally meaning "welfare," *svasti* was an auspicious expression intended to "ensure success of the undertaking" (Sircar 1966: 331). It can appear alone or in conjunction with *śrī* (good fortune, prosperity), another word expressing the hope that all would go well.

22. At a number of Andhra temple sites, one customarily donated small plots of land

along with milk-bearing animals when endowing a perpetual lamp, which was lit continuously in the vicinity of an image.

23. A *khaṇḍuga* was a unit of measurement for unirrigated or dry land. Ten *tūmus* equaled one *khaṇḍuga*. A *māna* was a unit of liquid measurement, and several specific standards for the *māna*, like the *nandi-mānika* measure, are mentioned in Andhra inscriptions of this period.

24. Perhaps the only large category of Indian literature from the era 1000 to 1500 that might be compared to inscriptions in their sociological purview are texts dealing with popular religion—that is, Puranic and devotional literature, especially when composed in regional languages. Additionally, a small group of historical writings were produced through the patronage of local-level political leaders. While the kind of literature I have just mentioned is less elite than *dharmaśāstra* or courtly *kāvya*, it still does not reveal much about groups such as herders and merchants.

25. I am grateful to Phillip B. Wagoner for suggesting this particular comparison. Subsequent to my writing this introduction, Wagoner also directed my attention to an excellent archaeological analysis of a body of Indian inscriptions as an artifact assemblage (Morrison and Lycett 1997).

26. The only exception is the inscriptional corpus of Chola-period Tamil Nadu, due largely to the efforts of Noboru Karashima and his collaborators as well as others like James Heitzman and Leslie C. Orr. The copper-plate inscriptions of Bengal have also been systematically treated by Barrie M. Morrison (1970).

27. François Dosse makes this point among others in his critique of quantitative history (1994: 153–63). Another opponent of quantitative methods is Lawrence Stone (1981: 29–43). Roger Chartier, on the other hand, urges historian to adopt other approaches but concedes that quantitative history should not altogether be abandoned (1988: 58–59, 102).

28. Unlike the situation with copper-plate grants, it is rare to find a spurious stone inscription, largely because stone inscriptions were situated in the public arena of the temple, whereas copper-plate grants were retained privately by the brahman recipient(s). Because stone inscriptions had an official character, they were used increasingly to record not only religious endowments but also other types of property transfer, such as the selling or leasing of land. Tax assessments that departed from the norm, generally attempts to attract business or labor by means of lower rates, were also sometimes recorded in inscriptional format, particularly in the sixteenth and seventeenth centuries.

29. In Sanskrit inscriptions numerical dates are sometimes indicated by the citing of body parts, natural phenomena, or mythical figures that represent set numbers. In this instance the word *dinakara*, "maker of the day," means "sun," which stood for the number 12 (as in the 12 Adityas of myth who represented the sun in the 12 months of the year). I have changed the sequence of nouns to make things clearer for the reader but should note that the enumeration in this inscription, as usual, actually proceeds in reverse order (i.e., the eyes, the arms, and the sun).

Chapter 1

1. The Archaeological Survey of Southern India began collecting Telugu inscriptions within the territories governed by the British in 1892 (published in *South Indian Inscriptions*, vol. 4). The first Kakatiya-period inscription published by the Nizam's Government of Hyderabad appeared in the early twentieth century (Barnett 1919a and b).

2. The majority of Andhra inscriptions are published, but I also examined hundreds of transcripts of unpublished inscriptions collected by the epigraphical branch of the Archaeological Survey of India, as well as by the Department of Archaeology and Museums, Government of Andhra Pradesh. Unpublished inscriptions are identified by the number

assigned to them in the year their existence was reported by these organizations in the *Annual Reports on Epigraphy* (ARE) and *Andhra Pradesh Reports on Epigraphy* (APRE), respectively. I occasionally used the summaries of unpublished inscriptions provided in ARE and APRE in compiling the data for the tables and maps in this chapter, mainly in cases where I was unable to collect a transcript. Since the summaries are sometimes inaccurate, however, I read the actual texts of the inscriptions used in this chapter whenever possible; in subsequent chapters I utilized *only* those inscriptions whose published texts I had read or whose unpublished transcripts I had examined.

3. In addition to the sources cited in the body of the text, I have also consulted Alam 1968, Spate 1954: 670–92, and Geddes 1982: 72–90 for geographic information.

4. The rainfall amounts for each Andhra Pradesh district have been converted from the metric measures reported in Babu 1990. Other sources list slightly different average figures.

5. Details on Andhra rivers are based on Spate 1954: 35 and 690, Babu 1990: 29, and Vasantha Devi 1964: 14–16.

6. On soils, see Raychaudhuri 1963: 1–19 and Venkateswaran 1961: 1–22.

7. The chronological distribution of Telugu and/or Sanskrit inscriptions in Andhra by century is as follows: eleventh century, 96 inscriptions; twelfth century, 911; thirteenth century, 1,072; fourteenth century, 602; fifteenth century, 499; sixteenth century, 962. From the 50 years between 1600 and 1649, 197 inscriptions survive.

8. Lists of all dated inscriptions utilized in compiling table 1 appear in Appendix A. When inscriptions have been published in more than one venue, in the body of this book I refer only to the version I relied on but have identified the other versions in the appendixes. Although different readings of the same inscription typically do not vary greatly, in cases where they do I generally chose the reading by the staff of the Chief Epigraphist's Office (Archaeological Survey of India) over that of the Department of Archaeology and Museums (Government of Andhra Pradesh), because the former organization usually collected the inscription earlier and was therefore able to provide a more complete text.

9. Many Telugu inscriptions from this era (and particularly from the eleventh and twelfth centuries) have an introductory portion in the Sanskrit language. For that reason, it would be impossible to strictly differentiate Telugu from Sanskrit inscriptions, even if my main interest here was not rather in tracing the expansion of the Telugu linguistic sphere at the expense of Kannada and Tamil. Another 623 records that fall into the Telugu-Sanskrit category also survive from medieval Andhra but cannot be accurately dated, either because that information was never recorded or because the relevant portions of the inscriptions have been damaged.

10. My figures in the "Other" category should be considered conservative estimates since I have undoubtedly undercounted the true number of Tamil inscriptions. This is partly due to the practice of using regnal years in place of the Shaka era, which makes it difficult to accurately date Tamil inscriptions; also, I did not include the numerous Tamil inscriptions found in the Tirupati area and published in *Tirumala Tirupati Devasthanam Inscriptions*. The statistics relating to non-Telugu inscriptions in Andhra were compiled through examination of *Nellore District Inscriptions*, various publications of the Andhra Pradesh Government, and the abstracts in ARE and Desai 1989. There are another 332 undated or undatable inscriptions composed in languages other than Telugu and/or Sanskrit written in Telugu script, which were probably composed between 1000 and 1650.

11. The only notable difference caused by the inclusion of non-Telugu inscriptions is a change in the relative ranking of Periods I and III. Whereas Period I yields the smallest number of Telugu inscriptions followed closely by Period III, if non-Telugu inscriptions are also considered, Period III yields the smallest number.

12. The following summary of Andhra political history is based on my own understanding. Recommended secondary sources for the entire time span are Nilakanta Sastri 1966 and

Sundaram 1968: 1–16. For Period I, also see Nilakanta Sastri and Venkataramanayya 1960; for Period II, Parabrahma Sastry 1978, Venkataramanayya and Somasekhara Sarma 1960; for Periods III and IV, Ramachandra Rao 1988, Ramesan 1973, Richards 1975: 1–34, Sherwani 1973a, b, Somasekhara Sarma 1945 and 1948, and Venkataramanayya 1935 and 1942: 3–90.

13. Carol Breckenridge has also analyzed the replacement of earlier gift objects by food, although her discussion relates solely to the provision of food offerings to a temple deity and not the feeding of brahmans at large feasts (1986). She dates the full-fledged development of this trend to the late fifteenth century. However, her study is based only on the site of Tirupati, which is not a representative institution.

14. See chapter 4 for further discussion of the religious patronage of the Kakatiyas.

15. The provenance of all records has been adjusted to correspond to the administrative boundaries in effect for the 1971 Census of India. Since that time extensive administrative reorganization has occurred, which greatly increased the number of taluks. Because the taluks in existence in 1971 were old and well-known, I have chosen to retain them. I was not able to verify the location of approximately 6 percent of the reported provenance sites (77 out of a total of 1,260) in the 1971 census district handbooks and reverted to the original attribution in these cases. Additionally, the Hyderabad Museum owns a number of inscriptions collected from the vicinity of Hyderabad whose exact provenance is unclear. These are depicted in maps 5–8 in their current location in the Hyderabad Urban Taluk, but they most probably originated in the larger Hyderabad District.

16. Maps of the expansion of Kakatiya polity can be found in chapter 4.

17. In fact, the earliest Telugu inscriptions were issued by the Renati Choda kings of Cuddapah and their affiliates starting in the sixth century and continuing on until the late eighth century. Other Telugu inscriptions from Rayalasima were produced by the political networks of the Vaidumba and Bana dynasties during the ninth and tenth centuries. See Nagaraju 1995 for a discussion of the context of their production.

18. *South Indian Inscriptions*, vol. 16 (*Telugu Inscriptions of the Vijayanagara Dynasty*) contains numerous Telugu records found outside Andhra Pradesh. Examples of sixteenth- and seventeenth-century inscriptions in Telugu are SII 16.118, 141, 177, 211, 217 from Bellary District of Karnataka; SII 16.325 from North Arcot District of Tamil Nadu; SII 16.80 from South Arcot District of Tamil Nadu; and SII 16.100 and 328 from Chingleput District of Tamil Nadu.

19. Map 5 does not reflect the true extent of Tamil usage, since numerous Tamil inscriptions most probably from this era but not precisely datable are also found in Nellore District along the southern coast.

20. E.g., ARE 68 of 1961–62, IAP-W.17, and HAS 13.23.

21. The two Telugu records are HAS 13.6 and IAP-W.25; the others are HAS 13.7 and 12; IAP-K.14, 15, 19, 22, and 24; IAP-W.14, 22, and 29.

22. These records are ARE 126 of 1958–59; HAS 13.3 and 56; IAP-W.37; SII 4.1071, 1095, and 1107; SII 6.212.

23. Persian and Arabic are a good case in point. Modern Telugu has adopted many lexical items from Perso-Arabic but only after centuries of coexistence. Muslim polities began to influence western Andhra in the early fourteenth century, but the borrowing of words from Persian and Arabic did not begin until the late fifteenth century (Iswara Dutt 1967: cxxv).

24. Kannada and Tamil are regarded as closer to each other than Telugu is to either. Whereas Kannada and Tamil are grouped together as South Dravidian languages, the situation with Telugu is less clear. Telugu is sometimes classified as a Central Dravidian rather than a South Dravidian language (Trautmann 1981: 11).

25. Personal communication, Phillip B. Wagoner; see also Wagoner 1997.

26. Derrett 1957: 35, 43; e.g., IAP-K.14, IAP-W.14, and IAP-W.22 from Telangana.

27. Lorenzen 1972: 141–72; HAS 13.7 and 12 from Telangana.

28. The extent of Tamil influence is often overrated. Burton Stein, for instance, included the Krishna-Godavari River deltas and southern coastal Andhra within the South Indian macroregion, his euphemism for an enlarged Tamil sphere. One justification Stein offered for this classification is the Chola overlordship over this portion of Andhra during the reign of Kulottunga I. Short interludes of hegemony are scarcely sufficient grounds for asserting coastal Andhra's unity with the Tamil country, especially since Stein failed to advance any evidence of cultural or social uniformity. Moreover, his characterization of Telangana, which he deemed not part of the macroregion, was based on faulty understanding and cannot be accepted (Stein 1980: 30–62). I discuss this aspect of Stein's ideas further in the last section of chapter 4.

29. Note that the final long vowels of feminine nouns in Sanskrit are often shortened in Telugu, as we see in the Telugu *bhāṣa* (from Sanskrit *bhāṣā*).

30. The term Telugu, however, is first found in Tamil and Kannada inscriptions of the eleventh and twelfth centuries (Iswara Dutt 1967: iv).

31. The Malapaha is described in other Reddi inscriptions as flowing through portions of Krishna District and may be the same as the modern Pulleru. Bhimarathi is a synonym for the Bhima River (Iswara Dutt 1979: 247, 258).

32. The exception is Malayalam, whose literary development came slightly later. See Freeman 1998 for an interesting analysis with relevance to my present discussion. According to Freeman, the late-fourteenth-century *Līlātilakam* text differentiated the Tamil language domain into the three separate dialects, Chola, Pandya, and Kerala, using the labels of political communities to denote varieties of language. Despite its differences from the Tamil language that lay to its east, however, the text presents the language of Kerala (i.e., Malayalam) as sharing a Dravidian character with Tamil that distinguished them both from the languages of Andhra and Karnataka (1998: 51–52, 57).

33. I should emphasize that this statement only applies to the production of inscriptions recording endowments to temples and brahman villages. The links between the temple institution and the agrarian society it was embedded in are further explored in chapter 3. Other kinds of inscriptions, notably hero-stones recording death in a cattle raid, are associated with a pastoral rather than agrarian milieu (Dandekar 1991).

34. The percentages given here were calculated from the statistics provided in Babu 1990.

35. On irrigation see Singh 1974: 45–56, Venkateswaran 1961: 254–67, Vasantha Devi 1964: 31–37, and Williamson 1931.

36. See the section titled "Agrarian Expansion through Temple and Tank Construction" in chapter 3 for more discussion of this point.

37. Cuddapah was also the center of Rayalasima epigraphic activity in the centuries prior to 1000 C.E.

38. Between Periods I and II, the number of inscriptions in Prakasam District rose from 62 to 212, while they rose from 2 to 116 in Nellore District. The number of village sites yielding inscriptions followed a similar ascending pattern, from 23 to 73 sites in Prakasam District and from 2 to 60 sites in Nellore District. The third greatest level of change between periods occurred in Guntur District, just to the north of the Krishna River, which includes Palnad Taluk.

39. How much is unclear, but one estimate for the Mughal empire suggests that only 60 percent of the land that would come under cultivation by 1900 was actually cultivated in 1600 (Habib 1982: 164). Since the Mughal empire included extensive territories within the long-settled Gangetic region, the proportion of cultivated land was probably higher there than in Andhra during the same period.

Chapter 2

1. Among the leading revisionist works are Bayly 1989, Dirks 1987 and 1989, Fuller 1977, Pederson 1986, and Washbrook 1981 and 1988.

2. The fourteen districts covered here are Cuddapah, East Godavari, Guntur, Karimnagar, Khammam, Krishna, Kurnool, Mahbubnagar, Medak, Nalgonda, Nellore, Prakasam, Warangal, and West Godavari.

3. The rough figure of 1,000 is smaller than the 1,500 dated inscriptions noted for Andhra during Period II in chapter 1. Many inscriptions included in the Period II count are excluded from consideration here either because they come from areas outside Kakatiya Andhra and/or because they are composed in languages other than Telugu and Sanskrit in Telugu script. Another reason for the smaller corpus of inscriptions here is the unavailability of transcripts for some unpublished inscriptions. Thus, I was able to collect only 1,074 (91 percent) out of the total of 1,179 dated inscriptions in Telugu and/or Sanskrit reported as existing in the fourteen districts of Kakatiya Andhra (as well as about 150 undated records that can be assigned to the period), and just those inscriptions that I have actually read were utilized in setting up databases for statistical analysis of the various issues examined in chapters 2, 3, and 4. I have also generally eliminated heavily damaged inscriptions from consideration, further reducing the size of the inscriptional corpus analyzed.

4. However, note that there are a few instances in Sanskrit literature where the word *jāti* is used to signify *varṇa* and vice versa (Jaiswal 1986: 47; Sharma 1978: 296).

5. Families claiming descent from the Eastern Chalukyas of Vengi traced their ancestry to the lunar grouping (e.g., SII 4.735, SII 5.61, SII 6.96), while minor Telugu branches of the Pallava and Chola dynasties belonged to the solar division of the *kṣatriya* order (e.g., IAP-C 1.137; APAS 31.15; HAS 19 Mn.26).

6. *Śūdra* origin continued to be a source of pride in the émigré Telugu culture of later centuries (Narayana Rao, Shulman, and Subrahmanyam 1992: 7–8).

7. E.g., CPIHM 1.10; EA 1.7; EI 5.17; EI 12.22, EI 18.41; HAS 4, HAS 13.25; SII 10.395. Copper-plate inscriptions are usually longer and stylistically more elaborate than stone inscriptions. Since the language used in them is typically Sanskrit, it is not surprising that they should contain references to pan-Indic concepts and status claims. Copper plates most often record land grants to brahmans, although this is not always the case in thirteenth-century Andhra.

8. A similar phrase is also found in Kannada inscriptions (Stein 1980: 219).

9. The notion of 18 social units is widespread in Telugu popular literature of the medieval period (Narayana Rao 1990: 304n. 3). The number 18 is also found in Tamil traditions relating to the Vellalars (Dirks 1987: 140).

10. We get references to a Manma *kula* (e.g., HAS 13.27; IAP-W.53; SII 6.602), Ayya *kula* (EI 3.15), Matturu *kula* (APAS 38.15), Durjaya *kula* (e.g., SII 4.743 and 1333, SII 10.269), Matsya *kula* (SII 4.1368), Kayastha *kula* (SII 10.346), and Karikala *kula* (SII 10.409 and 417).

11. Brahman *gōtras* are cited by lineages of chiefs in APAS 31.15; ARE 26 of 1953–54; SII 6.588 and SII 10.278. Nonbrahman *gōtras* are mentioned in ARE 349 of 1937–38; NDI Rapur 20; SII 5.183, 216 and 217; SII 6.99; SII 10.264, 293, 299, 357, 446, and 456.

12. According to Stein, this is the conclusion reached by B. Suresh in his doctoral dissertation on the geography and ethnology of the Chola period (1980: 102–3). Y. Subbarayalu, on the other hand, enumerates 16 different castes figuring in the inscriptions of Chola Tamil Nadu. Although the term *jāti* was often used in reference to them, Subbarayalu admits that "many of the so called castes were found rather as professional groups than as kinship groups" (1982: 275).

13. *Uttarāyaṇa-saṅkrānti* was a very popular time to make endowments in Kakatiya Andhra. It marks the beginning of the six-month period when the sun is moving north of the equator and is the same as *makara-saṅkrānti*, or the day the sun moves into the zodiacal sign Capricorn. Hence I translate it elsewhere as "winter solstice," although the observance

of *uttarāyaṇa-saṅkrānti* in this era had diverged from the actual winter solstice due to calendrical inaccuracies. This inscription is dated on March 25, however, which corresponds to *mēṣa-saṅkrānti*, the day the sun enters the sign Aries, rather than to *makara-saṅkrānti*.

14. Personal communication from Malathi Rao.

15. For more on Telugu names, see Sjoberg 1968.

16. Cheraku Bolla Reddi is one such instance (APRE 133 of 1966; SS: 169–70).

17. The suffixes-*peddi* and -*manci* on a personal name appear to mark brahmans (personal communication, S. S. Ramachandra Murthy).

18. Only those records with adequate information on the donors were considered in this chapter, comprising a corpus of 1,024 inscriptions. The majority of these inscriptions (892 records, or 87 percent) were issued by individual donors rather than by groups. Because some inscriptions document multiple sets of endowments, individual donors were actually responsible for a total of 1,019 different acts of religious gifting (i.e., endowments), as enumerated in table 4. The number of donors is smaller than the number of endowments because some donors made more than one gift. The relevant inscriptions are marked in pt. 1 of Appendix B.

19. Brahman *amātyas* appear in SII 10.325 and 337; brahman *mantris* are found in APRE 408 of 1967, IAP-W.69, SII 4.1366, and SII 10.406; and *pregaḍas* who are definitely brahman are donors in HAS 19 Mn.46, SII 4.715, SII 5.146, SII 10.318 and 453. Brahman *varṇa* status has been ascribed only when membership in pan-Indic brahman *gōtras* is specified or when the donor explicitly states that he is a brahman.

20. ARE 324 of 1930–31 and 293 of 1932–33; SII 4.718 and 728.

21. E.g., the Telugu Pallava lineage of Guntur and Prakasam Districts (NDI Darsi 69, Kanigiri 24, Kandukur 61; SII 6.588; SII 10.278 and 362); the Yadavas of Addanki in Prakasam District (NDI copper plate 17, Darsi 72, and Ongole 28); several Telugu Choda lineages in Prakasam, Nellore, and Cuddapah Districts (ARE 285 of 1949–50 and 18 of 1968–69; IAP-C 1.159; NDI Atmakur 7, Darsi 28, Kandukur 60, and Ongole 17–B); and the Kanduri Chodas of Nalgonda and Mahbubnagar Districts (APAS 31.15; ARE 224 of 1935–36; HAS 19 Mn.17 and 34; SS:162–63 and 167–68). The title usually appears in the honorific plural form *mahārājulu* in Telugu inscriptions.

22. Among the dynasties that preferred this status title are the Parichchhedis of Krishna and Guntur Districts (SII 4.969 and 985; SII 6.120; SII 10.269, 282, and 426), the Chagis of Krishna District, the Kolani princes of West Godavari District, and the Kota dynasty of Guntur District.

23. E.g., SII 5.111, 112, and 141; HAS 13.25; and EI 4.33.

24. *Nāyuḍu* is the singular form of *nāyaka* in Telugu, *nāyakulu* is the plural and/or honorific form.

25. Other miscellaneous status titles are *bhakta* (Shaiva sectarian allegiance), *dāsa* (indicating Vaishnava sectarian allegiance), *dēsaṭi* (possibly referring to a segment of the *reḍḍi* community), *ōju* (from the Sanskrit word *upādhyāya* and used by master artisans), and *vaidya* (Ayurvedic doctor).

26. The singular form in Telugu is *bōyuḍu*, individual *bōyas* do not typically use the honorific plural.

27. Certain *bōyas* are referred to as *gōpa* in SII 4.1370, SII 10.284 and 333; *bōya* and *golla* are equated in SII 5.197. *Bōyas* often appear in Kakatiya-period inscriptions as the persons who are entrusted with livestock endowed to temples.

28. The meaning of *bōya* has changed considerably over time. During the seventh century, it appears appended to village place-names as an alternative designation for brahman recipients of religious grants (EI 8.24, 18.1, 31.12). It may have either meant "resident" or denoted a particular village office. By the eighteenth century, the label *bōya* was used for a Telugu-speaking community in the Kurnool-Anantapur region, resembling the Kannada-

speaking Bedars, who were associated with hunting and often served in local armies (Thurston 1975, 1: 180–93).

29. See the discussion in Rudner 1994: 17–25. Rudner himself disagrees, believing that castes, defined as "corporate kin groups with enduring identities, a variety of rights over property, and crucial economic roles" have functioned at supralocal levels over the last few centuries (p. 25).

30. My impression is that a similar social typology existed in medieval Karnataka, with, for instance, *gavuḍa* replacing the Telugu *reḍḍi*, and *heggaḍe* instead of *pregaḍa*.

31. These figures differ from those in Talbot 1992 for two reasons: I have since collected more inscriptions and, for the sake of consistency, I have only enumerated individual male donors here whereas I had formerly also included men appearing as donors in joint groups. The inscriptions used in compiling table 5 are marked in pt. 1 of Appendix B.

32. They figure in the following inscriptions: APRE 184 of 1966; ARE 26 of 1929–30, 251 of 1935–36, 131 of 1951–52, 20 of 1957–58, 18 of 1968–69, 4 of 1973–74; HAS 13.18; HAS 19 Mn.17 and 18; IAP-C 1.156 and 159; NDI Kanigiri 24; NDI Kandukur 61, 64, 65, 66; SII 4.712, 756, 1178, 1367; SII 10.231, 291, 300, 319, 325, 331, 355, 367, 451, 452, 483, 487, 536.

33. Ranabir Chakravarti reports that the Sanskrit title *śrēṣṭhī*, from which the Telugu *seṭṭi* was probably derived, denoted a rich or successful merchant in inscriptions from the Konkan dated between 997 and 1144 C.E. The term for a trader in general was *vaṇik* (1986: 209).

34. That is, just as Upendra stole the wish-fulfilling tree to give to another, so too did Ambadeva seize the treasures of enemy kings for the purpose of making gifts.

35. Gangaya Sahini's grant is recorded in IAP-N 1.71. Female members of the family appear in ARE 21 of 1929–30, 10 of 1941–42; IAP-C 1.141 and 144.

36. A well-known tradition, recorded in the *kaifiyat* of Oguru, notes that Gangaya Sahini was first in the service of Manuma Siddhi's father, Tikka, the king of Nellore. Gangaya Sahini is said to have been defeated by the Vaidumba chief Rakkasa Ganga soon after King Tikka's death and only then became a subordinate of Kakatiya Ganapati (Venkataramanayya and Somasekhara Sarma 1960: 619; Parabrahma Sastry 1978: 113–14). Inscriptional evidence does not support this tradition, however, since Gangaya Sahini declares his allegiance to the Kakatiyas as early as 1242. Furthermore, he is not active in southern Andhra, the sphere of the Nellore kings, until the mid 1250s.

37. ARE 21 of 1929–30, 269 of 1937–38, 274 of 1949–50; IAP-C 1.141; IAP-N 1.70 and 71; SII 10.332, 334, 343, 346. He also figures in ARE 201 of 1892, 69 of 1929–30, 314 of 1930–31, 10 of 1941–42, 267 of 1949–50, 4 of 1973–74; IAP-N 1.67.

38. Jannigadeva, Tripurarideva I, and Ambadeva II. Other male members of the family appearing in inscriptions are their father Ambadeva I (who was Gangaya Sahini's sister's husband) and Ambadeva II's son Tripurarideva II.

39. ARE 3 of 1973–74; IAP-N 1.70 and 71.

40. The translation of *biruda* as "epithet" is not strictly accurate, for a *biruda* was not only a title but often also a physical emblem or insignia. *Birudas* could be transmitted hereditarily, bestowed on an individual by an overlord, or acquired through conquest. I say more about them in chapter 4.

41. Revanta was the son of the sun-god Surya, conceived when his father assumed the shape of a horse. He is considered a consummate horseman (Fleet 1898–99: 236n.1).

42. For a translation and discussion of the epic, see Roghair 1982; for a short summary of the story, see Blackburn 1989: 245–47.

43. Verses 116–26 in the original Telugu text (Prabhakara Sastri 1988: 32–35), translated in Roghair 1982: 80–81.

44. Discussion of this construct of village India can be found in Inden 1990: 131–61 and Ludden 1993.

45. On the significance of regions, see Subbarayalu 1973 and the essays collected in Crane 1967 and Fox 1977. For merchants, artisans, and trade, see Hall 1980, Ramaswamy 1985, and Abraham 1988.

46. Some examples are Leshnik 1975, Leshnik and Sontheimer 1975, Sontheimer 1989, and Ratnagar 1991.

47. EI 12.22, ll. 135–46, based on the translation from Sanskrit of E. Hultzsch (1913–14: 196).

48. The Reddi king Anavota also issued an inscription in Motupalli about a century later, exempting foreign merchants from certain taxes (SII 10.556).

49. The previous few sentences are based on Habib 1990: 373–74, Childers 1975: 247–51, Dandekar 1991: 321, and Thurston 1975, 4: 207.

50. I am following Parabrahma Sastry (1978: 242–43) in translating the term *prabhu-mukhyulu*, which literally means "leading lords" or "primary owners," as "licensed traders." He believes the Pekkandru held the trade license in Hanumakonda town as well as in Pakanadu (Nellore and southern Prakasam Districts) and Vengi (West Godavari, Krishna, and Guntur Districts). See also NDI Ongole 139, in which a merchant associated with the Pakanadu 21,000 calls himself a *prabhu-mukhyuḍu*.

51. A *magama* is a voluntary levy of a set fraction of goods or income made by collective groups of merchants as a religious endowment, a term also figuring in CTI 35, IAP-C 1.156, and SII 10.429.

52. The words *kēsari-pātika*, *vīsa*, and *kēsari-aḍḍuga* most probably refer to coins. The prefix *kēsari-* is associated with Kakatiya coins and measures, while the remaining terms signify fractions and may therefore indicate coins made of base metals. An *aḍḍuga* is one-half, a *pātika* or *pādika* one-fourth, and a *visa* one-sixteenth—but it is not clear which coin is the standard. See Parabrahma Sastry 1975, Yasodadevi 1968, and Gopala Reddy 1971–72 for a discussion of Kakatiya-period coins and measurements.

53. The word I have translated as "bullock-load" is *peṟuka*, which means a "sack slung over the body of a bullock" (Iswara Dutt 1967: 199). Judging from the rates levied in this record, a bullock-load comprised half the amount of a cart-load.

54. Ubhaya Nanadeshi is another name for Pekkandru, but its meaning is not clear. See the discussion in Narasimha Rao 1975: 114–17.

55. Although *samaya* can mean a "customary practice," "contract," or "group of people," here it should be understood as the association of merchants who follow established rules in their business activities. The phrase *samaya-kāryamu* figures in SII 10.473 in the sense of the "affairs relating to the guild of merchants" (Iswara Dutt 1967: 303). Cf. ARE copper plate 10 of 1919, which records the granting of trade privileges by a collective of merchants to Puliyama Setti in reward for his having killed Karapakala Kati Nayaka, a *samaya-drōhi* (betrayer of the *samaya*).

56. The practice of assessing a fraction of a sales tax suggests that these merchant bodies were in charge of collecting the sales taxes. In addition to merchant collectives, numerous individuals appear to have acted as tax-farmers in this period, at least for commercial revenues. The reliance of South Indian states on tax-farming has been noted for later centuries (Subrahmanyam 1990: 330–32), but once again we see that these trends had begun to develop by the thirteenth century.

57. Vira Balanjya records are ARE 87 of 1929–30, 277 and 278 of 1934–35; CTI 37; HAS 13.55, HAS 19 Km.6; IAP-K.38; IAP-W.71; SII 4.935, SII 5.200, SII 5.202, SII 6.120, SII 10.435, SII 10.473. See also SII 10.528.

58. Personal communication, fall 1995. I am grateful for his generous sharing of field notes and patience with my questions. It should be noted that Claus's research will considerably advance our present understanding of pastoralists as reflected in Murthy and Sontheimer 1980, Murthy 1993, and Sontheimer 1975.

59. Examples of hero-stones from Cuddapah and Anantapur are IAP-C 1.177 Devapatla 4 and 5; IAP-C 1.31; and ARE 726, 734, 746, 747, 748, and 759 of 1917.

60. The editors' reading of the inscription's Shaka date (1170 or 1248–9 C.E.) does not match the year of the Jupiter cycle that is recorded. There is further doubt on the attributed date because Prataparudra's reign did not begin until the late thirteenth century. Unfortunately, the inscription itself seems to have vanished since its contents were noted by Alan Butterworth and V. Venugopaul Chetty around 1900.

61. Mss. 117 sect. 14; 148 sect. 2; and 144 sect. 2, respectively, in Mahalingam 1976. Similar traditions appear in Mss. 109 sect. 6; 115 sects. 8 and 11a; 117 sect. 13; 128 sect. 9.

62. However, several village histories collected ca. 1800 relay such events about their pasts (Mss. 114 sect. 9 and 9c; 115 sect. 9; 127 sect. 12 in Mahalingam 1976).

63. For a discussion of Vijayanagara-period inscriptions from Tamil Nadu that complain about unjust taxation, see Karashima 1992: 141–58.

64. APRE 407 of 1967; ARE 268 of 1952–53; *Bhārati* 54: 56ff.; HAS 19 Km.1 and 2; Mn.19 and 21; IAP-K.36; SII 5.176, SII 10.377.

65. Endowments made by *nagaram* (also called *nagaramu*, *nakaram*, and *nakharamu*) are recorded in ARE 252 of 1935–36; HAS 13.11 and 14; IAP-W.71; and SII 10.429. *Pekkaṇḍru* made gifts in ARE 277 and 278 of 1934–35, 300 of 1936–37; HAS 13.55; IAP-C 1.156; SII 4.935 and 939; SII 10.381, 422, 427, 473, 480, 495. See also EI 3.15; NDI Darsi 70 and Kanigiri 24.

66. ARE 313 of 1932–33; EA 4.14; HAS 13.26, 30, 53; HAS 19 Km. 6, 7, 14; IAP-W.86 and 90; NDI Ongole 58; SII 10.489, 495; SS: 258–64. (Related inscriptions are ARE 330 of 1924; SII 10.526 and 533.) References to the various *praja* are limited in their chronological and geographical distributions, occurring primarily in Telangana and only in the years from 1300 to 1323. Previous scholars who have interpreted the *praja* as a village assembly have not noticed the restricted extent of the phenomenon within Andhra. The term *samasta-praja* is found in Karnataka as well, however.

67. Manuru-sthala in HAS 13.53 and Tangeda-sthala in SII 10.495.

68. See Derrett 1964: 105–6, Kane 1946: 590–94 and 770–802.

69. E.g., APRE 193, 194, 197, and 198 of 1965; EA 1.7; IAP-W.46, 59 and 60; SII 10.254.

70. Other markers of female gender were *amba*, *ambika*, and *ammagāru*, usually but not exclusively used by aristocratic women. In a couple of instances, women did incorporate the status titles of their husbands into their names—as with Peda Potana Boyusani, the wife of Peda Potana Boya (SII 4.1259), and Surama Redisani, whose husband was a *reḍḍi* (SII 5.153).

71. Most intriguing are the women who mention no other kin but their mother (ARE 398 of 1932–33; SII 4.1251, 1261, 1357, 1372; SII 5.85, 192, 1053, 1094, 1280, 1304, 1326, 1330; SII 6.178; SII 10.108 and 110; TIAP 213 and 223). A few are associated with temples but not uniformly, and so they cannot be construed as the precursors of the modern *dēvadāsi*, who were sexually active but unmarried (and whose families were matrilineal). While the data are inconclusive because of the small size of the sample, they do raise the possibility that there were alternatives to the patrilineal model.

72. This subject has been treated in far greater depth for Tamil Nadu; see Orr 2000.

73. Note that Susan Bayly argues for a similar fluidity in South Indian religious identities of the precolonial period, although with scant evidence (1989: 1–70).

Chapter 3

1. See the critique of Appadurai and Breckenridge in Dirks 1987: 286–89.

2. I should clarify that I am referring to the period from the late third century onward. Prior to that time, there are numerous stone inscriptions in Andhra that record gifts made

at Buddhist *stūpas* by a range of donors. The two most renowned Buddhist sites of Andhra were Amaravati and Nagarjunakonda, both in the lower Krishna River valley.

3. The inscription is called the Kondamudi Plates of Jayavarman (EI 6.31). I am adopting K. Nilakanta Sastri's dating for this record (1966: 105), but D. C. Sircar believes it was composed in the fourth century (1965: 107).

4. During the second half of the fourteenth century alone, kings and chiefs of the Kondavidu Reddi and Recherla Nayaka lineages and of Vijayanagara's Sangama dynasty cited Hemadri in the following inscriptions: EI 14.4; HAS 19 Mn.35; IAP-C 2.6; NDI Kanigiri 10; SII 10.555.

5. Copper-plate grants from the Kakatiya period are ARE A.5 of 1915, A.10 and A.11 of 1918–19, A.1 of 1961–62; *Bhārati* 15: 555ff., 36: 4ff., 37: 11ff.; CPIHM I.10 and 11; EA 4.11, 4.12-A and B; EI 18.41 and 38.16; HAS 6; IAP-K appendix; NDI copper plate 17. Traditional grants of brahman villages that were formerly recorded on copper were sometimes inscribed in stone in the thirteenth century, however; see APAS 38.14 and 15; ARE 282 of 1935–36 and 16 of 1943–44; EI 34.13; IAP-C 1.109; NDI Kavali 35 and 39, Ongole 17; SII 6.204, 228, 229, 237; SII 10.248.

6. E.g., APRE 5 of 1966; ARE 282 of 1935–36; CTI 22; IAP-W. 57; NDI Kandukur 60 and 62; SII 10.259 and 312.

7. The use of Tamil terms in some Vaishnava grants of the Kakatiya period is evidence for the growing impact of Shrivaishnava doctrine. Several different terms with the Tamil honorific prefix *tiru* appear. The word *tirupratiṣṭha* (meaning "installation of a form of Vishnu") occurs in NDI Kanigiri 24 (Prakasam District) and HAS 19 Ng.2 (Nalgonda District). The term *tirumuṭṭamu* occurs in NDI Kanigiri 24, ARE 26 of 1929–30 (Guntur District), and SII 4.700 (Guntur District). It designates a Vaishnava temple (Iswara Dutt 1967: 12).

8. Donations were sometimes given to provide for lamps lit only at the times of worship and several of these specify that the *sandhya* was performed twice daily (NDI Kavali 23, 29, 31, and 43). ARE 39a of 1929–30 refers to three periods of worship, however, while a midday service (*ardhajāmu avasaramu*) is endowed in SII 5.131.

9. Besides the Sanskrit term *naivēdya*, it is also referred to as *amudupaḍi* or *ōgirālu* (e.g., SII 4.979; SII 10.218). Endowments also provided for the offering of flowers, for decorating the image, or for supplying sandalwood paste and unguents.

10. For more on the role of women in temple ritual, see Orr 1993 and forthcoming.

11. E.g., SII 6.162 (*dama tanḍri Ritta Nalle Bōyunikin dama talli Nūṅkkāsānikini dharmārthamugā)* and SII 10.456 (*tama tallidanḍrulakum bunyamugānu*).

12. *Śiva-lōka* appears in APRE 116 of 1965; ARE 13 of 1973–74; EI 3.17; HAS 13.48; SII 6.144; and Parabrahma Sastry 1974. Other terms for "heaven" are *puṇya-lōka, para-lōka,* and *Vaikuṇṭha-lōka* (the Vaishnava heaven), figuring in ARE 366 of 1915; HAS 13.50, HAS 19 Mn.18; IAP-W.69; NDI Ongole 150; SII 10.471 and 472.

13. EI 3.16, vv.16–17; based on the translation from Sanskrit of E. Hultzsch (1894–95b: 102).

14. Phillip B. Wagoner has identified a particular style of Telangana temple architecture from the Kakatiya era that embodies funerary and memorial connotations (1995).

15. The actual *number* of temples built in Andhra at this time is not large when compared to other regions and eras. In the 150 years between 1300 and 1450, for instance, 358 new temples were constructed in only a portion of the Tamil country, according to a study conducted by Burton Stein (1978: 21). But the *percentage* of inscriptions recording the establishment of new temples in Andhra is high, evidence that a substantial proportion of resources were diverted to this end.

16. The temple corpus of this chapter contains 963 distinct acts of religious gifting (by individuals, joint groups, and corporate bodies) contained in 814 separately inscribed epigraphs. Because my emphasis is on endowments here, I have chosen to consider the 963

instances of religious gifting as separate records and use the word "inscription" to describe them although it is not strictly accurate. Only inscriptions situated at the temples to which they document endowments are included; see column C of Appendix B, pt. 1 for a list. Occasionally, inscriptions were also placed at the village where land was being given away, in order to publicize the transfer of ownership embodied in the gift.

17. This is the first line of an often-quoted benedictory-imprecatory verse. The complete verse would run, "He who steals land, whether donated by himself or by another, will be reborn as a maggot living in excrement for the (next) 60,000 years." Note that the beginnings and endings of inscriptions are the portions most likely to be abraded and hence difficult to read.

18. APRE 93 and 198 of 1965 and 408 of 1967; HAS 3.1; HAS 13.41, 42, 52; IAP-K. 29 and 38; IAP-W. 39 and 54—all from Telangana—and also SII 10.289 from Guntur District.

19. I have found about twenty instances of it from the Vijayanagara period, including IAP-C 2.106 and 3.215; NDI Udayagiri 46; ARE 369 and 397 of 1940–41.

20. The following inscriptions all record the excavation of a tank: APAS 31.26; APRE 193, 197, and 198 of 1965, 286 of 1966; APRE 408 of 1967; ARE 19 of 1971–72; EA 1.7; EI 34.13; HAS 3.1; HAS 4; HAS 13.1, 41, 42, 43, 51, and 52; HAS 19 Km.1, Km.15, Mn.17, Mn.18; IAP-C 1.131, 1.159; IAP-K.29 and 38; IAP-W.38, 39, and 54; NDI Darsi 24, Darsi 74, Nellore 106, Ongole 138, Ongole 139 and Udayagiri 3; SII 10. 289, 10.312, 10.340, and 10.472.

21. Vv. 17–20, translation from Sanskrit by Sreenivasachar (1940: 120–21). This inscription comes from Pillalamarri, Nalgonda District.

22. Kakatiya-period inscriptions that mention the *sapta-santāna* include APRE 194 of 1965 and 192 of 1996; EA 1.7; EI 3.15; HAS 13.56; IAP-W.49 and 50; SII 6.100, 620, and 628. The concept also appears in several post-Kakatiya inscriptions and literary works (Somasekhara Sarma 1948: 91, 370n.25).

23. The tank foundation inscriptions are distributed throughout Telangana, the southern coastal districts, and Cuddapah in Rayalasima. They are most concentrated in Telangana, however, particularly in Warangal and Khammam Districts.

24. Warriors used the term in reference to land over which they had proprietary rights and could alienate—*nija-vritti* or *tana-vritti*, "my subsistence grant" (ARE 317 of 1934–35 and 346 of 1937–38; NDI Atmakur 55; SII 5.55; SII 10.291, 321, 388).

25. Pilgrims from other areas might also purchase lands for donation near a popular temple, as sometimes happened at Draksharama—a situation where local land-controllers received personal gain from their proximity to a temple (Krishna Kumari 1987: 427).

26. In SII 4.751, for example, only 7 cows were required in order to establish a *sandhya* lamp at the Malleshvara temple in Vijayavada. For a perpetual lamp, 25 cows were always given at this temple.

27. Similar points have been noticed by George W. Spencer (1968) in relation to the livestock grants at the Tanjavur Rajarajeshvara temple, where all assignments were to groups of herders and 361 men were named, to whom thousands of animals donated by 32 people were given.

28. APRE 248 of 1965; HAS 19 Mn.46; IAP-K.38; SII 5.116, SII 10.314, 358, 413, 427, 447, 455, and 528.

29. For Tirupati, see Stein 1960 and Breckenridge 1986; on Madurai, Appadurai and Breckenridge 1976, Fuller 1984; on Tanjavur, Spencer 1968, Heitzman 1997: 121–42; on Puri, Eschmann et al. 1978.

30. The figures here are slightly different from those in Talbot 1991, an earlier treatment of the topic. Because I have been able to collect more unpublished inscriptions since that time, the corpus I study here is larger.

31. The three *liṅgas* are those at Srisailam and Kaleshvaram (Karimnagar District), besides

Draksharama; while the five *ārāmas* consist of Kumararama at Samalkot-Bhimavaram (East Godavari District), Kshirarama at Palakol, Amararama at Amaravati, and Bhimarama at Gunupudi-Bhimavaram (West Godavari), in addition to Draksharama.

32. In a variant of this story, Taraka actually had a Shiva *liṅga* in his throat. Pieces of this *liṅga* shattered and landed at the five sites in Andhra (Ramesan 1962: 90–92).

33. Inscriptions from Kshirarama are discussed by Ramachandra Murthy 1981. A temple at a fourth *ārāma*, the Chalukya-Bhimeshvara temple of Kumararama in East Godavari District, received several endowments during the Kakatiya period, although it does not rank among the major institutions.

34. This is true of the *liṅgas* at Kumararama (Samalkot-Bhimavaram), Bhimarama (Gudipudi-Bhimavaram), and Draksharama, according to Rao (1973: 222), and of the Amararama *liṅga*, according to Ramesan (1962: 88). I have not been able to ascertain the shape or size of the Kshirarama *liṅga*.

35. See discussion in Sundaram 1968: 46; Nilakanta Sastri and Venkataramanayya 1960: 300; Ramachandra Murthy 1983a: 307.

36. On the grounds of the Rameshvara temple at Velpuru is a stone pillar bearing an inscription of the sixth- and seventh-century Vishnukundin dynasty (SII 10.1). This temple was patronized from the beginning of the twelfth century onward by the Kota kings based in Amaravati. The Vallabha temple at Srikakulam received a few donations from members of the Parichchhedi family, another minor dynasty of the coastal area. It may have roots in the Eastern Chalukya period since one of the favorite dynastic titles of those kings was "*pṛthvī-vallabha*." Eluru, where the Someshvara temple is located, was the capital of the chiefs known as the Saronathas or Kolani Mandalikas. Tadikalpudi was the capital of a minor noble family of Vengi, claiming descent from the Eastern Chalukyas, between the twelfth and fourteenth centuries (Yasodadevi 1949–50: 142–43 and 1950–52: 66). The Bhimeshvara temple at Mogallu can also tentatively be dated to the era of the Eastern Chalukyas, when several other Bhimeshvara temples (as at Draksharama) were constructed.

37. Simhachalam inscriptions are listed by Sundaram in his book on that site (1969) and are discussed in Berkemer 1992. Inscriptions from temples in Srikakulam District have been published in Ramesan and Mukunda Row 1980. Ramachandra Murthy has analyzed the records from the Srikurman temple in that district (1983b).

38. Because the inland districts received so little in the way of religious patronage as compared to those on the coast, the actual numbers of minor temples found in them are quite small. But minor temples were very significant institutions for most of the interior, in the sense that they received a large share of all the religious gifts made there. The more centrally located districts of Guntur, Prakasam, Nellore, Nalgonda, and Mahbubnagar fall somewhere in between the two extremes described above.

39. The remaining one-third of all individual donations, covered in the category "other" in table 9, were made by men who either possessed no status title or who possessed a status title other than *bōya*, *seṭṭi*, *rāju*, *reḍḍi*, *mahārāja*, or *nāyaka*. Numerous endowments were also made by corporate bodies and joint groups of donors but are not included in table 9.

40. For example, ARE 76 of 1958–59; IAP-K.38; SII 5.136, 137, 148, and 152.

41. V.33, translation from Sanskrit by Sreenivasachar 1940: 151.

42. APRE 358 of 1966 and 407 of 1967; ARE 325 of 1934–35 and 322 of 1937–38; EI 3.15; HAS 13.49, HAS 19 Mn.41 and 46; IAP-W.61 and 69; SII 10.373. In one case the deity was named after the overlord's religious teacher (ARE 40 of 1942–43).

43. They are APRE 286 and 358 of 1966; ARE 21 and 26 of 1929–30, 321 of 1930–31, 261 of 1932–33, 274 and 285 of 1949–50, 89 of 1958–59; *Bhārati* 54:56; EA 4.14; EI 3.15 and 6.15; HAS 13.11, 18, 25, 34, 41, 43, 53, HAS 19 Mn.4, 5 and 41, Ng.1 and 2; IAP-C 1.137, 1.156; IAP-K.38; IAP W.40, 61, 65, 73; NDI Atmakur 24, Darsi 35 and 70, Kanigiri 24, Kavali 31 and 51; SII 4.933 and 939, SII 5.70 and 131, SII 6.120, 165, 214, 228, SII

10.274, 275, 276, 282, 289, 295, 309, 331, 333, 334, 351, 352, 373, 375, 377, 386, 412, 420, 422, 427, 452, 465, 475, 489, 526, 533, 544.

Chapter 4

1. Within the fourteen districts of Andhra that are being considered in this chapter (see dotted area on map 3), Kakatiya inscriptions comprise slightly less than one-third of all dated inscriptions (350 out of 1,190, or 29 percent). There are also close to 100 undated Kakatiya inscriptions, listed in pt. 2 of Appendix B. But it is likely that Kakatiya influence was more extensive than indicated by these figures, since subordinates sometimes issued inscriptions without citing their overlords.

2. The political chronology in the following pages is largely based on Venkataramanayya and Somasekhara Sarma 1960 and Parabrahma Sastry 1978. The two works agree on most matters. Where they differ, I have followed Parabrahma Sastry, since he collected and edited many previously unknown Kakatiya-period inscriptions.

3. Although the building of the Svayambhudeva temple has been ascribed to Ganapati in the secondary literature (Yazdani 1960: 743), its positioning at the center of the original planned city provides strong evidence to the contrary. Aside from inscriptional evidence, later historical memory as manifested in the fifteenth-century *Śivayōgasāramu* text also attributes the construction of Warangal to Rudradeva.

4. IAP-W.37, SII 10.241, HAS 13.52; Raghavan 1979: 104.

5. These are recorded in SII 10.241 and SII 4.1155, respectively. Rudradeva's other benefactions are documented in CTI 26, IAP-W.37 and 41.

6. Two other records from Draksharama do mention Rudradeva's name, but they both predate Rudradeva's own inscription of 1186. Neither the inscription issued ca. 1158 by one of his ministers (SII 4.1107) or that of his queen dated ca. 1168 (SII 4.1095) state that Rudradeva was ruling the area. I therefore must disagree with Venkataramanayya and Somasekhara Sarma (1960: 591), who assert that Rudradeva conquered the area around Draksharama. Similarly, there is little hard evidence of Rudradeva's presence in Guntur. An early inscription dated in 1170 from Tsandavolu in that district does cite Rudradeva as overlord. But the Kakatiya conquest of the Kotas has been inferred by Andhra historians from an epithet borne by one of Rudradeva's generals. Kota inscriptions themselves do not acknowledge Kakatiya overlordship until several decades later.

7. Out of the 13 endowments, 10 are gifts made directly by Ganapati alone, 1 was made in conjunction with daughter and successor Rudramadevi, and 2 more endowments were made by his subordinates on his order. The ones from Guntur and Prakasam are ARE 310 of 1930–31; EI 27.35; NDI Darsi 27 and Ongole 17; SII 6.204, 206, and 214; SII 10.248, 371, and 395. The others are ARE 132 of 1954–55; *Bhārati* 37: 4; and *Indian Antiquary* 21: 197–202.

8. The damaged inscription that documents the establishment of the Kumara-Ganapeshvara temple (EI 27.35) is located in the nearby village of Nayanapalli, where presumably some lands endowed to the new temple were situated. At present, no known temple at Motupalli houses a deity named Kumara-Ganapeshvara. But it seems quite likely that the temple where Ganapati's only inscription from Motupalli (the one that addresses tolls on the sea trade) is located might have been the one he had constructed, although its deity is today known as Virabhadreshvara.

9. Rudramadevi actually seems to have shared the throne with her father for the two-year period 1261–1262. She became sole ruler in 1263.

10. This is the position taken by Parabrahma Sastry (1974), on the basis of an inscription discovered fairly recently. Venkataramanayya and Somasekhara Sarma (1960), on the other hand, believe that Rudramadevi lived until 1295.

11. The 350 dated Kakatiya inscriptions figuring in tables 11 and 12 are indicated in

column D of Appendix B, pt. 1, while 829 other dated (but non-Kakatiya) inscriptions from the territory of Kakatiya Andhra are indicated in column E.

12. He was, however, a considerable patron of literature. The most famous work composed at his court is the text on Sanskrit poetics and dramaturgy (*alaṅkāra)* by Vidyanatha known as *Pratāparudrīya* or *Pratāparudra Yaśōbhūṣaṇa*, which circulated widely in the peninsula up to the twentieth century. Each verse that illustrates a principle of poetics in this treatise eulogizes its royal patron Prataparudra, an innovation that was imitated by some later authors (Raghavan 1979: 2).

13. Prataparudra's gifts are recorded in EA 4.13; SII 4.759, SII 10.492 and 496.

14. Inscriptions in Tamil and Kannada are not enumerated in table 12. Since they are found primarily in Nellore and Cuddapah Districts, including them would not significantly affect the conclusions to be drawn from the table. Anantapur and Chittoor Districts also yield a number of non-Telugu records.

15. Medieval literature also mentions the performance of gift ceremonies known as *mahādānas*, in which sovereigns gave stupendous quantities of valuable goods to brahmans (Inden 1978). But since the ceremonies were one-time affairs and involved the alienation of movable items, they were not recorded in inscriptions.

16. We can assume this temple was also constructed by Rudradeva, although we cannot say for certain since so little of it remains.

17. The neglect of Telangana by the Kakatiya rulers was somewhat mitigated by the religious activities of a few female members of the royal family. Two of Ganapati's sisters, Mailama and Kundamba, made numerous gifts in various parts of Telangana during the early part of his reign (APAS 31.20; APRE 193, 194, 197, and 198 of 1965; EA 1.7; IAP-W.46, 57, 58, 59, 60). Lakmadevi, Prataparudra's queen, also made a donation to a Telangana temple (IAP-K.37).

18. In one of his last published works, Stein identified Nicholas B. Dirks's study of Pudukkottai as the best explication of ritual sovereignty, one that is "more clearly and better specified than in my work" (1995: 156). He also rejected his own earlier insistence on two separate spheres of ritual and political sovereignty, stating that "I am now convinced that in India the proposition is incorrect, that lordship for Hindus always and necessarily combined ritual and political authority" (p. 160).

19. Indeed, Stein has criticized Kulke on these very grounds: "Kulke proposes something he calls an 'integrative polity' where the sole specified means of royal incorporation seems to be the symbolic capture of local, 'tribal' godlings by the royal cult of Jagannatha of whom the first worshipper was the Ganga or Gajapati ruler. How this incorporation was achieved and whether it was or can have been the sole political process at work is left unclear" (1995: 142). Despite its lack of specificity, however, Kulke's work is groundbreaking in its recognition that states expanded by absorbing tribal peoples and deities. He has also consistently emphasized the growth processes of states in a way that few other scholars have.

20. We see this twice in the case of the Kakatiyas, with Ganapati's gift at the Ekamranatha temple at Kanchipuram and Prataparudra's endowment to the Srirangam temple in the Kaveri River delta. Such inscriptions attested to the intruding king's presence in his enemy's turf. At other times, kings chose to appropriate images from temples within their rivals' territories (and particularly from those within enemy capitals) and bring them back home so that their own subjects would witness their might (Davis 1997: 51–87).

21. The same can be said of the Tamil epithets of the imperial Chola kings. See SII 2.1 for Rajaraja's titles and SII 2.11 for those of Rajendra.

22. Both *calamarti* and *jagadāḷa* are archaic terms and have been translated somewhat differently. See, for example the differing translations of *jagadāḷa* in HAS 13.52 and NDI Darsi 35. My rendering of *calamarti-gaṇḍa* is based on the discussion of the term in Sreenivasachar 1940: 202.

23. Rahu is a legendary demon whose head was severed from his body by Vishnu after the sun and moon discovered that he was deceitfully trying to drink the ambrosia that the gods had churned from the ocean. Because Rahu had managed to imbibe some of the ambrosia before being caught, his head became immortal and remains fixed in the sky. From there, he periodically revenges himself on the sun and the moon by swallowing them (i.e., by causing eclipses).

24. Translation from Sanskrit by E. Hultzsch (1894–95a: 92).

25. Jaya Senapati actually was quite learned and wrote a Sanskrit treatise on dance-drama called the *Nṛttaratnāvali* later in his life (Raghavan 1965: 9).

26. Through the use of puns, the poet suggests that the king deserved jewels both because of his innate greatness and because he was like the traditional sources of precious gems—mountains (i.e., mines) and oceans.

27. The reality of an overlord's dependence on his subordinate, despite "the latter's rhetoric of renunciation and histrionic self-abasement," has been noted in an analysis of the relationship between the Vijayanagara emperor Krishnadeva Raya and Vishvanatha Nayaka, the lord of Madurai (Narayana Rao, Shulman, and Subrahmanyam 1992: 52).

28. Elsewhere *baṇṭu* may have just meant a warrior or soldier who had sworn a personal oath of allegiance to someone, since several *nāyakas* attached to non-Kakatiya rulers call themselves their lord's *baṇṭu* (e.g., SII 5.203, SII 10.301).

29. Individual *rautus* figure in APAS 31.33; IAP-N 1.89; IAP-W.42; and SII 10.287.

30. Note that elephants also played a significant role in Kakatiya-period warfare and numerous Kakatiya donors bear the title of *gaja-sahiṇi*. But while these men may have been in charge of elephant troops, they do not appear to have ridden elephants themselves. Elite warriors are consistently praised as horse riders and never in reference to elephants.

31. The figures come from Amir Khusrau and Isami, who wrote in the early and mid fourteenth centuries, respectively. However, Peter Hardy notes that early Indo-Muslim chroniclers were known to disregard the facts at times (1982: 115–21).

32. Its main weakness relative to the Khalji and Tughluq armies of the Delhi sultanate, which it shared with other South Indian armies, was the absence of mounted archers (Deloche 1989: 34; Wink 1997: 81–82).

33. See Michell 1992 for maps and photographs of the fortifications.

34. Among the few scholars to rigorously examine political intermediaries are James Heitzman, Noboru Karashima, and Y. Subbarayalu.

35. I counted as subordinates only those people who cited a Kakatiya overlord and also wielded political power. All men of noble lineage (as defined in the following paragraphs) were deemed to possess political power, but among non-nobles only those men who held administrative titles, possessed *nāyaṅkaramu* rights, and/or bore the status titles of *leṅka* and *aṅgarakṣa* were included.

36. The Chalukyas claimed a lunar pedigree, while the Cholas and Pallavas claimed descent from the solar race. Examples of claims to solar/lunar ancestry appear in SII 4.735; EI 38.16; and IAP-C 1.137. Yadava descent is asserted in HAS 13.34.

37. HAS 13.17, ll.1–9; see also HAS 13.37 and 43.

38. About one-fifth of all Kakatiya officers (18 out of 87) paid some form of respect to another lord or officer in addition to the Kakatiya overlord.

39. The formulaic phrase "ruling the earth enjoying friendly interchanges" originally appeared in the records of many chiefly lineages that were subordinate to the Chalukyas of Kalyani (Desai 1951: 310). The Kakatiyas had used this phrase and the epithets *pati-hita-carita* (whose actions are for the good of his lord) and *vinaya-bhūṣaṇa* (for whom modesty is an ornament) since the days when they acknowledged Chalukya overlordship, and retained them even afterward, despite their inappropriateness.

40. The *gaṇḍa-peṇḍāra* was an anklet worn as a badge of honor by distinguished warriors

and an epithet included in the list of *birudas*. Images of defeated foes were occasionally affixed to this anklet (Somasekhara Sarma 1948: 248).

41. Table 13 enumerates only people who made individual endowments that were recorded in relatively undamaged inscriptions (listed in column F, pt. 1 of Appendix B). Since some of the donors cannot be classified as either officers or nobles, the numbers under the column "Total" are larger than the combined sums of these two categories of subordinates. The figures in this table are smaller than those in table 11 both because collective and joint endowments are omitted and because they are based on the number of donors rather than on the number of inscriptions they issued.

42. Because it is often unclear whether an official title applies to the donor in an inscription or to the male relative whose name is mentioned beforehand, all men from a particular family have to be included in the count. Since I am mainly interested in the comparative importance of the noble class versus the officer class, I also counted female family members.

43. Ten different men bearing the *aṅgarakṣa* title seem to be referred to in the following records: ARE 240 of 1935; *Bhārati* 54: 56ff.; SII 4.705 and 707, SII 6.591, SII 10.423, 424, 451, 425, 375, 444, 539.

44. A sample of *leṅka* records is found in HAS 19 Mn.18; IAP-C 1.157; SII 10.491, 509, and 520. *Leṅkas* are discussed in Mahalingam 1955: 64–65 and Settar 1982: 197.

45. See APRE 248 of 1965; HAS 13.35, HAS 19 Ng.2; IAP-K.38; SII 10.450 and 505.

46. Devari Nayaka figures in NDI Darsi 35; SII 10.495, 505, and 526, SII 26.617; and EA 4.13 (the latter gift is also recorded in EI 27.48).

47. Kota subordinates appear in ARE 293 and 304 of 1932–33, ARE 299, 318, 325 of 1934–35; SII 4.933; SII 6.216, SII 10.208, 289, 291, 406.

48. Between 1211 and 1269, inscriptions from this region that did not mention the Kakatiyas far outnumbered those that did (62 non-Kakatiya to 20 Kakatiya). From 1270 onward, the number of non-Kakatiya inscriptions was still larger (22 non-Kakatiya to 20 Kakatiya), but the proportion of inscriptions that mentioned the Kakatiyas had increased.

49. Officers were more likely as a class to consistently acknowledge the Kakatiyas than were nobles, as is evident in the instances when subordinates issued more than one record. Of the 19 nobles who commissioned two or more inscriptions, two-thirds (13) failed to mention the Kakatiyas on at least one occasion; only one-fifth of such officers (3 out of 15) failed to do so.

50. ARE 19 of 1971–72 contains another reference to *rāca-siddhāya*, while a second village collective endowing a proportion of a cash tax due to a lord (*rācavārikim beṭṭeḍi pahiṇḍi)* appears in IAP-N 1.101.

51. Plots of land from "my own" maintenance grants were given in NDI Kandukur 29 (*dama jīvita-vargamaina*) and SII 10.377 (*tama jītāla-polamu*).

52. The inscriptions documenting remissions of taxes are ARE 303 of 1932–33, 307 and 328 of 1934–35; IAP-K.37; NDI Darsi 35; SII 4.952, SII 10.304, 492, 496, 497, 509, 521, 540. Gifts of tax incomes are ARE 26 and 94 of 1929–30, ARE 314, 321, 324, 332 of 1930–31, ARE 240 of 1935–36, ARE 295 of 1936–37, ARE 28 of 1961–62; APRE 248 of 1965; CTI 35; EA 4.14; HAS 3.2, HAS 13.2 and 54, HAS 19 Mn.32 and 33; IAP-C 1.157, IAP-K.38, IAP-N 1.84, 89, 101; SII 6.652, SII 26.617, SII 10.314, 317, 328, 413, 427, 443, 445, 447, 455, 528, 530. Damaged inscriptions that seem to record tax gifts (but were not included in the count) are ARE 25 of 1941–42; HAS 19 Km.5; IAP-K.36, IAP-N 1.92, IAP-W.93; SII 10.401.

53. Whereas only 11 tax grants or remissions occurred in the sixty years of Ganapati's reign, there were 14 instances when Rudramadevi ruled, and 23 while Prataparudra was king.

54. Stein has noted that South Indian dynasties based in the dry inland expanses—a phenomenon noticeable from the thirteenth century onward—relied more heavily on revenues from trade than did earlier polities centered in the fertile wet lands with their ample agricultural revenues (1989: 15–17).

55. There is an isolated occurrence of the phrase *nāyaṅkaramu* in an early-twelfth-century inscription from Tripurantakam (SII 10.68). The epigraphist N. Mukunda Row believes *nāyaṅkaramu* also appears in another twelfth-century record from Narayanapuram (1991: 73), but an earlier reading of this inscription (SII 10.761) differs from his version. Even if the latter case were proven true, a total of two occurrences is insignificant. While the concept of *nāyaṅkaramu* could conceivably have predated the Kakatiya period, its meaningful implementation evolved only under Rudramadevi.

56. ARE 39a of 1929–30; NDI Ongole 98; SII 10.499. Another inscription relating to the *nāyaṅkaramu* holder in the first of these inscriptions makes it clear that he actually was a Kakatiya subordinate, however (ARE 13 of 1941–42).

57. ARE 39a of 1929–30 and 278 of 1935–36; *Bhārati* 54: 56ff.; CTI 35; EA 4.14; HAS 13.26, HAS 19 Mn.41 and Ng.4; IAP-K.38, IAP-N 1.93; NDI Kandukur 1 and 23, Kavali 36, Ongole 98; SII 4.705, SII 10.422, 423, 424, 451, 459, 499, 509, and 526.

58. One *nāyaṅkaramu* holder was a *cakravarti*, possibly a Chalukya prince related to Rudramadevi's husband (IAP-N 1.93). The other calls himself a *mahārāja* but is not a member of a known family and appears in only one record (IAP-K.38).

59. Note that Rudramadevi is the monarch signified in this record, although the masculine name Rudradeva is used. "Winter solstice" is my translation for *uttarāyaṇa-saṅkrānti*, which was observed on January 6 in 1270 C.E. See note 13 in chapter 2 for more on *uttarāyaṇa-saṅkrānti*.

60. See *Bhārati* 54: 56ff.; SII 4.705, SII 10.423, 424, and 451. There were two other possessors of *nāyaṅkaramu* rights during Rudramadevi's reign, who both appear in HAS 19 Mn.41.

61. CTI 35; IAP-K.38; SII 10.422, 499, 509; and EA 4.14.

62. Because previous analyses of Kakatiya-period *nāyaṅkaramu* were not based on systematic examination of the term's usage and context, they failed to recognize that it was a relatively late phenomenon (Venkataramanayya and Somasekhara Sarma 1960: 668–69; Parabrahma Sastry 1978: 195–96). They also assume that *nāyaṅkaramu* was awarded to all Kakatiya military officials in exchange for tribute and the maintenance of troops, as described in relation to the Vijayanagara empire (Sewell 1982: 281, 374, and 389), but this assumption cannot be justified on the basis of the existing evidence.

63. Inscriptions issued before Rudramadevi's reign are ARE 244 of 1935–36; SII 4.934, SII 10.381. Those from Rudrama's reign: ARE 775 of 1922; *Bhārati* 54: 56ff.; IAP-N 1.80; SS: 239–43. Prataparudra is cited by village collectives in the following records: ARE 317 of 1930–31 and 313 of 1932–33; EA 4.14; HAS 13.26, 30, 53, HAS 19 Km.6, Km.7, Km.14; IAP-N 1.92, 93, 100, 101, IAP-W.86 and 90; NDI Darsi 35 and Ongole 58; SII 10.489, 495, 526, 533; SS: 258–64; TS 2 Kak.11. ARE 330 of 1924 was also issued when Prataparudra was king but does not mention him. There are an additional four instances during Prataparudra's reign where village collectives give their consent to gifts, all involving the granting of taxes by Kakatiya officers (ARE 28 of 1961–62; *Bhārati* 55: 40; EA 14.14; HAS 13.54).

64. For discussion and bibliography on feudalism in India, see Kulke 1995b: 6–18 and Chattopadhyaya 1994: 185–95. Among the more noteworthy critiques of the feudalistic model are Kumar 1985, Mukhia 1981 and 1985, and Wink 1990. John Deyell's impressive monograph on early medieval North Indian monetary history (1990) refutes one of the central tenets of the school of Indian feudalism.

65. This aspect of Stein's formulation—the artificial distinction between a "real" form of physical dominance and a "symbolic" form of ritual dominance—was rightly criticized by

Kulke (1982: 253–55). Also see Inden 1990: 208–9 and Dirks 1987: 404. For Stein's retraction, see 1995: 160.

66. Kulke doubts that the *nāḍus* of the Tamil country were as autonomous as Stein has suggested (1982: 255–62), while Karashima believes they were not as important (1984: xxv–xxviii). It should also be noted that Stein's assertion that the *nāṭṭār* peasant assembly was the typical governing body of the Chola wet zone is questionable. Heitzman reports that Pudukkottai, the driest of the five subregions he studied, yielded half the references to the *nāṭṭār* in his corpus of Chola inscriptions (1987: 53). Karashima observes that inscriptional references to the *nāṭṭār* are more common in Pandya and Vijayanagara inscriptions than in those from the Chola period (1984: xxvi).

67. The *sthala*, ranging from roughly 20 to 60 villages, is the only Andhra territorial unit of the Kakatiya period that is comparable in size to the Chola *nāḍu*, but only 13 of them are named. A slew of designations for other territorial units are found, including *viṣaya*, *rāṣṭra*, and *nāḍu*. Most localities named in inscriptions appear only for brief periods. Among the longer-lasting names are Vengi (coastal taluks in Krishna and Godavari Districts), Kammanadu (Bapatla and Narasaraopet Taluks in Guntur District along with Ongole and Chirala Taluks in Prakasam District), Natavadi (portions of Nandigama and Vijayavada Taluks in Krishna District and Madhira Taluk in Khammam), Pakanadu (contiguous regions of Cuddapah and Nellore Districts), Renadu (parts of Cuddapah and Chittoor Districts), and Velanadu (Tenali and Repalle Taluks in Guntur District). The territories just listed were all mentioned prior to 1000 C.E. and lasted into the Kakatiya period, although the exact area encompassed within each varied over time. See Mangalam 1986 for further details.

68. For example, we are never told that a particular *sthala* lies within a larger territorial unit such as a *nāḍu* or *viṣaya* (although certain villages are located within a *sthala*). Vijayanagara-period inscriptions contain many more references to territorial units, but it is again difficult to discern the various levels of reference. This lack of clarity in Andhra inscriptions stands in sharp contrast to the Tamil practice of carefully citing the location of a village within one or more larger territorial units.

69. For a more detailed discussion, refer back to the section on the agrarian frontier in chapter 1.

70. Stein (1985) has applied a patrimonial model to Vijayanagara, which he concluded was a protopatrimonial state.

Chapter 5

1. Of the large body of literature on social memory and historical writing, I have been most influenced by Fentress and Wickham 1992 and Spiegel 1993. See also Halbwachs 1992, Lowenthal 1985, Connerton 1989, and Comaroff 1992.

2. The three most important are Isami's *Futūḥ-al-Salāṭin*, Amir Khusrau's *Khazā'in-al-Futūḥ*, and Barani's *Ta'rīkh-i-Fīrūz Shāhi*. Excerpts from all three are provided in Venkataramanayya 1942. English translations of the relevant portions of the *Khazā'in-al-Futūṭḥ* and *Ta'rīkh-i-Fīrūz Shāhi* are included in vol. 3 of Elliot and Dowson 1966.

3. The ostensible aim of the campaign was the restoration of Sundara Pandya to his throne, but it coincided with the Kakatiya desire to quell disturbances in southern Andhra.

4. This and the following paragraph are based on Venkataramanayya 1942: 23–24, 31–43, 83–85, 99–108, 115–19. The same material is summarized in Venkataramanayya and Somasekhara Sarma 1960: 644–57.

5. The one exception is Kolani Rudradeva, a Kakatiya warrior whose last inscription is dated in 1326 (SII 10.535). M. Somasekhara Sarma believes two other Kakatiya generals, Anna Mantri and Recherla Singama Nayaka, also survived the fall of the kingdom (1945: 25–30). Neither appears in an extant inscription, however.

6. There is some disagreement on the exact dating of these events. Here I follow the chronology set forth in Somasekhara Sarma 1945.

7. The Recherla Reddis derived their name from the village Recheruvula (Parabrahma Sastri 1978: 142). According to much later tradition, the Recherla Nayakas were named after an untouchable retainer, Rechadu, who gave up his life so that the founder of the lineage might acquire a buried treasure and asked in return only that the lineage henceforth adopt his name and that a marriage be performed for his descendants every time the lineage was conducting a marriage of its own (Venkataramanayya 1939: 1–6; Rama Row 1875: 3–6). Nonetheless, this version of Recherla Nayaka origins implies an awareness of the earlier Recherla Reddis, for not only does the Nayaka lineage founder start out with the status title *reḍḍi*, but he also establishes a village called Recherla and acquires the alias "Pillalamarri Betala"—Pillalamarri being one of the main sites where the Recherla Reddis had previously flourished.

8. The most detailed discussions of fourteenth-century Andhra political history are to be found in Somasekhara Sarma 1945 and 1948, while Bahmani history is treated in Sherwani 1973a. General coverage of the post-Kakatiya period can be found in Richards 1975: 7–30, Sundaram 1968: 11–16, and in portions of Nilakanta Sastri 1966: 227–312.

9. Published with an analysis and English summary by Venkataramanayya and Somasekhara Sarma 1958. The text itself appears in Somasekhara Sarma 1945: 100–10.

10. The relevant portion of the inscription is published in Somasekhara Sarma 1945: 111–12 and discussed in Ramesan 1974: 354–55.

11. Comparisons to Varaha are common in post-Kakatiya Andhra inscriptions; for example, see EI 36.22, v. 23, a Reddi record from 1403 C.E. that likens Vema Reddi to Vishnu's boar incarnation. Vema was also often praised as an Agastya to the ocean of barbarians, in an allusion to the sage's conquest of the *rākṣasas* (demons) who infested South India (NDI Ongole 73; EI 8.3; CPIHM 1.16). See Pollock 1993: 283n.25 for similar examples from elsewhere in India.

12. Line 19. The text is published in Somasekhara Sarma 1945: 113–17 and discussed in Ramesan 1974: 353–54.

13. Ironically, the Kakatiyas themselves issued very few copper-plate grants.

14. The same *biruda* was claimed by the Kondavidu Reddis of the Panta clan (EI 36.22, v. 21).

15. Venkataramanayya cites one case of a Kakatiya warrior who later became a military officer under Ulugh Khan (1942: 122n.44). There must have been several other such instances, if evidence from the western Deccan can be extrapolated to Andhra. Richard M. Eaton has shown that the Tughluqs incorporated minor chiefs in the former Yadava domain of the northwestern Deccan as *iqṭādārs* (holders of *iqṭā* military service assignments), while recognizing former subordinates of the Hoysalas in the southwestern Deccan as *amīrs*. Among the latter, in his view, were the Sangama brothers Harihara and Bukka, who later repudiated their allegiance to the Tughluqs and founded the Vijayanagara kingdom (Eaton 1997). However, these areas came under much more thorough Muslim control than did Andhra for another two centuries (Richards 1975: 6).

16. In the 1480s Bahmani power disintegrated upon the death of Muhammad Shah II, while Vijayanagara was in the throes of a dynastic usurpation by Saluva Narasimha.

17. Additional secondary sources on Andhra political history after 1450 C.E. are Ramachandra Rao 1988, Subrahmanyam 1973b, and Sherwani 1973b.

18. Fifteenth-century references to Prataparudra are found outside of Telangana as well. One example, a Sanskrit and Kannada inscription from Bellary District, Karnataka, dated ca. 1466 C.E. (ARE 434 of 1923), records the construction of a dam by a man whose father was allegedly born in the family of Prataparudra. A further instance comes from Telugu literature. The *Bhīmēśvara Purāṇamu*, possibly composed around 1430, was dedicated to the minister of a

Reddi king from Rajahmundry in coastal Andhra. The minister's grandfather is said to have been the commander of Prataparudra's elephant corps (Somasekhara Sarma 1948: 523 and 1945: 11).

19. Quotations from vv. 27, 33, and 34 of the grant, translated in Sastri 1932: 23–24.

20. The physical layout of Warangal in the era of Kakatiya Prataparudra, as well as its social and religious life, is further described in the *Krīḍābhirāmamu*, a Telugu work from the early fifteenth century written by a Vijayanagara subordinate called Vallabharaya. While it is noteworthy that a remembrance of Prataparudra's capital should have been produced by a man dwelling outside of Telangana, the work is supposedly based on a Kakatiya-era original composed in Sanskrit (Venkataramanayya and Somasekhara Sarma 1960: 657).

21. This is true, for instance, in the material from ca. 1800 contained in the Mackenzie Collection.

22. Details on Colin Mackenzie are derived from Wilson 1882, Cohn 1992, and Dirks 1993.

23. Letter by Colin Mackenzie dated 1802, cited in full in Johnston n.d.: 69. This version of Kakatiya history is included in the India Office Library and Records, Mackenzie Collections, General Collection (hereafter, Mack. Gen. Coll.) vol. 7, as item 9, "History of the Ancient Rajahs of Waruncull."

24. Report by C. V. Ram included in Mackenzie Collections, Translations (hereafter, Mack. Transl.), Class 12 and cited in Dirks 1993: 297. I am unable to identify which version of Kakatiya history was collected by Ram.

25. The one exception is the short story translated in Mack. Gen. Coll. 8.6 (untitled). It narrates the construction of Pakala Lake by Prataparudra (accomplished through magical means) and the siege of Warangal by the Delhi sultan. Not until a dream helped the sultan to identify two great warriors was Warangal fort successfully assaulted and seized. Prataparudra is said to have died while in captivity in Delhi.

26. Other versions of Kakatiya history collected by Mackenzie are Mack. Transl. 7.22, Mack. Transl. 7.53, and Ms. 97 summarized in Mahalingam 1976: 26–33. See also India Office Library and Records, Elliot Collection, Mss. Eur. D.327, Eur. F.46, and Eur. F.48.

27. Both begin their narratives with the Hidimba ashram, said to be located southwest of the first Kakatiya capital, Hanumakonda, which is directly adjacent to Warangal and is described in the *Siddhēśvara Caritramu*. Its author, Kase Sarvappa, gives his birthplace as Cheruvupalli village in the Bolikonda-sima, located by the editor of the text in the neighborhood of Hanumakonda (Lakshmiranjanam 1960: vi). Ekamranatha, the author of the *Pratāparudra Caritramu*, may also have come from the Warangal area, since he worshiped the same Shaiva deity as did the Kakatiyas (Ramachandra Rao 1984: 4).

28. The *Sōmadēva Rājīyamu* is a mixed verse and prose (*campu*) composition that elaborates on an ancillary tale included within the *Pratāparudra Caritramu*. It has been dated around 1700, providing a terminal date after which Lakshmiranjanam and Ramachandra Rao believe the *Pratāparudra Caritramu* could not have been produced. The *Rāyavācakamu*, a Telugu prose narrative about the Vijayanagara king Krishnadeva Raya, similarly contains material that resembles episodes in the *Pratāparudra Caritramu*. It has recently been dated to about 1600 (Wagoner 1993: 17–23, 41–44, 130).

29. These kings are called the Narapatis (Lords of Men or Infantry) and/or Rayas in the text but the name of their capital, Vidyanagara or Vijayanagara, is explicitly mentioned in numerous places.

30. In her analysis of old French prose chronicles, Gabrielle Spiegel similarly considers that "although the product of clerical writers, [they] nevertheless represent the aspirations and anxieties of the French aristocracy responsible, by its patronage, for their creation" (1993: 6).

31. The relevant inscriptions are ARE 305 of 1920 and 284 of 1932–33; IAP-C 2.69, IAP-K.48; NDI Atmakur 3 and Darsi 73; SII 5.1260, 6.1184, and 10.755.

32. ARE 305 of 1920 and 284 of 1932–33; SII 10.755.

33. For example, the equivalence of the Padmanayakas with the Recherla Nayaka clan is assumed, without any discussion, in the book *Rēcaṟla Padmanāyakulu* (Sastri 1991).

34. They are probably the equivalent of the *kā(m)pu* corporate body of peasants that figures in other Kakatiya-period inscriptions (e.g., ARE 313 of 1932–33; *Bhārati* 54 p. 56ff.; NDI Ongole 58; SII 4.934 and 10.533).

35. Although this Telugu text is traditionally ascribed to Shrinatha, an author who lived in the late fourteenth and early fifteenth centuries, many later works have been falsely attributed to him, including the written version of the Palnad epic (Roghair 1982: 8–12).

36. Bastar had experienced Telugu warrior rule as early as the late first millennium, when a number of Telugu Choda inscriptions were issued there (Nagaraju 1995: 14).

37. The 785 records were culled from a larger body of 921 Andhra Vijayanagara inscriptions in Telugu or Sanskrit and represent those inscriptions that could be firmly dated and located geographically. Copper-plate grants and heavily damaged stone inscriptions are not included in these figures.

38. See SII 16.53, 109, 165, 169, 181, 199, 299.

39. Again we see echoes of the sixteenth-century reality in this recollection of the fourteenth century. The Krishna River *was* the traditional northern boundary of the Vijayanagara sphere in Andhra, but only after the decline of the Reddis in the early fifteenth century. Bidar was indeed a Muslim center in Karnataka, but it did not become the capital of the Bahmanis until about 1425 (Sherwani 1973a: 165).

40. One historical account collected by the Mackenzie team, which continues the narrative found in the *Pratāparudra Caritramu* up through the eighteenth century, states that the Vijayanagara king Krishnadeva Raya drove the Muslims out of Warangal and then provided maintenance to the "chiefs of the Kakatiya dynasty" (Nilakanta Sastri and Venkataramanayya 1946, 3: 114; summarized in Mahalingam 1976: 26–33). In this version, the histories of Vijayanagara and the Kakatiyas are hence brought into conjunction again in a later time period, reinforcing the notion of a connection between the two.

41. Mirroring the reduction in Vijayanagara power after 1565 is the drop in number of Vijayanagara inscriptions produced within Andhra. Whereas 574 records dated between 1500 and 1565 survive, there are only 116 inscriptions issued from 1566 to 1649. The decline is particularly noticeable from the 1580s onward. The area within which Vijayanagara inscriptions are found also steadily diminishes. Virtually no records are found outside Rayalasima and the neighboring coastal district Nellore after 1565. The majority were issued in Anantapur, in the modern state's southwestern corner.

42. See discussion in chapter 1, where the gradual southward movement of Telugu inscriptions was identified as one of the major trends of the post-Kakatiya centuries.

43. Bellary: SII 16.99, 177, 216, 254. North and South Arcot: ARE 30 of 1933–34; SII 16.68, 245, 325.

44. E.g., ARE 573 of 1916, 341 of 1950–51, 322 of 1952–53; SII 16.312.

45. Map 1 in Irschick 1994 shows the distribution of Telugu speakers in Tamil Nadu in 1931 in relation to the elevation of the areas where they resided.

46. Wagoner believes that the story of the foundation of Vijayanagara city in the *Rāyavācakamu* also bears strong structural similarities to the Madhavavarman story in the *Pratāparudra Caritramu*. In the former, the city itself empowers the Vijayanagara kings, whereas in the latter the sword and shield Madhavavarman receives from the goddess Padmakshi are the source of the Kakatiya dynasty's power (Wagoner 1993: 41–44).

47. The memories of Prataparudra were not always positive, however. For example, the

late Telugu ballad called *Kumāra Rāmuni Katha*, which narrates the life story of a prince of the short-lived Kampili kingdom of early-fourteenth-century Karnataka, depicts Prataparudra as an enemy of the Kampili king and a tributary of the Delhi sultan. (I thank David Shulman and Sanjay Subrahmanyam for providing me with an unpublished English summary of this work.) Late Kannada historical works like the *Kumāra Rāmana Sāṅgatya* similarly portray relations between the Kampili and Kakatiya kings as ultimately hostile, although Kakatiya assistance had initially been sought by Kampili in its struggle against the Hoysalas (Venkataramanayya and Somasekhara Sarma 1960: 652). The significant aspect of the Kampili traditions for our purposes is that they attempt to prove the greatness and legitimacy of the Kampili kings by portraying them as victorious over, and thereby superior to, several other kingdoms of the period including the Kakatiyas.

48. The *Rāyavācakamu* also uses the title Narapati (Lord of Men; i.e., Lord of Infantry) for the Vijayanagara kings, as does the *Pratāparudra Caritramu*. However, the earliest occurrence of this title is in the 1423 inscription of the Reddi queen Anitalli (Somasekhara Sarma 1945: 111), where it is applied to Kakatiya Prataparudra. When or how usage shifted and the label Lord of Men began to signify the Vijayanagara rather than Kakatiya kings is unclear. But use of the same title for both groups of rulers again suggests that Telugu society perceived a certain continuity between them.

49. Some of them, including the *Vidyāraṇya Kṛti*, are discussed in *Annual Report of the Mysore Archaeological Department* 1932: 100–23, a copy of which was kindly provided to me by Phillip B. Wagoner. Robert Sewell has also recorded several variants of the story (1982: 20–21).

50. This narrative forms part of a longer manuscript volume known as *Vidyāraṇya Kālajñāna* (Vidyaranya's Prophecies), which is preserved in the Mysore Oriental Library—not to be confused with the text of the same name that is extracted in Nilakanta Sastri and Venkataramanayya 1946, 3: 13 (Wagoner, forthcoming).

51. For a discussion of the dating of these texts, see *Annual Report of the Mysore Archaeological Department* 1932: 101. However, it should be noted that Fernão Nuniz, who visited Vijayanagara in the 1530s, was acquainted with a version of the story of the capital's founding that involved the sage Vidyaranya, although he says nothing about the Sangama brothers' alleged prior service with the Kakatiyas (Sewell 1982: 299–300).

52. It is noteworthy that Vidyaranya is explicitly linked with Warangal in at least one of these texts, the *Vidyāraṇya Vṛttānta*, where he is said to be the son of a brahman living in Prataparudra's Warangal (Nilakanta Sastri and Venkataramanayya 1946, 3: 9).

53. For example, Venkataramanayya and Somasekhara Sarma 1960: 642, Parabrahma Sastry 1978: 129 and 195.

54. The *Pratāparudra Caritramu* is not the only text ascribing 70-odd *nāyaka* subordinates to the Kakatiyas. The *Śivayōgasāramu*, a family history of the Induluri chiefs, speaks of 72 Kakatiya *nāyakas*, whereas the *Cāṭupadyamaṇimañjari* (a collection of popular verses) mentions the number 77. One of the Mackenzie manuscripts contains the list of epithets possessed by the Desatla family, who claim to be descended from one of Prataparudra's 72 *nāyakas* (Somasekhara Sarma 1948: 19, 56).

55. Perhaps because of the strong Telugu influence in early modern Tamil Nadu, we also find some memories of Kakatiya Prataparudra transmitted within the Tamil country. There are stories, for example, alleging that the most famous Tamil poet, Kamban, traveled to Prataparudra's court and was honored there (Desikar 1932–33: 103–5). In its narrative covering the first Khalji expedition to the Tamil region, in 1311, the chronicle of the Srirangam temple briefly mentions that the Turkic king defeated Prataparudra in battle and then proceeded to Srirangam (Hari Rao 1961: 24; I am grateful to Vasudha Narayanan for bringing this reference to my attention). Interestingly, there is also a Tamil proverb referring

to the Kakatiyas in a pejorative manner. The expression "I am not a Kakatiya" implies that the speaker is not foolish or helpless (Desikar 1932–33: 107).

56. *Kaifiyat* is a Perso-Arabic word meaning "description, account, remarks." Its singular form in Telugu is *kaifiyyatu*. The Mackenzie project used the term for the village histories that were collected under its auspices, and these Mackenzie accounts continue to be known as *kaifiyats* today.

57. The relevant *kaifiyats* are found in the following, sometimes summarized, formats in Mahalingam 1976: Mss. 90 sect. 1, 95 sect. 1, 99 sect. 1, 99 sect. 4, 105 sect. 3, 106 (a) sect. 6, 106 (b) sect. 8, 106 (c) sect. 10, 110 (a) sect. 1, 110 (b) sect. 2, 114 (a) sect. 1, 114 (b) sect. 2, 114 (c) sect. 7, 114 (d) sect. 7b, 114 (e) sect. 8, 114 (e) sect. 8a, 114 (f) sect. 9c, 114 (g) sect. 9e, 114 (h) sect. 10, 114 (i) sect. 11, 114 (j) sect. 12, 114 (k) sect. 9a, 114 (k) sect. 14, 115 sect. 7, 115 sect. 13a, 116 sect. 2, 117 sect. 8, 117 sect. 16, 118 sect. 9, 118 sect. 11, 120 sect. 6, 121 sect. 7, 123 sect. 12, 124 sect. 10, 124 sect. 12, 127 sect. 11, 128 sect. 1, 128 sect. 10, 132 sects. 1 and 2, 135 (a) sect. 1, 135 (b) sect. 2, 136 sect. 1, 138 sects. 5–19, 140 sect. 1, 141 sect. 5, 144 sect. 12, 144 sect. 15, 146 sect. 28, 147 sect. 6; in Mack. Transl. 7.5, 7.6, 7.11, 7.12, 7.57, 7.59, 8.8, 8.11, 8.20, 8.37, 8.39, 8.42; the *kaifiyats* of Garapadu, Kopparu, Prattipadu, and Turlapadu in Parthasarathy 1982; Nilakanta Sastri and Venkataramanayya 1946, 3: 47 and 114; Sitapati 1982b.

58. I was able to identify the village or taluk locations of 62 out of the total of 68 *kaifiyats* that refer to the Kakatiyas: 29 are in Kurnool District, 19 in Cuddapah District, and 8 in Guntur District. The remaining 6 *kaifiyats* come from four different districts.

59. Inscriptions preserved in local temples are sometimes explicitly said to be the source of information. It is unclear whether the local people decided on their own to utilize inscriptions in composing their village histories or were prompted to do so by the Mackenzie crew. Since the Telugu script had not changed much between the thirteenth and eighteenth centuries, it is quite possible that the contents of inscriptions were already known to the literate.

60. A *kaulu* was a written guarantee of tax rates for a number of years. Often they were intended to promote agrarian settlement in areas that had never been cultivated or had been depopulated for some reason. In these instances, the taxes usually started out very low and gradually increased over the years. Merchants and artisans could also receive a *kaulu* (SII 4.711 and 10.753). The term is borrowed from Perso-Arabic, and the earliest Andhra occurrence is in a Telugu inscription of 1494 C.E. (APAS 31.27).

61. Paraphrased from the versions in Mack. Transl. 8.39 and Mahalingam 1976: 131–32.

62. Summarized and paraphrased from the version in Mack. Transl. 7.11. Prataparudra's son Haripalaka is also mentioned in the *sthala-purāṇa*, or local history, of Kocherlakota, Darsi Taluk (Butterworth and Venugopal Chetty 1990: 336). Ongole, Addanki, and Kocherlakota are all in northern Prakasam District.

63. He is also credited with promoting Shaivism against Jainism and Buddhism, and this anti-Jain aspect of Mukkanti has been attributed to Prataparudra in one account (Mack. Gen. Coll. 8.8a).

64. For a discussion of Thurston's place in the colonial sociology of India, see Dirks 1992: 69–70.

Conclusion

1. Most of the languages are named after regions (i.e., Sindhi, Kashmiri, Bengali), but two other cities, Lahore and Delhi, are also associated with specific languages. This list is found in the work known as *Nuh Sipihr*.

2. Translation by Richard M. Eaton from Firishta 1864–65, 1: 10. I thank him for alerting me to this passage and providing me with a translation.

3. I must therefore disagree with Pollock's statement that "nowhere in the manifold data on language, identity, and polity for precolonial South Asia does anything like ethnicity—which for purposes of this discussion we may define as the politicization of group sentiment—seem to find clear expression" (1998: 64). He goes on to say that South Asia lacked a linkage between "blood" and "tongue," as opposed to Europe, where the vernacularization of language was accompanied by a quest for authenticity and a vision of tribal unity. But I am doubtful whether his description of Europe can be accepted for the time period from 1000 to 1500. Similarly, I feel that Pollock has exaggerated the differences between medieval India and Europe in stating that "the political as an overt territorial project is unspoken" in Indian sources as opposed to European (1998: 65).

References

Abraham, Meera. 1988. *Two Medieval Merchant Guilds of South India.* New Delhi: Manohar Publications.

Abu-Lughod, Janet L. 1989. *Before European Hegemony: The World System* A.D. *1250–1350.* New York: Oxford University Press.

Alam, S. Manzoor. 1968. "Telangana." In *India: Regional Studies*, ed. R. L. Singh. Calcutta: Indian National Committee for Geography, 288–306.

Allchin, F. R. 1963. *Neolithic Cattle-Keepers of South India: A Study of the Deccan Ashmounds.* Cambridge: Cambridge University Press.

Anderson, Perry. 1974. "The Asiatic Mode of Production." In *Lineages of the Absolutist State.* London: N. L. B., 462–549.

Appadurai, Arjun. 1977. "Kings, Sects and Temples in South India, 1350–1700 A.D." *Indian Economic and Social History Review* 14, 1: 47–73.

———. 1981. *Worship and Conflict under Colonial Rule.* Cambridge: Cambridge University Press.

———. 1988. "Putting Hierarchy in Its Place." *Cultural Anthropology* 3: 36–49.

Appadurai, Arjun, and Carol A. Breckenridge. 1976. "The South Indian Temple: Authority, Honour and Redistribution." *Contributions to Indian Sociology* 10, 2: 187–212.

Babu, Satish, ed. 1990. *Andhra Pradesh Yearbook 1990.* Hyderabad: Data News Features.

Barnett, Lionel D. 1919a. *Inscriptions at Palampet and Uparpalli.* Hyderabad Archeological Series no. 3. Hyderabad: H.E.H. the Nizam's Government.

———. 1919b. *Pakhal Inscription of the Reign of the Kakatiya Ganapatideva.* Hyderabad Archeological Series no. 4. Hyderabad: H.E.H. the Nizam's Government.

Basham, A. L. 1959. *The Wonder That Was India.* New York: Grove Press.

Bayly, Susan. 1989. *Saints, Goddesses and Kings: Muslims and Christians in South Indian Society, 1700–1900.* Cambridge: Cambridge University Press.

Beck, Brenda. 1972. *Peasant Society in Konku: A Study of Right and Left Subcastes in South India.* Vancouver: University of British Columbia Press.

Berkemer, Georg. 1992. "The 'Centre Out There' as State Archive: The Temple of Simhacalam." In *The Sacred Centre as the Focus of Political Interest*, ed. Hans Bakker. Groningen: Egbert Forster, 119–30.

Blackburn, Stuart, et al. 1989. *Oral Epics in India.* Berkeley: University of California Press.

Bloch, Marc. 1961. *Feudal Society.* Vol. 1, *The Growth of Ties of Dependence.* Trans. L. A. Manyon. Chicago: University of Chicago Press.

Breckenridge, Carol A. 1985a. "Scale and Social Formations in South India, 1350–1750." In *Studies of South India: An Anthology of Recent Research and Scholarship*, ed. Robert E. Frykenberg and Pauline Kolenda. Madras: New Era Publications, 51–66.

———. 1985b. "Social Storage and the Extension of Agriculture in South India, 1350 to 1750." In *Vijayanagara—City and Empire: New Currents of Research*, ed. A Dallapiccola and S. Z. Lallemant. Stuttgart: Steiner Verlag Wiesbaden, 41–72.

———. 1986. "Food, Politics and Pilgrimage in South India, 1350–1650 A.D." In *Food, Society and Culture*, ed. R. S. Khare and M. S. A. Rao. Durham, N. C.: Carolina Academic Press, 21–53.

Butterworth, Alan, and V. Venugopal Chetty. 1990 [1905]. *A Collection of the Inscriptions on Copper-plates and Stones in the Nellore District*. Reprint, Madras: Asian Educational Services.

Chakravarti, Ranabir. 1986. "Merchants of Konkan." *Indian Economic and Social History Review* 23, 2: 207–15.

Chandrasekhara Reddy, R. 1994. *Heroes, Cults and Memorials: Andhra Pradesh, 300 A.D.–1600 A.D.* Madras: New Era Publications.

Chartier, Roger. 1988. *Cultural History: Between Practices and Representations*. Trans. Lydia G. Cochrane. Ithaca, N.Y.: Cornell University Press.

Chatterjee, Partha. 1992. "History and the Nationalization of Hinduism." *Social Research* 59, 1: 111–49.

Chattopadhyaya, B. D. 1977. *Coins and Currency Systems in South India, c. A.D. 225–1300*. New Delhi: Munshiram Manoharlal.

———. 1994. *The Making of Early Medieval India*. Delhi: Oxford University Press.

Chaturvedi, B. N. 1968. "The Origin and Development of Tank Irrigation in Peninsular India." *Deccan Geographer* 6, 2: 57–85.

Chaudhuri, K. N. 1985. *Trade and Civilization in the Indian Ocean: An Economic and Political History from the Rise of Islam to 1750*. Cambridge: Cambridge University Press.

Childers, C. H. 1975. "Banjaras." In *Pastoralists and Nomads in South Asia*, ed. L. S. Leshnik and G. D. Sontheimer. Wiesbaden: Otto Harrassowitz, 247–65.

Cohn, Bernard S. 1971. *India: The Social Anthropology of a Civilization*. Englewood Cliffs, N. J.: Prentice Hall.

———. 1984. "The Census, Social Structure and Objectification in South Asia." *Folk* 26: 25–49.

———. 1992. "The Transformation of Objects into Artifacts, Antiquities and Art in Nineteenth Century India." In *Powers of Art: Patronage in Indian Culture*, ed. Barbara Stoler Miller. Delhi: Oxford University Press, 301–29.

Comaroff, John, and Jean Comaroff. 1992. *Ethnography and the Historical Imagination*. Boulder, Colo.: Westview Press.

Connerton, Paul. 1989. *How Societies Remember*. Cambridge: Cambridge University Press.

Crane, Robert I., ed. 1967. *Regions and Regionalism in South Asian Studies*. Durham, N.C.: Duke University Press.

Crone, Patricia. 1989. *Pre-Industrial Societies*. London: Basil Blackwell.

Dandekar, Ajay. 1991. "Landscapes in Conflict: Flocks, Hero-Stones, and Cult in Early Medieval Maharashtra." *Studies in History* 7, 2: 301–24.

Davis, Richard H. 1997. *Lives of Indian Images*. Princeton: Princeton University Press.

Deloche, Jean. 1989. *Military Technology in Hoysala Sculpture*. New Delhi: Sitaram Bhartia Institute of Scientific Research.

Derrett, J. Duncan M. 1957. *The Hoysalas: A Medieval Indian Royal Family*. Madras: Oxford University Press.

———. 1964. "Law and Social Order in India before the Muhammadan Conquests." *Journal of the Economic and Social History of the Orient* 7: 73–120.

Desai, Dinkar. 1951. *The Mahamandalesvaras under the Calukyas of Kalyani*. Bombay: Indian Historical Research Institute.

Desai, Visakha N. 1993. "Beyond the Temple Walls: The Scholarly Fate of North Indian Sculpture, A.D. 700–1200." In *Gods, Guardians, and Lovers: Temple Sculptures from North India A.D. 700–1200*, ed. Visakha N. Desai and Darielle Mason. New York: Asia Society Galleries, 18–31.

Desai, Ziyaud-din A. 1989. *A Topographical List of Arabic, Persian and Urdu Inscriptions of South India*. New Delhi: Indian Council of Historical Research and Northern Book Centre.

Deshpande, Madhav. 1993a. "Nation and Region: A Sociolinguistic Perspective on Maharashtra." In *Sanskrit and Prakrit: Sociolinguistic Issues*. Delhi: Motilal Banarsidass, 109–27.

———. 1993b. "Rajasekhara on Ethnic and Linguistic Geography of India." In *Sanskrit and Prakrit: Sociolinguistic Issues*. Delhi: Motilal Banarsidass, 83–107.

Desikar, Soma Sundara. 1932–33. "Kakatiyas in Tamil Literature." *Journal of the Andhra Historical Research Society* 7: 103–7.

Deyell, John. 1990. *Living without Silver: The Monetary History of Early Medieval North India*. Delhi: Oxford University Press.

Dharampal-Frick, Gita. 1995. "Shifting Categories in the Discourse on Caste: Some Historical Observations." In *Representing Hinduism*, ed. Vasudha Dalmia and Heinrich von Stietoncron. New Delhi: Sage Publications, 82–100.

Diehl, Carl Gustav. 1956. *Instrument and Purpose: Studies on Rites and Rituals in South India*. Lund: CWK Gleerup.

Digby, Simon. 1971. *War-Horse and Elephant in the Delhi Sultanate*. Oxford: Oxford University Press.

Dirks, Nicholas B. 1976. "Political Authority and Structural Change in Early South Indian History." *Indian Economic and Social History Review* 13, 2: 125–57.

———. 1982. "The Pasts of a Palaiyakarar: The Ethnohistory of a South Indian Little King." *Journal of Asian Studies* 41: 655–83.

———. 1987. *The Hollow Crown: Ethnohistory of an Indian Kingdom*. Cambridge: Cambridge University Press.

———. 1989. "The Original Caste: Power, History and Hierarchy in South Asia." *Contributions to Indian Sociology* 23, 1: 59–77.

———. 1992. "Castes of Mind." *Representations* 37: 56–78.

———. 1993. "Colonial Histories and Native Informants: Biography of an Archive." In *Orientalism and the Postcolonial Predicament: Perspectives on South Asia*, ed. Carol A. Breckenridge and Peter van der Veer. Philadelphia: University of Pennsylvania Press, 279–312.

Dosse, François. 1994. *New History in France: The Triumph of the Annales*. Trans. Peter V. Conroy Jr. Urbana: University of Illinois Press.

Duara, Prasenajit. 1995. *Rescuing History from the Nation: Questioning Narratives of Modern China*. Chicago: University of Chicago Press.

Dumont, Louis. 1970. *Homo Hierarchicus: The Caste System and Its Implications*. Chicago: University of Chicago Press.

Eaton, Richard M. 1978. *Sufis of Bijapur 1300–1700: Social Roles of Sufis in Medieval India*. Princeton: Princeton University Press.

———. 1992. Review of *Saints, Goddesses and Kings*, by Susan Bayly. *Indian Economic and Social History Review* 29, 2: 234–38.

———. 1993. *The Rise of Islam and the Bengal Frontier, 1204–1760*. Berkeley: University of California Press.

———. 1997. "The Rise of Deccani Cultures." Paper presented to South Asia Seminar Series, University of Pennsylvania, November.

Elliot, H. M., and John Dowson. 1966 [1871]. *The History of India as Told by Its Own Historians, the Muhammadan Period*. Vol. 3. Reprint, New York: AMS Press.

Erndl, Kathleen M. 1993. *Victory to the Mother: The Hindu Goddess of Northwest India in Myth, Ritual, and Symbol*. New York: Oxford University Press.

Eschmann, Anncharlott, Hermann Kulke, and Gayan Charan Tripathi, eds. 1978. *The Cult of Jagannath and The Regional Tradition of Orissa*. New Delhi: Manohar Publications.

Feldhaus, Anne. 1986. "Maharashtra as a Holy Land: A Sectarian Tradition." *Bulletin of the School of Oriental and African Studies* 49: 532–48.

———. 1995. *Water and Womanhood: Religious Meanings of Rivers in Maharashtra*. New York: Oxford University Press, 1995.

Fentress, James, and Chris Wickham. 1992. *Social Memory*. Oxford: Blackwell Publishers.

Filliozat, Pierre. 1982. "The After-Death Destiny of the Hero according to Mahabharata." In *Memorial Stones*, ed. S. Settar and G. D. Sontheimer. Dharwar: Karnataka University, 3–8.

Firishta, Muhammad Qasim. 1864–65. *Tarikh-i-Firishta*, 2 vols. Lucknow: Naval Kishor.

Fleet, J. F. 1898–99. "Inscriptions at Ablur." *Epigraphia Indica* 5: 213–65.

Fox, Richard G. 1971. *Kin, Clan, Raja and Rule*. Berkeley: University of California Press.

Fox, Richard G., ed. 1977. *Realm and Region in Traditional India*. Durham, N.C.: Duke University Press.

Fox, Richard G., and Allen Zagarell. 1982. "The Political Economy of Mesopotamian and South Indian Temples: The Formation and Reproduction of Urban Society." *Comparative Urban Research* 4: 8–27.

Freeman, Rich. 1998. "Rubies and Coral: The Lapidary Crafting of Language in Kerala." *Journal of Asian Studies* 57, 1: 38–65.

Fuller, Chrisopher J. 1977. "British India or Traditional India? An Anthropological Problem." *Ethnos* 3–4: 95–121.

———. 1984. *Servants of the Goddess: The Priests of a South Indian Temple*. London: Cambridge University Press.

———. 1988. "The Hindu Temple and Indian Society." In *Temple in Society*, ed. Michael V. Fox. Winona Lake, Ind.: Eisenbrauns, 49–66.

———. 1992. *The Camphor Flame: Popular Hinduism and Society in India*. Princeton: Princeton University Press.

Furer-Haimendorf, C. von. 1985. *Tribal Populations and Cultures of the Indian Subcontinent*. Leiden-Koln: E. J. Brill.

Fussman, Gerard. 1987. "Central and Provincial Administration in Ancient India: The Problem of the Mauryan Empire." *Indian Historical Review* 14, 1: 43–72.

Garuda Purana. 1978–80. 3 vols. Ancient Indian Tradition and Mythology Series. Delhi: Motilal Banarsidass.

Geddes, Arthur. 1982. *Man and Land in South Asia*. New Delhi: Concept Publishing.

Gopal, Lallanji. 1963. "Samanta—Its Varying Significance in Ancient India." *Journal of the Royal Asiatic Society* 5: 21–37.

Gopala Reddy, Y. 1971–72. "Some Measures and Weights in Medieval Andhra." *Journal of the Andhra Historical Research Society* 32: 102–14.

———. 1973. "Agriculture under the Kakatiyas of Warangal." *Itihas: Journal of the Andhra Pradesh Archives* 1, 1: 57–65.

Gopalachari, K. 1941. *Early History of the Andhra Country*. Madras: University of Madras.

Gordon, Stewart. 1993. *The Marathas, 1600–1818*. Cambridge: Cambridge University Press.

Goudrian, T. 1969–70. "Vaikhanasa Daily Worship." *Indo-Iranian Journal* 12: 161–215.

Gough, Kathleen. 1981. *Rural Society in Southeast India*. Cambridge: Cambridge University Press.

Guha, Ranajit. 1989. "Dominance without Hegemony and Its Historiography." In *Subaltern Studies* VI, ed. Ranajit Guha. Delhi: Oxford University Press, 209–310.

Habib, Irfan. 1982. "Population." In *Cambridge Economic History of India*. Vol. 1, *c.1200–c.1750*, ed. Tapan Raychaudhuri and Irfan Habib. Cambridge: Cambridge University Press, 163–71.

———. 1990. "Merchant Communities in Precolonial India." In *Rise of Merchant Empires*, ed. James D. Tracy. Cambridge: Cambridge University Press, 371–99.

Habib, Mohammad. 1931. *The Campaigns of Alauddin Khalji Being the English Translation of the "Khaza'inul Futuh" (Treasures of Victory) of Amir Khusrau*. Bombay: D. B. Taraporewala Sons.

Halbwachs, Maurice. 1992. *On Collective Memory*. Ed. and trans. Lewis A. Coser. Chicago: University of Chicago Press.

Hall, Kenneth R. 1980. *Trade and Statecraft in the Age of the Colas*. New Delhi: Abhinav Publications.

Hanumantha Rao, B. S. L. 1973. *Religion in Andhra*. Guntur: Welcome Press.

Hardy, Peter. 1982 [1960]. *Historians of Medieval India: Studies in Indo-Muslim Historical Writing*. Reprint, Westport, Conn.: Greenwood Press.

Hari Rao, V. N., ed. and trans. 1961. *Koil Olugu: The Chronicle of the Srirangam Temple with Historical Notes*. Madras: Rochouse and Sons.

Hasnain, Nadeem. 1983. *Tribal India Today*. New Delhi: Harnam Publications.

Hazra, R. C. 1940. *Studies in the Puranic Records on Hindu Rites and Customs*. Dacca: University of Dacca Press.

Heitzman, James. 1987. "State Formation in South India, 850–1280." *Indian Economic and Social History Review* 24: 35–61.

———. 1997. *Gifts of Power: Lordship in an Early Indian State*. Delhi: Oxford University Press.

Hellman-Rajanayagam, Dagmar. 1995. "Is There a Tamil 'Race'?" In *The Concept of Race in South Asia*, ed. Peter Robb. Delhi: Oxford University Press, 109–45.

Hultzsch, E. 1894–95a. "Ganapesvaram Inscription of the Time of Ganapati." *Epigraphia Indica* 3: 82–93.

———. 1894–95b. "Yenamadala Inscription of Ganapamba." *Epigraphia Indica* 3: 94–103.

———. 1896–97. "Pithapuram Pillar Inscription of Mallapadeva." *Epigraphia Indica* 4: 226–42.

———. 1913–14. "Motupalli Pillar-inscription of Ganapatideva; A.D. 1244–45." *Epigraphia Indica* 12: 188–97.

Inden, Ronald. 1976. *Marriage and Rank in Bengali Culture*. Berkeley: University of California Press.

———. 1978. "The Ceremony of the Great Gift (Mahadana): Structure and Historical Context in Indian Ritual and Society." In *Colloques Internationaux du Centre National de la Recherche Scientifique*, no. 582. Paris: Editions du Centre de la Recherche Scientifique, 131–36.

———. 1982. "Hierarchies of Kings in Early Medieval India." In *Way of Life: King, Householder, Renouncer*, ed. T. N. Madan. New Delhi: 99–125.

———. 1985. "The Temple and the Hindu Chain of Being." *Purusartha* 8: 53–73.

———. 1990. *Imagining India*. London: Basil Blackwell.

Irschick, Eugene. 1994. *Dialogue and History: Constructing South India, 1795–1895*. Berkeley: University of California Press.

Iswara Dutt, Kunduri. 1967. *Inscriptional Glossary of Andhra Pradesh*. Hyderabad: Andhra Pradesh Sahitya Akademi.

———. 1979. *Pracinandhra Caritraka Bhugolamu*. Hyderabad: Andhra Pradesh Sahitya Akademi.

Jaiswal, Suvira. 1986. "Studies in Early Indian Social History: Trends and Possibilities." In *Survey of Research in Economic and Social History of India*, ed. R. S. Sharma. Delhi: Ajanta Publications, 39–108.

Jayasree, K. 1991. *Agrarian Economy in Andhra under Vijayanagara*. New Delhi: Navrang.

Johnston, E. H. n.d. "Catalogue of Mss. in European Languages Belonging to the Library of the India Office." Vol. 1, "The Mackenzie Collections," Pt. 2, "The General Collection." Unpublished typescript at India Office Library.

Kane, P. V. 1938. "Naming a Child or Person." *Indian Historical Quarterly* 14: 224–44.

———. 1941. *History of Dharmasastra*. Vol. 2, Pt. 2. Poona: Bhandarkar Oriental Research Institute.

———. 1946. *History of Dharmasastra*. Vol. 3. Poona: Bhandarkar Oriental Research Institute.

———. 1953. *History of Dharmasastra*. Vol. 4. Poona: Bhandarkar Oriental Research Institute.

———. 1975. *History of Dharmasastra*. Vol. 1, Pt. 2. Rev. ed. Poona: Bhandarkar Oriental Research Institute.

Karashima, Noboru. 1984. *South Indian History and Society: Studies from Inscriptions*, A.D. *850–1800*. Delhi: Oxford University Press.

———. 1992. *Towards a New Formation: South Indian Society under Vijayanagar Rule*. Delhi: Oxford University Press.

Kasturi, N. 1940. "The Hero Stones of Mysore." In *Professor K. V. Rangaswami Aiyangar Commemoration Volume*. Madras: G. S. Press, 203–7.

Kaviraj, Sudipta. 1992. "The Imaginary Institution of India." In *Subaltern Studies VII*, ed. Partha Chatterjee and Gyanendra Pandey. Delhi: Oxford University Press, 1–39.

Kolenda, Pauline. 1978. *Caste in Contemporary India: Beyond Organic Solidarity*. Menlo Park, Ca.: Benjamin/Cummings Publishing.

Kolff, Dirk H. A. 1990. *Naukar, Rajput and Sepoy: The Ethnohistory of the Military Labour Market in Hindustan, 1450–1850*. Cambridge: Cambridge University Press.

Krishna Kumari, M. 1987. "Land Transactions as Seen in the Draksharama Inscriptions." *Indian Economic and Social History Review* 24, 4: 424–47.

Kulke, Hermann. 1978a. "Early Royal Patronage of the Jagannatha Cult." In *The Cult of Jagannath and The Regional Tradition of Orissa*, ed. Anncharlott Eschmann, Hermann Kulke, and Gaya Charan Tripathi. New Delhi: Manohar Publications, 139–55.

———. 1978b. "Jagannatha as the State Deity under the Gajapatis of Orissa." In *The Cult of Jagannath and The Regional Tradition of Orissa*, ed. Anncharlott Eschmann, Hermann Kulke, and Gaya Charan Tripathi. New Delhi: Manohar Publications, 199–208.

———. 1978c. "Royal Temple Policy and the Structure of Medieval Hindu Kingdoms." In *The Cult of Jagannath and The Regional Tradition of Orissa*, ed. Anncharlott Eschmann, Hermann Kulke, and Gaya Charan Tripathi. New Delhi: Manohar Publications, 125–37.

———. 1982. "Fragmentation and Segmentation versus Integration? Reflections on the Concepts of Indian Feudalism and the Segmentary State in Indian History." *Studies in History* 4, 2: 237–63.

———. 1985. "Maharajas, Mahants and Historians: Reflections of the Historiography of Early Vijayanagara and Sringeri." In *Vijayanagara—City and Empire: New Currents of Research*, ed. A. L. Dallapiccola and S. Z. Lallemant. Stuttgart: Steiner Verlag Wiesbaden, 120–43.

———. 1995a. "The Early and Imperial Kingdom: A Processural Model of Integrative State Formation in Early Medieval India." In *The State in India, 1000–1700*, ed. Hermann Kulke. Delhi: Oxford University Press, 253–62.

———. 1995b. "Introduction: The Study of the State in Pre-modern India." In *The State in India, 1000–1700*, ed. Hermann Kulke. Delhi: Oxford University Press, 1–47.

Kulke, Hermann, and Dietmar Rothermund. 1990. *A History of India*. 2nd ed. London and New York: Routledge.

Kumar, Dharma. 1985. "Private Property in Asia? The Case of Medieval South India." *Comparative Studies of Society and History* 25: 340–66.

Lakshmiranjanam, K. 1974. "Language and Literature," Pt. viii, "Telugu." In *History of Medieval Deccan*, vol. 2, ed. H. K. Sherwani and P. M. Joshi. Hyderabad: Government of Andhra Pradesh, 147–72.

Laksmiranjanam, K., ed. 1960. *Sri Siddhesvara Caritramu of Kase Sarvappa*. Hyderabad: Andhra Racayitala Sanghamu.

Lal, Hira. 1907–8. "Inscriptions from Bastar State." *Epigraphia Indica* 9: 160–66.

Lariviere, Richard W. 1997. "Dharmasastra, Custom, 'Real Law' and 'Apocryphal' Smritis." In *Law, State, and Administration in Classical India*, ed. Bernhard Kölver. Munich: R. Oldenbourg, 97–110.

Leavitt, John. 1992. "Cultural Holism in the Anthropology of South Asia: The Challenge of Regional Traditions." *Contributions to Indian Sociology* n.s. 26, 1: 3–48.

Leshnik, Lawrence S. 1974. *South Indian "Megalithic" Burials: The Pandukal Complex*. Wiesbaden: Steiner Verlag.

———. 1975. "Nomads and Burials in the Early History of South India." In *Pastoralists and Nomads in South Asia*, ed. L. S. Leshnik and G. D. Sontheimer. Wiesbaden: Otto Harrassowitz, 40–67.

Leshnik, Lawrence, and Gunther-Dietz Sontheimer, eds. 1975. *Pastoralists and Nomads in South Asia*. Wiesbaden: Otto Harrassowitz.

Lingat, Robert. 1973. *The Classical Law of India*. New Delhi: Thomson Press.

Lorenzen, David. 1972. *The Kapalikas and Kalamukhas*. New Delhi: Thomson Press.

Lowenthal, David. 1985. *The Past Is a Foreign Country*. Cambridge: Cambridge University Press.

Ludden, David. 1978. "Ecological Zones and the Cultural Economy of Irrigation in Southern Tamilnadu." *South Asia* n.s. 1, 1: 1–13.

———. 1979. "Patronage and Irrigation in Tamil Nadu." *Indian Economic and Social History Review* 16: 347–65.

———. 1985. *Peasant History in South India*. Princeton: Princeton University Press.

———. 1993. "Orientalist Empiricism: Transformations of Colonial Knowledge." In *Orientalism and the Postcolonial Predicament: Perspectives on South Asia*, ed. Carol A. Breckenridge and Peter van der Veer. Philadelphia: University of Pennsylvania Press, 250–78.

———. 1994. "History outside Civilization and the Mobility of South Asia." *South Asia* n.s. 17, 1: 1–23.

Luders, H. 1900. "Two Pillar Inscriptions of the Time of Krishnaraya of Vijayanagara." *Epigraphia Indica* 6: 108–33.

Mahalingam, T. V. 1955. *South Indian Polity*. Madras: University of Madras.

Mahalingam, T. V., ed. 1976. *Mackenzie Manuscripts: Summaries of the Historical Manuscripts in the Mackenzie Collection*. Vol. 2, *Telugu, Kannada, and Marathi*. Madras: University of Madras.

Mandelbaum, David G. 1970. *Society in India*. Berkeley: University of California Press.

Mangalam, S. J. 1976–77. "Tula-purusa Mahadana." *Bulletin of the Deccan College Research Institute* 36: 89–96.

———. 1979–80. "Vengi—A Study of Its Historicity and Historical Geography." *Bulletin of Deccan College Research Institute* 40: 96–107.

———. 1986. *Historical Geography and Toponomy of Andhra Pradesh*. New Delhi: Sundeep Prakashan.

Marglin, Frederique Apffel. 1985. *Wives of the God-King: The Rituals of the Devadasis of Puri*. Delhi: Oxford University Press.

Marx, Karl. 1972. "The British Rule in India." In *On Colonialism; Articles from the* New York Tribune *and Other Writings*. New York: International Publishers, 35–44.

Mauss, Marcel. 1967. *The Gift*. New York: W. W. Norton.

McGilvray, Dennis B. 1982. "Mukkuvar Vannimai: Tamil Caste and Matriclan Ideology in Batticaloa, Sri Lanka." In *Caste Ideology and Interaction*. Cambridge: Cambridge University Press, 34–97.

Meister, Michael W., and M. A. Dhaky, eds. 1986. *Encylopedia of Indian Temple Architecture*. Vol. 1, pt. 2, *South India: Upper Dravidadesa*. Philadelphia: American Institute of Indian Studies and University of Pennsylvania Press.

Michell, George. 1992. "City as Cosmogram: The Circular Plan of Warangal." *South Asian Studies* 8: 1–17.

Mill, James. 1826. *The History of British India*. 3rd ed. London: Baldwin, Cradock and Joy.

Mines, Mattison. 1994. *Public Faces, Private Voices: Community and Individuality in South India*. Berkeley: University of California Press.

Morrison, Barrie M. 1970. *Political Centers and Cultural Regions in Early Bengal*. Tucson: University of Arizona Press.

Morrison, Kathleen D., and Mark T. Lycett. 1997. "Inscriptions as Artifacts: Precolonial South India and the Analysis of Texts." *Journal of Archaeological Method and Theory* 4, 3/4: 215–37.

Mukhia, Harbans. 1981. "Was There Feudalism in Indian History?" *Journal of Peasant Studies* 8, 3: 274–310.

———. 1985. "Peasant Production and Medieval Indian History." *Journal of Peasant Studies* 12: 228–51.

Mukunda Row, N. 1991. *Kalinga under the Eastern Gangas*. Delhi: B. R. Pub. Corp.

Murthy, M. L. K. 1982. "Memorial Stones in Andhra Pradesh." In *Memorial Stones*, ed. S. Settar and G. D. Sontheimer. Dharwar: Karnatak University, 209–18.

———. 1993. "Ethnohistory of Pastoralism: A Study of Kuruvas and Gollas." *Studies in History* n.s. 9, 1: 33–41.

Murthy, M. L. K., and Gunther D. Sontheimer. 1980. "Prehistoric Background to Pastoralism in the Southern Deccan in the Light of Oral Traditions and Cults of Some Pastoral Communities." *Anthropos* 75: 163–84.

Murton, Brian J. 1973. "Some Proposition on the Spread of Village Settlement in Interior Tamil Nadu before 1750 A.D." *Indian Geographical Journal* 48: 56–66.

———. 1989. "An Inquiry into Agrarian Differentiation in Interior South India before A.D. 1342." Paper presented at 18th Annual Conference on South Asia, Madison.

Nagaraju, S. 1995. "Emergence of Regional Identity and Beginnings of Vernacular Literature: A Case Study of Telugu." *Social Scientist* 23, 10–12: 8–23.

Narasimha Rao, R. 1975. "The Pekkamdru: A Medieval Merchant Guild." In *Aspects of Deccan History*, ed. V. K. Bawa. Hyderabad: Institute of Asian Studies, 113–30.

Narayana Rao, Velcheru. 1989. "Tricking the Goddess: Cowherd Katamaraju and Goddess Ganga in the Telugu Folk Epic." In *Criminal Gods and Demon Devotees: Essays on the Guardians of Popular Hinduism*, ed. Alf Hiltebeitel. Albany: State University of New York Press, 105–21.

———. 1990. *Siva's Warriors: The Basava Purana of Palkuriki Somanatha*. Princeton: Princeton University Press.

———. 1992. "Kings, Gods and Poets: Ideologies of Patronage in Medieval Andhra." In *The Powers of Art: Patronage in Indian Culture*, ed. Barbara Stoler Miller. Delhi: Oxford University Press, 142–59.

———. 1995. "Coconut and Honey: Sanskrit and Telugu in Medieval Andhra." *Social Scientist* 23, 10–12: 24–40.

Narayana Rao, Velcheru, David Shulman, and Sanjay Subrahmanyam. 1992. *Symbols of Substance: Court and State in Nakaya Period Tamilnadu*. Delhi: Oxford University Press.

Nath, R., and Faiyaz "Gwaliari." 1981. *India as Seen by Amir Khusrau (in 1318 A.D.)*. Jaipur: Historical Research Documentation Programme.

Neustupny, Evzen. 1993. *Archaeological Method*. Cambridge: Cambridge University Press.

Nilakanta Sastri, K. A. 1955. *The Colas*. Madras: University of Madras.

———. 1966. *A History of South India*. Madras: Oxford University Press.

———. 1972. *Foreign Notices of South India*. Madras: University of Madras.

Nilakanta Sastri, K. A., and N. Venkataramanayya. 1946. *Further Sources of Vijayanagara History*. 3 vols. Madras: University of Madras.

———. 1960. *The Eastern Chalukyas and the Chalukyas of Vemulavada*. London: Oxford University Press.

O'Hanlon, Rosalind. 1985. *Caste, Conflict, and Ideology: Mahatma Jotirao Phule and Low Caste Protest in Nineteenth Century Western India*. Cambridge: Cambridge University Press.

Olivelle, Patrick. 1998. "Caste and Purity: A Study in the Language of the Dharma Literature." *Contributions to Indian Sociology* n.s. 32, 2: 189–216.

———. 1999. *Dharmasūtras: The Law Codes of Ancient India*. Oxford: Oxford University Press.

Orr, Leslie C. 1993. "Women of Medieval South India in Hindu Temple Ritual: Text and Practice." In *Annual Review of Women in World Religions*, vol. 3, ed. Arvind Sharma and Katherine K. Young. Albany: State University of New York Press, 107–41.

———. 2000. *Donors, Devotees and Daughters of God: Temple Women in Medieval Tamilnadu*. Center for Asian Studies, University of Texas at Austin, South Asia Research Series. New York: Oxford University Press.

———. Forthcoming. "Women in the Temple, the Palace, and the Family: The Construction of Women's Identities in Pre-colonial Tamilnadu." In *Structure and Society in Early South India: Essays in Honour of Noboru Karashima*, ed. Kenneth R. Hall. Delhi: Oxford University Press.

Pandey, Gyanendra. 1990. *The Construction of Communalism in Colonial North India*. Delhi: Oxford University Press.

Pant, Rashmi. 1987. "The Cognitive Status of Caste in Colonial Ethnography: A Review of Some Literature on the Northwest Provinces and Oudh." *Indian Economic and Social History Review* 24, 2: 145–62.

Parabrahma Sastry, P. V. 1974. "Did Kakatiya Rudramadevi Die on the Battle Field?" *Studies in Indian Epigraphy* 1: 38–49.

———. 1975. *Kakatiya Coins and Measures*. Hyderabad: Government of Andhra Pradesh.

———. 1978. *The Kakatiyas of Warangal*. Hyderabad: Government of Andhra Pradesh.

———. 1982. *Srisailam, Its History and Cult*. Hyderabad: privately published.

Parasher, Aloka. 1991. *Mlecchas in Early India*. New Delhi: Munshiram Manoharlal.

Parthasarathy, R., ed. 1982. *Grama Kaifiyyatulu, Gunturu Taluka* (Pt. 2). Hyderabad: Andhra Pradesh State Archives.

Pederson, Paul. 1986. "Khatri: Vaishya or Kshatriya, an Essay on Colonial Administration and Cultural Identity." *Folk* 28: 19–31.

Pollock, Sheldon. 1985. "The Theory of Practice and the Practice of Theory in Indian Intellectual History." *Journal of the American Oriental Society* 105: 499–519.

———. 1989. "Mimamsa and the Problem of History in Traditional India." *Journal of the American Oriental Society* 109, 4: 603–10.

———. 1993. "Ramayana and Political Imagination in India." *Journal of Asian Studies* 52, 1: 261–97.

———. 1995. "Literary History, Indian History, World History." *Social Scientist* 23, 10–12: 112–42.

———. 1996. "The Sanskrit Cosmopolis, 300–1300: Transculturation, Vernacularization, and the Question of Ideology." In *Ideology and Status of Sanskrit*, ed. Jan E. M. Houben. Leiden: E. J. Brill, 197–247.

———. 1998. "India in the Vernacular Millennium: Literary Culture and Polity, 1000–1500." *Daedulus* 127, 3: 41–73.

Prabhakara Sastri, Veturi, ed. 1988 [1928]. *Kridabhiramamu*. Reprint, Hyderabad: Manimanjari Pracharanalu.

Prasad, B. Rajendra, and O. Sambaiah. 1983. "Brahmanayudu and Vira Vaishnavism." In *Srinidhih: Perspectives in Indian Archaeology, Art and Culture*, ed. K.V. Raman et al. Madras: New Era Publications, 239–42.

Prasad, Pushpa. 1990. *Sanskrit Inscriptions of the Delhi Sultanate*. Delhi: Oxford University Press.

Preston, Laurence W. 1989. *The Devs of Cincvad: A Lineage and the State in Maharashtra*. Cambridge: Cambridge University Press.

Quigley, Declan. 1993. *The Interpretation of Caste*. Oxford: Clarendon Press.

Radhakrishna Sarma, M. 1972. *Temples of Telingana*. Hyderabad: Osmania University.

Raghavan, V., ed. 1965. *Nrttaratnavali of Jaya Senapati*. Madras: Government Oriental Manuscript Library.

———. 1979. *Prataparudriya of Vidyanatha*. Madras: Sanskrit Education Society.

Raheja, Gloria Goodwin. 1989. "Centrality, Mutuality and Hierarchy: Shifting Aspects of Inter-caste Relationships in North India." *Contributions to Indian Sociology* n.s. 23, 1: 79–101.

Raju, P. T. 1944. *Telugu Literature*. Bombay: International Book House for P.E.N. All-India Centre.

Ramachandra Murthy, S. S. 1981. "Kshiraramesvara Temple Inscriptions: A Study." *Journal of the Epigraphical Society of India* 8: 105–8.

———. 1983a. "Kanakadurga Mallesvara Temple Inscriptions: A Study." In *Srinidhih Perpectives in Indian Archaeology, Arts and Culture*, ed. K. V. Raman et al. Madras: New Era Publications, 307–10.

———. 1983b. "Srikurmanatha Temple Inscriptions: A Study." In *Rangavalli: Recent Researches in Indology*, ed. A. V. Narasimha Murthy and B. K. Gururaja Rao. Delhi: Sundeep Publications, 113–19.

Ramachandra Rao, C. V. 1976. *Administration and Society in Medieval Andhra, A.D. 1038–1538*. Nellore: Manasa Publications.

———. 1988. *The Suryavamsa Gajapatis of Kalingotkala: A Political History*. Nellore: Manasa Publications.

Ramachandra Rao, C. V., ed. 1984. *Ekamranathuni Prataparudra Caritramu*. Hyderabad: Andhra Pradesh Sahitya Akademi.

Ramana, Y. V., ed. 1982. *Draksharama Inscriptions*. Hyderabad: Andhra Pradesh State Archives.

Rama Rao, M. 1966. *Select Kakatiya Temples*. Tirupati, A. P.: Sri Venkateswara University.

———. 1967. *Ikshvakus of Vijayapuri*. Tirupati, A. P.: Sri Venkateswara University.

———. 1971. *Krishnadeva Raya*. New Delhi: National Book Trust Press.

———. 1974. *Karnataka-Andhra Relations (220–1323 A.D.)*. Dharwar: Kannada Research Institute, Karnatak University.

Rama Row, T. 1875. *Biographical Sketches of the Rajahs of Venkatagiri*. Madras: Highland.

Ramaswami, N. S. 1975. *Amaravati: The Art and History of the Stupa and the Temple*. Hyderabad: Government of Andhra Pradesh.

Ramaswamy, Vijaya. 1985. *Textiles and Weavers in Medieval South India*. Delhi: Oxford University Press.

Ramesan, N. 1962. *Temples and Legends of Andhra Pradesh*. Bombay: Bharatiya Vidya Bhavan.

———. 1973. "The Reddi Kingdoms and Other Minor States." In *History of Medieval Deccan*, vol. 1, ed. H. K. Sherwani and P. M. Joshi. Hyderabad: Government of Andhra Pradesh, 517–46.

———. 1974. "Epigraphy," Pt. 1, "Sanskrit-Telugu." In *History of Medieval Deccan*, vol. 2, ed. H. K. Sherwani and P. M. Joshi. Hyderabad: Government of Andhra Pradesh, 345–59.

Ramesan, N., and N. Mukunda Row, eds. 1980. *Temple Inscriptions of Andhra Pradesh*. Vol. 1, *Srikakulam District*. Hyderabad: Government of Andhra Pradesh.

Rangaswami Aiyangar, K. V. 1941. *Krtya-Kalpataru of Bhatta Laksmidhara*. Baroda: Oriental Institute.

Rao, B. V. 1973. *History of the Eastern Calukyas of Vengi*. Hyderabad: Andhra Pradesh Sahitya Akademi.

Ratnagar, Shereen. 1991. "Pastoralism as an Issue in Historical Research." *Studies in History* 7, 2: 181–93.

Raychaudhuri, S. P., et al. 1963. *Soils of India*. New Delhi: Indian Council of Agricultural Research.

Richards, John F. 1975. *Mughal Administration in Golconda*. Oxford: Clarendon Press.

Rocher, Rosanne. 1993. "British Orientalism in the Eighteenth Century: The Dialectics of Knowledge and Government." In *Orientalism and the Postcolonial Predicament: Perspectives on South Asia*, ed. Carol A. Breckenridge and Peter van der Veer. Philadelphia: University of Pennsylvania Press, 215–49.

Rodgers, W. A. 1991. "Environmental Change and Evolution of Pastoralism in South Asia: A Discussion." *Studies in History* n.s. 7, 2: 195–204.

Rogers, John D. 1994. "Post-Orientalism and the Interpretation of Premodern and Modern Political Identities: The Case of Sri Lanka." *Journal of Asian Studies* 53, 1: 10–23.

Roghair, Gene H. 1982. *The Epic of Palnadu*. Oxford: Clarendon Press.

Rudner, David W. 1987. "Religious Gifting and Inland Commerce in Seventeenth-Century South India." *Journal of Asian Studies* 46, 2: 361–79.

———. 1994. *Caste and Capitalism in Colonial India: The Nattukotai Chettiars*. Berkeley: University of California Press.

Sahlins, Marshall. 1972. *Stone Age Economics*. Chicago: Aldine.

Sanyal, Hitesranjan. 1976. "Temple Promotion and Social Mobility in Bengal." In *History and Society: Essays in Honour of Prof. Niharranjan Ray*, ed. Debiprasad Chattopadhyaya. Calcutta: K. P. Bagchi, 341–70.

Sarma, K. V. H., and K. Krishnamurty. 1965–66. "Annavarappadu Plates of Kataya Vema Reddi." *Epigraphia Indica* 36: 167–90.

Sastri, B. N. 1991. *Recarla Padmanayakulu*. Hyderabad: Musi Publications.

Sastri, Hirananda. 1932. *Shitab Khan of Warangal*. Hyderabad Archeological Series no. 9. Hyderabad: H.E.H. the Nizam's Government.

Schopen, Gregory. 1996. "What's in a Name: The Religious Function of the Early Donative Inscriptions." In *Unseen Presence, The Buddha and Sanchi*, ed. Vidya Dehejia. Mumbai: Marg Publications, 60–73.

Schwartzberg, Joseph. 1977. "The Evolution of Regional Power Configurations in the Indian Subcontinent." In *Realm and Region in Traditional India*, ed. Richard G. Fox. Durham, N.C.: Duke University Press, 197–233.

———. 1978. *A Historical Atlas of South Asia*. Chicago: University of Chicago Press.

Settar, S. 1982. "Memorial Stones in South India." In *Memorial Stones*, ed. S. Settar and Gunther D. Sontheimer. Dharwar: Karnatak University, 183–97.

Sewell, Robert. 1982 [1900]. *A Forgotten Empire*. Reprint, New Delhi: Asian Educational Services.

Sharma, Arvind. 1978. "The Purusasukta: Its Relation to the Caste System." *Journal of the Economic and Social History of the Orient* 21, 3: 294–303.

Sharma, R. S. 1965. *Indian Feudalism, c.300–1200*. Calcutta: University of Calcutta.
———. 1985. "How Feudal Was Indian Feudalism?" *Journal of Peasant Studies* 12: 19–43.
Sherwani, H. K. 1973a. "The Bahmanis." In *History of Medieval Deccan*, vol. 1, ed. H. K. Sherwani and P. M. Joshi. Hyderabad: Government of Andhra Pradesh, 141–206.
———. 1973b. "The Qutb Shahis." In *History of Medieval Deccan*, vol. 1, ed. H. K. Sherwani and P. M. Joshi. Hyderabad: Government of Andhra Pradesh, 411–90.
Singh, Jasbir. 1974. *An Agricultural Atlas of India: A Geographical Analysis*. Kurukshetra: Vishal Publications.
Sircar, D. C. 1965. *Indian Epigraphy*. Delhi: Motilal Banarsidass.
———. 1966. *Indian Epigraphical Glossary*. Delhi: Motilal Banarsidass.
Sitapati, P. 1982a. *Sri Ahobila Narasimha Swami Temple*. Hyderabad: Government of Andhra Pradesh.
Sitapati, P., ed. 1982b. *Srisailam Temple Kaifiyat, Andhra Pradesh*, vol. 2. Hyderabad: Government of Andhra Pradesh.
Sivaramamurti, C. 1962. *Indian Bronzes*. Bombay: Marg Publications.
Sivasankaranarayana, Bh. 1967. *Cuddapah*. Hyderabad: Government of Andhra Pradesh.
Sjoberg, André F. 1968. "Telugu Personal Names: A Structural Analysis." In *Studies in Indian Linguistics: Professor* M. B. *Emeneau Sastipurti Volume*, ed. Bhadriraju Krishnamurti. Poona: Centres of Advanced Study in Linguistics, Deccan College and Annamalai University, 313–21.
Smith, Anthony D. 1986. *The Ethnic Origins of Nations*. Oxford: Basil Blackwell.
Somasekhara Sarma, Mallampalli. 1945. *A Forgotten Chapter of Andhra History: History of the Musunuri Nayaks*. Madras: Ananda Press.
———. 1948. *History of the Reddi Kingdoms*. Waltair: Andhra University.
Sontheimer, Gunther-Dietz. 1975. "The Dhangars: A Nomadic Pastoral Community in a Developing Agricultural Environment." In *Pastoralists and Nomads in South Asia*, ed. L. S. Leshnik and G. D. Sontheimer. Wiesbaden: Otto Harrassowitz, 139–70.
———. 1985. "Folk Deities in the Vijayanagara Empire: Narasimha and Mallanna/Mailar." In *Vijayanagara—City and Empire*, ed. A. Dallapiccola and S. Z. Lallemant. Stuttgart: Steiner Verlag Wiesbaden, 144–58.
———. 1989. *Pastoral Deities in Western India*. Trans. Anne Feldhaus. New York: Oxford University Press.
Sopher, David. 1962. "Indian Peoples and Their History." In *India: A Compendium*, ed. Raye R. Platt. New York: American Geographical Society, 46–128.
——— . 1975. "Indian Pastoral Castes and Livestock Ecologies: A Geographic Analysis." In *Pastoralists and Nomads in South Asia*, ed. L. S. Leshnik and G. D. Sontheimer. Wiesbaden: Otto Harrassowitz, 183–208.
Spate, O. H. K. 1954. *India and Pakistan: A General and Regional Geography*. New York: E. P. Dutton.
Spencer, George W. 1968. "Temple Money Lending and Livestock Distribution." *Indian Economic and Social History Review* 5, 3: 277–93.
———. 1969. "Religious Networks and Royal Influence in Eleventh Century South India." *Journal of the Economic and Social History of the Orient* 12, 1: 42–56.
———. 1982. "Sons of the Sun: The Solar Geneology of a Chola King." *Asian Profile* 10, 1: 81–95.
———. 1983a. *The Politics of Expansion: The Chola Conquest of Sri Lanka and Sri Vijaya*. Madras: New Era Publications.
———. 1983b. "When Queens Bore Gifts: Women as Temple Donors in the Chola Period." In *Srinidhih Perspectives in Indian Archaeology, Arts and Culture*, ed. K. V. Raman et al. Madras: New Era Publications, 361–73.

Spencer, George W., and Kenneth R. Hall. 1974. "Toward an Analysis of Dynastic Hinterlands: The Imperial Cholas of Eleventh Century South India." *Asian Profile* 2, 1: 51–62.

Spiegel, Gabrielle M. 1993. *Romancing the Past: The Rise of Vernacular Prose Historiography in Thirteenth-Century France*. Berkeley: University of California Press.

Sreenivasachar, P., ed. 1940. *A Corpus of Inscriptions in the Telingana Districts of H.E.H. the Nizam's Dominions*, Pt. 2. Hyderabad Archaeological Series no. 13. Hyderabad: H.E.H. the Nizam's Government.

Srinivas, M. N. 1971. *Social Change in Modern India*. Berkeley: University of California Press.

Srinivasachari, M. S. 1971. "Draksharama Bheemeswara Temple in Literature—A Critical Historical Study." *Quarterly Review of Historical Studies* 10, 4: 217–23.

Stein, Burton. 1960. "The Economic Function of a Medieval South Indian Temple." *Journal of Asian Studies* 14: 163–76.

———. 1977. "The Segmentary State in South Indian History." In *Realm and Region in Traditional India*, ed. Richard G. Fox. Durham, N.C.: Duke University Press, 3–51.

———. 1978. "Temples in Tamil Country, 1300–1750 A.D." In *South Indian Temples*, ed. Burton Stein. New Delhi: Vikas Publishing, 11–45.

———. 1980. *Peasant State and Society in Medieval South India*. Delhi: Oxford University Press.

———. 1985. "Vijayanagara and the Transition to Patrimonial Systems." In *Vijayanagara — City and Empire*, ed. A. Dallapiccola and S. Z. Lallemant. Stuttgart: Steiner Verlag Wiesbaden, 73–100.

———. 1989. *Vijayanagara*. Cambridge: Cambridge University Press.

———. 1995. "The Segmentary State: Interim Reflections." In *The State in India, 1000–1700*, ed. Hermann Kulke. Delhi: Oxford University Press, 134–61.

Stevenson, H. N. C. 1954. "Status Evaluation in the Hindu Caste System." *Journal of the Royal Anthropological Institute* 84, 2: 45–65.

Stone, Lawrence. 1981. *The Past and the Present*. Boston: Routledge and Kegan Paul.

Subbarao, B. 1958. *Personality of India; Pre and Protohistoric Foundation of India and Pakistan*. Baroda: University of Baroda Press.

Subba Rao, R. 1930–31. "History of Padmanaiks." *Journal of the Andhra Historical Society* 5: 50.

Subbarayalu, Y. 1973. *Political Geography of the Chola Country*. Madras: Tamilnadu State Department of Archaeology.

———. 1982. "The Cola State." *Studies in History* 4, 2: 265–306.

Subrahmanyam, R. 1973a. "Dynastic Introduction to the Inscriptions." In *Corpus of Inscriptions in the Telangana Districts*, Pt. 4. Hyderabad: Government of Andhra Pradesh, viii–xxiii.

———. 1973b. "Vijayanagar." In *History of Medieval Deccan*, vol. 1, ed. H. K. Sherwani and P. M. Joshi. Hyderabad: Government of Andhra Pradesh, 77–137.

Subrahmanyam, Sanjay. 1990. *The Political Economy of Commerce, Southern India, 1500–1650*. Cambridge: Cambridge University Press.

Subrahmanya Sastry, Sadhu. 1930. *Report on the Inscriptions of the Devasthanam Collection*. Madras: Tirupati Sri Mahant's Press.

Sundaram, K. 1968. *Studies in Economic and Social Conditions of Medieval Andhra*. Machilipatnam and Madras: Triveni Publishers.

———. 1969. *Simhacalam Temple*. Simhacalm, A.P.: Devasthanam Publication.

Talbot, Cynthia. 1987. "Golaki Matha Inscriptions from Andhra: A Study of a Saiva Monastic Lineage." In *Vajapeya: Essays on the Evolution of Indian Art and Culture*, ed. Ajay Mitra Shastri and R. K. Sharma. Delhi: Agam Kala Prakashan, 130–46.

———. 1991. "Temples, Donors and Gifts: Patterns of Patronage in Thirteenth Century South India." *Journal of Asian Studies* 50, 2: 308–40.

———. 1992. "A Revised View of 'Traditional' India: Caste, Status and Social Mobility in Medieval Andhra." *South Asia* 15, 1: 17–52.

———. 1994. "Female Donors and Their Families in Andhra, 1000–1649." Paper presented at 23rd Annual Conference on South Asia, Madison, Wisconsin.

———. 1995a. "Inscribing the Other, Inscribing the Self: Hindu-Muslim Identities in Pre-colonial India." *Comparative Studies in Society and History* 37, 4: 692–722.

———. 1995b. "Rudrama-devi, the Female King: Gender and Political Authority in Medieval India." In *Syllables of Sky: Studies in South Indian Civilization in Honour of Velcheru Narayana Rao*, ed. David Shulman. Delhi: Oxford University Press, 391–430.

Tapper, Bruce. 1987. *Rivalry and Tribute: Society and Ritual in a Telugu Village in South India.* Delhi: Hindustan Publishing.

Thapar, Romila. 1974. "Social Mobility in Ancient India with Special Reference to Elite Groups." In *Indian Society: Historical Probings in Memory of D. D. Kosambi*, ed. R. S. Sharma. New Delhi: People's Publishing House, 95–123.

———. 1981. "Death and the Hero." In *Mortality and Immortality: The Anthropology and Archeology of Death*, ed. S. C. Humphrey and Helen King. London: Academic Press, 293–315.

———. 1995. "The First Milliennium B.C. in Northern India." In *Recent Perspectives of Early Indian History*, ed. Romila Thapar. Bombay: Popular Prakashan, 80–141.

Thomas, Nicholas. 1991. *Entangled Objects: Exchange, Material Culture, and Colonialism in the Pacific.* Cambridge, Mass.: Harvard University Press.

Thurston, Edgar. 1975 [1909]. *Castes and Tribes of Southern India.* 7 vols. Reprint, Delhi: Cosmo Publication.

Tinker, Hugh. 1990. *South Asia: A Short History*, 2nd ed. Honolulu: University of Hawaii Press.

Tirumalai, R. 1981. *Studies in the History of Ancient Townships of Pudukottai.* Madras: Tamilnadu Department of Archaeology.

Trautmann, Thomas R. 1971. *Kautilya and the Arthasastra.* Leiden: E. J. Brill.

———. 1981. *Dravidian Kinship.* Cambridge: Cambridge University Press.

———. 1997. *Aryans and British India.* Berkeley: University of California Press.

Trautmann, Thomas R., et al. 1985. "The Study of South Indian Inscriptions." In *Studies of South India: An Anthology of Recent Research and Scholarship*, ed. Robert E. Frykenberg and Pauline Kolenda. Madras: New Era Publications, 1–29.

Tripathi, Gaya Charan. 1978. "The Daily Puja Ceremony of the Jagannatha Temple and Its Special Features." In *The Cult of Jagannath and the Regional Tradition of Orissa*, ed. Anncharlott Eschmann, Hermann Kulke, and Gaya Charan Tripathi. New Delhi: Manohar Publications, 285–307.

van der Veer, Peter. 1994. *Religious Nationalism: Hindus and Muslims in India.* Berkeley: University of California Press.

Vasantha Devi, M. N. 1964. "Some Aspects of the Agricultural Geography of South India." *Indian Geographical Journal* 39, 1–2: 1–41.

Venkataramanayya, N. 1929. *Trilochana Pallava and Karikala Chola.* Madras: R. Ramaswamy Sastrulu and Sons.

———. 1935. *Studies of the Third Dynasty of Vijayanagara.* Madras: University of Madras.

———. 1942. *The Early Muslim Expansion in South India.* Madras: University of Madras.

———. 1990 [1933]. *Vijayanagara: Origin of the City and the Empire.* Reprint, New Delhi: Asian Educational Services.

Venkataramanayya, N., ed. 1939. *Velugotivari Vamsavali.* Madras: University of Madras.

Venkataramanayya, N., and M. Somasekhara Sarma. 1958. "Vilasa Grant of Prolaya-Nayaka." *Epigraphia Indica* 32: 239–68.

———. 1960. "The Kakatiyas of Warangal." In *Early History of the Deccan*, ed. G. Yazdani. London: Oxford University Press, 575–713.

Venkatasubba Ayyar, V. 1947–48. "Nayanapalle Inscription of Ganapatideva." *Epigraphia Indica* 27: 193–97.

Venkateswaran, P. A. 1961. *Agriculture in South India*. New Delhi: Directorate of Extension, Ministry of Food and Agriculture.

Viraraghava Charya, T. K. T. 1982. *History of Tirupati (The Tiruvengadam Temples)*. Tirupati: Tirumala-Tirupati Devasthanams.

Wagoner, Phillip B. 1986. "Mode and Meaning in the Architecture of Early Medieval Telangana." Ph.D. dissertation, University of Wisconsin-Madison.

———. 1992. "Warangal's Bastions in Literature." *South Asian Studies* 8: 17–18.

———. 1993. *Tidings of the King: A Translation and Ethnohistorical Analysis of the Rayavacakamu*. Honolulu: University of Hawaii Press.

———. 1995. "Modal Marking of Temple Types in Kakatiya Andhra: Towards a Theory of Decorum for Indian Temple Architecture." In *Syllables of Sky: Studies in South Indian Civilization in Honour of Velcheru Narayana Rao*, ed. David Shulman. Delhi: Oxford University Press, 431–72.

———. 1997. Review of M. A. Dhaky, *Encyclopedia of Indian Temple Architecture*, Vol. 1, Pt. 3, *South India, Upper Dravidadesa, Later Phase,* A.D. *973–1326*. *Journal of the Society of Architectural Historians* 56, 3: 371–73.

———. forthcoming. "Harihara, Bukka, and the Sultan: The Delhi Sultanate in the Political Imagination of Vijayanagara." In *Beyond Turk and Hindu: Rethinking Religious Identities in Islamicate South Asia*, ed. David Gilmartin and Bruce B. Lawrence. Gainesville: University Press of Florida.

Walters, Jonathan S. 1997. "Stupa, Story, and Empire: Constructions of the Buddha Biography in Early Post-Asokan India." In *Sacred Biography in the Buddhist Traditions of South and Southeast Asia*, ed. Juliane Schober. Honolulu: University of Hawaii Press, 161–92.

Washbrook, D. A. 1981. "Law, State and Agrarian Society in Colonial India." *Modern Asian Studies* 15, 3: 649–721.

———. 1988. "Progress and Problems: South Asian Economic and Social History c. 1720–1860." *Modern Asian Studies* 22, 1: 57–96.

———. 1991. "'To Each a Language of His Own': Language, Culture, and Society in Colonial India." In *Language, History, and Class*, ed. Penelope J. Corfield. London: Basil Blackwell, 179–203.

Westphal-Hellbusch, S. 1975. "Changes in Meaning of Ethnic Names as Exemplified by the Jat, Rabari, Bharvad and Charan in Northwestern India." In *Pastoralists and Nomads in South Asia*, ed. L. S. Leshnik and G. D. Sontheimer. Wiesbaden: Otto Harrassowitz, 117–38.

Williamson, A. V. 1931. "Indigenous Irrigation Works in Peninsular India." *Geographical Review* 21, 4: 613–26.

Wilson, H. H. 1882 [1828]. *A Descriptive Catalogue of Oriental Mss. Collected by Colin Mackenzie*. Reprint, Madras: Higginbotham.

Wink, André. 1990. *Al-Hind: The Making of the Indo-Islamic World*. Vol. 1, *Early Medieval India and the Expansion of Islam*. Delhi: Oxford University Press.

———. 1997. *Al-Hind: The Making of the Indo-Islamic World*. Vol. 2, *The Slave Kings and the Islamic Conquest, 11th–13th Centuries*. Leiden: E. J. Brill.

Yasodadevi, V. 1949–50. "History of the Andhra Country, 1000 A.D.–1500 A.D., Pt. 2." *Journal of the Andhra Historical Research Society* 20: 115–60.

———. 1950–52. "History of the Andhra Country, 1000 A.D.–1500 A.D., Pt. 3." *Journal of the Andhra Historical Research Society* 21: 56–94.

———. 1968. "Coin Terms in Andhradesa Inscriptions." *Journal of the Numismatic Society of India* 30: 122–32.

Yazdani, G. 1960. "Fine Arts: Architecture, Sculpture, and Painting." In *Early History of the Deccan*, ed. G. Yazdani. London: Oxford University Press, 715–82.

Index

aḍḍavaṭṭa, 162, 163
Adil Shahs, 27, 196–97
administrative title, 56, 58, 154, 156–57
agrahāra, 89, 139, 161, 179
agrarian settlement, 22–23, 38–39, 41–43, 43–44
Ahobilam, 195, 204
Amaravati, 23, 91, 108, 109
amātya, 56–57
Ambadeva
    inscriptions of, 64–65, 68, 146, 148, 201
    relations with Kakatiyas, 67, 133–34, 135, 153
Amir Khusrau, 153, 212, 275n. 31
Āmuktamālyada, 195
Anapota Nayaka, 177, 179, 190–91, 191
Andhra region, 10–11, 19–22, 36–37
Andhra Pradesh, 4, 259–60n. 8, 260n. 9
aṅga-bhōga, 90
aṅgaḍi, 162
aṅgarakṣa, 159, 165
Appadurai, Arjun, 142, 143
Aravidus, 27, 196–97
aṣṭādaśa-praja, 52, 82, 167, 269n. 66

Bahmani sultanate, 27, 176, 180–81, 186, 281n. 39
Bairi Setti, 96, 161
Banjara, 74
baṇṭu, 69, 151, 275n. 28
Bastar, 193, 281n. 36
Beck, Brenda, 118
bhaṇḍāru, 156
Bhatraju, 207
bhaṭṭa, 56, 57
bhṛtya, 148
birudas
    of Kakatiya subordinates, 147–48, 155, 157
    (*see also* Kākatīya-rājya-sthāpan=ācārya)
    martial character of, 65, 69, 144, 145
    miscellaneous, 115, 151, 179, 275–76n. 40, 279n. 14
bōya
    as donor, 102, 112, 113–14, 117, 118
    as status title, 58, 59, 64, 266n. 26, 266–67n. 28
    as trustee of livestock, 103–4, 266n. 27, 271n. 27
    See also golla; pastoralists
brahman
    position in society of, 3, 48, 66
    as recipient of gift, 88–90, 98, 99
    status claims of, 50, 51, 56–57
Breckenridge, Carol A., 97, 117, 142, 143, 263n. 13

cakravarti, 58, 154
camūpati, 58, 68
caste
    group, 58–59, 59–60, 86, 191
    system, 2, 50, 52, 54, 60
cavalry, 68, 145, 151–52
Chagis, 53, 266n. 22
Chalukya Bhima I, 107, 109
Chalukyas of Badami, 24
Chalukyas of Kalyani, 25, 26, 35, 127, 128
Chalukyas of Vengi, 58, 62, 156, 272n. 36
Chattopadhyaya, B. D., 5–6
Chenchus, 46, 195
Cherakus, 155
Chola dynasty
    religious patronage of, 119, 139, 140, 141
    status claims of, 51, 274n. 21, 275 n. 36
Chola-period Tamil Nadu, 54, 81, 102, 116–17, 265n. 12

Between the years of 1000 and 1650, thousands of temple donors in the Andhra region of South India had the details of their charitable gifts recorded for posterity on stone pillars, rock slabs, and temple walls. Cynthia Talbot uses these records to reconstruct precolonial Andhra as it existed in practice—as opposed to the normative ideal portrayed in religious and courtly literature—during the era when India's distinctive regional societies were taking shape.

Talbot begins by examining the historical process that led to Andhra's 650-year age of inscriptions, a time when the religious patronage of temples both reflected and stimulated an expanding agrarian economy. The old historical consensus has it that the medieval period produced an ossified India resistant to reform and enfeebled by foreign conquest. Talbot asserts that this time was actually a dynamic period of progressive change that witnessed a rise in the number of religious institutions, an expansion of commercial activity, and several evolving political systems and networks.

Talbot focuses on the years from 1175 to 1324, when the Kakatiya polity flourished. This era yielded the largest number of temple inscriptions. During this formative period, the Telugu-speaking region of South India was politically unified by the upland warriors who would continue to dominate its society for centuries. As Talbot demonstrates, patronage of temples was one means by which the new social identities and communities were formulated. Because of the expanding agrarian frontier and widespread warfare, the world of Kakatiya-era Andhra offered far more